Grass Roots Music

AMERICAN POPULAR MUSIC ON ELPEE:

Grass Roots Music

Other volumes:

- *Black Music*

- *Jazz*

- *Contemporary Popular Music*

Grass Roots Music

Dean Tudor

Chairman
Library Arts Department
Ryerson Polytechnical Institute
Toronto, Canada

Nancy Tudor

Head
Cataloguing Department
Toronto Public Library
Toronto, Canada

Libraries Unlimited, Inc. - Littleton, Colo. -1979

LIBRARIES UNLIMITED, INC.
P.O. Box 263
Littleton, Colorado 80160

Library of Congress Cataloging in Publication Data

Tudor, Dean.
   Grass roots music.

   (American popular music on Elpee)
   Includes index.
   1. Folk music, American--Discography. 2. Folk-
songs, American--Discography. 3. Country music--
United States--Discography. 4. Bluegrass music--
United States--Discography. 5. Music, Popular
(Songs, etc.)--United States--Discography. I. Tudor,
Nancy, joint author. II. Title. III. Series.
ML156.4.N3U7   016.7889'12   78-31686
ISBN 0-87287-133-9

PREFACE

This book is a survey of and buying guide to one aspect of American commercial popular music on discs: grass roots music. Three other modes—contemporary popular music, black music, and jazz—are detailed through three companion books, all published by Libraries Unlimited. Coverage of the four volumes of "American Popular Music on Elpee" extends to all worthwhile discs since the advent of recorded sound that are presently available on long-playing records or tapes. Recently deleted items are included when they are still available from specialist stores, and the labels are international in scope, for many reissued records of American music are currently available in France, Scandinavia, West Germany, Japan, and in other countries.

For this book, approximately 1,700 recordings have been pre-selected and annotated, representing relatively current thought expressed through thousands of reviews and articles, plus hundreds of books, that we have read. This is fully explained in the section "What This Book Is All About. . . ." Thus, the recordings selection librarian can base his or her choice upon informed evaluation rather than random choice. In some respects, then, *Grass Roots Music* is to recordings what the H. W. Wilson *Standard Catalog* series are to books, or what Bill Katz's *Magazines for Libraries* is to periodicals. Our criteria have been noted through discographic essays and comments, mainly emphasizing musical development, "popularity," repertoire indexes, artistic merits of discs, and extra-musical developments.

Arrangement includes a division by anthologies, different stylings, different time periods, diverse instrumentation and vocal techniques, etc., along with explanatory narrative essays that present short musicological descriptions, definitions, brief histories, roots of development and progressions, and a discussion on the written literature (reviews, articles, books). Each album is numbered, and sometimes a few are grouped together for ease of discussion. All relevant order information is included: name of artist, title, label, last known serial number, and country of origin. A directory of specialty stores and label addresses appears at the rear of the book, also. Each annotation averages 300 words and specifically states why that record and/or material is significant. In each grouping, anthologies have been presented together, "innovators" have been carefully separated into their own section, and important discs have been starred to indicate a "first purchase."

This book can be used by both libraries and individuals to build a comprehensive record collection reflective of grass roots music, within the constraints noted in each section. Other uses include tracing the background of musical interactions in the explanatory notes and annotations, gaining an overview of grass roots music in general, and establishing criteria on which to base *future* purchases. Obviously, this aid is only as current as are clearly defined musical developments; thus, while the physical discs are, for the most part, "in-print," the actual performed music is lagging behind this book's printing date, because no one knows what "fresh" music of 1977 or 1978 will be the leader in the years to come. Other limitations include the placement of discs within the four books.

Our intent has been to select recordings indicative of a style, regardless of convenient popular (and often simplistic) classifications of an artist or group. The over-riding condition for each selection has been its manner of presentation—whether a pop or a jazz item, a country or a rock item—with serious consideration given to its ultimate placement. (But all classification schemes seem to have their exceptions.) However, we are confident that in our four books, viewed as a whole, no important available material has been overlooked.

For *Grass Roots Music*, this meant keeping strict control over what is known as the "folk process." Black rural blues, which is legitimate folk music, was moved to the *Black Music* volume of this set for consistency, and other aspects of blues were incorporated into *Jazz*. White folk blues are here, but "blues rock" went to *Contemporary Popular Music*. Still adhering to the folk process, "troubador" music is here, as it is most consistent with grass roots music; yet quite often it employs the rock music procedure. Similarly, modern British "electric folk" uses distinct British folk songs but employs the rock format with electric amplification. "Folk rock," however, is related more to rock music. (The motives, intent, and audiences for "electric folk" and "folk rock" are quite separate—or they were until quite recently.) Lately, there also has been a trend for country music to invade the pop arena (and, of course, vice versa). We are thankful, though, that a clear split exists between "gospel music" (found in *Black Music*) and "sacred music" (found here); however, to get a proper overview of popular religious music, the reader needs to consult both books. The marketing patterns of cross-overs and fragmentation in the music world are, as indicated in the introduction, further examples of regional breakdowns in musical styles.

ACKNOWLEDGMENT AND THANKS

While this book is basically a summation and synthesis of existing thought about grass roots music (as revealed through books, periodical articles, record reviews, and the music itself), we also sought guidance from collectors in the field through letters and conversations. All are knowledgeable critics; some are even librarians. In no way did they comment on the text itself; that was our responsibility alone. Our thanks, then, go to: Andrew Armitage (bluegrass, country, troubador), Dick Flohil (folk), Paul Hornbeck (folk, troubador), Tom McCreight (bluegrass, old time, country, sacred), Rober Misiewicz (bluegrass, sacred), and Paul Steuwe. Our gracious thanks go also to Nan Ward, who typed a good part of the manuscript.

Dean Tudor
Nancy Tudor

1978

"Popular music in America never was taken seriously by anyone other than the people who produced it or bought it."
—Mike Jahn, *Rock* (1973)

TABLE OF CONTENTS

WHAT THIS BOOK IS ALL ABOUT
AND HOW TO USE IT

"Of all the arts, music has always been nearest
to the hearts of Americans and the most expressive of their
essential needs, fears, and motivations."
—William O. Talvitie

"Music is music and that's it. If it sounds good,
it's good music and it depends on who's listening
how good it sounds."
—Duke Ellington

"It's all music, no more, no less."
—Bob Dylan (1965)

This reference tool offers a complete pre-selected evaluative guide to the best and most enduring recorded grass roots music (largely American) available on long-playing discs and tapes. It can be used by both libraries and individuals to build up a comprehensive collection reflective of every area of grass roots music (except black music, in another volume in this set). About 1,700 discs are annotated within a space of 300 (average) words each indicating musical influences, impact, and importance. This represents about a $7,500 investment. However, about 220 key albums are identified and suggested as a "first purchase" (about $1,000). These are seminal recordings. The interested individual can use the selection guide to buy for instance, the key albums followed by the balance. Then this person could start purchasing all other discs by favorite bluegrass performers, or perhaps move on to a related field such as old time music or troubador music. The approach is by ever-widening circles.

This book also is concerned with the preservation of recorded popular music through the long-playing disc. The commercial disc, even though it does not adequately reflect the total characteristics of musical genres, is a very convenient way to scrutinize popular music and audience reactions in an historical perspective. A disc preserves exactly the manner of a performance, with absolutely no chance of change through future progression—except for the most recent materials that have been altered by remixing or tape dubbing (e.g., Hank Williams with strings or Simon and Garfunkel's "Sounds of Silence" with a soft rock background). Records are constantly available around the country; some may be difficult to acquire, but the waiting is worth the aggravation. By the 1970s, audiences for all types of music have been fully catered to in some form or another. However, at some point in the development of a genre, musical minorities can become cult fanatics who insist on having every single note a particular artist performed. At this point, the cult audience must seek out bootleg records, taped concerts, airshots, and so forth, most of which are outside the mainstream of the recording industry.

The discographic essays in this book provide information on the basic elements of musical genres, criticisms, and analysis, as well as literature surveys for book and magazine purchases. The introductory essay presents an overview of popular music generally; the bibliography lists core books and magazines dealing with popular music that were especially chosen to show broad historical trends of importance and influence. The narrative discographic essays head each category, beginning with musicological descriptions, definitions, and continuing with brief histories and roots of development, reasons why it succeeded, musical hybrids, recording company policies, leading proponents in the field, criteria for inclusion of records, a discussion of record critics, and the tendencies of specialist review magazines. A useful by-product of this mechanism is that significant data and criticism are presented on which the record librarian can base popular music phonodisc selection for future recorded issues and reissues. The *Annual Index to Popular Music Record Reviews* can serve to update this book for record purchasing.

ARRANGEMENT AND FORMAT

All records in this volume are arranged under such categories as anthologies, stylings, time periods, instrumentation, vocal techniques, and so forth, as laid out in the table of contents. Narrative essays not only introduce grass roots music (see page 31), but also head each category within. These essays include short musicological descriptions, definitions, brief histories, roots of development and progressions, the leading proponents in the field, general criteria for inclusion of the specific records that follow, and a discussion of relevant books and existing periodicals (plus some detail on record reviewing and critics).

Each album discussed is entered in abbreviated discographic style: an internal numbering scheme to pinpoint its location within the book; entry by group, individual or title (if anthology) with commonalities collected for comparison purposes; album title, the number of discs in the package, label and serial number; country of origin if *not* American. Prices have been omitted because of rapid changes, discounts, and foreign currencies. Annotations, which average 300 words, specifically state why the record and/or material is significant, with references to personnel and individual titles.

There are three clear special indications: one, the "innovators" have been carefully separated into their own section; two, important discs have been starred (*); and three, the anthologies have been collected (see the short essay on the anthology, page 27). In terms of budgets, the suggested order of purchasing is: 1) within each genre desired, the starred anthologies (approximately $250 total for each genre); 2) within each genre desired, the other anthologies (approximately $750); 3) within each genre desired, the starred recordings of the innovators (approximately $500); 4) within each genre desired, the rest of the innovators (approximately $500); 5) within each genre desired, the balance of the starred items (approximately $750); 6) within each genre desired, the rest of the recordings (approximately $4,750).

The repackaged anthology represents the best choice for even the smallest of libraries. This maximizes the dollar so that libraries can get a reasonable "flavoring" of the widest repertoires or themes in an attempt to manage on the smallest of budgets. Larger libraries which, for whatever reason, prefer not to collect in a particular genre could still supplement their collection by purchasing the worthwhile anthologies in those genres for about $250 a grouping. These books will not include "classical" music, spoken word and humor, children's, marching bands, foreign language, religious (except for gospel and sacred music, both exceptionally popular religious music), and non-commercial items such as instructional recordings, educational records if the commercial form co-exists on album, and field trips (except for significant folk music).

Additional information is provided after the text: a directory of latest known addresses for record companies, plus an indication of their albums that we have starred in label numerical order; a short list of specialist record stores; a bibliography of pertinent books and periodicals; and an artist index with entries for both musical performances in diverse genres and musical influences.

METHOD OF RATING

Written materials about important popular music phonodiscs exist in a variety of forms: scattered discographic essays; scattered citations as footnotes; short biographic essays of leading performers; books with lists of records; discographic "polls"; annual "best of the year" awards; "tops of the pops" lists and chart actions; and passing references in ordinary reviews. Written material about popular music genres in general—at an introductory level—exists mainly in books, but such books were not written with the intention of assembling a representative historical core collection of phonodiscs.

The basic method we have used is a manual version of citation analysis by consensus. Through the 1965-1976 period, we studied about 60 popular music periodicals, which contained over 50,000 relevant reviews and over 10,000 articles. We also read more than 2,000 books on popular music, some dating from the 1920s, and we actually listened to 14,000-plus long-playing albums. Although we didn't know it at the time, work began on this book in 1967—a decade ago. We started out by identifying, for personal use, *all* the important performers in popular music, and we then read widely and bought all of that person's material *before* going on to anyone else. The rationale here was that, since these performers are acknowledged as the *best*, even their "off" material might be considerably better than a second-generation or derivative imitator. By moving in ever-widening circles (somewhat akin to a Venn diagram), we then began to investigate influences, impacts, and importance—for whatever reasons. At the same time we began to categorize performers so that we could make some sense out of the profusion of records by time, place, and influence. Generally, the slotting of performers by genre does not really affect one's appreciation of them at all but rather produces common groupings for the novice listener. What has developed is the categorization of available records rather than of the performers. Thus, this book is about significant recordings rather than significant artists (although the two do coincide fairly often). By *not* first choosing artists and then seeking out important discs (which is what we started to do) but instead seeking important recordings first, we have neatly avoided the "star" approach, which has two main disadvantages: first, that individual reputations may rise and fall without reference to artistic merit; and second, that styles of performance rapidly change from fashionable to unfashionable.

Reading and listening widely, we developed several criteria for evaluation:

1. Musical development
   a) musical quality of the recording
   b) importance in relation to music history
   c) musical standards of musicians (soloists, sidemen, session artists)
   d) musical creativeness, inventiveness, devotion, drive
   e) each musical genre is considered on its own terms as being equally important

2. "Popularity"
   a) airplay listings since 1920s
   b) reviews of records
   c) purchases
   d) critics' notes
   e) amount of material available
   f) longevity of the artist
   g) music itself (words and/or melodies)
   h) indication of "influence on" and "influenced by"—the links in a chain

3. Index to repertoires
   a) the favorite tunes of the performers
   b) the tunes most recorded and performed constantly
   c) what was re-recorded and why
   d) what was best remembered by fans and friends
   e) sheet music and songbook availability
   f) the tunes still being performed by others

4. Artistic merit of a record
   a) the way the song or tune is structured
   b) the relation between its structure and meaning
   c) the manipulation of the medium
   d) the implications of its content
   e) art criticism

5. Extra-musical developments
   a) the record industry and media manipulation
   b) the concept album or one with a thematic or framing device (both original, long-playing recordings and reissued collections of singles)
   c) the impact of radio and regional breakdowns

5.   Extra-musical developments (cont'd)
     d)   the folklore process of oral transmission
     e)   consideration of differences in listening appreciation between singles (78 and 45 rpm) and albums (33-1/3 rpm)

Citation analysis revealed that certain artists and tunes keep appearing, and hence any important record is important by virtue of its historical worth, influence, best-selling nature, trend setting, and so forth. We have deliberately restricted ourselves to long-playing discs, believing that most of the major records of the past (available only as single plays before 1948) are now available in this format.

We would not be honest, though, if we stated that we personally enjoyed every single album. Each individual's cultural upbringing places limits on what he can enjoy completely, and these restrictions can be overcome only by an extensive immersion into the society that created the genre of music. Attempting to understand what the artist is saying will help build a vocabulary of listening. For example, rockabilly has less impact on a British folk fan, and British folk has less impact on a rockabilly fan. Thus, we must treat each musical genre as being equally important in terms of what it attempts to do, with an eye to cross-fertilization among different horizontal structures. It must be recognized that we are *not* rating a troubador item against a sacred music recording. Rather, we are comparing similar genre recordings against each other, such as an old time music recording against another old time music item.

One difficulty we faced was that there is no historical perspective for the recordings of the past decade; this is particularly noticeable for troubadors. We have no idea how this music will be accepted ten years from now, but we certainly know that these recordings should have a prominent place because of their current importance. It was a different world fifty, forty, thirty years ago; of course, the artists of a prior generation seem funny-strange today. Let us hope that the future will still remain kind.

PROBLEMS IN SELECTING FOR A COLLECTION

The selection of better pop recordings poses a problem because of the profusion of unannotated "best listings," the current trend toward reissuing and repackaging, and the unavailability of some records due to sudden deletions. Record librarians, most of whom lack a subject knowledge of popular music, usually select the most popular recordings without turning to evaluations. With the impact of the music and its general availability at low prices, the record librarians may end up with a current collection without an historical core. Where can record librarians turn for the back-up record evaluations of older discs? The same problems of continuity and historical perspective exist with respect to best-selling books. A disc that received rave reviews a decade ago might be consigned to the wastebasket today.

There is another reason that libraries end up with purely contemporary collections of popular music. Records do wear out and get lost or stolen; replacements may be sought. However, the original record could be deleted and the librarian lacks a source for locating an appropriate and perhaps better record by the same artists. For lack of a better alternative, the selector usually chooses an artist's latest recording, if that artist is still to be represented in the collection. This means a continually contemporary collection with no historical perspective.

The problem of choosing older records (or new reissues of older records) becomes one of selecting blindly from the *Schwann–1* or *Schwann–2* catalogs, or else hunting for the occasional discographic essay or lists in whatever periodicals are at hand. Fortunately, the librarian can also turn to *Popular Music Periodicals Index, 1973-* (Scarecrow, 1974-) or *Annual Index to Popular Music Record Reviews, 1972-* (Scarecrow, 1973-), but these are indexes only to the substance. Our book is a selection tool of that substance, enabling selectors to base their choices on informed evaluation rather than on random choice.

The balance of material in these books is not always in proportion to the importance of a genre or an artist, and this is mainly because there are so many examples of *good* music—"a good song is a good song." A greater proportion of materials is included for the minority offerings in blues, bluegrass, rockabilly, etc.—the same forms of music that laid the foundations for more commercial offerings in soul, country, rock music, respectively.

THE MARKET PLACE–IN BRIEF

The year 1977 was a very significant anniversary year for records. In 1877, Edison invented the phonograph by embossing sound on a piece of tinfoil wrapped around a *cylinder* and reproduced that sound through an acoustic horn. (Marie Campbell, the girl who recited "Mary Had a Little Lamb," died in 1974 at the age of 103.) Ten years after Edison's success, in 1887, Emile Berliner invented the gramophone for *flat* discs. In 1897 the first shellac pressings were created, and in 1907, the first double-sided record was created by Odeon, the record company. In 1917, the first jazz disc was recorded by Victor (original Dixieland Jazz Band, January 30), and ten years later, in 1927, the first modern country music was recorded (Jimmie Rodgers and the Carter Family, August 2). That same year saw two inventions: the first sequential recording device (magnetic paper tape, by J. A. O'Neill) and Edison's development of the long-playing record. Also in 1927 came the first record changer, the first transmission of television, and the first feature-length talking picture. This book, then, is about some of those events and the impact on modern popular music of today and it appears at a time in which more discs from the past are currently available than in any other previous year.

Records have always been popular purchases, despite their original high costs. And the market has always been flooded with as many discs as it could hold. For instance, in 1929, about 1,250 old time music 78 rpm discs were released; by 1976, this number was about 850 for 45 rpm discs (the modern equivalent of country and bluegrass music). In terms of 1929 dollars, though, this music now costs less than a dime. At that time, there were 10 million phonographs; now, there are about 70 million phonographs. In 1929, there were about 100 record companies, but by 1976, the industry numbered over 1,500.

During those years, four types of companies have developed. First, there are the *majors* (CBS, MCA, RCA, UA, Capitol, Mercury, etc.), who have shared the bulk of the market. The *independents* (King, Imperial, Arhoolie, Savoy, etc.) arose as an alternative source of music, catering to musical minorities; these companies were interested not in getting rich but in promoting good music. A third category is the quasi-legal *bootleg* outfits. Some of these are sincere companies interested in reissuing treasures of the past by performers long since dead or missing (e.g., Biograph, Yazoo, Old Timey), while some are dubious operations that issue taped concerts and other unpublished items they feel should not be withheld from fans (e.g., Bob Dylan's *White Wonder* set, Rolling Stones' concerts, jazz and dance music airshots). The fourth grouping consists of *pirates*, who reproduce in-print records and tapes in the lucrative rock and country fields, and who, by false and misleading claims, make a high profit since they pay no royalties and no studio costs are collected. The records included in this book were produced by an uncommonly high percentage of independent and bootleg labels. This is because the roots of each musical genre lie in the beginning steps taken by independent companies and by the innovative performers themselves, who first recorded for these labels early in their careers.

It should certainly be noted that the historical worth of disc recordings will increase even more in the years to come. One reason that older recordings have not been popular is that modern higher fidelity equipment amplifies the poorer reproduction of bygone years. An early compensation from the late 1950s was the "electronically processed stereo" disc, in which the highs went to one channel and the lows to the other. This suited stereo consoles but not the hi-fi components market. By 1976, though, RCA had developed its "sound stream" process, in which a computer reduces not only surface scratch from older discs but also faulty resonance and reverberation. This computer "justification" works on the same principles as NASA's clarification of the 1976 pictures of the surface of Mars. RCA's first such disc was of Caruso recordings; within the next few years, certain forms of popular music may be added.

POST-1974 RECORDINGS: POTENTIAL CLASSICS

Although the discographic information and availability of albums are current with this book's imprint, *most* of the music described here had been recorded before 1974. This lead time of five years allows for settling/detecting trends rather than fads and letting the jury, as it were, have sufficient time to arrive at decisions. Recognizing, however, that certain modern discs just *might* be significant in the long run, we list those recent innovative records that have drawn exceptionally fine current reviews.

Bluegrass

Bill Monroe and James Monroe. Father and Son. MCA 310

Red, White and Blue (Grass). Very Popular. GRC GA 5002

Country

Mac Davis. Stop and Smell the Roses. Columbia KC 32582

Skeeter Davis. The Hillbilly Singer. RCA LSP 4818

Jerry Reed. Koko Joe. RCA LSP 4560

Charlie Rich. The Silver Fox. Epic PE 33250

Tanya Tucker. MCA 2141

Conway Twitty and Loretta Lynn. Louisiana Woman—Mississippi Man. MCA 335

Contemporary Country

David Allen Coe. The Mysterious Rhinestone Cowboy. Columbia KC 32942

Freddy Fender. Before the Next Teardrop Falls. ABC DOSD 202

Flying Burrito Brothers. Last of the Red Hot Burritos. A & M SP 4343

Emmylou Harris. Pieces of the Sky. Reprise MS 2213

Leon Russell. Hank Wilson's Back. Capitol SW 8923

Troubador

Jackson Browne. For Everyman. Asylum 5067

Jackson Browne. The Pretender. Asylum 7E 1079

Ry Cooder. Chicken Skin Music. Reprise MS 2254

Anna and Kate McGarrigle. Warner Brothers BS 2802

Joni Mitchell. For the Roses. Asylum SD 5057

Phoebe Snow. Shelter 2109

James Talley. Got No Bread. Capitol ST 11416

Tom Waits. Nighthawks at the Diner. two discs. Asylum 2008

REFERENCES AND INDEX

In the introductory comments to each section, reference will be made to the literature on the topic of grass roots music. When a name appears followed by a number in parentheses—e.g., Ewen (25)—the reader should consult "Book Citations" for a full entry and a description of the book. When a title is followed by a number—e.g., *Country Music* (4)—the "Periodical Citations" should be consulted. (Items such as "62a" represent updates or new entries and are filed in proper numerical sequence.)

The alphanumeric code preceding each entry first locates that item in the overall classification used for the four volumes (F here denotes the "folk process" music in *Grass Roots Music*, B is used for *Black Music*, and J for *Jazz*). The number immediately following the letter code then indicates the major section of this book in which an item/artist can be found. Additionally, the artists' index references all of the recordings listed in this book by that code number.

INTRODUCTION TO POPULAR MUSIC

"Time has a way of making the style stick out,
rather than the music, unless
that music is exceptional."
—Joe Goldberg

Popular music is a twentieth century art form made available to the masses through records, radio and, to a lesser extent, nightclubs, concerts, festivals, and television. As an art form, it is in a state of constant evolution in which each generation redefines its own music. One's perception of popular music is based only on what is heard or what is available to be heard. "Access," then, becomes a key word that was not found before either the breakdown of regional barriers or the advent of mass media. Previous to bulk production of commercial recordings (about 1920), different styles had arisen to meet the moods of geographic areas and of the times. All that these diverse styles had in common were the elements of rhythm, melody, harmony, and form; each style went its separate way in emphasizing one of these elements over the other. Sorting out the musical strains and streams is confusing, then, because of the vast number of musical and extra-musical influences shaping the styles. Some of these will be explored in the introductions to the various volumes on specific musical genres, but it should be noted that there are five general statements that appear to be incontrovertible when discussing styles of popular music:

1) Styles persist past their prime, and often they are revived by a new musical generation, perhaps in a series of permutations.

2) One development in a style leads to another development through constant evolution.

3) Each style and stream of music influences the other styles and streams through the artists' awareness of trends in all areas, this caused by the exposure that the mass media give to such a variety of artists.

4) Styles are as much shaped by extra-musical influences (such as the recording industry and radio) as by other styles themselves.

5) To the novice, all music performed in one particular style may sound the same, but each stream is a language or form of communication, and to become familiar with it, the listener must consciously learn this new language.

Each of these statements will be further explored in this section and with the appropriate genres of popular music.

Schoenberg once wrote (in a different context): "If it is art it is not for all; if it is for all it is not art." Popular music relates to the existing mores of an era, and it falls in step with a current culture by reflecting popular tastes. In this sense, popular music is relevant to its audience's interests. But listeners evolve with time, for society never stands still. Popular music changes in response to audience manipulation or demand; consequently, *all* popular music styles of the past may make little sense to a modern audience. There appears to be little need *today* for the sentimental ballads of the late nineteenth century, the New Orleans jazz sound, the Tin Pan Alley pop music of the 1920-1950 period, and so forth, in terms of what that music meant to *past* generations. However, it is important to note the older styles of popular music because these styles have revivals that show an interest in the past (for stability or nostalgia) and also show the evolution of modern streams of music. In recordings, for each genre there exist at least three types of similar music: the original recordings of by-gone days; a revival of the style reinterpreted in modern terms; and the modern equivalent that evolved from that early style. An example would be the slick group singing of the 1930s and 1940s, as exemplified by the Andrews Sisters (in the original form), the Pointer Sisters (in the revival), and the Manhattan Transfer (in the modern equivalent). Through the phonograph record, all three co-exist, and future singers in this genre could borrow a different emphasis from each of the three closely-related styles to project a fourth synthesis of, to continue the example, the vocal group singing slick, catchy lyrics.

Over a period of years, each style of popular music loses much of the original drive, mood, and inventiveness that came from its roots in tradition. As a minority music style catches on with wider audiences, and as this style becomes influenced by both other genres and urban cultures, the original excitement of the innovation becomes diminished considerably. This is inevitable as styles evolve and as performers add something "a little different" to distinguish themselves from the increasing number of other similar musicians interpreting the same genre. This creates permutations and sub-genres, resulting in the creation of yet other musical streams. As these styles become commercially successful, performers self-consciously appraise their music as found in shows, concerts, or on record, and they become concerned over their image and saleability. They are frightened that they might fall into a rut (or, more appropriately, a groove). However, seeking reappraisal by becoming observers defeats both the spontaneity and the emotional impact of the music, and no emerging musical sub-genre would long survive if it stayed with a narrow conception of its style. This is what happened to the Beatles, and, to their credit, they split up when they recognized that they could no longer develop musically as a group. An emerging style at its beginnings can offer real excitement, emotion, and exuberance, all of which tend to fade (or be jaded or tired) in its mature years. This, then, is a prime rationale for the preservation and retention of early and historical recordings that helped to produce fanatical enthusiasm among both the performers and the audiences who knew and recognized new, emerging popular music styles.

It was David Reisman who identified two groups of performers and listeners as early as 1950 ("Listening to Popular Music," *American Quarterly* 2:359-71). There was the majority audience, which accepted the range of choices offered by the music industry and made its selections from this range without considering anything outside of it. And there were also the "cults," or minority audiences, more active and less interested in words and tunes than in the arrangement, technical virtuosity, and elaborate standards for listening and analysis. This audience (now scattered among the forms of early country music, jazz, blues, musical shows, rockabilly, etc.) preferred "personal discovery" of the music, and usually arrived at such listening pleasures by painstakingly searching for the roots of modern popular music. Their outlook was international, and they had a sympathetic attitude to black musicians, whom they considered to be the prime source of material. It was the cults that promoted "early music," wrote the books and magazines, and produced reissues of original recordings and issues of rediscovered early performers. The latter were past their prime but still active and often better in the musical style than current interpreters. The recordings cited in this book are based on both the cult image and the emerging musical stylings.

On a personal basis, as members of the cult, we have found that one of the most maddening things about loving minority musical styles is the frustration we feel when we try to share that love with others who are both ignorant of the form and apathetic towards it ("I don't know and I don't care"). In addition, there is an equally disheartening feeling—when that favorite minority musical style either changes into another form of expression which becomes more popular than the original while still being imitative, or when it gets raped by enterprising producers and performers who then try to pass it off as theirs alone. The circle becomes complete and the frustrations compounded when we try to convince others that this more "popular" music is but a pale imitation of the originals. We admit, therefore, that there is a proselytizing tone to the construction of this book.

The most dramatic influence upon the popular music of the twentieth century has been black African music. Its characteristics have pervaded all forms (except perhaps most musical comedies). Jazz, blues, and soul, of course, have direct roots. But the important innovators in other fields have had direct contact with black musicians and had assimilated black sounds, such as Bill Monroe (bluegrass music), Woody Guthrie (folk and protest music), Bob Wills (western swing), Jimmie Rodgers and the Carter Family (country music), Benny Goodman (big bands), Elvis Presley (rockabilly), the Yardbirds and the Beatles (blues rock), and Led Zeppelin (heavy metal music). Without this assimilation, there would have been no popular music as we know it today.

All of this relates to the essential differences between European (Western) and African (black) music. Black music, in its components, prefers an uneven rhythm but in strict time, and with a loose melody that follows the *tone* of the words. This tone is explained by the fact that the same syllable of a word can connote different things depending on whether it is sung in a high, medium, or low pitch of voice. For the African singer or instrument, beauty resides in the *expression* of music (the *how* of performance). Western music, on the other hand, prefers an even rhythm (which explains why rhythm is the weakest element here) in loose time, with a strict melody that follows the *stress* of the words. For the Western performer, the music stands or falls on its own merits (the *what* of performance), and, ideally, the performance could be perfectly duplicated by others in another place and time.

Much has been written about the differences between Western and black music (see the bibliography section), but little about why white audiences did not accept black music. Three assumptions, however, have arisen. One involves social barriers denying white access to black music; that access was a phenomenon brought about by mass media. Another relates to the musical traditions of black music that were foreign to white audiences (e.g., sexuality, ghetto life). A third assumption is that basic differences in musical cultural upbringing produce preconceptions of what is music and what is not (for example, the white listener defines a tune by its melody, whereas a black listener thinks of it in terms of its chord progressions; white song lyrics are either sentimental or sophisticated, while black song lyrics are experiential and improvised).

As an incidental note, it appears that the state of Texas is actually the well-spring of much of today's popular music. Most of the significant innovators were born and raised in Texas, where they perfectly assimilated the diverse musical stylings of the blues, ethnic materials (Chicano, Caribbean, Cajun), jazz, and so forth, to create and fashion swing jazz, western swing, urban blues, country music, troubador songs, rhythm 'n' blues, rock and roll, and country rock music. No appropriate written materials have yet emerged to explain this complex cross-fertilization of musical ideas, but it is important to remember that the vertical separation of white and black music did not exist in Texas (i.e., both groups shared a common heritage) and that literally all kinds of musical influences were at work virtually simultaneously—a true melting pot.

It is not our intention to present a history of the recording industry or of radio (elementary surveys can be found in Schicke's *Revolution in Sound* [80] for records, and in Passman's *The Dee Jays* [66] for radio), but we view these industries as being equally important as the music itself towards the shaping of popular music. Both recordings and radio had the power to encourage and to deny by their manipulation of public tastes. A brief overview of the highlights follows:

1917-1925—limited retention of sound through the acoustic recording method. Many companies formed.

1925-1931—electric recordings begin, capturing the sounds of a piano and larger groups. 1929 was a peak year, with different markets for different recording styles of regional characteristics (largely ignored outside the geographic areas of marketing; no cross-fertilizations except by musicians who borrowed from other records).

1931-1934—The Depression meant fewer sales (in 1933, these were 7 percent of the 1929 peak), fewer recordings, and the rise of recorded sound on radio. This was the beginning of regional breakdowns.

1934-1941—This period saw cheaper records ($0.25 to $0.35), more recording activities, and the beginning of *professional* musicians who aided in the shifting of the geographic centers of recording activities (pop moved to Hollywood, swing jazz to the West and Midwest, western swing to the Midwest, folk to New York, etc.).

1942-1945—Musicians were drafted, shortage of shellac appeared, there was the ASCAP ban, and the musicians' union went on strikes. Very little new music recorded here, but this was also the beginning of independent companies.

1946-1950—The post-War era saw the establishment of hit parades, the popularity of juke boxes, records becoming full-time radio programming, a complete break in regional stylings, and expenses rising for touring groups.

1950-1959—This period brought a resurgence of *different* forms of music existing simultaneously for diversified but separate markets (blues, jump music, rhythm 'n' blues; jazz, swing, bop, cool; rock and roll; folk, country, bluegrass, etc.), this because of many competing independent companies. The situation is similar to the 1920s.

1959-1963—An age of imitation and derivative music, this was highlighted by a watered-down folk revival, the beginnings of soul music, and the decline of specialized markets in bluegrass, jazz, and rock 'n' roll.

1964-1970—An age of cross-overs, this period sees country music go pop and rock music emerge as a symbiotic co-existent through country-rock, blues-rock, jazz-rock, theatre-rock, soul-rock, folk-rock, etc.

1970-   —Now there is the simultaneous co-existence not only of separate musical styles, but also of merging styles and "roots" music. All three are widely known to a mass audience for the first time *ever*.

Recordings have had a troubled history, and it is a wonder at all that historically important recordings still remain. Many basic conflicts shaped audience appeal. First, it was the cylinder versus the disc, and then the conflict about early playing speeds that ranged from 60 to 85 revolutions per minute. Then, there were different types of materials used for the physical product (metal, shellac, paper, etc.). The method of reproduction varied from the "hill and dale" of the vertical groove cutting to the horizontal cutting, being compounded by the outward playing groove as against the inward playing groove. After World War II, further technological conflicts had to be resolved: tape versus disc; 45 rpm versus 33-1/3 rpm; ten-inch disc versus seven-inch disc; ten-inch disc versus twelve-inch disc; stereophonic sound versus monophonic sound; quadrophonic sound versus stereophonic sound; different configurations of quadrophonic sound (discrete, matrixed, compatible) and tapes (reel-to-reel, cartridge, cassette), and so forth. If an audience was expected to hear everything available and make judgments, then it would have to purchase a wide variety of equipment far too expensive for all but radio stations. Thus, unless recordings were issued and reissued in a variety of configurations, there would be music that people would simply never hear because they lacked the necessary play-back equipment.

Beyond the shape of the prime listening document, there were other conflicts. Various musician unions' strikes against the industry precluded hearing first-hand evidence of aural changes in music at crucial times. The various licensing bans called by ASCAP in the 1940s precluded listening to new records on radio and on the juke box. The rise of the disc jockey on radio led to an influence over what records the public could hear, which in turn resulted in scandals of "payola" and "drugola" for bribes that ensured that certain records were played (and others thus denied air time). And from time to time, there were various shortages of materials for reproducing the record, such as the wartime shellac crisis (to buy a new record, the customer had to turn in an old one for recycling) and the vinyl crisis of the 1970s. All of these slowed down the rate at which new music became acceptable.

The practices of the recording industry are also illuminating when trying to understand the popular music performer. The big schism in the industry occurred during World War II. Previous to this time, the type of singer the industry looked for was one who coupled low cost with better-than-average returns. Later, when the industry learned that it took money to make money, the shift would be to turn a fairly high investment into an astronomical return. Thus, the pre-war performers were largely middle-aged people who had already established for themselves a loyal fandom. These people were self-accompanied, and wrote or modified their own materials. Indeed, their major employment was not in records, or even in music. They were *not* "professional musicians," but simply better than adequate performers who were paid a flat recording fee and given no promotional tours for emphasizing any regional characteristics of their music. At this time, radio was viewed as a competitor, and each record was usually about 50 percent sold out within a year (and left in the catalog for up to 10 years or more). Post-war developments, taking into account the young returning servicemen and the later "war baby boom," concentrated on the under-30 performer, who then broke new ground with a solid financial investment behind him.

These singers and musicians usually performed other people's materials (except for the 1970s rock movement) and relied on great accompaniment from major studio session men. Their prime occupation was in music, especially records; they were "professionals" with a high profile from tours and promotions. They were paid royalties instead of a flat rate, no doubt as a result of collecting funds from radio stations that were now heavily dependent on records as a source of programming. As national markets were aimed for (there was obviously more money to be made here than in just one geographic or minority audience), the music's consistency became blander and more stylized. Tours and national exposure meant that record sales would peak in the first three months, and many records were generally withdrawn after a year. Economically, this meant that, of all elpees released in 1977, 85 percent *lost* money, with the remaining 15 percent being monster sellers that created the corporate profits.

Record companies are always quick to discover new audiences. The fast pace of the industry, plus the high failure rate, indicate which records sell and which do not. Whether they are *good* records or not is largely immaterial. Playlists of radio stations, and best-selling lists of trade magazines, provide an *index* to popular music rather than a *criterion*. This is in much the same way as lists of best-selling books, in that both reflect the interests of the time. Whether they are enduring or not is up to "history" to decide, and by tracing the development of musical styles, any record's impact and influence can be ascertained. As Robert Shelton (*Country Music Story*) has said: "Few popular music styles remain pure for long. Nothing can spread quite so quickly as a musical style that is selling." On this basis, each and every modern record must be regarded as a one-shot attempt. No matter what its popularity, just three months after its release few people appear to buy it. And if the record is successful, then it will generate hybrids and derivative imitations (in addition to making its originators duplicate their success with an exact follow-up copy). This is the determining factor in the preservation and continuation of music, despite the poor side effects caused by records.

There is a distinction that can be made between a *record*, a *broadside*, and the *oral tradition*. The latter is very limited, being based on one-to-one contact in a community, and changes in the music are prone to develop. The broadside, on the other hand, presents words only (it might have been sung at the time of sale), and the later "sheet music" added piano versions of the music. With a broadside, one had to find a tune. With sheet music, one had to find an accompanying instrument. Both, though, stabilized the texts. A record, on the other hand, has not only the words and melody but also the performance style: the text, tune, and style are together in one package, from one particular moment in time. It can be replayed and memorized, and the listener can learn from it—perhaps indicating variants in later performances—and also, of course, duplicate any of its success.

Not everybody could possibly buy all records. Originally, it was up to radio to provide a "free" service, which meant random selection until the days of "Top 40" playlists. Radio was the medium that not only transmitted older songs but also created the regional breakdown in styles, as one geographic area began to hear the songs of other adjoining areas. Radio used a lot of material, and because of its random nature, it created a demand for more and newer material. This was furnished by both new records and live performances. The latter were very important, for many programs were recorded off the air at home, and are now available via small reissue labels. Disc recordings have certainly never reflected any artist's entire repertoire, and it is questionable as to how many discs were actually favorites of the performer. It was up to the a. and r. men and producers to select the tunes for marketing, yet this interfered with the artist's natural choice of songs. This was the case with Uncle Dave Macon, who also never felt at home in the studio. With radio work, the performer could program what he or she liked to sing and usually (in the early days) performed in front of an audience. "Airshots," as they are called, could determine more about a performer's repertoire than discs, and they also plugged the gaps that existed when there were recording bans. This was absolutely crucial during the development of bop jazz because few people outside of New York were aware of the music (in its early period, it was not recorded because of the recording bans).

A graphic conceptual display of diverse major Western musical influences in the twentieth century is shown on page 26. There are, of course, many, many minor variations. (Relative size of boxes is not indicative of influence or importance.)

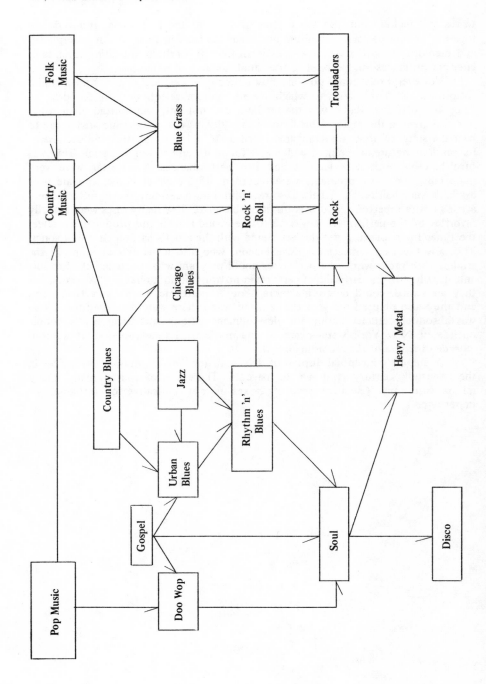

THE BEST OF THE BEST:
Anthologies of Popular Music on Records

"Anthology" is derived from Greek words meaning "flower gathering." Presumably, this means either the best that is available or a mixed bag, with some parts showing off the rest by means of contrast. Certainly the display should be stunning, for why else anthologize? In the music world, anthologies serve either as samplers or as introductions to a company's products. These collections of the works of popular performers sell to a captured audience that is used to having pre-selected convenience items before their eyes. At the same time, anthologies are invaluable for rapidly building up a music record library, or for fleshing out an area of music not already covered in the library. There will also be little duplication among the items in collections if the library does not already have the originals.

Within the past three years, aided by the soaring costs of studio time and performers' fees plus the recognized nostalgia fad, more anthologies and collections than ever before have been released. From a manufacturer's point of view, they are cheap to produce: the material has virtually paid for itself already; the liner notes are few (if any) or standardized; there is uniform packaging and design; a ready market exists, which the rackers and jobbers love, so little advertising is necessary; and anthologies act as samplers of the performer or to the catalog, hence promoting future sales. However, selection of the program depends on the cooperation of music publishers in granting reduced rates.

Personally, we are quite partial to anthologized performances. For a pure musical experience, there has been nothing quite like, say, on a hot and humid night, throwing on a pile of 45 rpm singles and sitting back guzzling beer while tapping to the rhythms. At this point, our attention span is about three minutes; thus a new record with a new voice comes on just as minds start to wander. With older records, the effect is one of familiarity, evoking fond, past memories. For the sake of convenience and better musical reproduction, though, a stack of anthologized long-play records makes this easier. Most new records today can be quite boring between the highlights, and it is not uncommon for a group to have an album with one hit single, fleshed out with nine duds. You really wouldn't want to hear it all again. Too, while most people might all like or remember one or two particular numbers, they also like other tracks individually. An anthology or "best" album attempts to take those most popular selections that we all enjoy and market them so that the most people might like the whole reissue album. One man's meat is not another man's poison in the case of the anthology.

Many reservations exist about compilations, especially with regard to trickery, motives, and shoddy packaging. Some of these are discussed here, but a few general comments are also necessary. In many instances, anthologies have only 10 tracks to a disc. This may be fewer tracks than the original albums had, and certainly it makes each number more expensive at a per selection cost. Yet, there are distinct advantages for a certain market that has low-fidelity equipment: the wider grooves give a full range of sound and increase the bass proportionately, thus making this particular type of disc virtually ideal for home stereo consoles and for older, heavier needle cartridges. Since these wider grooves don't wear out as quickly as compressed ones, the records may be played over and over again with less wear than on an "original" disc. In other instances, some "best" collections (especially multi-volume sets) almost equal the catalog material from which they are drawn and, hence, cost more in the long run.

Trickery involves a number of gimmicks, such as "electronic enhancement" for stereo, with its vast echoing sound being reminiscent of a train station lobby. These types are dying out, as it costs money to re-channel, some of the public are demanding original monophonic sound, and—the biggest marketing blow of all—these discs have been relegated to the semi-annual *Schwann–2* catalog with the mono discs. Sometimes the informative print is very small, or was printed say, yellow on orange, and the consumer virtually couldn't read the notice "enhanced for stereo." Some tricks are not solely for deception, though. Cute tricks include the title "The Worst of the Jefferson Airplane"—an obvious collection of best material. But what about an original first record by an unknown group that is titled "The Best of . . ." just to attract sales?

Another problem with the vinyl product is that anthologies are mostly regional pressings. Duplicate masters are used in factories not as careful as the home plant and are shipped directly to the regional distributor. Of course, a careless pressing sounds worse than a skillfully crafted product. And the polyvinyl chloride content can drop to below 85 percent. This is important, for the extender in a disc can be exposed to the stylus riding on the otherwise soft plastic and great harm can occur. Classical records are generally 95-99 percent vinyl, with pop recordings being around 90 percent. Anything lower than 90 percent can be detrimental to sound reproduction.

The material included in anthologies is another concern. It is usually selected by the producer or company, so that it may have no relation to what the performers themselves think is their best material. Many groups are anthologized *after* they leave one company for greener pastures, and the original manufacturer can keep churning out the reissues year after year, relying on the groups' future success to advertise the old reissued product. Some anthologies are shoddily passed off as memorials after a performer's death; others are issued if performers cannot produce an album in any one particular year, whether through accident (as in Bob Dylan's case), personal problems, laziness, or personnel changes. This keeps the name in front of the record-buying public, but too often the album is at full list price and the cover only mentions in passing that it is a reissue.

With the new packaging gatefold, is it likely that *all* notes on anthologies (as well as many others) will be inside the shrink-wrapped cellophane parcel. Thus, the consumer will not know what he is supposed to buy until he reads a review, ad, or opens the package (thus forfeiting a "return" if he already has the item). As these records rarely get reviewed or advertised, there is no certain way of knowing what is on them; Schwann does not often give track listings for them.

Anthologies are also notable for what they do not contain. The biggest performers are rarely anthologized while they are still under contract, and if they are, then the discs are sold at full price. There is no inexpensive introduction to the best material of Hank Snow, Charlie Pride, Elvis Presley, or the Rolling Stones.

When the latter group left Decca/London, the company released two anthologies at a full price of $10.98. Presley is available on a set of four discs, if you want virtually *all* of his better product. England is the best place to go for inexpensive reissues in all fields, particularly so if the reissue is not available on the North American market.

Mail order houses are a direct development from the recording companies, and some of the latter have gone into the business themselves. Being leased only for such a one-shot appearance, the selected items are pure gravy for the companies. Thus, with groove compression, 18 to 24 titles (2½ minutes long) can appear on some of these albums. Usually these discs are promoted only by television commercials or direct mail. Other reissue companies (prevalent in England) lease material from the original companies and repackage it as they see fit. Pickwick International is most successful at this, drawing on the large Capitol and Mercury catalogs (which is one reason why these two companies do not reissue many discs).

The anthologies listed in the musical genres herein consist of reissued material, either in the form of anthologies, "best" collections, or "live" versions of studio tracks that enjoy reasonably good sound. They are set apart as subsections entitled "anthologies." These records are offered as a pre-selected guide to really good performances, or as material that may lie outside of a library's main interest or collecting policy. For instance, a recorded sound library may want to capture a flavoring of the blues without exceptional expense and without culling lists of basic records, discographic essays, or even Schwann (which splits blues among "current popular" and "jazz"). Determining what records may be basic, essential, or important is not always an enjoyable listening experience; it is certainly expensive. What is being stressed here is quantity *with* quality: to get the best and most available at the cheapest price possible. In many instances, a well-rounded collection will result from buying anthologies, but not necessarily an in-depth collection.

Basic recordings are something else again—interesting for the derivative performers that will follow in the style, but mainly useful in a historical context. Such a collection is one to build on—to use the "basic" in its literal sense. These selections are listed to capture the whole field at once. The demise of the record shop's listening room has meant that the informed consumer can no longer hear an album before purchase; others might not have any real knowledge of music other than somewhat vague personal interests. How can they hear the "best" in another field? The same reasons for anthology production that are advanced by recording companies can be applied when libraries acquire such records: to introduce people to new listening pleasures (despite all the gimmicks of hard sell). Also, nearly all these records are also available on tape (except for most of the mono reissues).

GRASS ROOTS MUSIC:
The Folk Process

> "You hear people talking about folk songs.
> You hear people talking about the blues,
> like it's something else. It's all folk songs.
> You never hear horses sing 'em."
> —Big Bill Broonzy,
> Bluesman, 1956

The "folk process" is more important than "folk music." By process, we mean the manner of the creation, dissemination, and subsequent use of music. After a strenuous debate, the International Folk Music Council finally accepted these parameters of a definition in 1954:

> Folk music is the product of a musical tradition that has been evolved through the process of oral transmission. The factors that shape the tradition are: (i) continuity which links the present with the past; (ii) variation which springs from the creative impulse of the individual or the group; and (iii) selection by the community, which determines the form or forms in which the music survives. . . . The term can be applied to music that has been evolved from rudimentary beginnings by a community uninfluenced by popular and art music and it can likewise be applied to music which has originated with an individual composer and has subsequently been absorbed into the unwritten living tradition of a community. . . . The term does not cover composed popular music that has been taken over ready-made by a community and remains unchanged, for it is the re-fashioning and re-creation of the music by the community that gives it its folk character.

Thus, this definition provides for *continuity* (mainly the lyrics), *variation* (mainly the melody), and *selection* (for preservation) in the transmission of folk music from one generation to the next, or from one region to another. Overall, it has been found that travelers and/or gypsies have been the two groups highly involved in the preservation of folk materials. Such oral manifestations of heritage always develop through a process where an item's origin does not matter, but the treatment of it does. Thus, not *what* (repertoire) is played or *how* (style) it is played counts in the folk process; rather, what counts are the *circumstances* under which a song is performed, such as the relationship between artist, listener, and material. At this point, distinctions between "traditional folk," "folk revival," and "troubador" become very blurred. On the one hand is the common property of traditional songs; on the other is the traditional framework of lyrics and music, which is representative of the *then-current* community. Further, the impact of *electronic* culture has tended to even blur distinctions between the performer and the audience, whereby the oral tradition is becoming an aural tradition through mass exposure. This breakdown then resolves itself in a co-terminal fusion, with little to distinguish artist, audience, and repertoire. From this pool arises the constant attribution of material to past and different societies (e.g., British folk music from Celtic origins, American folk music from British folk music), which, although linked through arising from common eras, now exist all at the same time: traditional "folk" music, "old time" music, bluegrass music, country music, southwestern music, sacred music, and troubador offerings.

Change, then, is an integral part of the folk process, which makes it very difficult to arrive at some consensus on important and interrelated recordings. To pigeonhole any musical genre is at once to limit it and to prevent it from evolving. Yet, for purposes of this book, it had to be done. The ten sub-sections here all deal with the folk process, and while one form led to another, they all are interrelated and are still evolving. Grouping, then, is mainly by chronological emergence. There are thousands of recordings from which to choose, with a variety of styles, categories, languages, and repertoires. And there are constant triangulations that are difficult to reconcile, such as:

1. Traditional-style performances of professionals/amateurs at concerts and festivals.

2. Historically important/educationally valid/highly listenable.

3. American/British/non-English.

4. Traditional/Ethnic/Modern.

Thus, more than any of the other genres covered in this set of books, everything here must be viewed as part of an organic whole, for a folk *style* will persist long after the actual songs themselves are forgotten (e.g., rural songs are not popular in urban areas, but the rural style remains intact with the urban folk revivalist whose song might be more contemporary).

 ETHNIC OFFERINGS

ETHNIC OFFERINGS

INTRODUCTION

No account of the folk process would be complete without some examination of non-English influences. Many African antecedents are found in the blues, jazz, soul, and all forms of black music, and quite a few also mixed in with white music, as in folk blues, blues rock, Dixieland jazz, and so forth. Of all non-American sources of music, African music contributed the most ideas and innovations, and thereby became the most pervasive. Oriental music also has shown up, especially in Hawaii, with the Hawaiian guitar style influencing much of old time music and pop music, and eventually emerging as the pedal steel guitar in country and country-rock. Mysticism, the Indian sitar, and the raga form contributed to rock and jazz music in the late 1960s, as did Arabian (Middle East) music.

Beyond European and Latin dance forms (waltzes, tangos, polkas, etc.), the non-English language influence has been through Spanish music in the American Southwest (and in New York City); French music in Louisiana, New England, and Eastern Canada; and polyglot English-French-Spanish music in the Caribbean. On popular commercial recordings, these manifested themselves as chicano music and salsa, Cajun and fiddle dance tunes, and calypso and reggae, respectively. Of these, only chicano, Cajun and calypso have immediate folk roots.

The ethnic musical form closest to the American folk tradition has been Cajun music, with its oral transmission and (sometimes) cultural arrest. Primarily a dance music, it has been an influence on modern western music, and even on country music to some extent. It arose and became popular in Louisiana, Texas, Oklahoma, and Mississippi, and it is still a regional music today through such labels as La Louisianne, Goldband, Arhoolie, and Swallow (the latter an anglicization of owner Leo Soileau's name). Chicano music has become diversified through rock recordings in Los Angeles and San Francisco or through salsa music in New York City. Calypso and voodoo-type music, as well as Spanish and French, had profound impact in New Orleans, which, through jazz and r 'n' b, became a hotbed of musical interweaving. Both calypso and chicano music had dramatic impact on the western swing style, as did German waltzes and Middle European polkas. In fact, western swing has the most diverse roots of any musical form annotated in this book.

Other nationalities influenced popular music in America, but recordings are scarce and many were not "popular" in the commercial sense. The following short titles had their fans and markets, and are intended as very good examples of ethnic musical offerings.

ANTHOLOGIES
[largely non-English language]

F1.1   **Bahaman Songs, French Ballads and Dance Tunes, Spanish Religious Songs and Game Songs.** Library of Congress AAFS L 5.

F1.2   **Cajun Music.** Folkways Ethnic Library F 458.

F1.3   **Folksongs of the Louisiana Acadians, v.1/2.** two discs. Arhoolie 5009 and 5015.

These field recordings are samplers of influential non-English language music within the borders of the United States. The Library of Congress set is the widest ranging, incorporating six songs from the Bahamas (and, hence, Carribbean influences) and fourteen from Texas and New Mexico for the Spanish religious and game songs. The eight Cajun pieces were recorded in 1934 at New Iberia, Crowley, Angola, etc.—all in Louisiana—and all were blues or waltzes. The Folkways set was recorded in 1957 at Abbeville (LA), and it comes with good notes. The Arhoolie discs concentrate on Mamou (LA) during the same period—volume one here is a reissue of Harry Oster's Folklyric A4, which first came out in 1959. These two Arhoolies are excellent surveys of the music of the Acadians. The first side of volume one deals with the nineteenth century and afterwards; the second side deals with the eighteenth century and before and, covering the period before the Acadian expulsion from Canada, is the more lyrical. Both records have a spontaneous feeling, as if the performmers were entertaining for friends and not for a microphone. Extensive notes and English translations of the French songs are included, with only a few for the second volume, which is mainly waltzes and instrumentals ("Lance Meg Waltz," "French Jig," and "Empty Bottle Stomp").

F1.4   **Harry Belafonte. Calypso.** RCA LSP 1248.

F1.5   **Harry Belafonte. This Is Harry Belafonte.** two discs. VPS 6024.

Belafonte was instrumental in creating the calypso craze of the late 1950s as a form of commercial folk music (and indeed, he was swept up in the folk music idiom by presenting slick versions that were covers of other performers). His best work has always been his first album, the first noted above. It is a purer distillation of Caribbean rhythms and exuberance, containing such classics as "Banana Boat Song (Day-O)," "Brown Skin Girl," "Come Back Liza," "Jamaica Farewell," and "Mary's Boy Child." Later, he would branch out into original materials and sources from other countries, as found on the twofer compilation (which unfortunately duplicates some of the bigger selling items on the *Calypso* disc). Here are "I Do Adore Her," "Mama Look at Bubu," "Island in the Sun," and "Mathilda." He had a charming way with his audiences and with children, and he was ever-popular when touring.

F1.6   **The Cajuns: Songs, Waltzes and Two-Steps.** Folkways RBF 21.

F1.7   **Louisiana Cajun Music, v.1-5.** five discs. Old Timey X 108-111, and 114.

The Old Timey records are a series that deal with each decade from 1920-1960 to define the extent and commercialism of "Cajun" music. Volume one is subtitled "The 1920s—Early Recordings" and shows some of the roots of latter-day Cajun singers such as Vin Bruce, or the English commercialism of Doug Kershaw. And, of course, the roots of Cajun music itself go back to the Acadians in Canada after 1604 and, earlier, to France and the Norman (or Breton) traditions. Since the development of recordings, the instrumentation has remained basic: accordion, violin, and spoons, and triangle for percussion. Cajun music became widely known during the great field expeditions of the 1920s, when recording companies needed new singers and material to cash in on the market for records. As was typical in other folk fields, just about anybody who could sing was recorded, provided that they lived in a rural area. Cajun music, as a type of regional folk music, was first recorded by Columbia in 1928, with Joseph and Cleoma Falcon. Their first two recordings ("Lafayette" and "The Waltz that Carried Me to My Grave") are in the Old Timey set, and in all five selections of them on the fourteen tracks here, we hear the tremendous, soulful soaring cries of Joseph Falcon. On five others, we get his accordion. Lawrence Walker, another accordionist, gives the blues on "Alberta" and "What's the Matter Now," while a third accordion player—Amade Ardoin—is the only black artist on these discs. Fiddlers include Leo Soileau and Dennis McGhee (with two fiddles on "Mon Cherie Bebe Creole").

Volume two is subtitled "The Early Thirties," and continues the first volume (some of the titles quoted above come from this second disc). Unlike the first two albums, volume three ("The String Bands of the 1930s") does not feature the accordion. Country music influences by the mid-thirties led to a revival of the violin. Instrumentation here is thus a mixture of guitars, violins, dobros, banjos, drums, or washboard. Recording quality, again taken from 78 rpms, is better than the first two albums, and the groups appear to be more diversified in their performances here, including one instrumental and one English number ("Hand Me Down My Walking Cane," a black blues in the folk tradition). The fourteen tracks here, as on each and every album except for volume five, have notes, transcriptions and definitions, and translations. All five records are good educational experiences in listening. The themes of the songs in the 1920s concerned love, death, lullabyes, and rambling, but unlike other folk music in the United States, there are few bawdy songs and more marriage songs, perhaps reflecting the Roman Catholicism of the Cajuns. The string band album is more danceable, although almost everything on these discs was meant for the dance, with waltz, one-step, and two-step rhythms predominating. Several variants of the Cajun standard "Jole Blond" are presented, such as "La Valse De Guedan." The groups include Miller's Merry Makers, the Hackberry Ramblers, and Cleoma Falcon.

It is interesting to note that "Tu Pen Pas Ma Retter De Revere," which comes from the Folkways RBF set and is of the same period, translates as "You Can't Stop Me from Dreaming," and is a French-Cajun cover version of that popular 1937 song, recorded in the same year. The RBF set of fourteen tracks covers the 1930s in a brisk survey, from Falcon to the more country singers of the Alley Boys from Abbeville, who not only sang in English in order to garner the larger English market but also employed amplified steel guitar. By this time, the Cajun stringbands had some impact on the formative years of western swing. The RBF set has notes, but the poor sound of the transfers and the duplications in the Old Timey make it a low priority item. Volume four of the Old Timey set is subtitled "From the 30s to the Early 50s," but it doesn't present the more commercial offerings, concentrating instead on such groups as the Riverside Ramblers and the Oklahoma Tornados, or on soloists such as Nathan Abshire or Iry Le June. Volume five is "The Early Years, 1928-1938," and comprises newly uncovered records, including the original melody for "Jole Blond" in the Breaux Family's "Ma Blonde Est Partie." Others include Cajun blues, twin fiddle accompaniment, Cajun vocal duets, and the originals of such other standards as "Calinda" and "T'Es Petite."

F1.8 **Texas-Mexican Border Music; Una Historia de la Musica de la Frontera. v.1 (An Introduction: 1930-1960); v.2 (Corridos, Part 1: 1930-1934); v.3 (Corridos, Part 2: 1929-1936); v.4 (Norteño Acordeon, Part 1: The First Recordings); v.5 (End of a Tradition, 1928-1938: The String Bands); v.6 (Cancioneros Viejos, Part 1); v.7 (Norteño Acordeon, Part 2: From the 1940s to the 50s).** seven discs. Folklyric 9003/7 and 9011/12 (in progress).

Most of the recordings on this fine set of seven-plus discs were recorded during the "golden age" of folk music recording in the United States (from about 1927 through the mid-1930s). Almost any kind of music heard in South Texas was recorded, but especially the regional "corridos," which at that time generally took up both sides of a 78 rpm disc (or, about six minutes for the singers to relate their story). Corridos were seldom heard by anyone except for those in the lower economic classes, such as laborers and farmers. Workers had little to be proud of, except for their courage and honor, and this is reflected in their arrogant, exceptionally individualistic music. To the untrained ear, all the tunes sound the same, and indeed, appear to be comparable to American beer drinking songs—except that the lyrics are different. As an example of exasperation: "I am desperately tired/ of doing so much work/ of picking so many oranges/ I think I'm turning orange." The serious side is found in the story ballads, usually of some great personal tragedy. During this period, there apparently was little or no censoring of material.

Chris Strachwitz has done an admirable job in presenting a survey of music that illustrates the feelings, attitudes, and problems of the Mexican-Americans in the United States. He has wisely selected songs and tunes he found to be still of great interest to the people of South Texas, where some are still performed today. He chose recordings by artists who are representative of the rural tradition in contrast to trained, urban middle-class singers. Very important items include the original recordings of "El Huerfano," "La Zenaida," and "Corrido De Gregorio Cortez." The corridos series contains a 32-page oversized booklet, written by Philip Sonnichsen, that presents texts and translations to all the songs (plus explanatory footnotes), general commentaries, biographical information, several overviews, bibliographic footnotes, illustrations and photographs, and full discographic data.

The accordion collections emphasize the diatonic—or button—accordion. It was cheaper and easier to play than the piano accordion, and it gave forth a reedy vibrato sound characterized by sweetness and delicacy. The sixteen representative tracks are from 1930 through 1939, recorded at either San Antonio or Dallas; the second volume continues this pattern to 1950. Once again, as with all discs in this series, there are sixteen tracks with full discographic information and superb liner notes. These are important records in the history of ethnic popular music, and the series is in progress, ultimately to conclude with volume 10.

BRITISH FOLK TRADITION

BRITISH FOLK TRADITION

INTRODUCTION

British folk material is mainly lower class and rural, with motifs common through many songs. Anonymity and illiteracy were important in the transmittal of folksongs, at least until the age of the broadsheets in the urban areas. These broadsheets—or broadsides—developed in the early sixteenth century and flourished up through the late nineteenth century. A "broadside ballad" was a printed sheet of verse, falling historically and stylistically between the earlier folk ballad and the later newspaper. The British folk song had for quite awhile in the nineteenth century suffered from various problems of definition. Differences of interpretation would abound from country to country, county to county, scholar to scholar, and even era to era. It was not until Francis James Child's time that they were even codified. Child (1825-1896) was born in Boston but moved to England. Over the years, he collated folk song ballads, including variants of lyrics and music, and finally codified them in his book, *English and Scottish Popular Ballads*. This definitive collection of turn-of-the-century work was important because, before Child, accurate editions of ballad texts never existed.

There are four main types of materials in British folk song. In a rough chronological order, there were first the ceremonial *event* songs for festivals. Second came the *ballads* (mostly classified by Child) that covered love problems, stories, and nonsense, and also included carols. Third, by the time of print, came the extension of the ballads into *lyrical* songs covering scenery, love, identification with nature (pathetic fallacy), sex, military life, and labor. (Some of these were attributable; most of them had a standard tune.) And fourth came the *industrial* songs of urban life but based on classical rural forms (the broadsides).

Although Child was the first to collate *ballads*, of even more importance was the work done by Cecil Sharp (1859-1924). Whereas the American Child went to Britain, the Englishman Sharp went to the United States and collected folk songs and dances at the turn of the century. In twenty years, he noted and collected 5,000 songs (3,300 from England and 1,700 from the Southern Appalachian Mountains). His coverage was wider than ballads, and he thereby restored to the English the songs and dances of their country. He also attempted to grapple with the characteristics of folk songs. He found six principles that distinguished a folk song from any other. First, it was built on a non-harmonic principle. Second, it rarely modulated. Third, the modes were Dorian, Aeolian, or Mixolydian. Fourth, it contained bars of irregular lengths. Fifth, it made frequent use of wide intervals. And sixth, certain melodic figures recur, such as ascending scale passages of four quavers or semiquavers.

At roughly the same time as the American folk revival of the late 1940s, there was a similar British folk revival. In the 1950s, this was led by Ewan MacColl in England and by Hamish Henderson in Scotland. The impetus for this came from the American revival and Harry Smith's *Anthology* for Folkways Records. Singers thus worked backwards from American songs to British songs (Sharp and Child). MacColl began his "radio ballads" program (theatrical recreations of industrial folk music with tape recorded talks by actual workers) and the BBC began its programs *As I Roved Out* (which stressed traditional songs and dances through field recordings) and *Country Magazine*. Later, the best tracks from these programs were edited for a ten-volume record anthology, which furthered access to folk material of a wide variety of styles. Roots, then, were traced and sourced, and the folk revival blossomed far more than in the United States, never peaking but gaining momentum over a period of 25 years.

The best music of this period can be found on Bill Leader's Trailer and Leader labels, with Irish and English materials. Argo and Topic tend to be scholarly, while Transatlantic is more in the popular mode. Excellent labels for Irish and Scottish music include Claddagh for the former and Tangent for the latter. Many titles are also available in the United States through the Folkways licensing label and through Rounder Records as imports. On the following pages, we have listed only a small handful of British folk items to show some antecedents to the American folk tradition, and to present, as well, highly enjoyable music. (Later, we present electric folk music from Britain in order to ascertain its American influences—Dylan—and its American popularity; see F2.44-61.)

Electric Folk

Folk-rock is the combination of the contemporary folk idiom with rock music; electric folk music is the continuation of the folk tradition with electrically amplified instruments. The two are not the same. Electric folk music is a British phenomenon that never spread to the United States with American performers, but has since proven enormously popular on the American market with British singers.

By way of background, both the American Alan Lomax and Ewan MacColl (in the early 1950s) were part of the folk blues music scene in Britain. Along with jazzman Ken Colyer, they redefined American influences in Britain through *skiffle* music, which combined blues, folk, and jazz music by using a jug band, "good time" lyrics, and the concept of jazz clarinet interpolations into a fairly straightforward folk song. This interpolation was the direct ancestor of the electric guitar solos in the work of Fairport Convention and Steeleye Span. In 1953, Lomax and MacColl started the "Ballads and Blues Club," one of the first folk and blues coffee houses in Britain. In 1956, they further developed skiffle music through a group called the Ramblers, which included Peggy Seeger. The American link here was now enormous, as Alan Lomax was the same Lomax who previously had been in the U.S., and Peggy was Pete Seeger's half-sister.

Sometime in the late 1950s, there was a clear split between blues and folk. Followers of the former became entranced with Chicago blues and created the electric blues revival that led to the British blues bands' invasion of the United States— and changed the course of popular music. The followers of the latter sought "pure" British folk songs to reinterpret. There was the same dichotomy here as in the United States: the traditionalists versus the folk-blues singer-songwriters. But in the end, most of the latter group were also performing traditional items, an occurrence that never happened in the United States, where the split was permanent. A new folk club in the late 1950s called "Les Cousins" took a chance and hired such good acts as those of Bert Jansch, John Renbourn, Sandy Denny, and others. These newcomers developed their pleasing mixture of new and old songs while experimenting with new methods of presentation.

One of the causes of splits between groups of singers was the question of accompaniment. The strict traditionalists maintained that all folk songs are to be sung a cappella. Thus, the question of electric or acoustic is actually one of *whether to accompany or not* and for all intents and purposes, an electric guitar would do as well as an acoustic, once accompaniment is decided upon. The electric guitar's development by now included the wah-wah pedal, and this "vocalized" it to the point where the guitar could almost talk. Since one of the major reasons for any musical accompaniment was to furnish a second voice for the soloist, it was thus possible to rationalize an electric guitar as being a more suitable accompaniment than an acoustic guitar, inasmuch as the wah-wah pedal was a second voice. This also meant the complete elimination of such drones as percussion and keyboards. With the accompaniment issue nicely resolved, the next use of electricity was for the raw power to convey the urgency and importance of sexual and violent folk songs. A cappella singing can convey the stark nature of incest, decapitation, and matricide, but the potent story line had lost its dramatic impact in today's world. Harsh, amplified punctuation was needed.

All of this was clearly brought into focus by the 1966 appearance of Dylan and The Band at the Royal Albert Hall. He showed that "folk" could be done with electronics, even though he dealt with contemporary topics. Nevertheless, there is much of the contemporary in the five-hundred-year-old ballads and narrative stories still being worked with today.

Literature

We have definitely limited our choice of materials solely concerned with the British Isles folk tradition, preferring to concentrate on surveys that show its impact on American folk music. Howes (45) and Lloyd (54) give the best overviews, the latter especially so in the relationship of ritual song to epic song to industrial song. Laing (50) tries to uncover the reasons for electric folk music by covering the folk revivals in both England and the United States, with details on Dylan, Fairport Convention, Steeleye Span, and others. Karples (48, 49) examines the impact of Cecil Sharp and his work in tracking down Child ballads in America. Some good studies on the interrelationships between the British and American folk song are presented by Abrahams (1), Coffin (15), Wells (94), and Wilgus (98). Some further recommended readings and recordings are noted by Sandberg and Weissman (77). Periodicals give good coverage for British music. *Sing Out!* (20) will have an occasional story, while *Melody Maker* (12) has a weekly page. Other British periodicals such as *English Dance and Song, Folk Review,* and *Traditional Music* are fully indexed in the books *Annual Index to Popular Music Record Reviews* (3) and in *Popular Music Periodicals Index* (69).

For tracing of folk songs, the English Folk Dance and Song Society (London, England) through its Vaughan Williams Memorial Library maintains a comprehensive title index to traditional and some contemporary folk songs (English, Irish, Scottish and American). In 1976, this index totalled 20,000 entries. There is also a tune index and a dance index, plus a sound archive of 3,000 recordings.

ANTHOLOGIES

F2.1   **Boscastle Breakdown.** Topic 12T240 (British issue).

F2.2   **English Country Music from East Anglia.** Topic 12TS229 (British issue).

F2.3   **English Folk Dances.** EMI CLP 3754 (British issue).
All three records are good surveys of southern English country dance music, being performed by both groups and individuals. *Boscastle Breakdown* is the best here, with tracks from Scan Tester (concertina), Rabbidy Baxter (tambourine), Billy Cooper (hammer dulcimer), and the bands of the Tintagel and Boscastle Players. East Anglian instrumentals ("Old Joe, the Boat Is Going Over," "Step Dance," "Italian Waltz" and the polka "On the Green") are performed on diverse series of mouth organs, melodeons, and hammer dulcimers. The EMI set collates different styles recorded in 1958 and 1961 by McBain's Country Dance Band, Jack Armstrong and His Northumbrian Barnstormers, and The Country Dance Band.

F2.4   **The Female Frolic.** Argo ZFB 64 (British issue).

F2.5   **The Iron Muse.** Topic 12T86 (British issue).

F2.6   **Men at Work.** Topic TPS 166 (British issue).
All of these records concern work songs and songs about work (there is a good proportion of women's work songs on the *Female Frolic*, relating to life in the factories and weaveries). Traditional and contemporary songs are intermixed on the *Frolic* album, with contributions from Peggy Seeger, Sandra Kerr, and Frankie Armstrong, through "The Doffing Mistress," "The Blacksmith," "Geordie the Generous Lover," and "An Old Man Came Courting Me." The two Topic albums are close, containing many songs related to industrial folk material from factory life and the northeastern coal mines. Bert Lloyd sings "Pit Boots" and "The Poor Cotton Wayver"; Anne Briggs contributes "The Recruited Collier" and "The Doffing Mistress"; Louis Killen sings "The Banks of the Dee" and "The Blackleg Miners." There are even some dance tunes here, from the Celebrated Working Man's Band. Margaret Barry sings about "The Factory Girl," while Bob Davenport relates life "Between the Cages." Both Topic albums have a superb set of notes.

F2.7   **Folk Songs; an anthology, v.1/3.** three discs. Topic TPS 114,145,201 (British issue).

F2.8   **The World of Folk, v.1/2.** two discs. Decca SPA 102,307 (British issue).
The sixty songs on these five albums are welcome samplers of the vast folk catalogs of Topic and Argo records. The Topic set features A. L. (Bert) Lloyd on "Skewball," Ian Campbell on "The Cutty Wren," the Spinners' "Whip Jamboree" and other performers (Louis Killen, Shirley Collins, Ewan MacColl, et al.). Unlike most samplers, this set comes with full notes and texts. The Decca albums are more for the mass market, with exceptionally popular items sung by the Yetties, the Young Tradition, Ian Campbell, the Clutha, the Druids, Dave Goulder, Shirley Collins, Peter Bellamy, and Cyril Tawney.

F2.9*   **Folk Songs of Britain.** ten discs. Caedmon TC 1142-46, 1162-64, 1224-25.

This marvelous set of folk music in Britain was to the British Isles as Harry Smith's *Anthology of American Folk Music* (item F3.4) was to the United States: a direct impact on the impetus to a folk revival. In 1953, the BBC radio program *Country Magazine* asked   Peter Kennedy, son of the director of the renowned preservationist English Folk Dance and Song Society, to tour the country with a tape recorder and compile hours of tapes for radio transmission. Some of the "better" recordings were issued on this set, along with titles from Alan Lomax, Seamus Ennis, Hamlish Henderson, and Sean O'Boyle—all influential folklorists. These ten discs became the most comprehensive survey of living traditional music ever undertaken in England, and the set became one of the best sources for the electric folk songs of fifteen years later. When put together, the songs were arranged by categories and each separate disc had a hefty booklet added, comprising full lyric texts and backgrounds to each song, plus information about the performer and the recording.

Volume one—*Songs of Courtship*—included the love songs "Green Grow the Laurels," "Our Wedding Day," "As I Roved Out," "The Girl Too Smart for the Fiddler," "The False Bride." Volume two—*Songs of Seduction*—included songs of sexual situation and slightly bawdy songs: "Bundle and Go," "The Foggy Dew," "Rolling in the Ryegrass," "Molly Put the Kettle On," "The Cunning Cobbler." Volume three—*Jack of All Trades*—concerned ballads and songs of British trades and occupations—millers, weavers, cobblers and laborers. Volumes four and five concentrated on the essential *Child Ballads*: "The Elfin Knight," "King Orfeo," "George Collins," "Johnie Cock," "The Auld Beggarman," "The Golden Vanity," "The Baffled Knight," etc. Volume six related songs on *Sailormen and Servingmaids,* while volume seven concentrated on songs of the highwaymen, poachers, sportsmen, and butchers (*Fair Game and Foul*). Volume eight concerned songs about the British Army (*A Soldier's Life for Me*) with "When I Was on Horseback," "The Dying Soldier," "The Banks of the Nile," "Bold General Wolfe," "Napoleon's Dream." Volume nine was a collection of songs relating to seasonal ceremonies (*Songs of Christmas*), with a number of carols and wassail songs. The last volume (*Animal Songs*) was about hunting, but it also has a few children's songs.

There are a number of drawbacks to the set. First, there are at least six or seven separate folk traditions in Britain, yet this set treats them all as one. Second, the tight control of the BBC resulted in some of the bawdy songs being cut; and thus one cannot hear the melodic variations from one verse to the next. As well, unaccompanied singing was limited to just a few stanzas on the (false) assumption that a general audience would quickly grow bored with a lot of husky a cappella voices.

STANDARDS

F2.10*   **Boys of the Lough. Second Album.** Rounder 3006.

This is the American reissue of the British Trailer 2090 disc. The "Boys" are one of the most successful and popular of the revival groups, and perform mainly Irish, Scottish, and Shetland songs. Some of the thirteen tracks here include "Da

Lermick Lasses (Shetland Reels)," "Patsy Campbell," "Gold Ring Halting March," "Merrily Kiss the Quaker's Wife," and "Lovely Nancy."

F2.11   **Isla Cameron and Tony Britton. Songs of Love, Lust and Loose Living.** London 5808.

Both actress Cameron and actor Britton recreate and recapture the earthy, emotional moods caused by human relationships. Most of the tracks here are about the sensuous, bawdy, sexual life, but others are highly lyrical or full of cynical despair, while still operating on a sexual motif. Gerald Pratly accompanies on spinet at times, and there are two guitarists as well. Titles include their only duos "Oh, No John, No John No" and "Died for Love," plus solo voices on "Westron Wynde," "Take Me out of Pity" and "Blow the Candles Out."

F2.12   **Ian Campbell Folk Group. The Sun Is Burning.** Argo ZFB 13 (British issue).

This well-known, established revival group has had many successes in North America, especially via Electra records. The titles on this disc include "Come Kiss Me My Love," "Old Man's Song," "Alexander Somerville Dragon," and "Lover Let Me In."

F2.13*   **Martin Carthy.** Fontana STL 5269 (British issue).

Carthy has been hailed as England's finest revival singer and a great influence on many other performers. His guitar style is ideally suited to accompanied traditional English folk songs and has been copied by others. On this disc, his unique vocals are also accompanied by David Swarbrick's violin for "High Germany," "Sovay," "The Queen of Hearts," "Springhill Mine Disaster," "The Wind That Shakes the Barley," and "Lovely Joan."

F2.14*   **Shirley Collins. A Favourite Garland.** Deram SMK 1117 (British issue).

F2.15   **Shirley Collins. The Sweet Primroses.** Topic 12T170 (British issue).

Collins is one of Britain's best known and beloved traditional folk singers. The first album above comprises recordings that span a decade, all selected off of her albums for half a dozen different labels. Included are such important versions of "Lady Margaret and Sweet William," "Nottamun Town," "Just as the Tide Was Flowing," and "Over the Hills and Far Away." The Topic album also has her sister Dolly on the flute organ, which is an electric version of the medieval hand-pumped instrument. Thus, here, Shirley has the delicate breathy tone of the organ to match her voice, as on "All Things Are Quite Silent," "Spencer the Rover," "The Cruel Mother," "The Streets of Derry," and "Higher Germaine."

F2.16*   **Copper Family. A Song for Every Season.** four discs. Leader LEAB 404 (British issue).

Bob, Ron, John and Jill Copper come from a family that has been singing for over five generations. By the time of this recording (the late 1960s), the four of them had developed glee-type harmonies that are now in use by other groups in their ensemble singing. At the same time, Bob and Ron Copper played a firm hand in shaping the ideas of electric folk and promoting folk clubs in Britain. This album is an attractive physical product, as there is a 22-page illustrated booklet to accompany the fifty songs. Bob Copper breaks in between songs to reminisce about singing styles from the past, and about the agricultural communities of past eras. Titles here include "Dame Durden," "Spencer the Rover," "Sweep Chimney Sweep," "When Spring Comes On," "Brisk and Lively Lad," "Sheep Shearing Song," "Corduroy," and "Come All Ye Bold Britons."

F2.17   **Harry Cox. English Folk Singer.** English Folk Dance and Song Society LP 1004 (British issue).

F2.18*   **Harry Cox. Traditional English Love Songs.** Folk Legacy FSB 20.
    Harry Cox, who also appears on the Caedmon anthology (item F2.9) is perhaps the greatest English traditional singer of all times. He has been a strong influence on the electric rock movement both serving as a source of inspiration and providing it items from his vast repertoire. Both of these albums have notes, and the songs featured (with no duplications) include "Betsy the Serving Maid," "Spotted Cow," "Seventeen Come Sunday," "Next Monday Morning," "The Female Drummer," "A Week of Matrimony," and "Marrow Bones."

F2.19   **Davy Graham. Folk, Blues and Beyond.** Decca LK 4649 (British issue).

F2.20   **Davy Graham and Shirley Collins. Folk Roots, New Routes.** Decca LK 4648 (British issue).
    Both of these records come from 1965. Graham's solo album features his vocals, his guitar accompaniment, plus bass and drums. The program is mainly American and Eastern influences, such as "Leavin' Blues," which features Oriental sounds in the introduction before leading to Leadbelly's classic, or "Seven Gypsies," which has an elaborate blues motif added to an English traditional song. There are also some jazz items here, such as Bobby Timmons's "Moanin' "and Charles Mingus's "Better Git It in Your Soul." Moroccan instruments are frequently featured (as on "Maajun"), and there are some Dylan motifs. The album with Collins is quite similar, except that Collins does the singing here. Again, there are some jazz influences, such as Thelonious Monk's "Blue Monk" or Timmons's "Grooveyard." Collins sang unaccompanied on "Lord Gregory," and there is a five string banjo on "Cherry Tree Carol."

F2.21*   **Bert (A. L.) Lloyd. First Person.** Topic 12T118 (British issue).

F2.22   **Bert (A. L.) Lloyd and Ewan MacColl. English and Scottish Folk Ballads.** Topic 12T103 (British issue).
    First Person is a selection of favorite songs from Britain's leading folklore music authority, with accompaniment from Alf Edwards on concertina and Dave Swarbrick on violin. His persuasive charm is part of his idiosyncratic singing, and as he is less traditional than other singers, he became a good source for both electric folk material and inspiration. Tracks on the solo album include "The Deserter," "A Sailor's Life," "Reynardine," "Blackwaterside," "Jack Orion," and "The Handloom Weaver and the Factory Maid." With MacColl and Alf Edwards, Lloyd performs some Child ballads, such as "Henry Martin," "The Cruel Mother," "The

Bitter Withy," "The Demon Lover," "The Prickly Bush," and so forth. Accompanying this disc is a booklet containing the texts of the songs. When this recording was first released, it was heavily criticized at the time by folk musicologists for both the mannered singing and the edited tunes and texts.

F2.23* **Ewan MacColl and Peggy Seeger. The Long Harvest.** ten discs. Argo ZDA 66-75 (British issue).

 MacColl's real name was James Miller (his father, William, had a vast repertoire of song texts). MacColl came to folk music from crooning with a band and from street theater expressionist groups. He worked for the BBC on diverse shows dealing with English folk music, plus he did the occasional writing of articles and books. As mentioned earlier, he joined with Alan Lomax and Peggy Seeger in creating the folk revival scene in England. His early singing had been characterized by a histrionic, ebullient style; his use of political material had been limited to what he could borrow from songs in the true folk tradition and folk process. *The Long Harvest* is a collection of comparative balladry, faithful to the sources of the Child ballads. On these ten discs, MacColl and Seeger sing English, Scottish, and North American variations of 44 of the most important Child ballads (with sometimes as many as five or six different versions of each song). Accompaniment includes guitar, autoharp, five string banjo, and the Appalachian dulcimer. All texts are included, and some of the standard songs include "The Twa Sisters," "The Cruel Mother," "Lord Randall," "The Daemon Lover," "The Dreadful Ghost," "The Gypsy Laddie," "Bonnie Barbara Ellen," and "The Knight and the Shepherd's Daughter."

F2.24 **Jean Redpath. "Frae My Ain Countrie."** Folk Legacy FSS 49.

 Born into a musical family in Leven, Fife, Scotland, Jean Redpath is perhaps the most visible singer of Scottish music in the United States today. She has worked under Hamish Henderson but considers herself an interpreter of folk music, utilizing her flute-like voice to the fullest measure. This current disc comprises love songs, laments, children's songs, and Scottish country dances—a long program that is also well-rounded. She either sings unaccompanied or with a guitar, and as with all Folk Legacy records, there is a twenty-page booklet of song histories and texts, and even a glossary. The sixteen tracks include the title selection about a fugitive from Culloden, "Farewell He" (which in dry humor tells of a rejected maid who thumbs her nose at her ex-lover), "Wars of High Germanie" (sung unaccompanied), plus material from the Child ballads and Ewan MacColl.

F2.25 **Susan Reed. Old Airs.** Elektra EKL 126.

 Although born in Columbia, South Carolina, Susan Reed collected and performed traditional songs from the British Isles, mainly Irish airs that she played on the Irish harp. The zither is her other instrument. She was very prominent in the mid-1950s folk movement, playing to a specialized audience as did so many people in the pre-Kingston Trio years. The eighteen selections on the balanced program include "The Pretty Girl Milking Her Cow," "The Leprechaun," "Bendemeer's Stream," "Wraggle Taggle Gypsies," "The Boreens of Derry," and the "Irish Famine Song."

F2.26   **Isla St. Clair.** Tangent 112 (Scottish issue).
   This superb Scottish revival singer also plays a concertina on some tracks. Included are "Herring's Haid," "Lullin' the Littlun'," "O Charlie, O Charlie," "MacCrimmon's Lament," and "The Fisherman's Lassie."

F2.27   **Peggy Seeger and Ewan MacColl. The Angry Muse.** Argo ZFB 65 (British issue).

F2.28   **Peggy Seeger and Ewan MacColl. At the Present Moment.** Rounder 4003.

F2.29   **Peggy Seeger and Mike Seeger.** Argo ZFB 62 (British issue).
   The Angry Muse, despite its late coverage through 1968, was actually one of the very first of the British protest song collections. Material here comes from both British and American sources (the 1689-1968 period) and includes "Ballad of Accounting," "Epithalamium," "Grey October," "The Clan Song" and "Strike for the Better Wages." The Rounder album continues the story from 1968 through to 1972, with such new songs as "Student Edward," "I'm Gonna Be an Engineer," "Uncle Sam," and "Tall and Proud." With brother Mike, Peggy Seeger had devised a program of diverse traditional English and American folk songs in the same vein as earlier works with Tom Paley for Electra records. Here they sing (or accompany each other) on "Worried Man Blues," "Come All Ye Fair and Tender Ladies," and "John Riley."

F2.30   **Phil Tanner.** English Folk Dance and Song Society PLP 1005 (British issue).
   This traditional singer from Wales recorded in the 1930s and 1940s before dropping out of sight. The tracks here include "Young Henry Martin," "The Gower Reel," "The Oyster Girl," "Fair Phoebe and the Dark-Eyed Sailor," and "The Parson and the Clark," and most of them were to have an influence on the electric folk music revolution in England. Included with the record is a booklet with texts.

F2.31*   **The Watersons. Frost and Fire.** Topic 12T136 (British issue).
   The revival group here comprises two sisters (Norma and Elaine), one brother (Mike), and one second cousin (John Harrison). Their unaccompanied, close harmony style of singing had a great impact on the revival of British folk music. This particular album is enormously satisfying, as it deals with a theme revolving around a calendar of ritual and ceremonial songs from the British Isles. Included are "Here We Come A-Wassailing," "Jolly Old Hand," "Seven Virgins," "Earsdon Sword Dance Song," and "We Gets Up in the Morn."

F2.32   **The Yetties. World of . . .** Argo SPA 436 (British issue).
   This sampler-anthology introduces the more popular song stylings of this well-known British group, which appeals to the middle-of-the-road popular audiences. Included are "Out in the Green Fields," "McCann's Jug," "Lilting Fisherman," and "Drowsy Maggie."

F2.33   **Young Tradition.** Vanguard VSD 79246.
The fourteen tracks here are derived from two Transatlantic albums. This unaccompanied vocal ensemble comprised of Peter Bellamy and Heather and Royston Wood performed in the renaissance/medieval style of arrangements, and this too had an impact on the development of electric folk music. Tracks here include "Chicken on a Raft," "The Foxhunt," "Byker Hill," "The Barley Straw," "The Husbandman and the Serving Maid," and "The Loyal Lover."

IRISH MUSIC

F2.34   **Here's to the Irish.** Transatlantic SAM 1 (British issue).

F2.35*   **Irish Music in London Pubs.** Folkways 3575.

F2.36   **Paddy in the Smoke.** Topic 12T 176 (British issue).
Variety is the spice of life, and nowhere is there more fun or boisterousness than in singing or dancing to Irish music in a pub or tavern. The Transatlantic album is more a sampler of their catalog and features a number of bands that play in the pubs, such as the Dubliners, the Glenside Ceilidh Band, Sweeny's Men, plus Finbar and Eddie Furey and the Grehan Sisters. The Folkways album contains performances by Margaret Barry, Michael Gorman, Seamus Ennis, and Joe Heaney. The Topic album, also recorded live in a North London pub, features mainly dance music through fiddlers Martin Byrnes, Julia Cifford, Lucy Farr, and Andy O'Boyle. All records contain many traditional elements in reels, hornpipes and jigs.

F2.37   **Margaret Barry. Her Mantle So Green.** Topic 12T 123 (British issue).
Barry, vocals and banjo, works with a country band tradition of some flamboyance. Fiddler Michael Gorman, associated with dance music, is assisted by melodeon, whistle, and piano. Tracks include "The Cycling Champion of Ulster," "The Galway Shawl," some polkas ("Tralee Gaol" and "Maggie in the Woods"), the reel "Doctor Gilbert," plus some dance music hornpipes.

F2.38   **Martin Byrnes.** Leader 2004 (British issue).
Byrnes is an Irish fiddler of some renown. In this program of new and old songs, he recreates the dance music of "Paddy Fahey's Jig," "Tarbolten Reel" and "Irish Molly." Other songs include "Duke of Leinster," "The Sailor's Bonnet," "Stack of Barley," and "The Blackbird."

F2.39*   **The Chieftains. 5.** Island ILPS 9334.
This Irish instrumental group promotes good music of airs, jigs, reels, hornpipes and polkas. Paddy Moloney plays the uileann pipes and the tinwhistle; David Fallon plays the bodhran; Michael Tubridy plays the flute and concertina; Sean Potts plays the tinwhistle; and Martin Fay is the fiddler. Throughout, there is a chamberlike quality to their music, such as "The Timpan Reel," "Three Kerry Polkas," "The Humours of Carolan," and "The Chieftains Knock on the Door." They have also recorded four previous albums for the Irish label, Claddagh.

F2.40*   **The Clancy Brothers and Tommy Makem. Best.** Tradition 2050.

This group is the one most associated with happy Irish music in the United States, and they have done much to popularize the genre away from home. Makem, who joined in 1961, was better known as a Broadway performer (*A Hatful of Rain* and *Finian's Rainbow*). Patrick Clancy founded Tradition records, and along with brothers Liam and Tom, began to record many popular Irish melodies for a variety of labels such as Vanguard and Columbia. Typical tracks on this sampler-anthology include "Little Beggarman," "Kitty Magee," "Jug of Punch," "Rosin the Bow," and "Paddy Doyle's Boots." All of this is mainly transplanted Irish music.

F2.41   **Seamus Ennis.** Leader 2003 (British issue).

Ennis is a master performer on the uileann pipes, as well as being a noted Irish folklore scholar. All the material on this disc is musically correct, such as "The Pinch of Snuff," "The Gold Ring," "Ditherum Doodah," "The Lark in the Morning," and "The Fairies' Hornpipe."

F2.42   **Horslips. The Tain.** Atlantic SD 7039.

This is Horslips' second album, from 1974, and it is a concept piece based on the pre-Christian Celtic saga *The Cattle Raid of Cooley*. With the influence of electric folk and rock music, Horslips presents a rock interpretation of traditional Celtic melodies and tunes, including "Setanta," "Maeve's Court," "Charolais," "You Can't Fool the Beast," and "Faster Than the Hound."

F2.43   **Planxty.** Polydor 2383.186 (British issue).

This flash Irish group (Christy Moore, Andy Irvine, Liamm O'Flynn, and Donal Lunny) perform a wide variety of instrumentation similar to the Chieftains: guitar, bodhran, mandola, harmonica, bazuki, uileann pipes. Apart from jigs and reels, the material predominates with Irish and contemporary songs such as "Raggle Taggle Gypsy," "Planxty Irwin," and "Junio Crehan's Favorite."

ELECTRIC BRITISH FOLK

F2.44   **The Complete Dancing Master.** Island HELP 17 (British issue).

F2.45*   **The Electric Muse.** four discs. Island FOLK 1001 (British issue).

F2.46   **Rave On.** Mooncrest 17 (British issue).

These are the three leading anthologies of British electric folk music. The Island anthology is a survey of folk music in England that traces its development from traditional performers through the revival and thence to electric rock. The main emphasis, though, is on groups of the first and the last periods. Most tracks are collated from the vast Island and Transatlantic catalogs, and the set accompanies the book of the same name (Methuen, 1975). All 55 tracks are detailed in a booklet written by Karl Dallas. Groups include Steeleye Span, Gryphon, Hedgehog Pie, Fairport Convention, the Coppers, New Humblebums, Ian Campbell Folk Group, Pentangle, Mr. Fox, the Albion Country Band, and the Watersons. Individuals include Jack Elliot, Davey Graham, John Renbourn, Jackson C. Frank, Martin Carthy, and

Bert Jansch. *Dancing Master* is an engaging electric interpretation of early English dance music, interlinked with readings of famous early English writers on the subject of the dance. Contributing musicians include John Kirkpatrick, Simon Nicol, Ashley Hutchings, Dave Mattacks, Sue Harris, and Peter Knight (most of these were in Fairport Convention at one time or another). Instruments include bagpipes, crumhorne, pipe, tabor, accordion, electric guitar, bass guitar, rebec, tambourine, and drums. The *Rave On* is a sampler from the electric folk collection of Mooncrest, and it includes Tim Hart and Maddy Prior (preceding their Steeleye Span days), Shirley Collins, Martin Carthy, and Shelagh McDonald.

F2.46a* **Albion Country Band. Battle of the Field.** Island HELP 25 (British issue).
Fairport Convention paved the way for British "folk-rock"; Steeleye Span polished traditional folk songs in an electric setting. Both groups were highly motivated by the amazing Ashley Hutchings, who mixed traditional elements with contemporary expressions and feelings. Feeling dissatisfied with meandering events in the lives of these two groups, Hutchings went on to found a third group that took the folk-rock merger to its highest form yet. Alas, the musicians were together for just a short time in 1973—internal dissension yet again split them, and Hutchings went on to form a *fourth* group: The Albion *Dance* Band, and for the moment restricted himself to instrumental endeavors. One record came out of the ACB, finally released three years later in 1976. Superb musicians here included England's leading revival singer Martin Carthy, the noble concertina and accordion of John Kirkpatrick, oboeist Sue Harris (who also doubled on the hammered dulcimer), Simon Nicol from Fairport Convention on guitars, drummer Roger Swallow, and Hutchings on bass. All but Swallow sang within the group. The fusion of folk and rock here is virtually complete, with the instrumentation being used to pin down the melody. Compelling historical songs are complemented by two Richard Thompson compositions: "New St. George" and "Albion Sunrise."

F2.47* **Shirley Collins and the Albion Country Band. No Roses.** Antilles AN 7017.
This album is one of the most exciting ventures into the area of electric interpretations of traditional songs. All of the arrangements are by Sandy Robertson and Ashley Hutchings (one of the founders of Fairport Convention). A number of revival singers accompany Collins's vocals: Lal Waterson, Royston Wood, Richard Thompson, Maddy Prior, Simon Nicol, and so forth. Traditional titles include "Banks of the Bann," "Van Diemans Land," "The White Hare," "Poor Murdered Woman" and "Just As the Time Was Flowing."

F2.48 **Fairport Convention. Fairport Chronicles.** A & M SP3530.

F2.49* **Fairport Convention. Liege and Lief.** A & M SP 4257.
Fairport Convention, under Ashley Hutchings, began life as a good time jug band, often singing Dylan or Dylan-type material. In emphasis, they were a soft-rock band that gradually drifted into folk music as a manner of expression. Thus, they evolved the sound of electric folk music, but came from rock rather than from folk roots. (In other words, they were a rock-type band searching for material, rather than a folk band searching for a style.) The distinction is important, for quite often

Fairport wavered and produced so-so rock music. Their strongest point was the vocalizing of Sandy Denny, who came over with extensive club experience (notably at Les Cousins). She became responsible for the direct folk emphasis of the material. Other engaging members included Dave Swarbrick, one of the leading folk violinists of Britain, lead guitarist Richard Thompson, and Ian Matthews, who would later go on to create many other groups. In fact, the personnel of Fairport would leave through disputes over musical policy and start splinter bands. In this respect, the position of Fairport is quite similar to that of the American group, the Byrds.

The first "electric" folk song in England was "Nottamun Town," which introduced the guitar lead and added punch to the tragic story. The typical electric folk song has usually been defined by the treatment of "A Sailor's Life." In this song, Denny sings solo against light drumming and improvised guitars for a few bars; then a rock riff is introduced on the bass, and the song ends with an improvised jam session and the electric violin—quite overpowering. Fairport made use of the best of various music forms found in folk, country, and blues, plus some of their own creations. The *Liege* album is their pivotal one; this was the first to exploit completely the concept of electric folk music, right down to detailed notes about folk music in England. The *Chronicles* album collates the bulk of their folk works; and together, the three discs contain such important reworkings as "The Deserter," "She Moved through the Fair," "Book Song," "Matty Groves" (in a far cry from the version of Joan Baez), "Mr. Lacey," "Walk Awhile," "Bonny Black Hare," and "The Hen's March." Some contemporary material in the same vein includes Thompson's own "Meet on the Ledge."

F2.50*   **Bert Jansch and John Renbourn. Jack Orion.** Vanguard VSD 6544.

F2.51   **Bert Jansch and John Renbourn. Stepping Stones.** Vanguard VSD 6506.
Jansch is a premier member of the baroque guitar school, specializing in ornamentation. At the same time, he is a contemporary introspective composer, once working in the early Dylan days on drug songs and other surrealistic ventures. Coming together with romanticist John Renbourn in the immediate pre-Pentangle days of 1966, he recorded a number of albums for Transatlantic, available here in the United States through Vanguard. Both emphasized tradition. *Jack Orion* (titled from a folk song selection) contained "Nottamun Town" and "Black Water Side"; *Stepping Stones* also had a distinct jazz orientation through Charles Mingus's "Goodbye Pork Pie Hat," but it did contain "East Wind" and "Red's Favorite." Both instrumental albums showed the free-flowing scope of two acoustic guitars. Jansch was highly influential on Donovan and came himself from the club scene at Les Cousins.

F2.52   **Pentangle.** Reprise RS 6315.

F2.53*   **Pentangle. Cruel Sister.** Reprise RS 6430.

F2.54   **Pentangle. Solomon's Seal.** Reprise MS 2100.
Pentangle began in 1967 and lasted until 1973. It was founded by guitarists Bert Jansch and John Renbourn, both of whom came from the influential club scene (fostered by the club Les Cousins); and with Jacqui McShee's high pure voice

and Renbourn's harmony, they became the first progressive folk-based band to win international acclaim. They gave concerts all over the world, and their position was that what one heard on the stage was what was on the disc. No electronic gimmickry was used, except for the electric bass of Danny Thompson and drums. Acoustic instruments were normally used, but they were played directly into the microphones (guitars, sitar, recorder, banjo, dulcimer, harmonica, etc.). Their sophisticated folk base included traditional songs, blues, jazz instrumentals, and contemporary songs. From their first album came "Pentangling" (an eight-minute piece full of virtuoso solo works), "Let No Man Steal Your Tyme," "Mirage," and "Bruton Town." *Cruel Sister* introduced the electric guitar into Anglo-Saxon ballads. There are five such traditional songs here, including an eighteen-minute adaptation of "Jack Orion." Outstanding selections on *Solomon's Seal* included "Cherry Tree Carol," "People on the Highway" (a cross-current of expressive guitar melodies), and "Lady Carlisle," played in uptempo fashion with a sparse wah-wah pedal.

F2.55   **John Renbourn. Sir John Alot of Merrie Englandes Musyk Thyng and Ye Grene Knight.** Reprise RS 6344.
Renbourn is a romanticist who harkens back to medieval times. He evolved his style while playing at Les Cousins, and subsequently, he joined with Bert Jansch in forming the influential folk group Pentangle. But he also pursued a solo career, and this concept album from 1968 is his version of the medieval romance Sir Gwain and the Grene Knight. Atmospheric songs related to the story include a piece by William Byrd ("Earl of Salisbury") and some blues materials. Titles included "Lady Goes to Church," "Transfusion," and "My Dear Boy."

F2.56   **Steeleye Span. Almanack.** Charisma CS 12 (British issue).

F2.57*   **Steeleye Span. Below the Salt.** Chrysalis CHR 1008.

F2.58*   **Steeleye Span. Individually and Collectively.** Charisma CS 5 (British issue).

F2.59*   **Steeleye Span. Please to See the King.** Chrysalis CHR 1119.
When Ashley Hutchings, former bass player with Fairport Convention, was discouraged over the musical directions that Fairport was assuming, he broke with them and founded Steeleye Span in 1969 as an out-and-out electric folk group that would play nothing but traditional British folk music. He linked with the acoustic folk team of Maddy Prior and Tim Hart. Originally, they began as a folk ensemble that used electric instrumentation, but changes crept in (including differing personnel) and Hutchings split again to found yet another group, the semi-electric Albion Country Band. Span's early, basic material was a series of highly elaborate arrangements of traditional songs, some borrowed from versions collected by Harry Cox, Bert Lloyd, and from the *Folk Music of Britain* anthology. Their finest overall album was with Martin Carthy, *Please to See the King*, but most of this is now available through the two Charisma collations noted above, which have selections from their first five albums plus some duos and solos. Titles include "The Lark in the Morning," "Bryan O'Lynn," "The Hag with the Money," "Betsy Bell and Mary Gray," and "False Knight on the Road." The nine tunes on *Below the Salt*, their first nationally

distributed disc released in America, include "Spotted Cow" (from Harry Cox), Child 32 "King Henry," "Rosebud in June," "Sheep Crook and Black Dog" and the perennial "John Barleycorn." As with Fairport Convention, much reliance was placed on the female lead's (Maddy Prior's) superior vocals, which were in the same manner as those of Sandy Denny, Jacqui McShee, and Shirley Collins.

F2.60   **Alan Stivell. From Celtic Roots.** Fontana 6325.304 (British issue).

F2.61*   **Alan Stivell. Renaissance of the Celtic Harp.** Philips 6414.406 (British issue).

Stivell prefers to think of himself as a Breton nationalist, for he records traditional Breton music with his Celtic harp, playing originally as a solo performer. The Philips album was one of his first discs, and at the time it was fairly traditional in the Breton manner with "Ys" and "Mary Pontkalley." But since that time, he has begun to explore all of Celtic music, as found not only in Brittany, but also in Ireland, Scotland, Wales and the West Country of England. In time, he introduced rock rhythms into the music (on a 1-2-3, 1-2-3, 1-2 pattern), with instrumentation composed of drums, organ, violin, and the electric guitar of Dan ar Bras. Along with other instruments in a more traditional vein (bombard, dulcimer) he continued to project the songs from long lost roots, such as "Susy MacGuire," "She Moved Through the Fair," and "Oidhche Mhaith." Stivell was to have a good influence on the electric folk movement.

AMERICAN FOLK TRADITION

AMERICAN FOLK TRADITION

INTRODUCTION

"Traditional" refers to music and song that has been learned orally from a community in which the performer has lived all of his life. The range is broad: from the Child ballads to original compositions by an unknown author to medicine shows. In nearly all cases, the vocal music is a cappella (rigidly pitched, high, rubato, nasal) and the instrumental music is solo (fiddle, banjo, guitar, mandolin); most performers now are older persons, since mass media seriously restricted the oral tradition. There are four basic streams to the American folk tradition: the strongest influence came from the British ballad, and this is followed by African blues rhythms, Cajun music, and chicano music. Lyrics were exceptionally important, especially in ballad/story songs, and these were set to simple melodies. Later, near the end of the nineteenth century, social functions and new instrumentation extended the range of the music, with harmony singing developing now from shape note instruction.

The folk tradition in America, by the turn of the century, was creating the *group* of two or more performers, which necessitated rehearsal time or at least some prearranged understanding of common, set lyrics and melodies. Here was the beginning of a loss of individuality, polished renditions, standardization, and the eventual break-up of regional barriers. The material, though, remained basically the same—both the accumulated wealth of the past and songs on newly emerging topics or events. All lyrics in the American folk tradition were concerned with the aspirations of the community that produced them. Later, the community was replaced by the nation, with its minority differences of opinions. This meant a broad scale of "equal applicability" plus divergent streams of alienation, frustration, alternate lifestyles, and other topics reflecting minority opinions. In each case, though, the trials and tribulations of the singer or else the topics were revealed in poetic, realistic lyrics, often augmented by haunting melodies.

The folk tradition, however, is not popular music in the commercial sense, but this book *is* mainly concerned with that latter form of musical expression (old time music, folk revival, southwestern music, bluegrass, country, troubador, etc.). But by relating the folk tradition to the folk process, we can fairly represent the types of folk music available in America, both from the past and from contemporary scenes. Deliberate exclusions here are instructional records, educational records, ethnic music (but see the section "Ethnic Considerations"), and most field recordings except for the significant trips that resulted in the folk music revivals featuring the recorded singers themselves.

Field recordings are, of course, a twentieth century phenomenon. Their great importance is threefold: notation errors are avoided, all nuances were captured, and all aspects of vocal tone and inflections were preserved. Two major collections were assembled by the Library of Congress Archive of Folk Song and by Folkways records, and these are still in print. John and Allan Lomax did most of the former, while Mike Seeger did most of the work for the latter. The largest repository of the recorded American folk tradition is found in the Folkways Catalog of both field and studio recordings: regional songs, topical and protest songs, dances, children's songs, etc.

At the same time that field recordings were being made, folk music collectors were also active. Francis James Child was the first with his significant *The English and Scottish Popular Ballads* (revised by Bertrand Bronson), which codified 305 principal "classics" mainly for their literary content. Cecil Sharp brought to Britain over 1,700 pre-World War I songs derived from older British songs he had traced to the Cumberland Mountains of Kentucky. Carl Sandburg collected for his *American Songbag*. Charles Seeger extended the range of songs by collecting in an "ethnomusicology" context (in which folk music is studied in the context of a total culture). John A. Lomax and son Allan did field researches with cowboy music and Texas black music. Others who did immense work include Frank Proffitt, Samuel Bayard, Vance Randolph, John Jacob Niles, John Greenway, Archie Green, D. K. Wilgus, Frederick Ramsey, Sam Charters, Harry Oster, and Harry Smith, along with more commercial collectors such as Ralph Peer, Art Satherley, and Moses Asch.

But there were a number of dangers in field work (both recording and notations). For instance, when Cecil Sharp moved through Kentucky, he actually created a distortion of the instrumental tradition, for he detested "accompanied folk songs." Thus, grapevine warned people ahead of him to hide their banjos and guitars. There was also the related American collectors' passion for pure a cappella singing, and this even extended to their refusal to recognize the *drone* in American folk music. Examples here include the banjo's fifth drone string in pre-bluegrass music, the bagpipes, the dulcimer, the jew's harp, the country fiddle (deliberately brushing the bow on neighboring strings), and the piano (depressing the damper pedal to sustain the notes). A third problem was the commercial influence of radio and recordings, which distorted the field recordings of the 1920s and 1930s, because people would simply sing versions of these commercial songs and thus lend "authenticity" to the original commercial recordings. Thus, many collectors went out too late, when regionalism was already crumbling. A fourth problem was the use of cheap or broken recording equipment, so the instrumentation could not be heard too well (and this may relate to the collectors' aversion to accompaniment). There was no technical excuse for poor recording facilities because Peer and others made field trips to produce commercial recordings (usually made in a hotel room) and the resulting sound was just as good as studio recordings. The American folk tradition continues today primarily because it is a "live" music that is easy to sing and/or to play. There are many festivals and concerts (as with old time music, bluegrass, and country music, too), there are college campus circuits for performing, there are still coffee houses, and there are school programs and camps for singalongs.

By 1964, there were *three* kinds of folk music: one, the authentic, stressed by the purist; two, the commercial sounds; and three, the singer-songwriters (who either modified existing traditional material to fit needs of self-expression or created their own material in the folk mode). This section examines the first, the fourth section looks at the revival and commercial folk, and the last section examines the third stream, the troubadors.

Literature

The literature is voluminous, but the one book (published in 1976) that put the wraps on all types of books, records, songbooks, films, societies, etc., is

Sandberg and Weissman (77). (They also detail British folk, old time music, blues, ragtime, Canadian, and ethnic music.) In many ways, it updates Lawless (51), which still stands as the definitive book of its type. Haywood (38) and Laws (52) give bibliographic assistance and classification of event songs, but the former only extends to 1960. General works documenting the Anglo-American connection include Abrahams (1), Coffin (15), Karples (48, 49), Wells (94), and Wilgus (98). General survey books on all aspects of the folk tradition in America (including songs and some analysis) include Ames (2), Bluestein (8), Bronson (10), Coffin (14), Lomax (55, 56), Nettl (63, 64), Scott (81), Seeger (82), and Williams (99).

Biographical information is poor, with only Stambler's (86) book available, but it concentrates mainly on northeastern and revival singers. Other specialist materials include Denisoff (18, 19, 21, 22) on songs of protest, war, social discontent and change from the American Revolution to the present times, and Green (34), who studies recorded coal-mining songs. Catalogs of these and other field recordings are available from the Library of Congress (92, 93). The folk song revivals also lack many in-depth studies. Stambler (86) incorporates biographies; Williams (99) presents a concise gloss; and Brand (9) comments on the rise of modern folk song. The two best "surveys" are De Turk and Poulin's (23) collection of readings, and Laing (50), who traces the evolution of folk music into folk-rock in both England and the United States, paying particular attention to revivals.

Periodical literature is in excellent shape. Nearly every state has a folklore society that publishes, even though perhaps less than half of the articles deal with music. The *Journal of American Folklore* (10) is the most scholarly of its kind. The country, bluegrass and old time music magazines pick up the thread of folk traditions in searching for roots. *Broadside* is an excellent source for lyrics and music of the revival, as is *Sing Out!* (20), which also covers blues, bluegrass, ethnic songs, etc., in its many articles. The *Quarterly* of the John Edwards Memorial Foundation (9) also has details on song histories and the event ballad. *Popular Music and Society* (18) will examine folk roots and the various revivals in terms of sociological studies, while *Guitar Player* (7), in addition to *Sing Out!*, gives transcriptions and instructions. More data on records and periodical articles can be retrieved through the *Annual Index to Popular Music Record Reviews* (3) and *Popular Music Periodicals Index* (69).

GENERAL ANTHOLOGIES

F3.1   **Anglo-American Ballads.** two discs. Library of Congress AAFS L1 and L7.

F3.2   **Anglo-American Shanties, Lyric Songs, Dance Tunes, and Spirituals.** Library of Congress AAFS L2.

F3.3   **Anglo-American Songs and Ballads.** four discs. Library of Congress AAFS L12, L14, L20, L21.

These seven discs present a wide assortment of the ballads available as field recordings through the Library of Congress Archive of American Folk Song. Many thousands of recordings have been made all over the country, but principally in the

South, by various folklorists and researchers since the 1930s. L7 was edited by B. A. Botkin and recorded between 1937 and 1942 in the Southeast, featuring versions of traditional English and Scottish ballads: "The Golden Willow Tree," "The Two Brothers," "The Two Sisters." L1 was pulled together by Alan Lomax, with fifteen tracks in the same time frame, but also including the Southwest. Singers include Woody Guthrie and E. C. Ball, and typical titles are: "Pretty Polly," "Barbara Allen," and "Lady of Carlisle." L2 varies a little to consider non-balladic folk variations, collated by Lomax in the same time period: "Haul Away My Rosy," "Soldier Won't You Marry Me?," "Sally Goodin." The last four records are an immense contribution made available through the efforts of editor Duncan Emrich. These tracks were recorded from 1941-1946, in the South, and include "Lord Bateman," "Frank James the Roving Gambler," "Young Charlotte," "Old Smokey," "Darling Corey," and so forth. The last two albums in the set are mainly American originals from the Southwest. All of these seven discs were prime documents for the folk revival singers of the early 1960s and should be noted as being highly influential.

F3.4*   **Anthology of American Folk Music.** six discs. Folkways F 2951/3.
       This set is often referred to as *The Anthology*—perhaps the most significant issuance of any records at any time or place. It was released in 1951-1952, being put together by the eclectic Harry Smith, and was the first reissue of 78 rpm disc material in the 12-inch long-playing format of material not originating with the issuing company (that is, it contained older records recorded for other companies). It could be thought of as one of the first bootleg sets. At any rate, many city singers listened and discovered for the first time their heritage: blues, folk, country, bluegrass, etc. This collection is a most comprehensive one, giving an incisive look into the folk music or commercial recordings available from 1927-1932 (the "golden period" of electric recordings before the Depression caught up with the recording companies). This is an excellent representation of rural music, with many important artists. Smith annotates, providing a text and tracing the history of each song through various recorded variants and printed book passages in this massive documentation.
       Volume one covers *Ballads*. Here are 27 traditional ballads performed by the Carter Family, Clarence Ashley, Buell Kazee, the Carolina Tar Heels, Charlie Poole, and others, such as bluesman Furry Lewis's "Casey Jones." Many of these are Child ballads (all traced) sung as current or popular songs in the period 1927-1932. Volume two contains 29 selections embracing *Social Music*. This was dance and religious music, with many instrumentals abounding. Both black and white traditions are noted through Bascom Lamar Lunsford, Blind Willie Johnson, the Sacred Harp Singers, Cincinatti Jug Band, the Carter Family, etc. Volume three covers *Songs* in the country and blues genres. The 28 selections here are more in the "popular" tradition, being good selling records—tuneful pieces such as "East Virginia," "One Morning in May," "99 Year Blues," "K. C. Moan," "Fishing Blues," and so forth, performed by Uncle Dave Macon, Blind Lemon Jefferson, Cannon Jug Stompers, Mississippi John Hurt, Stoneman Family, Carter Family, et al. Throughout the set, Smith has intermingled both black and white influences, drawing no real distinctions between the two streams but accepting them as equal partners in the tradition of the folk process.

F3.5   **The Asch Recordings, 1939-1947, v.1/2.** four discs. Asch AA 1/4.

Moe Asch was the founder of Folkways records, but before that, he had recorded many individuals for a series of labels, including Asch and Disc, from 1939 through 1947. The catalogs show that this label had enormous breadth and depth when it came to exploring American music. Single artist anthologies have appeared on the Folkways label, with material derived from these war years. The first two discs in the set here document trends and changes in blues, gospel, and jazz. The artists include Leadbelly, Champion Jack Dupree, Josh White, Lonnie Johnson, Sonny Terry, and Brownie McGhee from the blues area; the Gospel Keys, the Thrasher Wonders, and Sister Ernestine Washington from gospel; and a variety of contemporary (at the time) jazz musicians, such as Muggsy Spanier, Pee Wee Russell, James P. Johnson, Sidney Bechet, Joe Sullivan, Art Tatum, Coleman Hawkins, etc. All the sung selections have their lyrics reproduced.

Volume two (the second two discs) is concerned with folksingers, such as Burl Ives, Alan Lomax, Pete Seeger, Woody Guthrie, Cisco Houston—all in the second generation category of folk interpretation or revivalism. It also has a good collection of original singers in a folk-old-time music area, performing country dance traditions or ballads (e.g., Richard Dyer-Bennet, John Jacob Niles, Bascom Lamar Lunsford) and some instrumentals—"Cindy, Cindy" by Hobart Smith, Champion Jack Dupree's "Stomp Blues," Sonny Terry's "Fox Chase," Woody Guthrie's "900 Miles," Rev. Gary Davis's "Civil War March," and Baby Dodds's "Tom-Tom." Indeed, these instrumentals clearly show the differences and similarities among the different "categories" of music, illuminating the devices by which one form borrows from another. The notes, however, are stronger for the folk side of the American musical tradition. The four records contain a total of 54 selections.

F3.6   **The Ballad Hunter.** five discs. Library of Congress AAFS L49-53.

F3.7*   **The Folk Box.** four discs. Elektra EKL-BOX.

These two sets provided instructional materials in the business of American folk music traditions. Both are self-contained and are highly structured. Both present thematic music on each side, and only vary according to the source of the original music. The Library of Congress set was put together in 1941 as lectures on American folk music by John A. Lomax, together with musical illustrations and excerpts compiled from the extensive holdings of field recordings at the Archive. The topics as revealed by disc titles include "Cheyenne: Songs from the Range and Hill Country," "Blues and Hollers," "Chisholm Trail Cowboy Songs," "Rock Island Line: Woodcutters and Prisoners," "Two Sailors' Sea Shanties and Canal Ballads," "Boll Weevil," "Spirituals," "Railroad Songs," "Jordan and Jubilee" and convict songs from Texas. This is a liberal interpretation of ballads.

Robert Shelton put together the Elektra set, using Elektra and Folkways recordings arranged topically, as follows: Songs of the Old World and Migration to the New; Settling, Exploring and Growing in the New World; Work Songs; Many Worshippers, One God; Country Music—From Ballads to Bluegrass; Nothing But the Blues; Of War, Love and Hope; and Broadside, Topical Songs, Protest Songs. There are an average of ten selections per side, all contributed by contemporary folk singers (Phil Ochs, Judy Collins, Pete Seeger) and others included in the folk revival since the founding of the Elektra and Folkways companies. Overall notes are included in the 48-page booklet, as well as specific notes, lyrics, drawings, bibliography, and recommended records. Both of these sets were major and lasting efforts.

F3.8   **Festival of American Folklife.** Smithsonian Institution SI 100.

Over the years, the Smithsonian Institution has sponsored many festivals in Washington, D.C. This set comprises several items of note collected through that time period (the sleeve contains detailed notes but omits dates). For recording quality (stereo) and choice of material, this is a hard record to beat as an illustration of the variety and vitality of American music in all genres. The sixteen tracks cover blues (Skip James's country roots in "Cherry Ball Blues," the Chicago stylings of Muddy Waters's "Long Distance Call"); traditional music in the Riendeau Family's "The Old Man and the Old Woman"; the country in Grandpa Jones's "Old Rattler"; sacred music in the three Monroe Brothers (Bill, Birch and Charlie) singing "I Know My Lord's Gonna Lead Me Out"; bluegrass with Monroe's "Uncle Pen"; jazz through the Preservation Hall Jazz Band and "Hindustan"; modern country in Jimmy Driftwood's "What Is the Color of the Soul of Man?"; and diverse ethnic representation in Chet Parker's hornpipes and reels, the Rodriguez Brothers' Cuban-Congo music, New York Spanish, Turkish, Cajun, etc.

F3.9*   **Folk Music in America. v.1/15.** fifteen discs. Library of Congress Recording Lab LBC 1-15. In progress.

This is the most recent attempt at coming to grips with the vast variety of folk music stylings available in America. Richard K. Spottswood was asked to assemble this set for the Library's Archive of Folk Song as a contribution to the Bicentennial celebration. He took a judicious mixture of field recordings, early commercial discs and cylinders, plus recent taped concerts. By close editing, he can cover 1900 through to 1975 and present an accurate cross-section of music in America. As of this writing, only the first five have been released, but they range from 1902 (Dinwiddie Colored Quartette's "Down by the Old Camp Ground") to 1971 (Lennville Ball's "The Lord Will Provide"), cover obscure but artistically justified performances (a Menominee Indian flute solo), and present a wide variety of roots (old time music, black and Anglo folk, Spanish, American, Indian, Amish, Yaqui fiddlers, Polish cantors, etc.). Many of the items will be out-of-print materials that have not even been reissued by small companies. There is good sound throughout, with excellent liner notes by Spottswood and "consulting experts," complete discographies, and bibliographic references.

Volume one is entitled *Religious Music—Congregational and Ceremonial* (LBC 1), covering a cappella Baptist songs, the Stoneman Family ("I Know My Name Is There"), Arizona Dranes ("God's Got a Crown"), F. W. McGee ("Fifty Miles of Elbow Room"). Volume two embraces *Songs of Love, Courtship and Marriage*, with bluesman Lonnie Johnson and several old time musicians, such as the Blue Sky Boys (an unissued track from after they retired), the Carter Family, the Carolina Tar Heels, and Bill Monroe. Volumes three, four and five are all concerned with dance music. Volume three, *Dance Music: Breakdowns and Waltzes*, concerns black migrant workers, native peoples ("Warm Wipe Stomp" from 1930), Appalachian string bands, East European dance orchestras, and Cajun (including an

Acadian brass band). Volume four covers *Reels, Polkas and More*—Irish, Mexican, Eastern European (e.g., harmonica-jew's harp duet), Cajun—and continues volume three. Featured on volume five, *Ragtime, Jazz & More*, are Ukrainian fiddling, Italian tarantella (from 1917), Hawaiian popular music, early western swing in ragtime, Earl Hines, Bob Wills, and Tampa Red.

The series, when completed, will comprise these additional volumes and topics: volume six, *Songs of Migration and Immigration*; volume seven, *Songs of Complaint and Protest*; volume eight, *Songs of Labor and Livelihood*; volume nine, *Songs of Death and Tragedy*; volume ten, *Songs of War and History*; volume eleven, *Songs of Humor and Hilarity*; volume twelve, *Songs of Local History and Events*; volume thirteen, *Songs of Childhood*; volume fourteen, *Solo and Display Music*; and, finally, volume fifteen, *Religious Music: Solo and Performance*.

F3.10   **Greatest Folksingers of the Sixties.** two discs. Vanguard VSD 17/18.

F3.11   **The Roots of America's Music, v.1/2.** four discs. Arhoolie R2001/2 and 2021/2.

Both these sets are adequate samplers from the folk catalogs of two recording companies; Vanguard was the more commercial of the two. The 31 tracks here are lifted from Newport Festivals and studio recordings and concentrate on contemporary written materials, such as Ian and Sylvia's "You Were on My Mind," Buffy Sainte-Marie's "Now That the Buffalo's Gone," the Roof Top Singers' "Walk Right In," Country Joe and the Fish's "I-Feel-Like-I'm-Fixin'-to-Die Rag," plus Joan Baez, the Fariñas, Phil Ochs, Eric Anderson, the Weavers, Judy Collins, etc. The Arhoolie set comes from the studio, and material is arranged by type. Thus, there is one side of country blues, another of city blues, another of jazz, one of gospel, one of country music and bluegrass, others of Cajun and "folk." The 56 or so songs cover the entire range of owner Chris Strachwitz's interests.

F3.12   **Music from the South.** ten discs. Folkways F 2650/9.

F3.13   **Southern Folk Heritage Series.** seven discs. Atlantic SDHS 1.

F3.14   **Southern Journey Series.** twelve discs. Prestige P 25001/12.

Obviously the American South contributed the bulk of the folk music traditions in America today. These three sets of a first-rate job of collating field trip activities, with no pretentions of tracing back through influences but simply presenting good music. All sets are divided by subjects. Folkways covers *Country Bands, Songs, Play and Dance, Religious and Secular, Elders, Youngsters, Worship, Been Here and Gone, New Orleans,* and *Addenda* (filling in gaps on the other nine). The Prestige set (now out-of-print) and the Atlantic set share the same collator: Alan Lomax made a massive sweep through the country in 1959, and recorded these nineteen discs at that time. The first two on Prestige covered the important Georgia Sea Islands; the next two presented *Ballads, Breakdowns, Banjos of Southern Mountains*; volumes five, seven, eleven, and twelve presented religious music (sacred harp, white spirituals, and a cappella choirs); the Ozarks, Delta, and Piedmont got their separate discs, as does *Bad Man Blues*.

The Atlantic series is a more concise statement, showing the crossovers and influences from one region or race to another. One of the best is the *Roots of the Blues* album, with Fred MacDowell singing both blues and religious items. It is comparable to *Blue Ridge Mountain Music*, where Lomax recorded the Mountain Ramblers for nine of the fourteen tracks here. This is bluegrass from Galax, Virginia, including the marvelous fiddle of Cullen Galyean, three separate lead vocalists, and a number of important instrumental breakdowns.

F3.15*   **Newport Folk Festivals** [as follows] :
1959: volumes 1/3. three discs. Vanguard 2053/5.
1959 and 1960: volumes 1/2. two discs. Folkways 2431/2.
1960: volumes 1/2. two discs. Vanguard 2087/8.
1963: **Blues at Newport**. Vanguard VSD 79145.
Country Music and Bluegrass at Newport. Vanguard VSD 79146.
The Evening Concerts, v.1/2. two discs. Vanguard VSD 79148/9.
Newport Broadsides. Vanguard VSD 79144.
Old Time Music at Newport. Vanguard VSD 79147.
1964: **Blues at Newport, v.1/2**. two discs. Vanguard VSD 79180/1.
The Evening Concerts, v.1/3. three discs. Vanguard VSD 79184/6.
Traditional Music at Newport, v.1/2. two discs. Vanguard VSD 79182/3.
1965: **Newport Blues**. Vanguard VSD 77219.
Newport Folk Festival. Vanguard VSD 79225.

Where to begin . . . ? The enormity of even commenting on this significant series of live folk-derived recordings makes us pause. Newport was the first large and most influential gathering of folkies in the late 1950s and early 1960s. It ran the whole gamut of the folk revival, and included all types of music associated with the genres: traditional, British and Scottish, blues, chicano, bluegrass, country, pop, protest and topical, gospel, etc., etc. The recording quality varies from good to excellent, and there is superior rapport with the audiences. Everyone of any significance appeared. The Folkways set is the most traditional of all the albums, with a smattering of revivalism through Mike and Pete Seeger, Pat Clancy, Alan Mills, and Frank Warner. The blues of Butch Cage and Willie Thomas are strictly in the primitive country mold.

The 1959 concerts were the first of the series, and Vanguard presents adequate renditions by the early folkies who passed through the scene before folk lost its impact: Martha Schlamme, Leon Bibb, Barbara Dane, Cynthia Gooding, Oscar Brand, Ed McCurdy, John Jacob Niles. Of particular interest here is Joan Baez's first appearance, with Bob Gibson singing alongside her ("Wayfaring Stranger"). The material on the long-playing (about eighteen tracks apiece) 1960 Vanguards is largely apolitical, introducing Jimmy Driftwood's contemporary creations and the French-Canadian fiddle of Jean Carignan. 1963 and 1964 saw massive releases here (six and seven discs respectively), effectively collated as to origins. Thus, there are blues, again largely in the country tradition and with many rediscoveries; old time music of Dock Boggs, Doc Watson, Clarence Ashley (serving to introduce them to a larger audience, and Watson's career really took off after Newport appearances); non-commercial folk in 1964 from originators such as Hobart Smith, Sarah Ogan

Gunning, the Ritchies, and Almeda Riddle; country and bluegrass influences with the Morris Brothers, Jim and Jesse, and Mac Wiseman; plus an album of topical songs in 1963. The five *Evening Concerts* discs served the more popular singers in the mass folk revival: Joan Baez, Bob Dylan, the Roof Top Singers, Ian and Sylvia, Buffy Sainte-Marie, Tom Paxton, etc. All discs provide a generous survey of what folk music involved in the early 1960s; they are also perhaps the most commercial offerings of any of the anthologies that show origins.

THEMATIC ANTHOLOGIES

F3.16*   **American Fiddle Tunes.** Library of Congress AFS L 62.

F3.17   **Hell Broke Loose in Georgia.** County 514.

F3.18   **Old Time Fiddle Classics, v.1/2.** two discs. County 507 and 527.

F3.19   **Texas Farewell.** County 517.

F3.20   **The Wonderful World of Old Time Fiddlers, v.1/2.** two discs. Vetco 104 and 106.
     These seven discs display the differences in regional stylings of violin/fiddle music in North America. The Library of Congress offering covers a wide range of tunes and performers from throughout the country, originally recorded in the 1937-1941 period. There are 28 performances, each painstakingly researched from thousands in the LC collection. Alan Jabbour did the work, and compiled a 36-page booklet outlining tune-histories, bibliographies and discographical information—an immense work. The other recordings here are all commercial releases but certainly no less impressive. The Georgia collation is a wild record, being mainly a survey of Atlanta bands—the most active groups in early old time music (Fiddlin' John Carson came from the Atlanta area; it was his records, originally released there, that started the recording of old time music). The two general collections from County stress the popular Clark Kessinger, Eck Robertson, Lowe Stokes, Earl Johnson, Gid Tanner, Burnett and Rutherford, Fiddlin' Doc Roberts, and others.
     The Texas fiddlers are examined from the 1922-1930 period. This is restrained music for dancing and not for vocal accompaniment. The music is melodic, ornamental, and quite often fluid. All twelve are instrumentals, with the Red Headed Fiddlers, the Lewis Brothers, Soloon and Hughes, Eck Robertson, Jim Pate. Good notes by Charles Faurot. Another general collection comes from Vetco, from the 1920s and 1930s, featuring Uncle Bunt Stephens, the Blue Ridge Highballers, the White Mountain Orchestra, the West Virginia Coon Hunters, and Gid Tanner (among others).

F3.21*   **American History in Ballads and Song.** six discs. Folkways 5801/2.

F3.22   **Songs and Ballads of American History and of the Assassination of Presidents.** Library of Congress AAFS L29.

F3.23   **Songs of the Civil War.** two discs. Folkways 5717.

F3.24   Entry deleted.
Historical and event songs have their place in popular music because they were
a logical extension of the older British broadside tradition: to spread the good or bad
news to others because of a general lack of literacy or the lack of the press. The
Library of Congress set was edited by Duncan Emrich from recordings of 1937-1949.
Side one relates events, such as the 1942 recording of "The Iron Merrimac" by
Judge Learned Hand. The assassination songs on side two were contributed by
Bascom Lamar Lunsford, who sang and played fiddle at the Library of Congress.
The more commercial offerings of Folkways involved an elaborate six-disc presen-
tation of such various singers as Pete Seeger, Woody Guthrie, Ed McCurdy, the
New Lost City Ramblers, Oscar Brand, Will Geer and Malvina Reynolds—inter-
spersed with the actual voices of Teddy Roosevelt, Lindberg, Franklin Roosevelt,
William Jennings Bryan, Eisenhower, and Hemingway. This set, all nicely collated
with notes and texts, worked its way around the other one concerning the Civil War.
In a similar presentation, concentrating on just that period and the songs written
soon afterwards, many of the same singers reappear: Pete Seeger, New Lost City
Ramblers, etc.

F3.25*   **American Sea Songs and Shanties, v.1/2.** two discs. Library of Congress
          Archive of American Folk Song AAFS L26/7.

F3.26   **Sea Shanties.** Topic 12T 234 (British issue).

F3.27   **Sea Songs and Shanties.** Topic TPS 205 (British issue).

F3.28   **Songs of the Great Lakes.** Folkways FE 4018.
The sea shanty is common to all sea-going nations. As was typical in much
laboring work, the element of song promoted a steady rhythm with which to pound,
haul, pull, push, cut, and so forth. Different types of work had different rhythms.
The most predominant work songs came from railroad laborers, lumbermen, and
seamen, with the latter being the most popular and most widely known around the
world (and even exchanged with others in the tradition of the true folk process). As
with any type of song, there are numerous forms of shanties. The *capstan* (outward
bound) shanty was sung when hoisting the anchor; the *short drag* type for pulling;
the *halyard* shanty for raising the topsail; the *stamp-and-go* for deck work; and the
hand-over-hand for light jobs. Choruses were repeated with certain emphases to
relate to the extra stress needed to complete work actions (such as extra tugs).
Pacing had to be effective, and there was always a leader of the shanties. A related
type was the *fo'c's'le song*, performed off-duty (mainly below in the forecastle;
hence, its name), and it concerned ballads, love, stories, etc., as in regular folk
songs.
    The five discs cited above cover a wide variety of ground. The Library of
Congress set is a collection of field recordings sung by actual sailors: "Haul the
Bowline," "Sailor's Alphabet," "Paddy Get Back," "When Jones' Ale Was New,"
"So Handy, Me Boys, So Handy," "Blow the Man Down," and "Roll the Cotton
Down," among others, from the late 1930s and early 1940s. The two Topic sets are

sung in the folk tradition. The 24 tracks here include Bert Lloyd's "Blood Red Roses," Ewan MacColl's "The Black Ball Line," and the Watersons' "The Greenland Whale Fishery." Other performers include Roy Harris, Ian Manuel, and Bernard Wrigley, singing "Rolling Down the Bay," "Haul Away the Bowline," and "Shallow Brown." These are good records to compare with the Library of Congress set for contrasting the origins of the songs. Booklets and descriptive notes accompany all four records. The Folkways effort is another field recording, but with a difference. The stress here is on "freshwater" songs. Edith Fowke, well-known Canadian musicologist working in the folk idiom, compiled this anthology of unaccompanied singing by Captains C. H. J. Snider and Stanley Baby, plus two ex-seamen from Toronto, Canada. Titles include "The Dreadnaught," "The Maggie Hunter," "The Merrimac," and "Homeward Bound." In a strict sense, these are not sea shanty work songs, but rather story ballads.

F3.29   **Anthology of the Banjo.** Tradition 2077.

F3.30*   **Folk Banjo Styles.** Elektra EKS 7217.

F3.31   **The Very Best of Country Banjo.** United Artists UALA 411 E.
    There are many, many instructional albums and books detailing various ways to play musical instruments. Although we do not wish to ignore them, this is after all a book on "popular" music, not "educational" or "personal." Thus, we have chosen some *commercial* examples of diverse stylings in the banjo mode. Folkways has a two-album set that relates the differences between old time and Scruggs-style banjo through field recordings and extensive notes (see the sections herein on Bluegrass and Old Time Music). The three discs here are perfectly acceptable introductions to the more popular city manner of interpretations. The Tradition set has selections from country music's Joe Maphis, Mason Williams, and Billy Cheatwood, in addition to folkie Jim McGuinn (later known as Roger McGuinn of the Byrds), Mike Seeger, and Erik Darling. The Elektra set has revival performances in a wide variety of traditional banjo tunes in different stylings, as by Eric Weissberg, Tom Paley, and Artie Rosenbaum (mostly in what are now known as urban performances). The United Artist disc presents most of the same artists as on the Tradition album, plus Dick Rosmini.

F3.32*   **Blacks, Whites and Blues.** CBS 52796 (British issue).
    This anthology illustrates the book *Blacks, Whites and Blues* (London, Studio Vista) and presents key recordings that clearly show the influences of both white and black music on each other as they developed through the 1920s and 1930s. The cross-fertilization and interaction have produced significant results, most notably of late in the soul-rock area and in the British white blues bands. Beginning with ragtime, this musical genre is traced through white and black records, with jug bands and guitar versions (Dallas String Band and Charlie Poole, the latter producing "Coon from Tennessee," based on the black "I'm Gonna Live Anyhow until I Die"). Minstrelsy, vaudeville, and medicine shows contributed their influences through good-time and hokum music, with comics and the development of the Grand Ole Opry. In a strictly blues sense, the white Allen Brothers had "Chattanooga Blues" released on the Columbia race label (for this, they launched an unsuccessful restraining law

suit), and Darby and Tarlton, plus Jimmie Rodgers, exploited the blues. Dance music was the same for both blacks and whites. Western swing, personified by Bob Wills, took urban blues, country music, and southwest jazz (itself a black creation) into another whole new bag ("Steel Guitar Rag" and "Brain Cloudy Blues"). This interacted with r 'n' b material and new manners of guitar expression, culminating in the great black blues guitarist Earl Hooker, who extensively borrowed western swing methods for such as "Walking the Floor over You" and other steel guitar rags. This is an important historical document.

F3.33   **Child Ballads Traditional in the United States, v.1/2.** two discs. Library of Congress AAFS L 57.
The works and texts here were edited by Bertrand H. Bronson, and the twenty tracks illustrate the spread of English balladry throughout Appalachia and the southern United States. These field recordings are derived from 1935 to 1950 outings, from a variety of spots, and mainly recorded by the Lomaxes. The arrangement is by Child number, to show its subsequent development, such as the opening track "The Two Sisters" (Child 10), which here is sung by Jean Ritchie, or the comparative versions of "Wild Boar" and "Bangum and the Boar," (both Child 18). In retrospect, it is a shame that such early work by Child was not substantiated by field recordings, for as pointed out in the sectional introduction, errors do creep into notational systems. Among the other Child ballads here are two versions of Number 53: "Lord Bateman" and "Lloyd Bateman"; and a remarkable "Andrew Batann," which combines segments of Child 167 and 150.

F3.34   **Come All You Coal Miners.** Rounder 4005.

F3.35   **Songs and Ballads of the Anthracite Miners.** Library of Congress AAFS L16.

F3.36   **Songs and Ballads of the Bituminous Miners.** Library of Congress AAFS L60.
These three discs provide adequate documentation of the rise of coal mining songs (and by extension, almost any mining). The history is fraught with violence and death; the genre is a good source of topical and protest material. The Rounder record is a current effort of twelve tracks of protest, recorded at a Highlander Center workshop with George Tucker, Sarah Ogan Gunning, Hazel Dickens, and Nimroad Workman. Titles include "Black Lung Blues," "Both Lungs Is Broke Down," and "Thirty Inch Coal." George Korson, author of two books detailing anthracite/bituminous mining songs, collected and collated the Library of Congress sets. There are excellent notes and transcriptions of the songs, with discographical information. The first disc has fourteen tracks, from various locations in Pennsylvania in 1946. Daniel Walsh and Jerry Byrne have several tunes apiece in the ballad tradition ("The Old Miner's Refrain," "A Celebrated Workingman," "The Miner's Doom," and "When the Breaker Starts up Full Time"). There are eighteen tracks on the second album, with more diverse forms such as blues: "Coal Loadin' Blues," "Coal Diggin' Blues," "Lignite Blues," and "Drill Man Blues," mostly performed by local miners.

F3.37*   **The Greatest Songs of Woody Guthrie.** two discs. Vanguard VSD 35/36.

F3.38   **A Tribute to Woody Guthrie.** two discs. Warner Brothers 2W 3007.
     These four discs highlight the importance, impact, and influence of the late, great Woody Guthrie in the world of popular music and revival folk. The Vanguard issue draws on their folk catalog for tunes written by Guthrie. There are 33 selections, including six by Guthrie himself, borrowed from Folkways records: "This Land Is Your Land," "Grassey Grass Grass," "Riding in My Car," "Dirty Overhalls," "Hard Travelin' " and "Hard Ain't It Hard." Cisco Houston, his first disciple, has nine selections, followed by the Weavers with five, Country Joe McDonald with four, Odetta with three, Jack Elliott (his second disciple) with two, and so forth. Somebody at Vanguard also had the bright idea of lumping together five children's songs with separate performances by Houston, Guthrie, and the Babysitters (with Alan Arkin). The cover has a marvelous "barn painting" by Eric Von Schmidt.
     The other set was originally recorded for the Woody Guthrie Tribute Fund at Carnegie Hall (1968) and the Hollywood Bowl (1970). The 23 selections here total 83 minutes of good music and narration (the latter by Will Geer, Robert Ryan, and Peter Fonda). Joan Baez sings one of Guthrie's favorite songs ("Hobo Lullaby," written by Goebbel Reeves); otherwise all the numbers are Guthrie's alone. The assortment of excellent back-up musicians includes The Band and Ry Cooder. The program itself is laid out to cover Guthrie's life history in song. There are some very interesting vocals here. Arlo Guthrie (his son) presents uptempo, rock-like versions of "Do Re Mi" and "Oklahoma Hills" as well as "This Train Is Bound for Glory." Dylan sounds just like Guthrie, but with electrification ("Dear Mrs. Roosevelt," "Grand Coulee Dam"). Judy Collins is extremely quiet, sounding like Joan Baez ("So Long It's Been Good to Know You," "Roll on Columbia," "Union Maid"). Odetta and Country Joe McDonald, as on the Vanguard set, are here, as well as Jack Elliott, Richie Havens, Pete Seeger, and Tom Paxton.

F3.39   **Hoboes and Brakemen.** Country Music History CMH 106 (West German issue).

F3.40*   **The Railroad in Folksong.** RCA LPV 532.

F3.41   **Railroad Songs and Ballads.** Library of Congress AFS L 61.

F3.42   **Songs of the Railroad.** Vetco 103.
     The railroad was very important in American life. For the West, it meant quickly opening frontiers and civilization; for the East, it was a cheap means of travel or hoboing. Many singers have had railroad songs up their sleeves, the most notable being Jimmie Rodgers. The CMH release does include an unissued Jimmie Rodgers song plus six by Harry ("Haywire Mac") McClintock. Salty hobo songs are here plus western pieces from Goebbel Reeves and Gene Autry. The RCA set includes the original "Orange Blossom Special" by the Rouse Brothers, plus songs by the Carter Family, the Tennessee Ramblers, and the Monroe Brothers. The Library of Congress set has 23 songs selected by Archie Green (who also provides an excellent booklet containing transcriptions, tracings, and discographic data). Aunt Molly Jackson and Harry McClintock are the best known names in this album

of field recordings, but the songs are indicative, as "Lining Track," "The Wreck of the Royal Palm," "Gonna Lay My Head Down on Some Railroad Line," and "The Lightning Express." The material on Vetco is derived from recordings of the 1920s and 1930s, mainly from Al Hopkins and His Buckle Busters, Vernon Dalhart, Gid Tanner, Roy Harvey, etc. All of these records are exceptional and needed for aurally exploring the opening of the frontiers.

F3.43   **Maple Sugar: Songs of Early Canada.** two discs. Springwater S1/S2
(Canadian issue).
    This folk song collection is lively and varied: there are voyageur paddling songs and Klondike Gold Rush songs, political songs and women's songs. The influence of early Scottish/Irish settlers is clearly seen. "Down East" (Atlantic Provinces) songs make a strong showing, including a number each from Stompin' Tom Connors and Harry Hibbs. Champion fiddle player Eleanor Moorehead plays some marvelous tunes. Despite the Canadian lyrics, many of the melodies will be familiar to U.S. listeners. For instance, the American "Orange Blossom Special" becomes "Apple Blossom Special" with an entirely different fiddling style. A bibliography is included on the slipcase, as well as a printed insert of song texts.

F3.44   **Mountain Music Played on the Autoharp.** Folkways FA 2365.
    A wide variety of singers and instrumentals are presented here to show the styles of the autoharp as it is adapted to North American music. Ernest Stoneman, Kilby Snow, and Neriah and Ken Benfield work through a program of "Bile 'Em Cabbage Down," "Wreck of Number 9," "May I Sleep in Your Barn Tonight?"— plus some real old tunes in "John Henry," "Red River Valley" and "Coming Round the Mountain."

F3.45   **The Unexpurgated Folksongs of Men.** Arhoolie 4006.
    This disc orginally came out in 1960. It is essentially a collection of songs sung by various amateurs (both black and white) and several professional singers, sitting around a microphone with a tub of beer. This is a free-style song-swapping atmosphere. Long-forgotten verses and songs came as one man's recollection prodded another's. At times, they offer contrasting versions of the same song or surprise each other with strange verses to certain favorite songs. The bawdy song in folklore is a valid genre, in much the same category as children's songs and grisly death songs that predominate, at times, in the British folk tradition. Materials here are derived from western songs, college humor, British tunes with American lyrics, and so forth, with such typical offerings as "Cocaine Bill and Morphine Sue," "Take a Whiff on Me," "The Bastard King of England," "No Balls at All," "The Merry Cuckold," and "Stavin' Chain." A booklet with notes and texts accompanies this record.

F3.46   **The Unfortunate Rake.** Folkways 3805.

F3.47   **Versions and Variants of "Barbara Allen."** Library of Congress AAFS
L 54.
    Popularity of music depends entirely on its influence and spread, and these two records do an excellent job in documenting the spread of two songs. The "older" is the "Barbara Allen" song. Many collectors recorded a total of thirty variations

for the Library of Congress from 1933 to 1954. During this 22-year period, though, many incursions were made by commercial phonographs; thus, the field recording here is not exactly a truthful device (many singers later admitted that they merely listened to a record or to a radio). *However,* in the long run, it is part of the folk process for it fits in neatly with the variations and changes in songs as they go through a transition stage. Noted ethnomusicologist Charles Seeger edited this collection and provided notes. Geographic locations include all of the South, the Midwest, and the West, with a variety of performance styles (some guitar, some violin, some unaccompanied) plus a variety of stanzas chosen. The Folkways set is very similar in that it presents sixteen commercially recorded (that is, recorded for Folkways distribution) variants by different performers of the Anglo-American ballad "St. James Infirmary."

STANDARDS

F3.48   **Beers Family. The Art of the Psaltery.** Prestige P 13028.

F3.49   **Beers Family. Dumbarton's Drums.** Columbia CS 9472.

F3.50   **Beers Family. Seasons of Peace.** Biograph BLP 12033.

F3.51   **Beers Family. Walkie in the Parlor.** Folkways 2376.
     Robert Beers was a revival singer who predominated on the psaltery and fiddle. His wife Evelyne and daughter Martha assisted in collecting materials from the Midwest that resulted in a rather highly specialized form of esoteric folk music, plus some original compositions. Through the 1960s, they appeared at many folk festivals, always stressing the authentic nature of folk music. Beers sang or recorded either alone or in combination with his family, son-in-law Eric Nagler, and others. The Biograph album features nine people in an array of strings and percussion (the other five were the Boyer family) on fifteen tracks: "Run Like a Deer," "Simple Gifts," "Fiddler's Green," "Green Gravel." Generally, the smaller the label, the more esoteric was their material. For instance, the Folkways album (the only one with superb notes) includes "The Leatherman" and "Return from the Deep."

F3.52   **Theodore Bikel. Folksinger's Choice.** Elektra 7250.

F3.53.   **Theodore Bikel. Songs of the Earth.** Elektra 7326.
     Actor Bikel also performed on the musical stage. An Austrian by way of Palestine, he could speak and sing in over seventeen languages. As a consequence, his music contained goodly quantities of "foreign" folk music. Perhaps more than any other folk singer in the 1950s and early 1960s, Theo Bikel personified the popular conception of what a folk singer ought to be: a traveler with a mixed bag of material.

F3.54   **Oscar Brand. Bawdy Sea Shanties.** Audiofidelity AFLP 1884.

F3.55   **Oscar Brand. Bawdy Songs and Back Room Ballads, v.1-4.** four discs. Audiofidelity AFLP 1906, 1806, 1824, 1847.

F3.56   **Oscar Brand. Bawdy Songs Goes to College.** Audiofidelity AFLP 1952.

F3.57   **Oscar Brand. Bawdy Western Songs.** Audiofidelity AFLP 1920.

F3.58   **Oscar Brand. Sing along Bawdy Songs.** Audiofidelity AFLP 1971.
     Collections of bawdy folk songs are as valid a manifestation of America's culture as any other. They've been sung around the country for hundreds of years while America was being constructed, and some of them date back hundreds of years before then. Oscar Brand, the well-known folk satirist who led a mini-revival in the 1940s through his WNYC folk music radio show, here contributes some 130 bawdy songs of every type and nature; and each album comes with fairly good liner notes of explanation. Bawdy songs developed mainly in male-oriented professions; thus, there are three specialized sets here: the western songs (including "Charlotte the Harlot," "Blinded by Turds"), the sea shanty ("Keyhole in the Door," "Backside Rules the Navy"), and the college fraternity song, the latter collected from around the country and mainly based on British drinking songs. The four-volume set is the core of the collection, and they are very sensibly arranged with short notes tracing the history of each song. Typical tracks include "Roll Your Leg Over," "No Hips at All," "Seven Old Ladies Locked in a Lavatory," "She'll Do It Again" (from Robert Burns, as in "Green Grow the Rashes"), and "The Money Rolls In."

F3.59   **Oscar Brand. Election Songs of the United States.** Folkways F 5280.
     This engaging collection by one of the most well-known singers of "folk songs" contains the definitive version of "M.T.A." Folkways, as always, presents superb notes tracing the songs, along with texts and photographs. Here are some of the most biting and satirical songs ever written, going back to the early 1800s.

F3.60   **Loman Cansler. Missouri Songs.** Folkways 5324.
     Cansler here sings of his home state. He has done much work in the schools and colleges as regards folk music, and titles include "When I Leave for to Take My Leave," "Charles Guitreau," "Arthur Clyde," "The Blue and the Gray," "I Told 'Em Not to Grieve after Me," and "Kickin' Mule."

F3.61   **Paul Clayton. Bay State Ballads.** Folkways 2106.
     Clayton is a folk song collector from Massachusetts who has also recorded prolifically for the Elektra, Riverside, Stinson, and Monument labels. He is best known for his sea shanties and sea songs, some of which are on this Folkways album. Other materials here show roots in British sources, some Cumberland items that made their way up north, and in general, the effects of the sea.

F3.62*   **Michael Cooney. The Cheese Stands Alone.** Folk Legacy FSI 35.
     Cooney has always been concerned with his own folk "purity"; but often, he is a folk eclectic—a stance in which anything is a folk song, so long as the artist recognizes it as such. These fourteen tracks also come with a 26-page booklet that has good notes, texts and histories, and documentary tracings of all the songs. Although he can play many instruments, Cooney normally performs on six and twelve string guitar, plus banjo. His music has been most affected by Leadbelly, and that is the largest part of his performing repertoire. He is one of the last of the

ramblers, showing up at all the folk festivals still current, both major and minor. In this manner, he collects his songs. The varied program here includes "Turkey in the Straw," with its traditional melody but with boys' camp lyrics; "Worried Blues," but in Hally Wood's transitional version; plus Leadbelly's "Fannin Street," the humorous "Jim Crack Corn," the popular "John Henry," Mississippi John Hurt's "Creole Belle," and even Malvina Reynolds's "The Barbers and the Diplomats Are Going into the Army." Throughout, if there is but one criticism, it is that his voice does tend to reach a little for the higher notes.

F3.63   **Barbara Dane. Anthology of American Songs.** Tradition 2072.

Dane is a union person, learning much from Pete Seeger and her various involvements with union strikers. She has done radio and television work, as well as a column and articles for *Sing Out!* magazine. At one time, she even worked for a Dixieland band in San Francisco. Her upbringing relates to Arkansas, and her husky voice is most attractive with blues material, as on some of her Folkways albums.

F3.64   **Fred Gerlach. 12 String Guitar.** Folkways 3529.

Gerlach has a strong reputation as an excellent performer on the big twelve string guitar. He was influenced by Leadbelly, and indeed, this whole album is full of such Leadbelly songs as "Gallows Pole" and "Fannin," in that blend of folk and blues for which Leadbelly was so famous. Gerlach developed through the mid-1950s urban folk scene at the beginning of the great revival.

F3.65   **Anne Laylin Grimes. Folksongs of Ohio.** Folkways 5217.

Collector-singer Grimes presents an interesting collection of songs from Ohio, her home state: "Battle of Point Pleasant, " "Lass of Rock Royal," "Boatman's Dance," "Girl of Ohio," "Ohio Guards," and "Ohio River Blues."

F3.66*   **Sarah Ogan Gunning. A Girl of Constant Sorrow.** Folk Legacy FSA 26.

Gunning was Aunt Molly Jackson's half-sister; they shared the same trials and tribulations about unions, mines, and capitalism. Gunning also helped to organize unions in Eastern Kentucky, and she composed new lyrics to traditional melodies in the true folk process. Between 1935 and 1940, she was recorded by Lomax for the Library of Congress. This album was issued in 1965 and culls some representative samplings from her repertoire. Traditional songs and ballads are covered by "Loving Nancy," "Old Jack Frost," and "Davy Crockett." Union songs from the 1930s include "I'm Going to Organize," "Down on the Picket Line," and "I Hate the Company Bosses"—the latter being a lament about family deaths caused by the mining situation. In common with Aunt Molly, she moved to New York when threats caused her to leave Kentucky. Her father—Oliver Perry Garland—was a preacher-unionist, and here she sings some of the religious songs from her family ("I Have Letters from My Father" and "Dreadful Memories," a reworking of "Precious Memories") plus other common hymns. All are sung unaccompanied in that typical high dry voice that is not easy to listen to; but then, the material should set one on edge anyway, even the Woody Guthrie song "Why Do You Stand There in the Rain?" Archie Green, a mining song scholar, contributes the extensive liner notes.

F3.67   **Sam Hinton. Sings the Songs of Men—All Sorts and Kinds.** Folkways
          2400.
This marine biologist presents a smattering of all kinds of songs about farmers,
churchgoers, hard laborers, soldiers, and so forth. The only thing holding it together
is its occupational basis and his own guitar accompaniment. Good notes allow for
tracing song titles and derivations. Previously, Hinton had recorded for the Library
of Congress and all of the major companies (CBS, MCA, RCA) since 1947.

F3.68*   **Aunt Molly Jackson. Library of Congress Recordings.** Rounder Records
          1002.

F3.69*   **Aunt Molly Jackson. Songs and Stories.** Folkways 5457.
For 47 years, from the age of five, Aunt Molly Jackson nursed, organized, and
fought for the miners of Eastern Kentucky. She went to jail for the first time at
ten; members of her family were maimed and killed in the mines. Aunt Molly wrote
songs for the union movement, in the flexible folk song format where either the
words or the tune was changed (this was quite common in the proletariat music of
the IWW and Communists). In 1931, she was forced to leave Kentucky and move to
New York, where her songs became well known among union organizers and folklorists, including the Lomaxes. For the latter, she recorded hundreds of titles at
the Archive of American Folk Song (Library of Congress). Though widely varying
in content, this Rounder sampling is mostly political and protest in nature, emphasizing the standards in her reportoire by which people remember her: "Join the
C.I.O.," "Fare Thee Well Old Ely Branch," and the 1910 "Hard Times in Coleman's
Mines." If Aunt Molly's unaccompanied voice is harsh and unpleasant, so are the
events she sings about. There is a booklet here, with pictures, texts, and lyrics, plus
some balance with her traditional ballads, hymns, and tales. These are better found
on the Folkways set, with John Greenway.

F3.70   **Kathy Kahn. The Working Girl; Women's Songs from Mountains, Mines
          and Mills.** Voyageur VRLP 305S.
Georgia-born Kahn sings in the old time mountain style, with a fiddle band
accompaniment. She is also the author of *Hillbilly Women*, a book that explores some
of the themes on this disc. Titles include "Babies in the Mill," "Brown Lung Blues,"
the traditional "Hard Times Cotton Mill Girls," "I Hate the Company Bosses,"
and "Too Young to Marry." The disc includes a descriptive booklet with notes and
lyrics.

F3.71*   **Buell Kazee. His Songs and Music.** Folkways FS 3810.
For Brunswick and Vocalion between 1926 and 1930, Biblical scholar Kazee
recorded fifty folk songs that have yet to be reissued, and in addition, he did some
field recordings for the Library of Congress in 1930. He played the piano, banjo,
and guitar with equal facility. His main impact has been as an influence on Pete
Seeger and Joan Baez during the folk revival as a source for such material as
"Waggoner's Lad" for Baez and "East Virginia Blues" for Seeger. His traditional
songs, recorded again in 1959 for Folkways here, included "The Lady Gay," "The
Butcher's Boy," "Dance around My Pretty Little Miss," and "Cumberland Gap,"

all showing tracings from British ballads and paced with a fast-picked five string banjo background. A significant record in terms of his impact.

F3.72*   **Bradley Kincaid. Mountain Ballads and Old Time Songs, v.1/4.** four discs. Bluebonnet 105, 107, 109, 112.

Kincaid claimed to be the first person to introduce folk songs and mountain ballads on the radio. He is primarily a collector and secondly a composer who has appeared many times on the National Barn Dance. The material on these discs is what would be categorized as strictly folk music, as the songs were re-creations made in the mid-1960s of songs he had collected over the years, such as "Methodist Pie," "I Gave My Love a Cherry," "Liza up a Simmon Tree," "Fatal Derby Day," "Two Little Orphans," "The Letter Edged in Black," and "The Gypsy's Warning."

F3.73   **Alan Lomax. Texas Folk Songs.** Tradition T 1029.

In addition to his many other activities of organizing, recording and writing, Lomax was a first-rate singer, performing in both the United States and Great Britain. In 1933, at age eighteen, he began to help his father John collect for the Library of Congress, becoming assistant curator in 1937. In 1939, he began the epic series with Leadbelly, Jelly Roll Morton, and Woody Guthrie, excellent models of the arts of oral history and folk music preservation. In the 1950s, he would have radio series on both CBS and the BBC. This disc is a typical effort from Lomax—generally low-keyed renditions of beloved songs from Texas and the Southwest, covering the cowboys and the story songs through "Billy Barlow," "Ain't No More Cane on the Brazos," "The Dying Cowboy," "All the Pretty Little Horses," "Rattlesnake," "Sam Bass," etc.

F3.74   **Margaret Crowl MacArthur. Folk Songs of Vermont.** Folkways 5314.

Collector-singer MacArthur was an acknowledged authority on Vermont music. All the selections here are sourced, traced, commented on, and provided with lyrics in the accompanying booklet. Titles include: "The Needle's Eye," "Carrion Crow," "Gypsy Dave," "Cherries Are Ripe," "Trot, Trot to Boston," "Mother in the Graveyard," and "The Scolding Wife."

F3.75   **Alan Mills. Songs of the Sea.** Folkways 2312.

F3.76   **Seafarer's Chorus. Salty Seafaring Chanties.** Legacy LEG 117 (British issue).

F3.77   **Yetties. All at Sea.** Argo ZFB 86 (British issue).

Materials on these three discs are more in the popular vein of shanties than those listed in the anthologies. Alan Mills is from Canada, and he has sung quite a few folk songs for Folkways records. Here he is accompanied by Gilbert Lacombe on guitar and a male quartet (The Shantymen), in a program that embraces "Rio Grande," "Sally Brown," "Johnny Boker" and "The Dead Horse." The 32 tracks all have sterling notes and texts adapted by Edith Fowke; the Seafarer's Chorus was directed by Milt Okun. They sing polished renditions of fo'c's'le songs, prayer songs, and some sea work shanties such as "Hand on the Bowline," "Clear the Track," and "Boney." The popular singing group from England, the Yetties, take a more liberal view of sea songs, and include in their program such titles as "Bosun's Hornpipe," "Trumpet Hornpipe," "Fiddler's Green," and "The Watchett Sailor."

F3.78   **John Jacob Niles. Ballads.** two discs. Tradition 1046-2.

F3.79*   **John Jacob Niles. Folk Balladeer.** RCA LPV 513.

Niles was an art song folk interpreter, popular in the 1940s when the minor folk revival was under way. He played the dulcimer, lute, and piano, in addition to being a composer. His greatest strength, though, was as a collector. During the 1920s and 1930s, he compiled the largest folk collections in the world, and he drew on this vast repertoire to assist him in his recording activities. He came from a musical family (his father was also an instrument maker) and himself invented several variations of dulcimers and lutes. Admittedly, much of his material was esoteric, particularly with his high, eerie voice. The three discs cited above reflect the broad range of common folk elements (other of his albums deal with more ephemeral materials). The RCA collation is derived from the 1940s; the Tradition issue is from the late 1950s. Included amongst the forty tracks are "Barbry Ellen," "Old Bangum," "Mary Hamilton," "Hangman," "Dreary Dream," "Jack O'Diamonds," "Black Is the Color," and "Go Way from My Window."

F3.80   **Milt Okun. Adirondack Songs.** Stinson 82.

Guitarist and banjoist Okun was a man of many talents: he was a musicology student; he taught folk music; he directed festivals; he was musical arranger for the Chad Mitchell Trio, and for Peter, Paul and Mary; he was a music consultant to Elektra Records and assisted many artists on their roster, such as Tom Paxton; and he was also an urban folk singer. This particular album is relatively authentic in an interpretative sense, with titles relating to actual events, such as "The Days of '49," "Dolan's Ass," "The Fatal Wedding," "The Banks of Champlain," and "The Lass of Glenshee."

F3.81   **Tom Paley and Peggy Seeger.** Elektra EKS 7295.

Accompanying themselves on the guitar, banjo, autoharp, and dulcimer, Paley and Seeger present a varied program of their own choosing: some Child ballads ("Who's That Knocking at My Window?" with the drowsy sleeper variation; "The Lass of Roch Royal," "The Heartless Lady"), nonsense songs, work ballads, instrumentals ("Buck Dancer's Choice," learned from Sam McGee), and so forth. Their voices blend well together when they duet. Seeger is from the ethnomusicological Seeger family; Paley is a mathematician who helped to create the New Lost City Ramblers.

F3.83*   **Almeda Riddle. Ballads and Hymns from the Ozarks.** Rounder 0017.

Riddle is one of the best of the traditional singers; her earlier records are out-of-print, but this set comes from 1972. She has not recorded any of the twelve titles before, half of which are common and well-known (e.g., "The Butcher's Boy," "The Nightingale Song," and several Child ballads including "Lady Margaret"). The rarer items are more localized in their development and contribute strongly to the folk genre—"Peggy of Glasgow," "How Tedious and Tasteless the Hours," "The Merrimac at Sea," etc. Excellent phrasing and emotion.

F3.84*   **Jean Ritchie. Child Ballads in America.** two discs. Folkways 2301/2.

Jean was the youngest of fourteen in the Ritchie Family, an essential group in the understanding of the folk process and transmission (see the next annotation). This is music of the Cumberland Mountains of Kentucky, as traced through Sharp's field recordings and sung by the Ritchie Family. Jean accompanies herself on guitar and dulcimer for "Lord Randall," "Unquiet Grave," "Sweet William and Lady Margaret," "The Wife of Usher's Well," and so forth. Jean began singing at church and social events before becoming swept up in the folk music revival. Through the years, she recorded for Elektra, Prestige, and Folkways, as well as creating songbooks that included her own crafted variations.

F3.85*   **Ritchie Family.** Folkways 2316.

The spotlight shines on the famous Ritchie Family. Their roots can be traced back to James Ritchie, who moved from England to Virginia in 1768 and musically helped to preserve such British ballads as "Nottamun Town" and "Lord Bateman." When Cecil Sharp visited the Cumberland Mountains area, he saw and heard Balis Ritchie and his offspring (later to number fourteen, with Jean Ritchie being the youngest) and made many notations. Other collectors subsequently gathered, including the Lomaxes who recorded them for the Archive of American Folk Song. Indeed, the Ritchies were very generous with their time and efforts early on, but later decided to seek emolument for their services. This Folkways disc is composed partially of their singing the older ballads and partially of interviews.

F3.86   **Tony and Irene Saletan.** Folk Legacy FSI 37.

Both artists pursued separate careers until they met and married. Irene Kossoy specialized in the mountain ballads, and once sang blended harmonies with her twin sister. Her great voice can cover the low notes and give a quick rise to falsetto. Her autoharp and guitar playing are excellent. This is an album of international folk songs. There are some originals, but most come from Nepal ("Biswo Ma Aglo"), Indonesia ("Ala Tipang"), and China ("K'ang Ting Love Song")—as adapted to Western ears—or from regions such as "Sydney Coal Fields" from Nova Scotia. One of the highlights is "Lady Margaret," an 8.5 minute ballad by Irene alone with her autoharp. This is a good record of folk songs heard around the world.

F3.87   **Carl Sandburg. American Songbag.** two discs. Caedmon 2025.

Sandburg was an exceptionally gifted poet, raconteur, author, political commentator and collector of folk songs. On occasion, he would himself sing, and these two records cover a wide variety of folk interpretations, as a true songbag would in a rummaging sense. The whole set is characterized by ramblings and mumblings of many songs, especially what he called "darn fool ditties."

F3.88   **Pete Seeger. American Industrial Ballads.** Folkways 5251.

F3.89*   **Pete Seeger. Broadsides.** Folkways 2456.

F3.90*   **Pete Seeger. Gazette, v.1/2.** two discs. Folkways 2501/2

F3.91   **Pete Seeger. Songs of Struggle and Protest, 1930-1950.** Folkways 5233.

Throughout his long career, Seeger excelled at topical and protest songs, especially songs that would convey meaning to proletariat workers. The *Broadsides* and *Gazette* albums are non-specific in their conception, and most of the tracks are of topical nature such as "The Dove," "The Flowers of Peace, " "Coyote," "Little Boxes," "Pretty Boy Floyd," "Tomorrow Is a Highway," and "The Dying Miner." The industrial songs album shows the rich and diverse history of American music, beginning with "Peg and Awl" from about 1805, "The Buffalo Skinners" from 1873, "The Eight Hour Day" from 1886, "Hard Times in the Mill" from 1890, and then many, many songs relating to union difficulties and working conditions. The *Struggle* songs abound in irony and contrasts. Most were adopted from existing, familiar tunes, with new words or added words, such as "What a Friend We Have in Congress" (from "What a Friend We Have in Jesus"), "Hymn to Nations" (from Beethoven's Ninth Symphony), and "I Don't Want Your Millions, Mister" (from "Greenback Dollar"). All albums come with excellent descriptive notes and most texts to the songs.

F3.92   **Hedy West, v.1/2.** Vanguard VRS 9124 and VSD 79162.

F3.93*   **Hedy West. Old Times and Hard Times.** Folk Legacy FSA 32.
West plays the banjo in the Piedmont style. Her home was the mountainous region of North Georgia, and she came from a "po' white" background. All of her music is traditional, and of course, she stands out because there are so few women banjoists. After playing in diverse coffee houses and festivals, she emigrated to England in the sixties. The Folk Legacy album was originally issued on Topic records in England during this period. The Vanguard items, from the 1960 cusp, contain a mixture of classic ballads, nonsense songs, and children's songs ("Mister Froggie," "Single Girl," "The Wife of Usher's Well," "Lord Thomas and Fair Ellender," "The Cotton Mill Girl," "The Brown Girl"). Her lonesome voice very easily crosses over into old time music (indeed, she sings "Old Joe Clark" on the Folk Legacy set). Just about all of her songs are derived from her family's repertoire; thus, these are mainly British ballads with American banjo and American pronunciation. As her father was a union organizer in the 1930s, and as she was given freedom to record what she wanted, the Folk Legacy set contains a fair number of coal mining songs ("The Coal Miner's Child," "Shut up in the Mines at Coal Creek"), plus the traditional "Barbara Allen" and "Fair Rosamund." The Folk Legacy disc comes with an 18-page booklet that outlines the notes, texts, and histories of all the songs.

★ ★ ★ AMERICAN FOLK REVIVALS ★ ★ ★

AMERICAN FOLK REVIVALS

INTRODUCTION

The modern American folk revival performer is quite often from an urban environment and learns materials: 1) from listening to live performances or records of traditional performers; 2) by studying the recorded or transcribed performances of traditional singers (as found by various collectors or other revival singers). This revivalist is self-accompanied or is accompanied on one or more instruments. The American folk revivals, unlike the British revivals, have followed a relatively narrow path that has resulted in the troubador style of singer-songwriters. In Britain, as noted earlier, the material remained traditional, but the presentation varied, with more instrumentation, electric amplification, and medieval instrumentation— all of which proved very effective. In America, the instrumentation remained relatively stable at the beginning of the 1960s, *but* the material was changing to the self-written compositions of the troubadors. Electrification came with this new material, almost as if the thought were that it was sacrilegious to "amplify" *real* traditional music. No one in America has yet attempted the electric folk approach of Steeleye Span toward American folk music. American revival singers, though, do create some exciting music as well as expose songs and tunes that have been forgotten for years. Many such people are also folklore scholars who have also advanced research into folk processes.

Every generation in America creates a folk revival of sorts. The early 1900s, through the new business of copyrights, discs and cylinders, sheet music sales, and so forth, saw the beginnings of a concern for preservation of the past (particularly when World War I broke out). Materials were collected to feed the newly emerging Tin Pan Alley from the 1896 success of sheet music sales ("After the Ball"). Sharp made his visits to Kentucky at this time as well. In the 1920s, the successful but commercial "old time music" form of recording led to a hunt for more material, including foraging by A. P. Carter, who probably spread more knowledge of songs about American folk music than any other singer of the day. When this material ran out, newly fashioned songs had to be created, ultimately leading to both country music and to the troubadors.

It is also significant that the revival of the late 1950s is based on this 1920s period. In the early 1950s, Harry Smith collated his *Anthology of American Folk Music* (entry F3.4) for Folkways Records, using 78 rpm discs from the 1920s plus discographic tracings, lyrics, and short notes. Previously, no such music had been reissued in the new long-playing format, and many folk singers listened to this set of blues and old time music. Then they began to record their own versions of works on this *Anthology* and thus present the music of the late nineteenth century to another generation, who were hearing it for the first time. The *Anthology* directly influenced such singers as Joan Baez and Bob Dylan, but in the end, this music came back on them. The listeners soon became aware that the performers were just one step ahead of them in transcribing songs, and eventually the folk or traditional purists by-passed the "interpreters" for the real thing, i.e., album reissues of 1920s old time music (which, of course, were also "interpretations" of yet another older music). . . . And so it goes. . . .

The next revival—the third in this century—came during the Great Depression, when everyone was looking for a better life. This was music of isolation, manifested by the working-class intellectual (e.g., Pete Seeger), the cultural transplant (e.g., Aunt Molly Jackson, Sarah Ogan Gunning, Leadbelly, Josh White), and the traveler (e.g., Woody Guthrie, Cisco Houston). All believed in anonymity yet stressed cohesion and togetherness in their topical protest songs. Labeled "radical" music, it had little influence on the mass music of the time. It sprang up in urban centers independent of rural or British roots, because the singers had never lived in rural America. Herein lie the roots of the present day *troubador*. The Depression was the catalyst for all laboring songs, while the Spanish Civil War crystallized many sentiments. The breakdown of regionalism through rural-urban conflicts, radio, and records was further extended both by the union organizing tours of Guthrie, Seeger, and the Almanac Singers and by the spread of Library of Congress field recordings of "folk" personalities (most of the singers already mentioned). Socialist causes provided both employment and audiences for the singers, and when the moment of respectability arrived, it was their choice to remain ideologically isolated or to seek music industry stardom, as Burl Ives did. Those who remained anonymous thought of music as a key to political success (utilizing the British broadside as a prime example). Technically, their work was in the simple three-chord progression with stress on those lyrics that were adaptable to their contemporary scene.

The fourth revival came about in 1949-1952, and it was apolitical, being based on a new group from New York City—the Weavers (Seeger, Hays, Gilbert, Hellerman)—that arose from the ashes of the Almanac Singers. Despite record sales of over three million, the Weavers had little influence on mass music until the era of the House of Representatives' Un-American Activities Committee and the "Red Scare." This gave Seeger and the Weavers a larger audience plus sympathy for the older, more traditional songs rather than their highly stylized commercial recordings arranged for MCA by Gordon Jenkins. Throughout this period, New York and Boston were centers for small but booming folk clubs and activities, particularly Oscar Brand's *Folk Song Festival* radio show on WNYC and in the Greenwich Village area.

The fifth revival (1957-1964) was the largest and most exciting, as it reached the widest audience. It began with the success of the Kingston Trio, who were considered a palatable alternative to rock and roll by parents; consequently, the Trio and similar folk groups were pushed by the industry: 1) for high sales; 2) for inexpensive productions (trios or soloists didn't cost as much as a whole group); and 3) for their use of free, uncopyrighted (public domain) material. The early part of the revival (until the Kennedy Era) was apolitical, in line with the "Red Scare" that frightened many folk singers into singing safe, old English ballads. In 1958, Robert Shelton became the folk music critic of the *New York Times*, and this stamp of authenticity bolstered traditional music's acceptability. The first Newport Folk Festival was held in 1959 as a spin-off of its jazz festival. It featured 75 musicians (Jean Ritchie, John Jacob Niles, Rev. Gary Davis, Ed McCurdy, Lester Flatt, Earl Scruggs, Oscar Brand, Leon Bibb, Pete Seeger, New Lost City Ramblers, Odetta, Jimmy Driftwood, Bob Gibson, Joan Baez, etc.) playing for 16 hours before 13,000 attendees.

The New York Greenwich Village scene was extended cross-country by the typical coffee house, college campus shows, concerts, and festivals. During this period, folk music was considered to be a spontaneous group activity having to do with people who didn't have to sing well and with easy chord changes on guitars. It was also regarded seriously by the media and the fans alike, even though it reflected another culture and another time (with no immediate relevancy). Alan Lomax's philosophy prevailed: to be folk you live folk, for the true folksinger had to experience the feelings that lay behind his art. Thus, "purism" was all-important, and there emerged a reverence for old bluesmen, rural singers, bluegrass music—anything "authentic." Transmitters and interpreters were frowned upon as being commercial rip-offs who exploited the market; classified here were Joan Baez, Bob Dylan, and Peter, Paul and Mary.

By 1964, a dichotomy had set in. On the one hand, the purist insisted on the authentic model (little realizing that all folk music comes through a process of transmission), while on the other hand, the commercial market (knowing that such public material was limited and would not sell) pushed for new, copyrighted, and controlled material of *contemporary* folk or protest song. As with country music in the 1930s, by its sheer weight, the latter won out and seemed to fulfill some of the folk process in that its creators (or troubadors) participated in the events they sang about (e.g., diverse protests from Baez, Dylan, and Peter, Paul and Mary). Thus began the troubador singer in earnest (see the last section).

The latest folk revival occurred after 1970, with the re-discovery of ten-year-old material by a newer generation of listeners (aided by the repackaging of songs into "twofer" albums) and by the upsurge of bluegrass music. The festival returned (over 400 bluegrass festivals alone each year), the college campus is quiet once again and amenable to concerts of apolitical folk songs, coffee houses have returned, and spontaneous group activities spring forth, such as bluegrass "parklot pickin' " and workshops. It seems worthwhile to note that, for all their diversity, each of the five folk revivals exhibits similar characteristics:

1. Self-identification difficulties in a fast-changing society (Roaring Twenties, Depression, War, Red Scare, Kennedy Era) made it easy to clutch onto a non-changing older song that promoted older values.

2. The material was easy to learn and to perform, with good tunes adaptable to new words if necessary.

3. The changing lifestyles (i.e., the counter-culture) of those who went against the mainstream created original writings in the style of older folk songs for public acceptability, and featured real experiences.

4. Major musical genres were created by commercial elements after most revivals ran out of traditional or "public domain" material (e.g., Tin Pan Alley popular music, country music, folk-rock, and troubador music).

5. Each revival occurred within a musical generation (of long duration originally, but now more swift because of mass media) and has added to its predecessors *without* replacing them—the true folk music process.

6. Each revival reiterated the differences between the printed "broadside" and the aural "record." The words-only broadside stabilized folk song texts and enabled singers to choose or compose diverse tunes. The record, on the other hand, presented a package of text, tune, and performance. Since it could be replayed and memorized, it enabled singers to learn a particular *style* of performance.

INNOVATORS

F4.1*   Almanac Singers. Talking Union. Folkways FH 5285.

The Almanac Singers were the first organizational attempt to put folk consciousness into musical practice. From 1940-1942, it was a loosely-knit group of New York singers that included Woody Guthrie, Lee Hays, Burl Ives, Pete Seeger, Millard Lampell, and Bess Lomax. They sang for entertainment, at political meetings, street corners, colleges, concerts, and so forth. It was basically a quartet, but on an ad hoc basis, as singers came and went, especially Cisco Houston and Josh White. In their format, they were the forerunners to the Weavers, although at this time, they emphasized union and anti-war songs, such as the classic "Talking Union," "Which Side Are You On?," "Solidarity Forever," and "Dear Mr. President." Some of their 200 titles (many expressly written for the group) also included materials on traditional elements and peace. They took their name from the Farmers' Almanac, and later formed Almanac House, which gave shelter and paid the bills. Maxine Sullivan did something similar thirty years later with Jazz House, as did the Jefferson Airplane for rock musicians. Here, at the House, hoots were given for Sarah Ogan Gunning, the Lomaxes, Josh White, Ives, Leadbelly, and Sonny Terry and Brownie McGhee. Other typical titles include "Washington Breakdown," "Strange Death of John Doe," and the popular "Round and Round Hitler's Grave." Their major contributions were three-fold: they initiated a form of presentation for folk music through shifting trios and quartets; they sang propaganda songs in an urban environment; and they provided a training ground for folk singers in the 1940s.

F4.2   Joan Baez. Vanguard VSD 2077.

F4.3*   Joan Baez. Ballad Book. two discs. Vanguard VSD 41/42.

F4.4*   Joan Baez. Lovesong Album. two discs. Vanguard VSD 79/80.

Baez was the highest selling female folksinger of her time. She was the first to place folk *albums* in the chart of best sellers (discounting the Kingston Trio's pop-oriented efforts). Since appearing at the 1959 Newport Folk Festival with Bob Gibson, she has constantly been in the limelight despite limiting her appearances. Later, in the early sixties, she was both influenced by Bob Dylan and helped to give him exposure. Her personal life was the subject of much discussion and gave credibility to passive resistance (non-payment of taxes and non-violent marching and singing). By these means, her influence took a lot of folk singers out of the coffee houses and onto the streets. She organized the singers while Peter, Paul and Mary organized the audiences. Throughout, credibility was very high. Yet, she is not well-known as a protest singer, and very few of her recorded items fall in this genre. Mostly, she reflected the pure virginal romantic with her classic soprano voice, waist-length hair, sad facial features, and lyrical paeans to life. When she switched labels to A & M, her protest singing began, and her record sales and influence drastically declined. It was one thing to be a symbol of the folk element to the audience; it was another to try to transfer her attempts at persuasion from other singers to the audience itself.

Vanguard has reissued most of her material around themes in a series of two-fers (see the Troubador section for her contemporary songs). Her first album from 1960 still remains her most influential work, with Fred Hellerman of the Weavers on second guitar. This was pure folk and apolitical, with "Silver Dagger," "East Virginia," "House of the Rising Sun," "Little Moses," "Mary Hamilton," and so forth, from among the thirteen generous tracks. The *Ballad Book* is really dedicated to those purists who wanted her to stick with classic British and American ballads. The 23 selections include "Matty Groves," "Barbara Allan," and "Waggonner's Lad." The *Lovesong* set is similarly derived. The eighteen tracks are mainly traditional, such as "Come All Ye Fair and Tender Ladies," "Once I Had a Sweetheart," "The River in the Pines," "Plaisir d'Amour," "Death of Queen Jane," "Unquiet Grave," and so forth, along with some non-controversial contemporary items such as "House Carpenter" or "The Wild Mountain Thyme."

F4.5*   **Oscar Brand. Best.** Tradition 2053.

Brand has recorded over sixty albums; it is very difficult to choose from among these, particularly as many dealt with themes such as bawdy songs or are long out-of-print. His radio program for WNYC in New York (from 1945 onwards) was highly influential in spreading the good news about folk music and in introducing many performers to the public. Later, this show would develop into *The World of Folk Music* that was syndicated to 1,880 (!) stations. He was born in a multi-ethnic area of Winnipeg, Canada, and studied psychiatry. He has traveled about the world with his guitar and banjo, and he has shown his diversity through acting, scoring, composing, writing books, and being a master of ceremonies. The list of companies he has recorded for includes Elektra, Impulse, MCA, ABC, Folkways, and Riverside. His "behind the scenes" work in folk music has been just as important as his singing and performing. The Tradition album appears to be the only one he ever made that has been labeled "best"; it includes "Arkansas" and his typical "Talking Guitar Blues." Other albums by Brand can be found in this book by topic, such as the bawdy songs.

F4.6*   **Judy Collins. Concert.** Elektra EKS 7280.

F4.7   **Judy Collins. Recollections.** Elektra EKS 74055.

Collins has been described as "sweet, sad, gentle and unrealistic," but despite this, she has been a determining influence in the shape of troubador singing through the 1960s. After playing around with traditional ballads of "pure" folk, she became influenced by Bob Dylan, Phil Ochs, and Tom Paxton, especially by what they wrote and what they did. She was by now a respected folk singer, second only to Joan Baez. Because of her popularity, it was possible for her to help and assist protest singers by performing their songs, such as Dylan's "The Lonesome Death of

Hattie Carroll," "Masters of War" (in which she eliminated the last verse and its references to Jesus Christ), plus his other items, "Mr. Tambourine Man," "Tomorrow Is a Long Time," etc.; Tom Paxton's "The Last Thing on My Mind," "My Ramblin' Boy," "Bottle of Wine"; Phil Ochs, Eric Anderson, and later, Donovan, Leonard Cohen, Joni Mitchell, and Randy Newman (see items F10.38-39). Her music can be divided into two phases: the acoustic, folk-like period, and the electric, theater art song period. Throughout, she gives expert attention to details, and all of her records have been exceptionally well-produced for the pop folk market.

F4.8*   Gateway Singers. At the Hungry i. MCA Decca 8671.
The Gateway Singers were one of the best known folk groups of the 1950s. They helped to popularize many folk songs; unfortunately, they disbanded in 1961, right at the height of the folk boom. One of the founders was Travis Edmondson, later to be part of Bud and Travis. In many senses, the Gateway Singers were precursors of the Kingston Trio, perhaps just lacking that initial thrust that would have propelled them to stardom. This Decca recording comes from San Francisco in 1956 at one of the first West Coast coffee houses (the Kingston Trio would be there themselves in a few years). Good time titles include "Hey Li-Lee," "Let Me Fly," "Big Rock Candy Mountain," "Rollin' Home," "All over This World," and "Kisses Sweeter Than Wine." They were in the solid progression from the Almanac Singers and the Weavers to the Kingston Trio and the Limeliters.

F4.9*   Bob Gibson. Where I'm Bound. Elektra 7239.

F4.10   Bob Gibson and Hamilton Camp. Elektra 7207.
Gibson was one of the first commercially successful urban folk singers, introducing Joan Baez to Newport in 1959 and starting other singers on their way, as well as performing and popularizing folk music and some gospel items (such as "Yes I See" and the "Civil War Trilogy"). He played guitar and banjo as so many others did, but he also worked on the immense twelve string guitar as well. He recorded for Elektra in the 1960s after doing earlier songs of the Midwest and Ohio for Stinsom and Riverside. His fluid, light voice took much of the sting out of presentations formerly given by "authentic" harsh voices. All of his material was strong, and it was always presented with good energy. Quite often, he was coupled with Ham Camp, and the second album presents a selection of vocal duos, such as "Two Brothers."

F4.11*   Kingston Trio. Folk Era. three discs. Capitol ST 2180.
The saleable commercialism of the Kingston Trio opened the doors for others in the late 1950s folk revival. Capitol Records took an immense chance with this unknown group, and to that company, some of the credit for revivalism must go. The Trio were the mass popularizers that spawned other such acts (as Peter, Paul, and Mary). In later years, they would be looked down on; but without their commercial success, many companies would not have recorded folk music and the roots would not have been explored. How many "folkies" found their way to folk from the Kingston Trio? Not everyone knew enough to tackle the immense Elektra and Folkways catalogs. In essence, the Trio was a rock and roll version of folk, using the beat and vocal stylings borrowed from studio techniques. Their material was

largely apolitical and full of catchy songs rearranged to fit the tastes of the crowds and the college market. They won acceptability from parents for being a refreshing change from rock and roll. They were also the very first of the long-playing record vocal artists, for they recorded albums *first* and had singles lifted from the albums, not vice versa, as was the case in rock and roll and r 'n' b, and even popular music.

The early trio comprised Dave Guard, Bob Shane, and Nick Reynolds, all dressed usually in buttoned-down short sleeves with a barbershop design. They recorded several dozen albums, both from the studio and from concerts. The triple disc set presents their "greatest hits" (such as "Tom Dooley," a song lifted from Frank Proffitt and Frank Warner, and turned around to create the market for folk in 1958). Others: "The Tijuana Jail," "M.T.A.," "Where Have All the Flowers Gone?" (treated as a commercial recording with no political overtones), "Greenback Dollar," "Oleanna," "A Worried Man," "Hard, Ain't It Hard," etc. Kingston, their adopted name, came from Kingston, Jamaica, a sidelight to the calypso boom then current. Dave Guard gained credit with the folk element when he left after a few years because of gross commercialism; his replacement was John Stewart. This set is an important document in the "liberation" of folk music from the collector to the public.

F4.12   **Peter, Paul and Mary. Best (Ten Years Together).** Warner Brothers BS 2552.

F4.13*   **Peter, Paul and Mary. In Concert.** two discs. Warner Brothers 2WS 1555.

Often called "PPM," this trio was the leader of the folk revival for the commercial elements. Peter Yarrow, the tenor, was a solo folksinger in the later 1950s; Paul Stookey, the baritone, was a natural born M.C. (hence, their effectiveness in live performances); and Mary Travers was the pure voice that joined Paul in a duo, and they with Peter in a trio. From 1961, when they coalesced into PPM, their formula was predictable, being based on a combination of the two then most successful types of "folksinging": the Kingston Trio and Joan Baez (for here were two guys and a long-haired girl together).

While attaining much commercial success, they did three things of note. First, they opened the doors to others, especially composers just barely known, by singing their material (e.g., Dylan, Lightfoot). Second, they participated in a vast number of political rallies, thus making these gatherings somewhat acceptable to both the folk crowd and the younger, commercially-inclined listeners (plus giving these rallies acceptance in the media and with parents). Third, through their exceptional live performances and recordings, they helped to form folk-rock by singing essentially non-folk material (i.e., self-composed or contemporary songs). The double album, compiled from five concerts given in 1964, shows them at their best with their stage act and their marvelous rapport with audiences. Included are traditional folk songs (blues and folk revival) including "One Kind Favor," "There Is a Ship," "If I Had a Hammer"; Dylan material such as "The Times They Are A'Changin'," "Blowin' in the Wind"; children's songs such as Woody Guthrie's "Car-Car," "It's Raining" and "Puff." The collation album comes from the studio, with their singles hits: "Lemon Tree," "Leaving on a Jet Plane" (John Denver), "Early Morning Rain" (Gordon Lightfoot), etc.

F4.14   Pete Seeger. American Ballads. Folkways 2319.

F4.15*   Pete Seeger. American Favorite Ballads. five discs. Folkways 2320-23,
           2445.

F4.16   Pete Seeger. World of . . . two discs. Columbia KG 31949.
           Pete Seeger has been the man most responsible for the folk revivals in the
United States. He was the son of Charles Seeger, the ethnomusicologist, and a
direct descendent of Colonial settlers. He began traveling in 1938, after two years
at Harvard, and assisted Lomax on his 1939-1940 field trips. His next big folk
event was to organize the Almanac Singers, but then after awhile, he left to drift
with Woody Guthrie. In 1946, he started a songwriters' union (People's Songs, Inc.),
which ultimately had 3,000 members including Guthrie, Sonny Terry, Lomax,
etc., who involved themselves in diverse projects through the union: films, documentary shorts, hootenannys, festivals, etc. In 1948-1949, he founded the Weavers,
and this quartet sold four million "folk" records by 1952, in addition to their
radio, early TV, and concert work. Then Seeger was blacklisted by the industry
for a few years; he returned to re-form the Weavers in 1955, after three years,
leaving again in 1957. At this time he began to assist in starting the Newport Folk
Festival and with *Sing Out!* magazine. He also involved himself with educational
television.
           Seeger's greatness can be seen in the above survey of his career. Without him,
there would be no revival. Through the years, he has collected material, and this
can be found on sixty or more albums that he has recorded. All are equally good
since they promote rapport with the audience (especially with little children),
and they are almost always other people's songs. Some of his own include "Where
Have All the Flowers Gone?," "If I Had a Hammer" (with Lee Hays), and "Kisses
Sweeter Than Wine." Two that have had special impact in the music world were
"The Bells of Rhymney" and "Turn! Turn! Turn!" Both had been recorded by
the Byrds, and along with Dylan's "Mr. Tambourine Man," these songs formed the
basis for folk-rock.
           Seeger plays a variety of instruments, but mainly guitar and banjo. He is
proficient in diverse styles, and he has produced several instructional records,
manuals, and books. The Columbia set is derived from his later career, and it is
a combination of live and studio versions of some of the songs he popularized,
such as "Little Boxes" (by Malvina Reynolds), "Talking Union," "We Shall Overcome,"
"Darling Corey," "Guantanamera," etc. The Folkways sets are an interesting documentary of ballads in American history. Each record comes with notes, and the
material (all played in a straight forward fashion) is traditional: "Gypsy Davy,"
"John Henry," "Pretty Polly," "Jesse James," "Barbara Allen," "Jimmy Crack
Corn," "Red River Valley," "Old Smokey," "Midnight Special," "John Brown's
Body," "Banks of the Ohio," "All My Trials," "Foggy Dew," and so forth, from
among the 100 or so tracks. Seeger's main value lay in being an organizer, a persuader,
and a rallying point. His apolitical stance has caused him much trouble through
his life, but the strength of his convictions prevailed.

F4.17   Doc Watson. Essential. two discs. Vanguard VSD 45/46.

F4.18*   **Doc Watson. On Stage.** two discs. Vanguard VSD 9/10.

F4.19*   **Doc Watson. Watson Family.** Folkways FTS 31021.

F4.20*   **Doc Watson and Jean Ritchie.** Folkways FA 2426.
    The blind, eclectic "Doc" has been influenced by Jimmie Rodgers, Merle
Travis, the Carter Family, Riley Puckett (also blind), the Delmore Brothers, and
many hundreds of musical records. He even named his son Merle, after Merle Travis.
His repertoire is, quite literally, "everything"; he is a true folk troubador, with
interest in all blues, jazz, folk and oldtime music, bluegrass, country, and pop.
He performs ballads, hymns, instrumentals, and uptempo selections. Bill Malone
has said of him, "A Doc Watson concert is a history of southern folk music in a
capsule form," and of course he is best live, as *On Stage* shows—a superb collection
from Town Hall and Cornell University, featuring his son on guitar, and tunes such
as "Wabash Cannonball," the Hank Snow "Movin' On," the folk blues "Lost
John," (from a program of traditional, originals, instrumentals, Jimmie Rodgers,
Mississippi John Hurt, and Hank Snow numbers). He is a true assimilator of the
folk tradition, similar to his black colleagues, Jack Jackson, Mance Lipscomb,
and Snooks Eaglin.
    Watson is also a product of the folk revival. He performed at dances until he
was discovered in 1960 for an Old Time Music Festival with Clarence "Tom"
Ashley. His first album included his family (mother, brother, brother's father-in-
law) in a serious selection of their family repertoire: "Every Day Dirt," "Lone
Pilgrim," "House Carpenter," "Bonaparte's Retreat" (with Gaither Carlton on
fiddle) plus popular items such as "Darlin' Corey" or "The Train That Carried My
Girl to Town." The album with Ritchie explored further folk roots, as on "Sugar
on the Floor," "Amazing Grace" and "Cripple Creek." (Roger Sprung accompanied
on banjo. Later, Doc was to appear on the album *Will the Circle Be Unbroken* as
a cohesive force, one that molded and shaped the sessions.
    In between he became an entertainer on the folk festival circuit of clubs,
campuses, and bluegrass get-togethers (he can be found on several Newport sets),
as well as making definitive reinterpretations for Vanguard records. On both banjo
and guitar, he is a superb flat picker and finger-picker, displaying so many styles
and influences that he is best thought of as "southern." His strongest influence
has been on bluegrass guitarist Dan Crary. Typical titles reveal his sources—"Miss
the Mississippi and You" and "In the Jailhouse Now" (from Rodgers), the bluegrass
"Little Maggie," the contemporary "Moody River," the traditional "Black Mountain
Rag" (as learned from Leon McAuliffe), plus diverse black blues. A phenomenal
performer who quite possibly has absorbed the total impact of all the musical genres
discussed in this book, he has invested different influences in their replaying.

F4.21*   **The Weavers. Best.** two discs. MCA2-4052.

F4.22*   **The Weavers. Greatest Hits.** two discs. Vanguard VSD 15/16.
    A place of honor has to be given to the Weavers for their contribution to
the folk revival, particularly the 1949-1950 revival that culminated with the Kingston
Trio less than a decade later. Pete Seeger and Lee Hays had been part of the old
Almanac Singers. They formed a group with Ronnie Gilbert and Fred Hellerman in

1948 and made a number of successful folk-pop hits with Decca records, in front of a big band put together by Gordon Jenkins. They were not too happy with this popularization, but the records became million sellers: the first big hits for the folk music world. No political or ideological songs were included: just the singalong type of "Goodnight Irene," "Wimoweh," "Kisses Sweeter Than Wine," "The Roving Kind," "Down in the Valley," "Hush Little Baby," "The Wreck of the John B.," "Hard, Ain't It Hard," etc. The MCA twofer has 25 selections (as does the Vanguard set).

This all lasted until 1952, when Seeger was put on the blacklist. During that two-year period, the Weavers sold over four million records. They proved that folk could sell, but rock and roll and rhythm and blues took over the market, and coupled with the Red Scare of McCarthy and the blacklisting of several folkies, the folk music revival was put back a few years. Seeger moved in and out of the group. Erik Darling, Frank Hamilton, or Bernie Krause replaced him from time to time. In 1955, they made an album of Carnegie Hall material that was not released until 1957 and 1958 (the industry was still being cautious), and this concert aided the impetus for the second folk revival of the decade. In 1963, the Weavers permanently disbanded. Much of their material was still apolitical, and the Vanguard set repeats many of the earlier successes, only adding a few socialist songs such as "Last Night I Had the Strangest Dream" (Ed McCurdy) and "Brother Can You Spare a Dime?" Newer songs included "Michael Row the Boat Ashore," "House of the Rising Sun," "Guantanamera," "If I Had a Hammer," and "Erie Canal."

STANDARDS

F4.23   **Leon Bibb. Folk Songs.** Vanguard 9041.

Bibb came to the folk revival from the musical stage; he was one of the first black singers to get involved in what was essentially white music, but he also performed black spirituals and an occasional sacred tune. Titles here include "East Virginia," "Rocks and Gravel," "Take This Hammer," the spiritual "Sinnerman," and "Turtle Dove."

F4.24   **Bud and Travis. In Concert.** Liberty LPM 11001.

F4.25   **Bud and Travis. Latin Album.** Liberty LRP 3398.

Bud and Travis were both engaging performers in the 1960s folk revival. They were, unlike others, instrumentally secure, and their voices entwined together with perfect pitch and harmony. Besides the traditionally-expressed "Sloop John B.," "Two Brothers," "Johnny I Hardly Knew Ya," and others in vogue at the time, Bud and Travis were very heavily Latin influenced. Their program included such items as "La Bamba," "Sin Ti" and the bayou "Anna." Their two greatest numbers were the long, seven minutes of "Malaguena Salerosa" with all of its sustained notes, and the rolling "Guantanamera."

F4.26*   **Ry Cooder. Boomer's Story.** Reprise MS 2117.

F4.27   **Ry Cooder. Into the Purple Valley.** Reprise MS 2052.

Ryland Cooder is the master of the laid-back feeling. He works with a bottle-neck guitar and a blues mandolin, plus a small rock arrangement. He is well versed in both folk and blues music, at one time playing with Taj Mahal before moving onto session work. The *Purple* album is mainly songs from the Depression Era, such as "How Can You Keep on Moving (Unless You Migrate)?," "Billy the Kid," Woody Guthrie's "Vigilante Man" (a Dust Bowl ballad), the 1909 "Taxes on the Farmer Feeds Us All," plus eclectic but related items such as Leadbelly's "On a Monday," Johnny Cash's "Hey Porter," and Lefty Frizzell's "Money Honey." There are also some instrumentals. *Boomer* is a little more open. Cooder has reworked older materials (such as Jimmy McHugh's "Coming in on a Wing and a Prayer") and traditional songs into a very pleasing but exciting combination of Tin Pan Alley, blues, and instrumentals. As with all his albums, session accompaniment varies from track to track—anyone is apt to appear.

The first album listed above is an extremely well-balanced program, and includes an instrumental version of Skip James's "Cherry Ball Blues," the blues of Sleepy John Estes ("Ax Sweet Mama"), in which Cooder plays the mandolin as Yank Rachell once did for Estes, and the instrumentals "Maria Elena" (with a superb Spanish guitar interplay with the piano) and "Dark End of the Street" (in which he shows off the stunning virtuosity that has made him perhaps the key session man in all of America). To continue the rural America theme, Cooder introduces the standard hobo song "Good Morning, Mr. Railroad Man." Cooder's eclectic success has been at finding material that he has a feel for rather than writing his own, as so many others try to do. The interpretations are unique, however.

F4.28 **Erik Darling. True Religion.** Vanguard VSD 79099.

Darling began on the coffee house circuit, often accompanying Ed McCurdy with his guitar and five string banjo. He helped to form the Tarriers, a short-lived group at the time of Belafonte's calypso period (they recorded "Banana Boat Song") in the mid-1950s, but by 1958, he was engaged in folk music full time as Pete Seeger's alternate in the Weavers group. In 1962, Darling founded the Roof Top Singers, another short-lived folk revival group that scored with "Walk Right In" (the bluesman Bo Carter's success from the 1930s). On the disc above, one of two he made for Vanguard, he projects his slick instrumentation and high-pitched voice through a variety of pretty folk items. The title track is the best, being a spinoff of the spiritual and showing some nifty twelve string guitar work.

F4.29 **Richard Dyer-Bennet. Essential.** two discs. Vanguard VSDB 95/96.

Dyer-Bennet is an eclectic folk personality, performing on both lute and guitar. He was British-born but later became an American citizen. Learning his Spanish guitar technique from Rey de la Torre, he succeeded in bringing the European tradition of minstrelsy to North America via his many recordings for different labels in the 1940s and 1950s. His repertoire of songs is vast, reaching back to the thirteenth century, and includes ballads and folk songs from England, Ireland and America, old German minnelieder, Swedish shepherd songs, and even Schubert airs. This Vanguard reissue collates many of those songs. One of his major contributions was to organize a 1944 Town Hall concert, promoting himself as a folk musician doing art songs; this was one of the first concerts of folk music in America. Some of his more commercial tunes can be found on MCA 79102, and more of his esoteric songs are on his own label, Dyer-Bennet DB 1000 (including a generous proportion of sea songs). On this present album, though, are 27 songs, including: "Venezuela," "The Lass from the Low Country," "Westryn Wynde," "Eggs and Marrowbone," "Edward," and "The Swapping Song."

F4.30*   **Jack Elliott. Hard Travellin' Songs by Woody Guthrie and Others.** two discs. Fantasy F 24720.

F4.31   **Jack Elliott. Young Brigham.** Reprise RS 6284.
What do Robert Zimmerman and Elliott Adnopoz have in common? They both desired the Woody Guthrie mantle. They both got it, but Bob Dylan made a success of it and Jack Elliott didn't. Elliott was too early for the folk revival of the late fifties, yet the Fantasy album, when released on the British Topic label largely in its present form, did affect British musicians coming out of the skiffle craze. Elliott is more proficient a singer and guitar player than Guthrie, yet these tracks are still Guthrie's pieces: he wrote them, or modified them. And that is where Elliott differs from Dylan as well—by and large, Elliott does not write songs. He began as a cowboy from Brooklyn with the urban-folk complex, and ran away from home to join a rodeo. He has been singing ever since, with over forty albums to his name scattered over many labels. He met Guthrie at a rodeo and became enchanted with the life of a drifter. Even at that time, he had an "old" voice that sounded experienced.
Typical material seems to have included all the rambling songs, the singer stopping just long enough to say goodbye. His most accessible album is the Reprise offering, with such folk-pop songs as Jimmy Driftwood's "Tennessee Stud" (a pseudo-folk song from 1959, originally sung by Eddy Arnold), Dylan's "Don't Think Twice, It's All Right," Guthrie's "Talking Fisherman" and Tim Hardin's "If I Were a Carpenter." The Guthrie album contains 26 tracks from 1960-1961, with good notes by John Greenway. Included are "Hard Travelling," "Tom Joad," "Talking Dust Bowl," "Pretty Boy Floyd," "This Land Is Your Land," "So Long," etc. Elliott sounds more like Guthrie than Guthrie ever did.

F4.32*   **John Fahey, v.1: Blind Joe Death.** Takoma C 1002.

F4.33   **John Fahey, v.2: Days Have Gone By.** Takoma C 1014.

F4.34   **John Fahey. Of Rivers and Religion.** Reprise MS 2089.
John Fahey, who did his master's work with bluesman Charley Patton, has played a role in rediscovering bluesmen, especially Skip James and Bukka White. He is also a guitarist of some note, with emphasis on the Southern styles of blues, jazz, country, and gospel. His cult following is so strong that individual bars have been taken apart in trying to analyze the music. He is the master of long, deep, fluid Southern plantation sounds tempered with a little melancholia. He has admitted taking stimulants to heighten his awareness and has recorded while high. Each of the Takoma albums has eleven long tracks on diverse themes. C 1002 is the more traditional: "St. Louis Blues," "Poor Boy Long Way from Home," "John Henry," "Uncloudy Day." C 1014 is more impressionistic, surrealistic, and original. The titles don't really mean anything but are simply reference labels on which to

hang a guitar motif (including several musical jokes and wild themes). A sixteen-page booklet accompanies this particular disc, and it is a satire on the usual liner notes.

Fahey owns Takoma; with Reprise, he toned down considerably to achieve a more commercial sound (as he also did with earlier Vanguard records). These eight selections on Reprise are mostly low-keyed, slow tempo, acoustic steel string guitar solos, sometimes accompanied by certain jazzmen (such as Nappy Lamare on "Texas Pacific Blues" and "Lord Have Mercy"). The music is either traditional or original embodying traditional themes or motifs. One of the better numbers is the langorous "Steamboat Guine 'Round de Bend" played as a solo slide, dripping with sentiment for magnolia blossoms. "Funeral Song for Mississippi John Hurt" is a very pleasant eulogy using Hurt's guitar styles.

F4.35*   **Ian and Sylvia. Greatest Hits, v.1-2.** four discs. Vanguard VSD 5/6 and 23/24.

Ian and Sylvia came out of Canada as a premier singing duo. Sylvia came from the country scene of Canada's Midwest (southwestern Ontario); Ian arrived from the western scene of British Columbia and the rodeos (he had hurt himself, forcing an early retirement from bronc busting). Together they merged their folk, country, and western roots (submerging their real feelings about music, which were not to emerge for a decade; in reality, Ian preferred country music and Sylvia liked pop, but neither could earn money in those fields in 1960). At the start, they concentrated on a variety of Canadian, British, and American folk music, all characterized by Ian's hungry lead vocal and Sylvia's clear, resonant vibrato harmony. These titles included "Ella Speed" (with Sylvia lead), "Royal Canal," plus blues, ballads, bluegrass, French-Canadian ("Un Canadien Errant"), etc. Later they started to write their own songs, such as "Four Strong Winds" by Ian. Sylvia was the better writer, with such as "You Were on My Mind," "Someday Soon" (covered by Judy Collins), "Circle Game," and some other country-derived songs. This resulted in some chart successes, but at the same time, they were still singing folk tunes such as "Brave Wolfe" or "Four Rode By" (British-Canadian songs). They also actively promoted other Canadian folksingers in the United States. Near the end of their Vanguard career, they developed electric instruments and promoted such folk-rock as Dylan's "This Wheel's on Fire." Throughout the mixture of solos and duos, they maintained a close harmony with synchronized words and phrases. The 47 tracks here cover all aspects of their Vanguard recordings, showing good if eclectic tastes.

F4.36   **Burl Ives. Best.** two discs. MCA2-4034.

Ives has been an actor, Broadway performer, and general traveler all of his life. He became involved with the Almanac House in New York City during the developmental period of "folk songs for the masses," but he proved too popular to be kept down. He had a radio show as early as 1940 and has recorded for MCA, CBS, UA, and Stinson. In addition, he has done much work with children's songs, has done Town Hall concerts since 1945, and has compiled books of folk songs. The 24 tracks here are "general" American favorites such as "Foggy Foggy Dew," "Blue Tail Fly," "The Fox," "Old Dan Tucker," "Git along Little Dogies," "Down in the Valley," plus such others as "Waltzing Matilda" and "Molly Malone." MCA also put out a second volume of this set, but that collates his early 1960s material that was more popular; and since that was not in the folk genre, that annotation may be found in *Contemporary Popular Music*.

F4.37*   Leo Kottke. 6 and 12 String Guitar. Takoma C1024.
This is one of the finest solo guitar albums about, an unusual surprise from the Takoma label, which seemed to be concentrating on surrealistic playing from John Fahey, Robbie Basho, and others. The notes are terrible and tell the listener nothing about the music. The fourteen selections, though, demonstrate all types of styles: blues, rags, folk, and classical ("Jesu, Joy of Man's Desiring"), with minor variations and stylistic changes as determined by his mood. The execution is flawless, particularly on "Vaseline Machine Gun," which is a piece for twelve strings and is played very fast in flash guitar fashion.

F4.38   Jim Kweskin Jug Band. Greatest Hits. two disc. Vanguard VSD 13/14.
Kweskin's group is a whole bag of tricks. They began in 1963 in Cambridge, Massachusetts, as folkies, and packed it in in 1968. Throughout the years, the various members have come from diverse folk roots, such as Richard Greene (violin) and Bill Keith (banjo and steel guitar), both now operating in the bluegrass mode. Geoff Muldaur (guitar, kazoo, and vocals) is now with Paul Butterfield and blues music; Maria D'Amato married and then divorced Muldaur and now is successfully mining the nostalgia popular music field. In effect, this group was a loosely-knit breeding ground for all kinds of "good time" music through a ragtime shuffle and old time music melodies. The closest comparison for their music is the English scene and the many skiffle groups of the 1950s that were playing exactly the same music.
The eclectic music here reveals wide influences from the past (Blind Boy Fuller, Mississippi John Hurt, Blind Blake, Chuck Berry, Lieber-Stoller compositions from the world of r 'n' b, and Uncle Dave Macon, plus jazz and rags). This down home music recreated a feeling of good time happiness, jug bands, cutting up, and so forth, preceding the impact of the Nitty Gritty Dirt Band, Holy Modal Rounders, Thin Lizzy, and other acts of the late 1960s, and Maria Muldaur and Ry Cooder of the 1970s. Good tracks here include: "Blues in the Bottle," "Christopher Columbus," Chuck Berry's "Memphis," "Blues My Naughty Sweetie Gave to Me," "Rag Mama Rag," "Jug Band Music," "Fishing Blues," "Boodle an' Shake," and "K.C. Moan."

F4.39   Limeliters. Best. RCA LSP 2889.
From 1959 to 1965, at exactly the same time as the folk boom, the Limeliters were together as a literate folk group. Alex Hassilev and Glenn Yarbrough ran a club in Aspen, Colorado, called The Limelite; hence their name, as the group started off here. Yarbrough was the lyric tenor, Hassilev was the linguist, and Louis Gottlieb provided the arrangements and the humor, as well as the master of ceremonies role. It was good formula folk while it lasted, with the group coming together in solos, duos, and trio work. Titles here include "Gari Gari," "When I First Came to This Land," "The Cumberland Mountain Bear Chase," "Molly Malone," and "The Hammer Song." When it was all over, Yarbrough was the only one to seek a solo career.

F4.40   Trini Lopez. Greatest Hits. Reprise RS 6226.
Texas-born Lopez played guitar through many Latin clubs in Dallas, and then began to tour the Southwest, eventually recording popular folk material for Reprise in 1963 and in the few years that followed. Heavily arranged versions by Don Costa were the items of the day: "If I Had a Hammer," "La Bamba," "Michael Row the Boat Ashore," "Lemon Tree," "Green, Green," "Kansas City," etc.

F4.41   Ed McCurdy. Best. Tradition 2051.

F4.42   Ed McCurdy. Treasure Chest of American Folksongs. two discs. Elektra 205.
As with those of Oscar Brand, the albums of Ed McCurdy have been prolific but are not that easily accessible. He has been characterized as a collecting drifter, spending several years in Canada (1945-1954) and running a children's show, *Ed's Place*, for Canadian television during the mid-fifties. His deep baritone was instantly recognizable, and he is one of the most authentic of folksingers. The Tradition album includes such as "Dear Evelina'" "Green Grow the Lilacs," and "Three Fishermen." His Elektra recordings had included a variety of bawdy songs, western ballads, and minstrel songs. This present double album includes a wide range of Americana in the popular tradition.

F4.43   Chad Mitchell Trio. Best. Kapp KL 1334.
An out-and-out imitation of the Kingston Trio, right down to their dress, the Mitchell trio took to the college campus circuit and sang songs that were a little more meaningful in a dry, humorous tone—"Away Away with Rum" or "The Ballad of Lizzy Borden." They were not as popular as the Kingston Trio because they looked too much like them, and their main impact today is as the breeding ground for John Denver.

F4.44   New Christy Minstrels. Greatest Hits. Columbia CS 9279.
Randy Sparks founded this exceedingly popular group according to a formula. His idea was to take the pre-Civil War group led by Edwin "Pops" Christy and his minstrels as a model (this was the premier group of black-faced singers that introduced many of Stephen Foster's songs to the public). He then developed old time folk songs with modern tempos and arrangements. The faces were always changing in this arranged group, as personnel would flit in and out. But overall, it was the most popular group in all of folk music, if popularity can be measured by sales (over thirteen million albums sold). Titles on this anthology of their songs include "Green, Green," "Liza Lee," "Today," and "Saturday Night."

F4.45*   Odetta. The Essential. two discs. Vanguard VSD 43/44.
Previous to 1960, Odetta had done some jazz singing for RCA and Riverside (mainly blues), plus the occasional folk for Tradition Records. In 1960, she shifted to Vanguard and the solo acoustic guitar, winning more fans and transmitting her brand of folk blues to a wide audience through recordings, college tours, folk festivals, and coffee houses. Some of these 31 tracks were recorded in Carnegie Hall, others at Town Hall; the balance are from the studio. Odetta has an exceptionally strong voice, and her microphone always had to be turned down; one

always can hear her voice booming out during a concert. In addition to the folk blues of "Water Boy" and "I've Been Driving on Bald Mountain," she also performed Bessie Smith material ("Special Delivery Blues") in an uptempo fashion with an irresistible guitar riff, plus pseudo-gospel, religious, and freedom songs ("If I Had a Hammer," "He's Got the Whole World in His Hands," "No More Auction Block for Me," "Freedom Trilogy").

F4.46 **Dave Van Ronk**. two discs. Fantasy 24710.

F4.46a **Dave Van Ronk. Black Mountain Blues.** Folkways FTS 31020.

Van Ronk is a mysterious figure; his name is often heard and read about, but nobody appears to know where he is. Musicians often cite him as a source, or as an aid, and many of them apparently know him. But fans—and potential fans—know next to nothing. He is a folk-type who worked in several genres of blues and jug bands, along with the folk tradition. He has a truck driver sound with a gritty voice, and perhaps for this reason, he was never too popular at the folk time. However, it is now customary that singer-songwriters have poor voices in the 1970s; unfortunately, Van Ronk does not create his own material. The Fantasy twofer comes from 1963 and 1964 and shows Van Ronk in two moods: folk, with "Lady Gay," "Come All Ye Fair and Tender Ladies," and other "la-la" songs; and the jug band sound of "Willie the Weeper," "Cocaine Blues" and "Bad Dream Blues." Two influences can be seen here: Josh White and Woody Guthrie. The Folkways album uses his voice to good purpose, and along with white blues of pity as "Careless Love" or "In the Pines," he also tackles the black blues of Jelly Roll Morton ("Winnin' Boy") and Bessie Smith ("Backwater Blues").

OLD TIME MUSIC

OLD TIME MUSIC

INTRODUCTION

An analysis of the 20,000 old time music recordings made from 1922 to 1941 shows that less than sixty titles are Child ballads. On this basis, we can safely say that this music is *not* folk music; however, it is in a folk-derived style that fully employs the folk process. Through artist interviews, it was also determined that pre-1900 old time music was largely a *dance* music for social events, parties, or outdoor affairs, and *not* unaccompanied hymns or ballads, as folk music is so often thought of as being (and as Sharp thought). The instrumental tradition in old time music was very strong, and this runs counter to the folk purist's view of what folk music is supposed to be and what it is not (see also the section on British folk music).

The roots of these 20,000 old time music discs are easily discernible. Many examples of the Anglo-ballad tradition abound in a variety of styles, and these are listed here in rough chronological order:

1. English, Welsh, Scottish, Irish, and general Celtic ballads derived from the "cultural arrest" of immigrants transmitting the forms they learned to their descendants.

2. Ballads from urban Britain after the Industrial Revolution.

3. Ballads and songs reflecting the pioneer life of early American settlers.

4. Religious, "sacred" music and shape note singing.

5. Fiddle tunes from the United Kingdom and French-Canadian sources.

6. Humor from traveling medicine shows or minstrel shows.

7. Blues from the southern black man, plus music from ethnic minorities— Cajuns and Texas-Mexican people.

8. The sentimental composed song of the late nineteenth century, learned in the youth of many older singers of the 1920s (thus, these were *not* folk derived tunes, but merely the popular songs of the time).

9. Diverse instrumental tunes reflecting black jazz and the ragtime rage of 1900-1920.

10. Original "hillbilly songs" that were written when the supply of traditional items ran out (this developed in the very late 1920s and provided much "grist for the mill").

Each of the preceding "roots" influenced the later developments as time passed, until the amalgam fused itself into country and bluegrass music. In addition to this "source" analysis, a breakdown of the *New Lost City Ramblers Song Book* showed a wide range of topics. The largest category was the rambling-gambling-hobo-train songs (15 percent), followed by sad love songs (11 percent), topical and protest songs (10 percent), dance tunes (10 percent), murder ballads (8 percent), children's songs (7 percent), humor (5 percent), sacred (3 percent), work songs

(2 percent), and a large number of miscellaneous (29 percent) items. Almost half of the old time songs dealt with tragedy of some kind. This was a definite inheritance from the United Kingdom which, when combined with fatalistic fundamentalist religion, produced songs of isolation and somber grace. It is significant that most of the songs are in the minor key.

In comparison to other musical forms, old time music was thus settled by the time that recordings were being made. Before 1900, community involvement had spread the music throughout the Southeast and Southwest. Socializing events brought people closer together—such activities as barn raising, apple-cuttings, quilting parties, church and social dances, log rollings, etc.—and also served the purpose of a song-swap gathering. Migrations from the Cumberland-Appalachian area to Arkansas, Louisiana, and Texas meant that the acquired music went with the pioneers. A typical occurrence was to impose an account of a recent happening onto a half-remembered melody—thus was born the *event* song, with local lyrics and a variation of a widely-known tune. Migration to industrial areas produced songs about textile mills, coal mines, dock yards, railroads, etc. By the mid-nineteenth century, a cappella songs gradually acquired instrumentation. The dulcimer and fiddle were used as accompaniment before the Civil War, as was the five string banjo (with basic chords borrowed from blacks) a little later. The guitar was a later arrival at the turn of the century, with added impetus from the spread of the Hawaiian guitar through the pop music world. The mandolin was acquired shortly before World War I. Solo vocals were augmented by the harmony singing evolving from shape note singing, a simplified musical notation used in nineteenth-century hymnals, particularly in rural areas. Church music, in addition to the call-and-response of lining out and shape notes (see **Sacred Music**), was also a strong influence on songs of unrequited love, this by the simple means of providing for the metaphorical transfer of the religious notion that peace is found in death to the notion of lonely resignation or death that is so characteristic of such secular music. The minstrel and medicine shows injected *humor* into the repertoire, particularly Uncle Dave Macon, Fiddlin' John Carson, and Clarence "Tom" Ashley.

The *fiddle* tradition coalesced by 1880 with the beginnings of fiddling conventions and competitions throughout the land. This spirit deemphasized the droning pipe sounds for the flash of virtuosity. The two greatest such festivals are now at Union Grove, North Carolina (now over fifty years old, and specializing in both modern and traditional music) and Galax, Virginia (concentrating on traditional). The added instrumentation noted above created a strong string band approach by 1920, and indeed, the first record in the old time field was cut by a country string band on an Edison cylinder (Fiddlin' Bob Haines and His Four Aces). The banjo assumed such regional variations as the three finger style in North Carolina and the thumb and first finger style of Kentucky. The basic string band comprised banjo, guitar, and violin. Later, when the mandolin was mastered by the younger generation and the bass violin became widely known through recordings, the string band became five instruments. This was the time of transition to bluegrass, through J. E. Mainer to Bill Monroe.

The basic conservatism and rural economy of the American South fostered both the development and retention of old time music. The cultural arrest brought on by lack of education and communication meant that the Anglo ballads remained in the southern musical mainstream with very slight modifications, while transitional elements were introduced in other parts of the country, most notably the Southwest and Texas. This same retention occurred in New England and the Maritime Provinces of Canada, although for different reasons. When Cecil Sharp began hunting through Appalachia for ballads in 1916-1918, he discovered survivals of British styles that were more intact than what he could collect in Britain. Such preservation fit in with the fundamentalist teachings of Calvin, but the music also included social and humorous songs that Sharp never collected. Why? Because early on in his work, Sharp declared that he was *not* interested in dance music and *frowned* on musical accompaniment. The grapevine picked this up and wherever Sharp went he ran into a cappella singing of those songs that people had learned from their parents, namely, the Anglo ballad. Sharp was misled, but not deliberately; the people only sang what they knew he wanted to hear. Later, for the Library of Congress Archive of Folk Song, all types of music would be recorded.

The old time music forms of pre-1900 began to break down with the influence of radio and records. Popular music introduced the Hawaiian guitar, while blues music introduced the steel guitar. New stylings arose, infiltrated, and reduced regionalism. Recordings began with southwestern fiddler Eck Robertson in June 1922, and with Virginia balladeer Henry Whitter in March 1923. Many performers traveled to New York to record, but the market was too small. Ralph Peer of Okeh made a field trip to Atlanta, Georgia, and there recorded Fiddlin' John Carson in June 1923. The disc was only released in Atlanta, but it proved to be such a popular record that it was distributed elsewhere. Exploitation began through field recordings, and this lasted until the Depression. Traditional, old time music was recorded away from the big centers, and mainly by older, well-known (to their local communities) artists who could assure local sales to recoup the company's expenses. Any national distribution sales were pure gravy to the company (such as Okeh, Victor, Vocalion). The same principles were used for blues recordings as well—on the "race" series of labels established by the recording companies. No unknowns were recorded, and no risks were taken.

The dramatic importance of this is the priceless heritage of direct documentation of pre-industrial United States. Virtually every artist was over fifty years of age, and all were settled in their pre-1900 stylings. Okeh had Carson, who was over 55, and several over 35 (Norris, Lunsford, Stoneman). Columbia had Riley Puckett, Gid Tanner and Ernest Thompson. Vocalion had Charlie Oaks and Uncle Dave Macon. For the companies, costs were kept to a minimum by using a hotel room, solo performers (especially fiddlers over seventy), and public domain material from the nineteenth century. Although they did not intend to do so, the companies gave America the results of preservation. Much of this material can be found today on anthologies, especially those of the Old Timey series, County, and RCA. The recordings—done under primitive conditions—were all acoustic and do not fare too well on our present day stereo systems.

At the same time as all this field recording activity, Vernon Dalhart was in the studio with "The Prisoner's Song" in 1924, which proved to be an immensely popular song that could have been followed up except for two things. First, the WSM Grand Ole Opry began in 1925 and soon blanketed the East Coast with its diverse, free music. Second, the development of the electrical recording process plus the profits of the past two years meant that string bands could now be both recorded (groups of more than two persons suffered under acoustic recording techniques) and paid. They provided a variety of material—fiddle songs, sentimental songs, lively dance music—to compete with Dalhart's ballads, the latter a form that WSM in Nashville also used to keep costs down. The Opry itself developed from the WLS (in Chicago) show, National Barn Dance, but WSM had more power. Chicago's old time music show used a wide range of instruments, such as the accordion, but it was never a popular show until the Depression. Later, in the 1930s, "border radio" would begin broadcasting from Mexico, and its power could blanket the entire continent of North America. The music on border radio was in keeping with the tone of the religious-dominated sponsors: old time and southwestern ballads.

By 1927, the traditional repertoire of old time music petered out, and new music had to be found. A. P. Carter dug around, refashioned many older songs, and recorded them with the Carter Family, taking the compositional credits. Jimmie Rodgers collected bluesongs and modified that material. In the border town of Bristol, Virginia/Tennessee, on the same day, Ralph Peer, now working for Victor, auditioned and recorded both the Carters and Rodgers. The Carters came from a solid, old time string band background, and they performed on guitars and autoharps; Rodgers was in the balladeer format as a soloist. This significant recording event changed the course of the music. Commercialism intruded, for previous to this time, most performers were amateurs with other jobs (the money from recordings was secondary). The Carters were successful in selling records of their own "compositions"; Rodgers's compositions were successful to the point that he became the first country "star," and his only job was singing as a professional.

The shift here, then, was to the introduction of non-folk-derived music to old time music, through the Carters, and to the birth of the star system, which would lead to a more commercial sounding country music, through Rodgers. That this shift occurred on the same day in the same place is even more dramatic. Henceforth, "country" music would be built around a "star" with especially *composed* material— the forerunner of modern country music (see that section herein).

By this time, the audience had pretty well rejected the minstrel-balladeer tradition of slow paced ballads sung by artists whose rural roots were dubious (e.g., they lived in cities, as Dalhart or Carson did, or they were exposed to urban life, as Riley Puckett was). In their place, through the Depression and after, there developed the male duet of brother teams, such as the Delmore Brothers, McGee Brothers, Callahan Brothers, Monroe Brothers, Mac and Bob, Blue Sky Boys, Bailes Brothers, Bailey Brothers, Louvin Brothers—right through to the Everly Brothers and the beginnings of rock and roll. With such combinations, both sang and played (two guitars or a guitar and a mandolin). Usually the guitar player did rhythm chords and sang the lower melody line, while the mandolinist played and sang high harmony. Material was almost always ballads and love songs, but some boogies and uptempo songs (particularly in the Delmores' and Monroes' repertoire) helped to create bluegrass music.

The regional centers of old time music in the 1920s naturally followed the recording industry's field trips. Of first importance was Atlanta, Georgia, with the discs of Fiddlin' John Carson, Gid Tanner and His Skillet Lickers, and Riley Packett. Here were the fiddle tradition, the stringband tradition, and the solo troubador. Galax, Virginia, ranked as the second most important, contributing singers Henry Whitter, Kelly Hawell, and Ernest V. Stoneman. Later, Galax would stress old time fiddling conventions (available on the Galax label for each competition since 1965).

The third level of development—and most enduring in terms of impact on modern country music—was the later-emerging center of North Carolina, through Charlie Poole, Dock Walsh, Snuffy Jenkins, and Earl Scruggs. This area emphasized the string band tradition and the single note banjo picking (both pre-eminent in bluegrass music), although old time fiddle was still emerging through the Union Grove, North Carolina, fiddle competitons (available since 1967 on the Union Grove label).

Texas was the fourth major area to develop, and over the course of many years, it would transform diverse musical styles into "southwestern jazz and swing" (employing the roots of folk, ethnic, blues music) and then into rock and roll. Unfortunately, the recorded legacy of Texans on albums is small. Many have been widely anthologized, but few have albums under their own names. Charles Nabell was the first singer of traditional cowboy songs (Okeh, 1924) but his career and even his life are largely unknown. Eck Robertson, born in 1887, was the first southern rural artist to make commercial folk music recordings (Victor, 1922), and the first performer to appear in western dress. His "Sally Goodwin," the all time classic from 1922, presented dozens of variations on a theme (syncopation, single string, double string harmonies, drones, blue notes, rapid noting like bagpipes, and different fingerings). Vernon Dalhart was the first country music recording artist to attain an *international* following, but his one-man factory approach weakened his impact (see entry F5.29a).

Old time music diffused throughout the nation, evolving into bluegrass, western, modern country, troubador sounds, and so forth. But the tradition still exists either in continuations by original groups on Rounder, County, or Folkways labels (along with festivals), or by recreations through the New Lost City Ramblers. These companies are continuing the pre-1900 forms of old time music, with the by-now traditional songs and instrumentation (or lack of it). Most of these singers are also non-professional. By the Depression period, most non-professionals of the time had retired, disappeared, or died. The professionals, beginning with the brother duets and the urbane, practiced string bands, had exhausted the traditional repertoire and began to write their own songs in the traditional style (and thereby augmented their earnings by collecting copyright royalties). The banjo declined in importance (it was too ringing in sound for a polished and urbane recording), while the mandolin and steel guitar ascended. When regional barriers collapsed, the music of both the Southeast and the Southwest merged into country and western music. Nobody, it seems, wanted old time music anymore, and it easily transmuted into bluegrass; western music became western swing. The blander elements of old time music and western music became the "c & w" of the 1940s.

Literature

As old time music is so closely entwined with folk music, many of the works cited in that section have application here for basic background. Further reading and recordings can be found through Sandberg and Weissman (77). Documentation is just beginning to be published on "commercially disseminated folk music" (as it was once called), beginning with a 1970 symposium offprinted from *Western Folklore* (book section, [16]). Russell (75a) investigates the interactions of black and white performers with emphasis on the blues. Wolfe (100) details the early history of the Grand Ole Opry to 1935 in the first of a series of books from the periodical *Old Time Music* (16). The Carter Family and their impact have been discussed in two recent publication (5, 12). Respectability for country music scholarship was achieved with the publication of Malone's (57) Ph.D. dissertation in 1968, a definitive survey of the whole scope of country music. This was augmented by Malone and McCulloh (58) and Shelton (83).

For periodicals, Britain's *Old Time Music* (16) is the leading publication, with feature stories, discographies, tracings and record reviews. The *Quarterly* of the John Edwards Memorial Foundation (9) is a well-established presentation of articles dealing with American folklore, old time music, and early country music. It too deals with discographies and song histories. The *Journal of Country Music* (11) has interpretive articles on all subjects that touch on country music. Historical background can be found in the *Journal of American Folklore* (10), and song transcriptions in *Sing Out!* (20). The two British periodicals *Country Music People* (5) and *Country Music Review* (6) will run occasional articles. At present, there is no one source for discographic data, as in the genres of jazz and blues, although such a work will be forthcoming. Such data and other articles, books, and reviews, can be retrieved through the *Annual Index to Popular Music Record Reviews* (3) and the *Popular Music Periodicals Index* (69) either by artist's name or under the genre **Old Time Music.**

ANTHOLOGIES

F5.1*   **Ballads and Breakdowns of the Golden Era.** Columbia CS 9660.

F5.2   **Paramount Old Time Tunes.** JEMF 103.
The 31 tracks on these two discs are derived from two companies. The Columbia 15000 series issues are electrical recordings from 1926-1931 devoted to old time music issues, most notable being those of the string bands. A wide variety of styles are covered, including such classics as Charlie Poole's "White House Blues" and "Bill Mason," Burnet and Rutherford's "Ladies on the Steamboat" and "Sally Johnson," Dock Walsh's "In the Pines," and Gid Tanner's "Soldier's Joy." Other performers included Clayton McMichen, Riley Puckett, the Carolina Buddies, Darby and Tarleton, and the Roane County Ramblers. The JEMF collation presents a sampling from over 300 titles recorded by Paramount for their old time music series. Paramount had few fiddle bands; consequently, these are all vocals from the 1927-1932 period. This set is somewhat hampered by the original poor quality of Paramount pressings and by the fact that they were the last recording company to get electrical equipment.

The hardest old time music records to track down were from Paramount. A variety of styles developed, including some cowboy music but this latter genre did not develop at Paramount until 1931, and the company shut down its old time music series the very next year. Wilmer Watts contributes "Banjo Sam" and "Cotton Mill Blues"; the Fruit Jar Guzzlers, with banjo and guitar, sing "Stack-O-Lee"; the Carver Boys do "Brave Engineer," a train wreck song; Emry Arthur sings "Reuben, Oh Reuben"; and the North Carolina Ramblers appear with Roy Harvey and Posey Rorer. The different groups did all types of songs: the event song, the sentimental ballad, breakdowns, etc. The JEMF record comes with a rather large booklet that examines the music of the Paramount Company and its contributions to old time music.

F5.3*   **Ballads and Songs.** Old Timey X 102.

F5.4   **Mountain Songs.** County 504.

F5.5*   **Native American Ballads.** RCA LPV 548.

F5.6   **Old Time Ballads from the Southern Mountains.** County 522.

F5.7*   **Smoky Mountain Ballads.** RCA LPV 507.
  These anthologies present the great diversity in the oral tradition of folk transmission. The Old Timey set presents sixteen tracks with Grayson and Whitter ("Little Maggie," "Handsome Molly," "Rose Conley"), Cliff Carlisle, Wade Mainer, Dixon Brothers, Blue Sky Boys—all with good notes. The two County records come from 1927-1930 and feature more of the "event" song, with many of the same performers as above plus Don Blackard's Moonshiners, Boyd Moore and His Hot Shots, Emry Arthur's "The Broken Wedding," the Carolina Buddies' "Otto Wood, the Bandit," and B. F. Shelton's "Pretty Polly." The multi-faceted nature of singing in the old time music period continues with the 32 tracks on the two Vintage sets. Here, both the notes and selections concentrate on the text of the song rather than on the performer. LPV 548 comprises soloists (Uncle Dave Macon, Carl T. Sprague, Kelly Harrell, Vernon Dalhart, etc.), duos (Dixon Brothers, Delmore Brothers) and groups (Skillet Lickers) in a broader program than LPV 507, the latter restricted to southern Appalachia, with J. E. Mainer, the Monroe Brothers, etc.

F5.8   **Ballads and Songs of the Blue Ridge Mountains—Persistence and Change.** Folkways 3831.

F5.9   **Mountain Music of Kentucky.** Folkways F 2317.

F5.10   **Singers of the Piedmont.** Bear Family FV 15.505 (West German issue).
  Regional preferences come to light in these collections of singers and ballads. The string bands had more flavor and style in their regional diversification, but, obviously, different areas contributed different modes of singing as well. The two Folkways albums comprise about forty tracks of field recordings with Roscoe Holcomb, Wade Ward, Glen Smith, Sarah Hawkins, Granny Porter, and Glen Neaves. The Bear Family set is a reissue anthology from the 1920s and includes all seven of the known Dave McCarn recordings (including "Hobo Life" and "Bashful Bachelor"), plus four duos of McCarn with Howard Long. Gwen Foster has two items, as do the Carolina Twins. Booklets accompany all three discs.

F5.11   **Blacks, Whites and Blues.** CBS 52796 (British issue).

F5.12   **Blues in a Bottle.** Rounder 1011.

F5.13　　**Early Country Music, 1928-1931.** Historical HLP 8002.

F5.14*　　**Mister Charlie's Blues.** Yazoo L1024.

F5.15*　　**Mountain Blues, 1927-1934.** County 511.

F5.16　　**Old Time Mountain Guitar.** County 523.

These six anthologies show the various interactions between whites and blacks during the 1920s and their subsequent influence. The CBS set was compiled by Tony Russell, chiefly to accompany his book of the same title. There are eight tracks by both groups, largely from 1927 to 1935, plus two performances from 1969. The theme is the blues, and illustrative material is derived from the Allen Brothers and Sam McGee, the two chief exponents of white blues during the 1920s and 1930s. For comparative purposes, there are "Brain Cloudy Blues" by Bob Wills, and the ultimate twist: a bluesy rendition of Ernest Tubb's "Walking the Floor over You" and "Steel Guitar Rag" by the noted blues guitarist Earl Hooker. He performed these two country classics live in London, England, and these are the versions heard here. In effect, they show a closing of the circle: blues and rags to country to blues again. Hooker was a respected blues and r 'n' b performer who never disavowed country music roots (Chuck Berry was another melder of r 'n' b and country to form rockabilly music).

The Yazoo anthology drives the point home. This reissue firm normally only releases black blues, but this time decided to produce an album of guitar blues performed by whites who played in a style very close to that of blacks. Given the early nature of the recording microphone, it is impossible—even with a trained ear—to describe racial origins here. The fourteen instrumentals and vocals (from 1926-1930) are done by the Auglin Brothers, South Georgia Highballers, Dick Justice, the Allen Brothers, Darby and Tarlton, Sam McGee, etc. In fact, some of these tracks were so "black" at the time that they were released in the "race" series of the company involved. Many of the titles are also in the "ragtime" vein. This comes to a head with *Mountain Blues*, an album that concentrates on the vocals and string bands of the Piedmont. The black-white mixture here is the topicality of the lyrics in addition to the strange rag-blues intricate picking of the Piedmont. Topical items dealt with railroad songs (e.g., Sam McGee's "Railroad Blues" or Frank Hutchison's "Cannonball Blues"), and there were strong instrumentals such as the fiddles of Doc Roberts or Willie Narmour. Other performances are given by Jimmy Tarleton and the Carolina Tar Heels.

Tracks on County 523 trace the history of white guitar playing from the advent of the "parlor guitar" of the nineteenth century through the blues. Excellent liner notes are written by Rob Fleder, and indicate the "Vastopol" D tuning of the parlor guitar and the "Spanish Fandango" G tuning of the Spanish guitar. Both appear to have been advantageous when adapting ragtime selections. The resultant thumbing produced an alternating bass to the syncopation of the treble strings. The thirteen selections include five tracks by Roy Harvey (of the North Carolina Ramblers) in a guitar duet with either Leonard Copeland or Jess Johnson. Copeland had a light touch; Johnson was more dramatic, as in "Guitar Rag," with his slide on "Jefferson Street Rag" showing good picking. The title "Take Me to the Land of Jazz" proved to be a remarkable synthesis of jazz, blues, ragtime, and old time music.

Frank Hutchison plays a very mean slide guitar on "Logan County Blues," while Uncle Dave Macon and Sam McGee trade licks on "Knoxville Blues."

The Historical set is chiefly mandolin, both black and white performers, and was recorded in both Texas and New York. Among the standouts is John Dilleshaw on "Spanish Fandango" and "Cotton Patch Rag," a white player performing black material. The black Matthew Prater takes on a stunning development of instrumental style in "Nothin' Doin' " and "Somethin' Doin' "—both basically in the white idiom. Joe Evans and Arthur McClain combine for the bluesy "Sittin' on Top of the World" and the old timey "Sourwood Mountain."

F5.17   **Clawhammer Banjo.** County 701.

F5.18   **More Clawhammer Banjo.** County 717.

F5.19*   **Mountain Banjo Songs and Tunes.** County 515.
County 515 covers the 1925-1933 period, with a vast range of style and tunings. Included are Uncle Dave Macon, Marion Underwood, W. A. Hinton, Bascom Lamar Lunsford, Buell Kazee, Frank Jenkins, Dock Walsh, and Riley Puckett. The other two Counties are subtitled "old time banjo and fiddle tunes" and "songs and tunes from the mountains," respectively. Both are modern examples of the banjo playing in the clawhammer style (various stylings and configurations). This style—also known as "frailing," "rapping," or "downpicking"—takes its name from the position of the fingers in the shape of a clawhammer. It has been the most influential of the various five string banjo styles, radically different from the bluegrass Scruggs picking or the so-called chromatic, single note picking. Wade Ward, heard on two traditional pieces—"June Apple" and "John Lover's Home"—is probably the best known performer. Ernest Stoneman's brother George follows with four tunes. Then Kyle Creed and Fred Cockerham tackle two solos apiece and later combine for four banjo-fiddle duets (both can play the fiddle). These are perhaps the most satisfying cuts on the albums. Other performers include Matokie Slaughter, Gaither Carlton, Oscar Wright, and Tommy Jarrell.

F5.20   **A Day in the Mountains—1928.** County 512.
A little levity goes a long way. These five two-part skits, square dance tunes, and so forth do a brilliant job of showing country folks having a solid good time at the various kinds of social events that might be held on a non-working day. Included are Gid Tanner, Lowe Stokes, Eck Dunford, etc.

F5.21*   **Echoes of the Ozarks, v.1/3.** three discs. County 518/520.
The material here covers the Ozarks of Arkansas, Missouri, and Oklahoma in the 1926-1932 recording period. According to the annotations (which are superb) the Ozarks were the freest from all outside influences. Thus, the music is relatively pure, and at the same time, the music is relatively rare, for if the Ozarks were little influenced, then they exerted little influence on other areas. There are a total of seventeen groups here, with fiddle-guitar combinations being the most common instrumentation. Four groups used a banjo, and there are a number of harmonicas, pianos, and string basses used. Most of the groups came from Arkansas and peaked in their recording careers in 1928. This is all richly varied music that has a distinctive

style all of its own. Included are Pope's Arkansas Mountaineers, the Carter Brothers and Son, and the Reeves White County Ramblers—all with five tracks apiece. The other groups have two or one track only. An excellent set of discs for regional examination.

F5.22*   **Early Rural String Bands.** RCA LPV 552.

F5.23   **Old Time String Band Classics.** County 531.

F5.24*   **The String Bands, v.1/2: Southern Dance Music, and into the 1950s.** two discs. Old Timey X100/1.
    The annotated RCA Vintage record covers the 1922-1949 period, and shows, through sixteen tracks, the regional diversification and wide coverage of the string band tradition, particularly in its transitional stage through to bluegrass music. Performances are given by A. C. Robertson, J. P. Nestor, the Carolina Tar Heels, Leo Soileau (for Cajun music), and the Allan Brothers. The 32 tracks on the Old Timey set cover a later period into the 1950s and concentrate more on blues and ragtime influences, such as the Spooney Five's "Chinese Rag," the Moatsville String Ticklers' "Moatsville Blues," the Three Stripped Gears' "Black Bottom Strut," and so forth.
    The County offering represents at least seven different and distinct regions typical of the 1927-1933 period. Most of the music is led by a fiddle, and there are only two vocals here. All of it is uptempo music, being meant for social dances when originally recorded. Included among the twelve tracks are Luke Highnught and His Ozark Strutters ("Sailing on the Ocean"), the Fox Chasers ("Eighth of January"), Ted Gossett, and the Floyd County Ramblers. The notes for the RCA and Old Timey anthologies are superb, but notes are non-existent for the County set.

F5.25   **Maple on the Hill.** RCA Camden 898.

F5.26   **Traditional Country Classics.** Historical HLP 8003.
    The Historical reissue comes from a variety of recording companies during the 1927-1929 period, acknowledged by many as being the best era of the string band. Performances are given by Earl Johnson, Charlie Poole, Grayson and Whitter, the Stonemans, Da Costa Woltz (with the exciting "Yellow Rose of Texas"), Dilly and his Dill Pickles ("Lye Soap Breakdown") and B. F. Shelton ("Oh Molly Dear"). The RCA set continues the pattern through the 1930s to the early 1940s, stressing transitional string bands, such as J. E. Mainer's Crazy Mountaineers, Riley Puckett, Bradley Kinkaid, and the brother duos of the Delmores and the Carlisles. The total number of tracks from both discs is 26.

F5.27   **Old Time Music of Clarence Ashley's, v.1/2.** two discs. Folkways F 2355 and 2359.
    Tom Ashley made over seventy recordings for Columbia, Okeh, Victor, Vocalion, and so forth in the 1920s, plus others with the Carolina Tar Heels and the Blue Ridge Mountain Entertainers. His best known song was the banjo tune "Coo Coo Bird," included on the Harry Smith *Anthology*. In the past, Ashley has

influenced both Roy Acuff and Doc Watson; he was a rediscovery of the Newport Festivals in the early 1960s. These two Folkways discs are almost a reunion of the Carolina Tar Heels. All tracks were recorded at Ashley's home, and such various people (not heard on every track) accompanied him as: Doc Watson, Jean Ritchie, Clint Howard, Fred Price, Dock Walsh, and Garley Foster. Tracks include the diverse traditional titles "Omie Wise," "Rising Sun Blues," the solemn "Amazing Grace," the buoyant "Way Downtown," "East Tennessee Blues," "Richmond Blues," and the lonely "My Home's across the Blue Ridge Mountains."

F5.28*   **Steel Guitar Classics.** Old Timey OT 113.
This anthology collates some sixteen pre-electric steel guitar music, showing the diverse styles of old time, Hawaiian, and blues music. Lemuel Turner does a bottleneck solo blues; Jimmy Tarlton picks a steel guitar lead over a rhythm guitar; Cliff Carlisle concentrates on the melody form of picking. Diverse Hawaiian influences are shown through the roughly jazz-equated work of Sol Hoopii, the original duo of Kanui and Lula singing in Hawaiian, and the cross-over potential embodied in "Hillbilly Hula" by Tex Carman. Of special note are the three cuts by Jimmie Davis, who is better known for "You Are My Sunshine" and other pop songs. In "Sewing Machine Blues," "Red Nightgown Blues," and "Down at the Old Country Church," he shows a rough and ready blues style augmented by noted black guitar picker Oscar Woods.

MINSTRELS

Innovators

F5.29*   **Fiddlin' John Carson. The Old Hen Cackled and the Rooster's Gonna Crow.** Round Records 1003.
Showman and musical pioneer Carson (1868-1949) was *most* responsible for commercial country music. He was an important influence in early country music (that is, influential on the likes of the Carter Family and Jimmie Rodgers, who in turn were directly influential on modern commercial country music). After winning several old time fiddle competitions, he was discovered in Atlanta by the ubiquitous Ralph Peer, and he recorded for Okeh beginning in 1923. Prior to this, recordings of folk ballads were haphazard and never sold well. Usually, they were covered by professional singers such as Vernon Dalhart and marketed as art songs to an urban audience. Rural people were ignored. In fact, Carson's first release ("The Little Log Cabin in the Lane" and the title of the above album; both heard on this sixteen selection disc) was not advertised and not even listed in the Okeh catalog; yet it sold fantastically well in Atlanta—the only place it was released. This success demonstrated to recording companies that there was "gold in them thar hills," and massive field recordings began. Carson was 56 at the time of his first sessions, and of course his style was fixed by then.
These are unique specimens of the old fiddle-accompanied singing style that was prevalent before the turn of the century. Carson was indeed a transmitter of the folk tradition, more so than others such as the Carter Family. Some 150 tunes were released by Okeh up to 1931, plus 24 items Carson did for Victor in 1934.

Analysis of these 174 titles shows a varied repertoire, with only a few from Europe. Two dozen were pop songs of the 1880-1910 period; another two dozen were British immigrant songs. The balance were sacred music, humorous, or topical (plight of the farmer, taxes, political songs, moonshine music). His erratic playing and pyro-technic, flashy style needed a backup group (The Virginia Reelers), but his singing could stand on its own: an ornate, often melismatic vocal line. This is the first album ever devoted solely to Carson, and it includes "The Bachelor's Hall," "The Honest Farmer," "It's a Shame to Whip Your Wife on Sunday," and "Watcher Gonna Do When the Licker Runs Out." A separate booklet with full notes, texts, and discographic data is included with the record.

F5.29a*   **Vernon Dalhart. Old Time Songs, 1925-1930, v.1.** Davis Unlimited
          DU 33030 [first of a projected 15-volume series].
     Vernon Dalhart (real name: Robert Marion Slaughter) was the first country music recording artist to attain an *international* following. He began recording for Victor in 1917 with pop ballads and light opera, but in 1924, he recorded "The Prisoner's Song" (over eight million copies sold), "The Wreck of the Old 97," and "The Death of Floyd Collins"—his lifetime sales between 1915 and 1939 were 75 million copies (2/3 of which were based on country music) in 5,000 releases of 1,000 songs under 110 different pseudonyms. He was a phenomenon because his Texas background stressed "serious" music; indeed, he was signed to Edison records in 1915 because of his clear diction—a definite plus in the days of acoustic recordings. Looking for new material, he scouted the "folk" field of ballads, topical songs, minstrel songs, and "standards." His success can be attributed to a number of factors—his prolific output and availability, his clear voice, his material, plus the fact that he was the first to exploit the sentimental song (such as "The Letter Edged in Black"). His profound effect on country music was distilled through the touring of Jimmie Rodgers and the rise of the country star system. Thus it is that national acceptance of old time country music came about through a trained ballad singer who had already honed his work and eliminated the rough edges of accents that only had regional appeal (such as the stringbands).
     Davis Unlimited has planned a fifteen-disc set denoting Dalhart's early popu-larity. It includes all the tunes mentioned above, as well as the topical "Frank Dupree," the minstrel song "Golden Slippers," and the sentimental "I'll Be with You When the Roses Bloom Again." Although novelties were rare with Dalhart, this disc does contain Uncle Dave Macon's "On the Dixie Bee Line" (along with Macon's opening monologue). Dalhart's versatility is clearly evident: all of the selec-tions are significant. While this first volume contains a set of general notes, it lacks basic discographical material. As well, the sound and production are not of the high caliber of Rounder or Arhoolie records (both of which usually include booklets describing texts, lyrics, history, discographies—all illustrated by rare photographs).

F5.30*   **Frank Hutchison. The Train That Carried My Girl from Town.** Rounder
          1007.
     Hutchison was a master of the dense guitar pattern. He specialized in fast fingering, employing a slide style with a knife, and used the blues in many of his recordings ("Worried Blues," "Stackalee," "Railroad Bill," "K. C. Blues"). He improvised some rags as well ("Hutchison's Rag"). Other items in his repertoire

included comic and dance songs ("Alabama Girl," "The Burglar Man"), and the sentimental event song, such as "The Last Scene of the Titanic." He was a unique artist who only recorded 32 tracks between 1926 and 1929 and was one of the first few white people to adapt to the black blues.

F5.31*   **Uncle Dave Macon. Ace of Hearts.** AH 135 (British issue).

F5.32*   **Uncle Dave Macon. RBF 51.**

F5.33*   **Uncle Dave Macon. The Dixie Dewdrop, v.1/2.** Vetco 101, 105.

F5.34*   **Uncle Dave Macon. Early Recordings, 1925-1935.** County 521.

F5.35   **Uncle Dave Macon. First Row, Second Left.** Bear Family 15-518 (West German issue).

F5.36   **Uncle Dave Macon. Fun in Life.** Bear Family 15.519 (West German issue).

F5.37   **Uncle Dave Macon. The Gayest Old Dude in Town.** Bear Family 15.520 (West German issue).

F5.38   **Uncle Dave Macon. 1926-1939.** Historical HLP 8006.
   "Uncle" Dave Macon (1870-1952) was a superb banjoist and leader of his occasional group, the Fruit Jar Drinkers, which contained such diverse personnel as Sam and Kirk McGee and Mazy Todd. He was the oldest member of the Grand Ole Opry, and as he did not start to record until 1918 (at the age of 48), he is regarded as a direct link with traditional music. Between 1924 and 1952, Macon recorded over 200 songs, mainly topical, sacred, popular, minstrel, and a mixed bag of parodies and breakdowns. His main importance was as a preserver of a large amount of pre-1900 material, for he was one of the first of the old time musicians to be recorded (and hence suffered from no commercial influences). He linked both centuries as he recorded everything from Civil War songs through to Eddy Arnold hits. One of his first recordings was of "Hill Billie Blues," which became synonymous with country music.
   Through 1930, he was prolific for his day, recording twenty titles a year. His Opry career spanned 26 years, and until the arrival of Roy Acuff in 1940, he was its first and most popular "star." He recorded alone, or with his group, which produced a driving rhythm line based on Macon's shouts of encouragement. When he did sacred songs, the same group's name was changed from the Fruit Jar Drinkers to the Dixie Sacred Singers. For most banjo solo works, he transposed traditional fiddle tunes (thereby showing that it could be done) such as "Carve That Possum" or "Sail Away Ladies." Overall, his eclectic tastes were mostly part of the transition from traditional to commercial music.
   An analysis of his recordings reveals six equal sources: *original* music, mainly banjo specialties where the words are secondary to his superb frailing style; *sacred* music, including some of his personal favorites; 1870-1900 popular *sentimental* ballads dealing with love and courtship; 1840s *minstrel* show pieces, dealing with

humor; American *fiddle and dance* tunes, such as "Soldier's Joy," "Arkansas Traveler," and "Hop High Ladies"; and British *ballads* in the folk tradition, augmented by topical and political descendents. Such a vast repertoire influenced Pete and Mike Seeger as authentic followers of his style, which included shifting verses around, a routine task now performed by serious folk and blues singers. On the other hand, his popularity spawned many imitators such as Grandpa Jones, Brother Oswald, Stringbean Akeman, and other humorous old men or "uncles."

One reason for Macon's popularity, besides drawing on the vast repertoire of successful nineteenth century songs, was that he needed an audience. He preferred touring and broadcasting to recording (many of his favorite tunes he never recorded), for then he could entertain at the same time as sing. This was one of the last times that "singing" and "entertainment" would be thought of as two different functions. Thus, on disc, he would identify the audience by telling jokes, narrative stories, or use appelatives such as "now, folks." Of course, it is *de rigueur* that this *never* be done today. To top all of this, Macon acted as his own booking agent, and he was the first country singer to do so—about forty years in advance of the rest.

The tunes on these albums have variety. The Ace of Hearts presents some blues, such as "Late Last Night When My Willie Came Home"; RBF51, with good notes by Norman Tinsley, contains "Hold the Woodpile Down" plus some later Bluebirds from the 1930s. The Vetco set includes 24 (e.g., "Rise When the Rooster Crows," "Poor Sinners," "Whoop Em up Cindy," "The Bum Hotel," "The Bible's True," and "Country Ham and Red Gravy"). County 521 contains seven tracks from his best session with the McGee Brothers (May 1927)—six others are on Ace of Hearts, and RBF51 has three more titles. Here, he has recorded vaudeville numbers such as "Rock about My Sara Jane," and such old time pieces as "Grey Cat on the Tennessee Farm" and "Rabbit in the Pea Patch." Heard are his pleasant medleys, where he recorded two, three, or more songs, melodies, and lyrics within the three-minute framework allowed for one tune. This was his effect of shifting verses. The three Bear Family discs span his entire recording career, including his first disc, "Keep My Skillet Good and Greasy," and his last, "The Grayest Old Dude in Town." All six of his various sources are revealed in this superb set of 48 tracks, including quite a few of his comic narratives that deal with spinsters. Just listing the titles of all the tracks in the above nine albums would constitute a mini-history of traditional music. Uncle Dave preserved more valuable American folklore through his recordings than any other folk or country music performer.

F5.39*   **Riley Puckett. Old Time Greats.** GHP 902 (West German issue)

F5.40*   **Riley Puckett. Story, 1924-1941.** Roots RL 701 (Austrian issue).
Puckett was tremendously influential on two fronts. First, he had a characteristic voice that was instantly recognizable: country inflections and strength, overpowering lines that were heard over the instrumental accompaniment, and compassion. Secondly, his guitar fingering was outstanding for the day. The bulk of his work may be heard with the Skillet Lickers, where this blind guitarist takes many of the vocals. But under his own name, he recorded for almost twenty years. The GHP collection is derived from 1925-1935, but most of its fourteen tracks come from his later career. The Roots reissue spans more time. Here are found nine vocal-guitar solos, four duets with Ted Hawkins (mandolin), and two with fiddles

(one being with Gid Tanner himself: "Bile Them Cabbage Down"). His solos come from 1924-1930; the other works are from RCA Bluebirds of 1936-1941. Thus, the two records nicely complement each other with no duplications. Puckett's RCA period is generally thought of as being more influenced by other commercial recordings, but then, there was more music to hear at that period rather than in the "purer" era of 1924-1930. One of his first solo works—"Sleep, Baby, Sleep"— was the first old time country recording to feature a yodel. Excellent notes are on both discs.

F5.41*   **Blind Alfred Reed. How Can a Poor Man Stand Such Times and Live?** Rounder 1001.
    Reed was a highly influential, but not so prominent recording artist from 1927-1929 for Victor. Of the 21 tunes recorded under his name, two were never issued and two are on other reissued albums. Here are fourteen of the remaining seventeen tracks, and they are a unique social document from the twenties. His songs— written as would-be hymns—criticize the materialism and the hypocrisy he found in many merchants, preachers, and flappers. He was deeply religious, and hence sang many sacred songs (e.g., "Walking in the Way with Jesus" and "I Mean to Live for Jesus"), but, as is the case with many godly servants, he berated those "preachers who preach for gold and not for soul," for everybody was "taxed and schooled and preached to death." None of his material was sexist, but he didn't like the faults that he attributed to women, such as being shrewish, over-dressed, sexy, and so forth. He was also a topical broadsheeter, getting material from newscasts on the West Virginia radio stations, and he worked over the older traditional ballads, such as the British "Don't Go down in the Mines Dear Dad," which comes across on this disc as "Explosion in the Fairmount Mines" (an incident in 1907). Topical items, like the title track, dealt with contemporary problems of inflation, and these are still with us (e.g., "a steak is all gristle and bone"). Instrumentation was usually two fiddles and a guitar, with his uniquely austere fiddle style that echoed his lyrics and strong, clear voice. Reed died in 1956. An illustrated booklet, with all the lyrics, is included.

F5.41a*   **Eck Robertson, Master Fiddler, 1922-1929.** Sonyatone Records STR 201.
    The phenomenal Robertson did not make many recordings in the 1920s heyday of old time music (there are fifteen tracks on this album, which is billed as being complete), yet his impact and influence were profound on the level of second generation fiddlers and string band units. The titles are all from direct folk roots, and include such as the 1922 "Sallie Gooden," one of the finest renditions of this tune, and concludes with the 1929 "Texas Wagoner." Most of the sessions are from the time of acoustical recordings, but the sound is not at all bad. The six tracks from 1922 also include two unaccompanied solos, two duets with piano, and two tunes with Henry Gilliland. Later in life, Robertson would record with his family in the down home tradition of old time music. Other stirring titles here : "Arkansas Traveler," "Turkey in the Straw," "Ragtime Annie," "Amarillo Waltz," and the superb "Brilliancy Medley."

Standards

F5.42   **Norman Blake. Home in Sulphur Springs.** Rounder 0012.

F5.43   **Brother Oswald.** Rounder 0013.

F5.44*   **Friar Tut.** Rounder 0011.
From our personal assessment, these discs can be played anytime and anywhere, and one's attention will immediately be riveted to the music. Most of the compositions are played on the Dobro, one of the few remaining stringed instruments left unamplified. Dobro is a guitar with an aluminum (usually) resonator under the bridge; it is played horizontally with a sliding bar. These three albums represent the state of the art in Dobro music, and pickin' generally. Guitars are also represented, as well as mandolins. These tracks are instrumentals except for one vocal on Taylor's album and half of Blake's album. Blake and Taylor appear on all three albums; Brother Oswald is only heard on the album bearing his name.
Norman Blake is steeped in old time music. He plays all plucked instruments, most notably of late with Kris Kristofferson, from Baez, John Hartford, and Johnny Cash (his Dobro intro is on Cash's "Understand Your Man"). His album includes a number of transposed fiddle tunes among the fifteen selections, and his lead guitar or mandolin is superbly followed by Taylor's Dobro. Pleasing vocals can be heard on "Randall Collins," "Orphan Annie," and "Little Joe."
Tut Taylor, who has recorded for World Pacific and Tune, and can be heard on Hartford's *Aeroplain* album, has the least commercial sounding set of the three, and probably the best album of the three. He is unique in that he uses *only* a flat pick; all others noted here used finger picks. This enables him to get a sharper metallic sound that is augmented by the slide bar, and the easily recognizable sounds produced are in the blues idiom. Of the seventeen selections, all but three are originals. Each tune has different stringed instrument configurations, usually all with Dobro except "Midnight at Beanblossom" (mandolin), and the title cut. Blake sings "Daisy Dean" for the album's only vocal. Bashful Brother Oswald (Pete Kirby) should be well-known as Roy Acuff's Dobro player and high tenor man ("Wabash Cannonball," "Precious Jewel," "Wreck on the Highway," and many others). His "country style" is produced by having three wound and three unwound strings, angling the bar for slide, and picking the first and third strings together in harmony. He plays Dobro on all his seventeen cuts (instrumentals), with Blake on second guitar and mandolin and Taylor on mandolin. There are three originals here, and the pop material includes a number of waltzes sich as "Tennessee Waltz." For a stunning introduction to Dobro styles, go no further than the instrumental "Wabash Cannonball"—a Dobro trio with Blake playing it straight, Taylor flatpicking his bluesy style, and the master, Brother Oswald, acting as bossman by concluding the session with the definitive choruses. He *owns* that tune.
All of the music was recorded at New Year's cusp 1971-1972 in Nashville. The sound is superb, the packaging is excellent, and the playing time is generous.

F5.45*   **Dock Boggs, v.1-3.** Folkways. FA 2351 and 2392; Asch Recordings AH 3903.

Moran Lee "Dock" Boggs first recorded with Brunswick ("Pretty Polly") in 1927. As with other old timey musicians, he culled the vast repertoire of traditional and sentimental material. As accompaniment, he had developed a unique five string banjo style—the melodies are picked out note for note in a lower tuning (learned from a Virginia black man). He also greatly used black blues stylings, reflected in "Mistreated Mama Blues" and "Down South Blues." The nasal twang in his voice was wavering (these three discs come from 1963-1966), due to a mixture of the traditional style, emotion, and his age. His ever popular favorites are here: "Country Blues" and "Pretty Polly" among the 52 different tunes. Mike Seeger had a real find when he rediscovered Boggs during a field-collecting trip, as Boggs had not played the banjo for about 25 years. Everything here has been recorded and edited by Seeger, with the usual scholarly notes, collage of pictures, texts to the songs, and histories of all the materials used. Typical items include not only such traditionals as "Loving Nancy," "John Hardy," or "Little Ommie Wise," but also blues and hard black numbers such as "Mean Mistreatin' Mama" or "Davenport."

F5.46　　**Rufus Crisp.** Folkways 2342.

The blues and ballads of banjoist Crisp were recorded in Kentucky in 1946, and reveal a charming style in the old time tradition ("Shout Little Lulu," "Ball and Chain," "Sourwood Mountain," "Shady Grove," "Old Joe Clark"). Blues were not often recorded by these musicians, so this is a good chance to hear some superb interpretive music. There are notes and texts to the songs by Margo Mayo, who also did the recording.

F5.47　　**Kelly Harrell. Complete, v.1-3.** three discs. Bear Family 15508/10 (West German issue).

Harrell was a Virginia singer, another Ralph Peer discovery for Okeh in 1924. In essence, he was a sweet and melancholy singer who played no instruments and had to rely upon the Okeh and, later, Victor studio musicians for sparse but satisfactory backup. Most of the material assembled on these 43 tracks falls into the sentimental ballad category: "I Wish I Was a Single Girl Again," "O! Molly Dear, Go Ask Your Mother," "Beneath the Weeping Willow Tree," "Case Love Has Gained the Day," etc., but all of them are in the strong traditional style of nineteenth century romantic lyricism plus older works made available as transitory documents. Some exceptions such as "Pretty Monkey"—a pre-World War I novelty item— were repeated in Harrell's later life, as he turned to composing (he wrote "Away out on the Mountain," recorded by Jimmie Rodgers). When the Depression settled in, Harrell was let go because it was uneconomical to keep him; for each record, the company would have to pay studio musicians. Self-accompanied vocalists were better for the cash-balanced books. Of note here is the early version of "Peg and Awl" and "The Cuckoo She's a Fine Bird."

F5.48　　**Roscoe Holcomb. Close to Home.** Foldways 2374.

F5.49　　**Roscoe Holcomb. The High Lonesome Sound.** Folkways 2368.

Holcomb performed equally well on the banjo and guitar in the typical southern mountain style. He knew over 1,000 songs, and played often at many square dances. In 1959, he recorded for Folkways as a major discovery and shortly appeared on the concerts and festivals circuit. Some of his typical renditions here include "Darling Cory," "Frankie and Johnny," "Roll on Buddy," "Barbara Allen Blues" (a particularly interesting variant), "Wandering Boy," "Train that Carried My Girl from Town," etc.

F5.50   **Bascom Lamar Lunsford. Minstrel of the Appalachians.** Riverside 645.

F5.51   **Bascom Lamar Lunsford. Smoky Mountain Ballads.** Folkways 2040.
Born in 1882, fiddler and banjoist Lunsford had a very crowded career in folk and old time music. He was a collector (there were over 10,000 songs in his files); a festival organizer since 1928, including the renowned Mountain Dance and Folk Festival at Asheville, North Carolina; and he sang over 400 songs for the Library of Congress and about 315 songs for Columbia University Library. Some of his typical transmittal tunes on these two albums include "Mr. Garfield," "Little Margaret," "On the Banks of the Ohio," "Death of Queen Anne," "I Shall Not Be Moved," "The Miller's Will," "The Old Man from the North Country," and "Weeping Willow Tree."

F5.52   **Sam McGee. Grand Dad of the Country Guitar Pickers.** Arhoolie 5012.
McGee (1894-1975) lived all his life near Franklin, Tennessee, and performed on the Grand Ole Opry from almost its earliest existence. His flat-top picking guitar style was immensely influential, being mainly blues-based breaks on the runs he learned from various local black musicians (he was one of the first to bring blues into old time music). He was responsible for bringing the guitar out of rhythm and into a lead role. He recorded with his brother Kirk as the McGee Brothers (see that annotation). In 1969-1970, Mike Seeger made some field recordings to reinstate the solo McGee guitar style. The fast, fluid instrumentals that were McGee's hallmarks are here ("Franklin Blues," "Buckdancer's Choice," "Sam McGee Stomp"), as well as carefully presented blues ("Fuller Blues," "Pig Ankle Rag," and the long six-minute "Railroad Blues"). Seeger's liner notes comment on all the songs, and there is a transcribed interview with McGee about his influences.

F5.53   **Frank Proffitt. Memorial Album.** Folk Legacy FSA 36.

F5.54   **Frank Proffitt. North Carolina Songs and Ballads.** Folkways 2360.
Proffitt had an excellent voice; he was also facile with the banjo and dulcimer. His major importance, though, was as a folk music transmitter. The folklore collectors Frank and Anne Warner recorded 120 of his folk songs, one of which, entitled "Tom Dooley," Proffitt picked up in the 1930s. This song subsequently went to the Kingston Trio and became the popular hit that sparked the second folk revival. It also had the advantage of prompting the rediscovery of Proffitt, who promptly went on the folk circuit, including Newport. Good, solid interpretations here include "Handsome Molly," "Rye Whiskey," "Sourwood Mountain," "Beaver Dam Road," and "Down in the Valley," plus biographical sketches of "Bo Lankin," "George Collins," and "Old Abe Dan Doo."

F5.55   **Mike Seeger. Music from True Vine.** Mercury SRM 1-627.

F5.56   **Mike Seeger. Old Time Country Music.** Folkways 2325.

F5.57   **Mike Seeger. Tipple, Loom and Rail.** Folkways 5273.
Seeger comes from an illustrious Washington, D.C., musical family, and had most of his early listening experiences in the LC Archives of American Folk Music. He has organized many folk festivals, sat on the Newport board, produces and annotates records for Folkways, and writes about folk music. He helped to found the New Lost City Ramblers (see their annotation), a trio dedicated to recreating old time music. His solo activities are in the same vein, but of course, they concentrate on solo forms of old time music. He is a multi-instrumentalist fluent with all variations of stringed instruments and the harmonica. If there is one criticism of his wide-ranging repertoire, it is that his recreations have little of his own personality in the music. The selections on *Old Time Country Music* are mainly those that have seemingly passed into folklore from their semi-commercial beginnings, such as "Don't Let Your Deal Go Down," "John Hardy," "Sourwood Mountain," "Bonapart's Retreat," "Man of Constant Sorrow," etc. The *Tipple* album is more a specialist one, as it concentrates on work songs (mainly dealing with the textile industry and the railroad). Both have the usual scholarly annotations with a tracing of sources and discographic data. The Mercury issue is but a representation of his work in the 1970s, covering a wide range of items (again, all sourced) with Seeger on eight different instruments. The fourteen selections include "Birmingham Tickle," "The Sailor and the Soldier," "Old Grey Mare," "Buck Dancer's Choice," and "Black Is the Color of My True Love's Hair."

F5.58   **Fiddlin' Arthur Smith. Great Violin.** Starday SLP 202.
Smith joined the McGee Brothers in 1930, but he made no records until 1936, with "There's More Pretty Girls Than One" and "Beautiful Brown Eyes." He also worked with the Delmore Brothers as violin accompanist but later dropped out until the folk revival. His strong flavor was continued on the Starday album, which is mainly composed of recreations of his prior recordings. Included are "Chittlin' Cookin' Time in Cheatham County," "Dusty Miller," and other assorted old folk tunes.

F5.59   **Hobart Smith.** Folk Legacy 17.
Hobart Smith played in a frailing banjo style: double-noting or double-thumbing. He also learned guitar from black sources, and he can play the fiddle as well. During the 1920s, he performed with Clarence Ashley and in touring minstrel shows. He later recorded for Lomax and the LC Archive. This disc features renditions of "Great Titanic," "Uncloudy Day," and "Sitting on Top of the World," three songs that show his interest in the event song, sacred music, and blues.

F5.60   **Kilby Snow. With Autoharp.** Folkways 3902.
Snow is the leading proponent of old time autoharp music. In this collection, put together with Mike Seeger (who also accompanies Snow on diverse instruments), the autoharp-vocals are heard in a standard program of "Greenback Dollar," "Shady Grove," "Cannonball," etc.

STRING BANDS

Innovators

F5.61*   **Da Costa Woltz's Southern Broadcasters.** County 524.
Woltz's group was a good influence on other string bands, even though they only recorded together once (May 1927, as found here on twelve tracks). Ben Jarrell plays fiddle and does most of the vocals; Frank Jenkins and Woltz accompany on five string banjos; and there is a twelve-year-old boy who has a harmonica solo ("Lost Train Blues") and a vocal outing ("Lonesome Road Blues"). This group was noted for its trio performances (fiddle and two banjos) on such items as "Old Joe Clark," "Yellow Rose of Texas," "The Sweet Sunny South," and "Merry Girl." Jarrell's high and lonesome voice predates bluegrass tenors, especially on the sentimental ballads, which formed a contract (high lonesome sentimentality?). The three instrumentals here include "Wandering Boy" and "Home Sweet Home," and they feature good violin solowork, clawhammer banjo, and harmonica in a fine expression of social dance tunes.

F5.62*   **Clark Kessinger. Legend.** County 733.

F5.63   **Clark Kessinger. Old Time Music with Fiddle and Guitar.** Rounder 0004.
Kessinger was probably the best old time fiddler—technically proficient from absorbing the classical method. The County disc (previously available as Folkways FA 2336) was his first with both banjo (Wayne Hauser) and guitar (Gene Meade) accompaniment. The group was expressly formed for the Thirtieth Old Time Fiddlers' Convention (1964) at Galax, Virginia. The eighteen tunes include the traditional "Flop Eared Mule," "Sally Goodwin," and "Sally Ann Johnson"—all part of the breakdown heritage. "Poca River Blues" is a virtuoso performance. With the large number of dances, this smooth disc emphasizes speed. The second disc was recorded by the Rounder Collective in 1971, during the other major fiddle festival—the Old Time Fiddlers' Convention at Union Grove. Kessinger though, suffered a serious stroke a few days later. "Rickett's Hornpipe," with Kessinger's flying fiddle, Gene Meade's flatpick guitar, and diverse whoops and hollers clearly indicate why Kessinger won first prize as World's Champion Fiddler the day that this record was made. His forte, though, is the waltz; "When I Grow Too Old to Dream" is but one of six here, and none are maudlin in the least. The trite "Waltz You Saved for Me" and "Tennessee Waltz" are invested with a pure genius for toned down sentiment. Meade has a vocal on "Sunny Side of the Mountain."

F5.64   **J. E. Mainer's Mountaineers.** Arhoolie F 5002.

F5.65*   **J. E. Mainer's Mountaineers, v.1/2.** two discs. Old Timey X 106/7.
Mainer is important for two distinct reasons. First, he created and preserved some influential instrumentals and country fiddling. Second, his string band was a transitional group that linked Gid Tanner and the Carter Family with World War II bluegrass. Born in North Carolina in 1898, Mainer grew up in a textile mill

environment that shaped his urban outlook toward music. He was both a banjoist and a fiddler. From 1934-1939, along with Homer Sherill, Steve Ledford, and two of the Morris Brothers, he recorded for Victor, and the better tracks have been reissued on the Old Timey label. With such items as "Maple on the Hill," or Daddy John Love's "Broken Hearted Blues" and "Looking for a Pair of Blue Eyes," he strongly resisted change at the Grand Ole Opry. To him, "Maple on the Hill" was advanced enough. He pursued his career with traditional songs and fiddle break-downs—such as "Run Mountain" or the lovely instrumental "Country Blues"—and sacred tunes. Occasionally, he would project a preoccupation with rural attitudes towards lust, such as "Kiss Me Cindy," "Why Do You Bob Your Hair, Girls," and "What'll I Do with the Baby-O?" Good fun, though. In the late sixties, he embarked on a momentous recording career, producing over twenty albums for the Rural Rhythm label.

F5.66*   **New Lost City Ramblers, v.1-5.** five discs. Folkways 2395-2389.

F5.67*   **New Lost City Ramblers. Play Instrumentals.** Folkways 2492.

F5.68   **New Lost City Ramblers. Remembrance of Things to Come.** Folkways FTS 31035.
           The NLCR are a great introduction to the field of old time music, especially for those who cannot stand older scratchy records, poor reproduction, or the lo-fi of field recordings. They began as old time music *recreators* in 1958 and were primarily responsible for the subsequent inclusion of this music in the folk music revival. They appeared at many folk festivals (including Newport). Their technique was simple: They would recreate 78 rpms and Library of Congress field recordings from the 1925-1935 period, giving due acknowledgment and copious notes for the record jackets. As such, then, they were not original and were heavily criticized for being completely derivative. Yet, if they did not exist, then few would have been exposed to old time music, and certainly there would be no interest in reissuing the originals.
           Their artful recreations, in good sound, have been somewhat superseded by the present availability of the (clean-sounding) originals on labels such as County, Voyageur, Rounder, Old Timey, etc. But they uphold the key folk tradition of *transmission*, the means for others to learn from (and after all, that's what the "original" performers from the 1920s did too). It was not long before other folk singers delved into the Library of Congress Archive of Folk Music and transmitted their own versions. The NLCR merely recreated; others, such as Joan Baez, resang tunes in their own styles and put them over on an unsuspecting audience. The NLCR were honest, for they credited their sources and surprised no one. Perhaps this is why they are still performing today, while the "folksingers" have since had their audiences turn their backs on them. Having performed for almost twenty years in various vocal-instrumental combinations (but usually always as a trio), the NLCR multi-instrumentalists bring a feeling of reverence to the earlier commercial or post-Appalachian ballads. Certainly they could have been making more money doing something else.
           For the first four volumes of the Folkways set, Tom Paley was with the group. He could not tour; consequently, he was replaced by Tracy Schwartz.

John Cohen and Mike Seeger are the other two members (Seeger has also pursued a successful solo career). Born into a Washington, D.C., musicologist family (father Charles, sister Peggy, half-brother Pete), Mike had continual access to the LC field recordings. He was on the board of directors at Newport, and he had Pete's influences. He produced field recordings for Folkways, as well as diverse notes. Thus, it was relatively easy to put forth the NLCR as a group, for they had the inside track.

Their most wide-ranging album is *Remembrance*. This full set of eighteen tracks includes multi-stylings, from such British traditional material as "Lord Bateman" through "Little Ball of Yarn," a Cajun "Parlez-Vous a Boire," an old riverboat song "Rock about My Saro Jane," some early bluegrass ("I'm Lonesome"), a few Carter Family epics like "The Titanic" and "Dark and Stormy Weather," and several fiddle tunes such as "Give the Fiddler a Dram." Instrumentation is diverse, with all three playing, at one time or another, fiddles, harmonicas, guitars, banjos, autoharps, mandolins, spoons, and even a triangle. This disc diversity shows the incredible range of white "folk" and old time music in America today. Not only are sources and texts quoted, but other recorded variations are noted as well. The five-volume Folkways set, being their first recorded efforts, is a little more restrictive in the scope of its material: "Old Joe Clark," "Nick Nack Song," "Forked Deer," "Dallas Rag," "Colored Aristocracy," "Whoop 'Em up Cindy," "Louisville Burglar," "Texas Rangers," "Coo Coo Bird," "Dollar's All I Crave," "Raging Sea," and "Talking Hard Luck." The *Instrumental* set is just that, collating some fine, proficient styles of playing through "Saddle up the Grey," "Victory Rag," "Black Eyed Susie," and "John Brown's Dream," among others.

F5.69*   **Charlie Poole and the North Carolina Ramblers, v.1-4.** four discs. County 505, 509, 516, 540.

F5.70   **Charlie Poole and the Highlanders.** Puritan 3002.

F5.71   **North Carolina Ramblers. 1928-1930.** Biograph RC 6005.
    The North Carolina Ramblers were authentically rural sounding in the string band tradition of North Carolina. Poole made 110 sides with the NCR (who recorded over 200 in all). After recording for Columbia in 1925 and striking gold with their most favorite and oft-requested song—"Don't Let Your Deal Go Down Blues" (on County 505), based on gambling traditions—they struck out for music *full time*, and became the first old time performers to quit their farms or laboring jobs for solely performing as "professional musicians." The group had Posey Rorer or Lonnie Austin on violin, Roy Hurley (who stayed the longest) or Norman Woodlieff on guitars, and Poole on banjo. Poole's three-finger style was the result of a serious hand injury, and his method of playing deeply influenced Snuffy Jenkins and Earl Scruggs, transforming itself into the modern "Scruggs style banjo." His widely imitated nasal twang, though, can grate even at the best of times.
    But this is early bluegrass picking at its best, in a wide variety of British ballads and songs, dance tunes, blues, Tin Pan Alley songs of the early 1900s, topical pieces, nineteenth century sentimental songs, and minstrel/medicine show pieces. Much emphasis was on "hard times for pore whites." This, the most disciplined string band performing, was highly organized and members knew what they were

going to do before entering the studio. They had to, for they were performing all the time. This "arranged" music meant that the listeners could hear all the instruments separately as soloists. There were no "egotists" that dominated the group; equal stress and prominence were given to the fiddle, banjo, and guitar. The traditional fiddling of Posey Rorer (repetitive patterns of long and short bow strokes), with old time cadences and inflections, soon developed into more polished urban sounds as the group traveled. Poole's picking style precluded strumming or brushing but introduced quick, brisk tempos. The vocals from guitarist Roy Harvey derived from pop and vaudeville. With his long bass runs close to the melody (like Riley Puckett, Maybelle Carter, Lester Flatt), Harvey's rolling guitar, in conjunction with the fiddle and banjo, soon produced what was then called slick "uptown music." The NCR performed *no* religious music (it didn't sell well).

County 505 has twelve tracks of fiddle tunes ("Mountain Red," "Shootin' Creek"), dance tunes, plus sad or happy vocals. Of note is the famous recreation of the earlier "White House Blues." County 509 has the dances "Ragtime Annie" and "Wild Horse," the story songs of "Baltimore Fire" and "Bill Mason," the humor of "My Gypsy Girl" and "If I Lose, Let Me Lose," and the seriousness of "One Moonlight Night" and "Can I Sleep in Your Barn Tonight?" (also a hit from their very first recording session). County 516 continues with "Goodbye Booze," "Look before You Leap," and "The Highwayman."

Poole died suddenly in 1931 at the age of 39 (he had pushed himself too hard), and soon afterwards the group disbanded. The Biograph reissue of fifteen tracks ("Flop Eared Mule," "Kitty Blye" and "Old Clay Pipe") features Poole's banjo on only six cuts, with vocals on two. The County reissues are Columbia products; Biograph draws from Paramount, Edison, Gennett, Champ, etc., emphasizing the varying collective personnel that had at one time or another played in the NCR. If anyone is featured on Biograph, it is Roy Harvey. The Puritan issue concentrates on Paramount recordings by a larger group (quintet). Poole had always wanted to create a more commercial sound by adding a piano and another fiddle. Columbia, in its wisdom, never allowed this, even though Poole's live performances had five or more instruments. This is an excellent opportunity to hear a transitional document leading to modern country music (especially with the piano). Included is a four-part skit, *A Trip to New York*.

F5.72*   **Stoneman Family. 1926-1928.** Rounder 1008.

F5.73*   **Stoneman Family. 1927-1928.** Historical HLP 8004.

F5.74*   **Stoneman Family. Banjo Tunes and Songs.** Folkways FA2315.

F5.75   **Stoneman Family. Memorial Album.** MGM 4588.

The Stoneman Family has been singing since the turn of the century, and in doing so, they have preserved old time music far beyond World War I. Their first American ancestor could be traced to a cabin boy, and strong familial ties led to a preservation of their heritage. Ernest V. Stoneman was called "Pop," and during 1924-1929, for a variety of companies, he and his groups recorded over 125 individual titles, such as "Little Old Log Cabin in the Lane," "The Raging Sea How It Roars," "Sweeping through the Gates," "Sourwood Mountain," "Me and

My Wife," and so forth (ultimately 200 songs, counting the inevitable duplications), with such names as the Dixie Mountaineers or the Blue Ridge Corn Shuckers. (The latter group is heard on Rounder 1008, in a program of sixteen tracks from 1926-1928.) The different materials here embrace ballads, instrumental dance tunes, sacred songs, and novelties. The record has an accompanying 12-page booklet of pictures, discographic information, and lyrics to all the songs.

The former group (Dixie Mountaineers) is on Historical HLP 8004 and comes from 1927-1928 for Edison records. These are ten long tracks, and include "Once I Had a Future," "Hop Light Ladies," "East Bound Train," "The Old Maid and the Burglar," all with Kahle Brewer's fiddle and George Stoneman's banjo. "Pops" Stoneman was ambitious. By 1924, he thought he could record better than any other such artists around, so he tried out his autoharp (he was the first to record with this instrument) with various companies, but he strummed only the basic chords. He sang in a plain, under-rated style, and he showed little influence from either the blues or other black music. He was a pure singer in the old time tradition, being a transmitter of folk materials as noted above, but specializing in British ballads, the sentimental ballads, and story songs.

When the Depression came, he went into semi-retirement and raised thirteen children. After World War II, he toured with any five or six of them, performing on radio and television. The MGM disc offers their more commercial records, with excellent fiddle bowing by son Scotty. The 1957 Folkways collection includes them performing "Say Darling, Say," "When the Springtime Comes Again," and "New River Train." Stoneman's contribution was mainly preservation of the story songs, and later in life, a highly entertaining family.

F5.76*   **Gid Tanner and His Skillet Lickers, v.1/2.** two discs. County 506, 526.

F5.77*   **Gid Tanner and His Skillet Lickers. A Corn Licker Still in Georgia.** Voyager VRLP 303.

F5.78*   **Gid Tanner and His Skillet Lickers. "Hear These New Southern Fiddle and Guitar Music."** Rounder 1005.

The Skillet Lickers were one of the most prolific string bands recording. Between 1926 and 1931, they recorded 88 tunes as a group. The key personnel (Tanner, McMichen, and Puckett) were involved in no less than 700 recordings during their long career (McMichen took his fiddle into Dixieland jazz during the 1940s), and the Skillet Licker appellative was used on 565 selections! Changing personnel meant that the productions were variable, but consistency can be found when at least two of the three key personnel played together. Fiddler Tanner was forty years old when first recorded; he made music for the fun of it, and he performed a wide variety of traditional items such as Bristol ballads, minstrel songs, fiddle tunes of the nineteenth century, and simple American folk songs. His was an old style that was already disappearing at that time. Clayton "Pappy" McMichen was a much younger fiddler who had already been influenced by jazz, and he was constantly at odds with the older Tanner as to how pieces were to be performed. This tension, plus the device of the twin fiddles (one "oldfashioned," and the other "modern jazz") made for some fine and responsive music.

The fifteen years' age difference was a lot greater than just in physical appearance. McMichen's fiddle produced definitive versions of "Wreck of the Old 97," "Down Yonder," and "Sally Goodwin." Along the way, he won many national fiddling contests. Riley Puckett was a true minstrel, being a blind guitarist who would play for his supper. He sang lead for the Skillet Lickers, and brought to the group a varied repertoire of tunes plus some very important single note bass runs that later influenced Lester Flatt. The group was basically a trio or a quartet (or more), and others who played with them included Arthur Tanner and Jimmy Tarleton. Thus, the instrumentation was two fiddles (doubling each other for the lead), a back-up guitar with bass runs, and a drone banjo at times. All three sang, but Puckett usually took the lead.

Some of the best and most influential string bands (such as Tanner's) came from Georgia where the tradition was largely one of minstrel or medicine show pieces. Often, their most enjoyable efforts from minstrels were the comedy sketches, and these proved to be best sellers. Between 1926 and 1931, Columbia released eighteen two-part skits. Of these, seven were entitled *A Corn Licker Still in Georgia.* This was about moonshining during the Prohibition, and was interspersed with forty short old time fiddling tunes and songs. This particular set sold well into the hundreds of thousands. Some good and little known tunes are marvelously handled by fiddlers Lowe Stokes and McMichen. The "show" concentrates on the varying fortunes of a band of mountaineers who try to make their living at both music and moonshining. As such, it is a revealing social document, providing some interesting commentary both on the futility of the federal government's efforts at prevention and on the complicity of the authorities, who themselves were not above sampling the brew. The excellent notes include a glossary to make listening easier for a modern audience. The loose-knit nature of the group allowed for some slight improvisation, and this led to conflict between the two fiddlers themselves, and the fiddles against the guitar. McMichen played lead while Tanner doubled in high harmony; with singing, Puckett's lead was harmonized by McMichen, and a falsetto was occasionally added by Tanner.

The Skillet Lickers were very well handled by Columbia records. The electrical recording process had just arrived, and *all* members of the band could be heard. Faithful sound reproduction also meant that more string bands could be recorded. Good promotion and marketing followed, and their name was easily established by their being one of the first groups to play on the radio and to tour widely. This group was the first old time talent to have recorded for Columbia. Besides the material Tanner brought with him, they dealt with dance songs and novelties, plus some pop. Many items were derived from the British tradition of nursery songs and reels (made into square dance calls). In live performance, though, they stressed much popular material. Tanner was the clown, and Puckett (with two leads—vocal and instrumental) was the virtuoso who actually found more success as a soloist (see his annotation). McMichen drove them into a more commercial jazz sound, with the result that Tanner left and split from the group in 1931.

The Skillet Lickers recorded each time Columbia made a semi-annual visit to Atlanta. From 1927, an obvious standout is "Big Ball in Town," a jazz type item emphasizing Puckett's voice. From 1928, there is "Cotton-Eyed Joe," and 1929 found "Rock That Cradle Lucy." This period concentrated on fiddle tunes. "Four Cent Cotton" and "Molly Put the Kettle On" (both 1931) showed the consistency of their earlier styles. Richard Nevins contributes strong liner notes to County 526, including an interview with Skillet Licker fiddler Lowe Stokes. This reissue contains "Rocky Pallet," "Watermelon on the Vine," and "Hell Broke Loose in Georgia." The Rounder reissue includes three 1934 tracks recorded for Bluebird (RCA has had the Lickers' 1934 records in the catalog in some form continuously for over forty years). "Keep Your Gal at Home" is one of their rare blues items. "Tanner's Boarding House" is a good story (as a skit), while "I'm Satisfied" relates to contentment of life. Enclosed are notes, photographs, lyrics and a discography. Although the Skillet Lickers' impact was phenomenal, it was very difficult to imitate this group because of their conflicts of style. Thus, there were few, if any, direct steals from the Tanner group, although many of their successes were re-recorded by others.

F5.79*   **Dock Walsh. Carolina Tar Heels.** Bear Family 15.507 (West German issue).

F5.80   **Dock Walsh. Carolina Tar Heels.** Folk Legacy FSA 24.

F5.81*   **Dock Walsh. Carolina Tar Heels.** GHP LP 1001 (West German issue).
      Walsh, a North Carolina banjo player, was a key performer with the Carolina Tar Heels. This group was a great dance combo in the string band tradition, although they never used a fiddle. The instrumentation was usually harmonica, guitar, and banjo. The first recordings from 1927 (Victor, on the GHP) were just a duo with Gwen Foster on both harmonica and guitar: "The Bulldog Down in Sunny Tennessee" and "I Love My Mountain Home." In late 1928, Garley Foster (no relation) and Clarence "Tom" Ashley were added for "There's A Man Going 'Round Taking Names" (a black song), "I Don't Like the Blues No How," and "Roll on Blues" (with good vocal by Ashley).
      The Tar Heels were very eclectic, with material such as ballads, novelties, blues, dance numbers, and sentimental tunes. Their instrumental skill led to much expression in the interplay amongst themselves. Ashley and Walsh split the vocals, and both had authoritative voices. Seven of the GHP tunes are from 1929, and they include the twitter of birds on "My Home's across the Blue Ridge Mountains." The Bear Family reissue augments other scattered reissues on anthologies, and its sixteen tracks include the memorable "Peg and Awl" work song, the novelty "Her Name Was Hula Lou," "My Mama Scolds Me for Flirting," and "Got the Farmland Blues." The Folk Legacy disc is a recent recording (1960s), with Dock, Drake Walsh (his son), and Garley Foster in a reunion. Archie Green did the recording, notes, and discography (along with Eugene Earle). These are all recreations, except for the inclusion of Drake's fiddle. Excellent notes accompany the Bear Family and GHP reissues.

Standards

F5.82   **The Blue Ridge Highballers.** County 407.
      Originally recorded in 1926 for Columbia, these twelve selections reflect

the popularity of the old time stringband dance music (they also recorded again in 1927 for Paramount). Charley LaPrade organized this Virginia group, and here, his fiddle is accompanied by guitarist Lonnie Griffith and banjoist Arthur Wells. LaPrade had some formal violin instruction, and he is obviously the leader in these sprightly selections, for the others provide only rhythm. Several familiar tunes are here, based on traditional songs (e.g., "Darneo" comes from "Sail Away Ladies"; "Green Mountain Polka" is derived from "Richmond Cotillion"). There are three vocals, capably handled by Luther Clarke, including "Wish to the Lord I Had Never Been Born." Good biographical liner notes are by C. Kinney Rorrer.

F5.83   The Bogtrotters. 1937-1942. Biograph RC 6003.
    This fine and historically interesting recording comes from the Lomax collection in the Library of Congress' Archive of American Folk Song. This old time band played locally in the Carolinas at dances for many years, and over this period made about 200 recordings for LC. Included here are "Jesse James" (learned first-hand from a relative of James), "John Henry" (learned first hand from the West Virginia mines), "Make Me a Pallet on the Floor," "Shoo Fly," and "Who Broke the Lock?" The twin fiddles of Crockett Wade and Uncle Eck Dunford highlight the craftsmanship of the superb musicians. Fields Ward, a guitarist of note, handles most of the vocals. Sound quality is only fair, as the original recording was done on wire recorders.

F5.84   Camp Creek Boys. County 709.
    This traditional string band of fiddles, banjo, guitars, and mandolin was one of the few to be of such a large size. The six performers included Kyle Creed, Ronald Collins, Ernest East, Verlin Clifton, Paul Sutphin and Fred Cockerham. Typical traditional items included "Fire on the Mountain," "Soldier's Joy," and "Cotton Eyed Joe" from among the twelve titles here.

F5.85   The Hill Billies. County 405.
    The importance of the Hill Billies is varied: they were one of the first string bands to make themselves known extensively in the Southeast; they drew their members from diverse regions (North Carolina, Tennessee, Virginia, West Virginia, etc.), thereby reducing variations; and they supposedly created the term "hillbilly" when Al Hopkins, leader, said to Peer at Okeh records: "we're nothing but a bunch of hill billies." In addition, they were one of the first entertaining showband organizations, with regular features and comedy routines that appeared in vaudeville houses and on radio shows. Their music was polished and sophisticated, and the vocals were highly arranged. This album concentrates on their dance tunes and emphasizes the twin fiddling of Elvis Alderman and Charlie Bowman. Hopkins played piano in a bouncy rhythmic style, particularly suitable for dancing.
All styles were apparently covered: there is quartet singing in harmony on "C. C. & O. 558" and "Silly Bill"; swing music of a sort on "Texas Gals" and the "Soldier's Joy Medley." These men were an extremely efficient organization that furthered the concept of popular country music. Joe Wilson wrote the included booklet, which is well-illustrated.

F5.86   Tommy Jarrell, Fred Cockerham, and Oscar Jenkins. Back Home in the Blue Ridge. County 723.

F5.87*   Tommy Jarrell, Fred Cockerham, and Oscar Jenkins. Down to the Cider Mill. County 713.

F5.88   Tommy Jarrell, Fred Cockerham, and Oscar Jenkins. Stay All Night. County 741.

Old time music continued through the 1970s, when records such as the above three are still being recorded. Two of the three performers are descendents of performers in the influential Da Costa Woltz's Southern Broadcasters group: Oscar Jenkins's father, Frank, and Tommy Jarrell's father, Ben. The twin fiddles of Jarrell and Jenkins predominate, with the former taking the lead. The unaccompanied "When Sorrow Encompass Me 'Round" shows Jarrell's great depth and sensitivity; Jenkins is good on the dance tunes such as "Dan Carter Waltz" and "Rustic Dance." Cockerham plays fiddle as well on some of the more traditional songs such as "Arkansas Traveler" and "Bile 'Em Cabbage Down." Jenkins and Cockerham also play clawhammer banjo, and Jarrell contributes some fine vocals. Some of the tracks scattered on these three fine discs harken back to the original Da Costa Woltz group. Other selections from among the 36 include "Boll Weevil," "Polly Put the Kettle On," "Ground Hog," "Fall on My Knees," and "John Brown's Dream." Along with notes and information by Richard Nevins and Ray Alden, these are first rate discs in the old time tradition.

F5.89   **Leake County Revelers. Saturday Night Breakdown.** County 532.

This quartet (guitar, mandolin, banjo and fiddle) recorded stringband music during the 1927-1930 period. Twelve tracks here include some interesting pre-bluegrass renditions of "Dry Town Blues," "Good Fellow," "The Sweet Rose of Heaven," and dance tunes "Wednesday Night Waltz" and "The Old Hat."

F5.90*   **Wade Mainer.** County 404.

Mainer is better known for his work as a "sacred" artist, and as a member of brother J. E.'s Crazy Mountaineers. Yet he did produce some of the most emotional and sentimental music of the 1930s—despite his gentle style. His repertoire included the usual mountain ballads, blues ballads, sacred items, and sentimental love songs. County has collated twelve choice items from the 1937 to 1941 span, when Mainer was leading the Sons of the Mountaineers group. Steve Ledford contributes strong violin, Clyde Moody single strings his blues guitar (and adds early pre-bluegrass harmony), and there are also assorted miscellaneous instruments ahead of their time for this kind of music—a harmonica on "Ramshackle Shack," a steel guitar on "Memory Lane." Ledford's fiddle has a pronounced blues swing on "I Won't Be Worried." In summary, the diversification of the material, the changing of the instrumentation from track to track, the pronounced blues feel—all of these show why Mainer was an early developer of the pre-bluegrass transitional period.

F5.91   **Mountain Ramblers. Mountain Dance Music from the Blue Ridge.** County 720.

F5.92   **Mountain Ramblers. Virginia Breakdown.** County 705.
Otis Burris (on fiddle), Sonny Miller, and Buddy Pendleton are part of the Concord, North Carolina-based, Mountain Ramblers. The first disc here is largely instrumental breakdowns for dancing, with Joe Drye on fiddle ("Sugar in the Ground"). The second album features more diversified material, such as Pendleton's "Florida Blues," or the titles "Fortune," "Whistlin' Rufus," and "Blackberry Blossom."

F5.93   **New Lost City Ramblers. American Moonshine and Prohibition.** Folkways 5263.

F5.94   **New Lost City Ramblers. Modern Times.** Folkways FTS 31027.

F5.95*   **New Lost City Ramblers. Songs of the Depression.** Folkways 5264.
In addition to their pioneering efforts at recreating old time music, the NLCR have also shown that not all was fun and dance or sentimental parlor songs. These three discs aurally illustrate the concerns of southern rural people. Perhaps a fourth one could have been produced, dealing with government legislation and/or taxes (although these topics come up in the *Depression* album). The most significant one is *Modern Times*, subtitled "rural songs from an industrial society," which documents (through songs) the movement of southern mountaineers and farmers during the first half of this century into the cities, coal mines, and textile mills. The songs concern themselves with changing environments and urbanization. Needless to say, this disc shows that musical styles changed with the impact of the Depression, resulting in topicality and immediacy. These are *event* songs, such as "Shut up in the Mines of Coal Creek," "That Little Lump of Coal" (a union song), "Got the Farm Land Blues," "Time Table Blues," "Dollar Down and a Dollar a Week," etc. All of the songs, recorded 1920s through 1965, are derived from commercial recordings, suitably traced for sources. The NLCR recorded these eighteen tracks in 1967/68. Sourcing occurs in the other two discs as well.
Moonshine is more lighthearted, with "The Old Home Brew," "The Teetotals," "Kentucky Bootlegger," "Goodbye Old Booze," and "Intoxicated Rat," although there is a certain amount of bitterness here because of government legislation and the "revenoors." *Depression* is a superb album of sad songs that often harken back to the reassuring past. Several are religious in scope, such as the Carter Family's "No Depression in Heaven." Others: "Breadline Blues," "NRA Blues," "Franklin D. Roosevelt's Back Again" (a song of hope), "Keep Moving," and "Sales Tax on the Women."

F5.96*   **George Pegram.** Rounder 0001.
From the opening bars, Pegram, banjoist (from Union Grove, North Carolina, but later a resident of Galax, Virginia), and Fred Cockerham, fiddler (from Bow Gap, North Carolina), tear into some of the most familiar of old time music. There are fourteen tracks of well-known tunes—"John Henry," "Little Old Cabin in the Lane," "Wildwood Flower," "In the Sweet Bye and Bye," the German polka "Just Because," and "Reuben." In their 60s, Cockerham and Pegram represent southern mountain music rather well. Pegram's vocals are augmented by his

two-finger style. Other accompaniment is given by Jack Bryant (guitar) and Clyde Isaacs (mandolin) to perfect a pre-bluegrass transitional style.

F5.97   **Red Fox Chasers.** County 510.
        This trio from North Carolina recorded in 1928-1930. The twelve tracks here by Cranford, Miles, and Thompson are reflective of the string band tradition. Typical dance tunes include "Pretty Polly," "Stolen Love," "The Blind Man and His Child," and "Goodbye Little Bonnie."

F5.98   **Roane County Ramblers.** County 403.
        This is another typical old time music string band. The twelve selections here—"Green River March," "Callaghan Rag," "High Step Waltz" and "Free a Little Bird" among them—are their complete recordings from 1928-1929. Dance instrumentals predominate.

F5.99*   **Fiddling Doc Roberts. Classic Fiddle Tunes Recorded during the Golden Age.** Davis Unlimited DU 33015.
        Phil Roberts was a bluesy fiddler from Kentucky who recorded prolifically for about ten years. The fourteen titles here are derived from 1927-1933, and were made for the Starr Reno Company and ARC. Doc's fiddle is accompanied by either Asa Martin's guitar or James Roberts's guitar. "Cumberland Blues" is the definitive selection here and shows off Doc's unique violin style. Roberts served as accompanist to many vocalists; however, all the tunes here are dance instrumentals. While some are rare ("New Money"), others are surprisingly unusual variations on classic folk themes ("Cripple Creek," "Sally Ann"). Good liner notes are by Ivan M. Tribe.

F5.100   **Tenneva Ramblers.** Puritan 3001.
        This quartet of guitar, banjo, mandolin and violin was the backup group for Jimmie Rodgers, but they broke up just before his audition with Peer. Perhaps if they had been along, Peer might have thought of the group as just another string band (and expensive at that, because of the number of personnel). The music here comes from 1927-1928 and was very commercial sounding: "Seven Long Years in Prison," "Sweet Heaven When I Die," "Tell It to Me," "The Lonely Grave," and "When a Man is Married"—all a pleasant mixture of the sentimental ballad and event song.

F5.101*   **Fields Ward. Buck Mountain Band.** Historical HLP 8001.

F5.102   **Fields Ward. Bury Me Not on the Prairie.** Rounder 0036.

F5.103   **Fields and Wade Ward. Country Music.** Biograph RC6002.

F5.104   **Wade Ward. Uncle Wade; A Memorial to Wade Ward, Old Time Virginia Banjo Picker, 1892-1971.** Folkway, FA 2380.
        The Ward Family were extremely valuable transmitters of the oral tradition of southeast Virginia. The Historical album collates sixteen items from March 12, 1929—Gennett sessions that featured Ernest Stoneman on a wide variety of

instruments (banjo, guitar, harmonica, fiddle). Titles included "I Got a Bulldog," "The New River Train," "John Hardy," "The Birds Are Returning," "The Sweetest Way Home." The Folkways tribute was recorded 1958-1964 by Eric Davidson. Its 22 tracks, including narratives by Granny Porter, Wade Ward, and Katy Hill, constitute an exemplary documentary of the pieces that Wade liked to play best. For contrast there is "Cluck Old Hen" from 1937, added here to emphasize his intricate banjo runs. Fiddle tunes that he played included "Billy in the Low Ground," "Sourwood Mountain," and "Chicken Reel." There are excellent liner notes here.

Both Fields and Wade got together in the late 1960s for Biograph. While nephew Fields worked on the banjo for the Buck Mountain Band, here he plays a guitar that is startlingly reminiscent of Riley Puckett's. Fields's voice is not as rich here as it had been, nor Wade's clawhammer as driving as in the past. But these tracks are played in a style identical to that of forty years earlier. This is living mountain music, ranging from "Winking Eye," "Riley and Spence," "Little Birdie," and "Sweet William" through "Cold Icy Floor," and the showpiece "Wade's Fox Chase" to the more modern (in terms of the music) "Don't Let Your Deal Go Down." The Rounder disc, recorded after Wade died, features Fields with a number of traditional items in the banjo-guitar instrumentation of string bands. Nancy Ward provides the vocals. Selections include: "Leaving Dear Old Ireland," "Sweet Bird," "Cotton Blossom," "Country Road Gang," and "Peekaboo Waltz."

DUOS AND GROUPS

Innovators

F5.105*   **Blue Sky Boys.** two discs. RCA Bluebird AXM 2-5525.

F5.106*   **Blue Sky Boys. The Sunny Side of Life.** Rounder Records 1006.
Bill and Earl Bolick began recording harmonic duets at an early age (fifteen and seventeen, respectively). They were largely responsible for and influential on the close harmony groups of brothers in the country field (e.g., Everly Brothers, Delmore Brothers, Louvin Brothers, Monroe Brothers, et al.). They were one of the few creators in this musical field to have heard virtually all the old time music records of the 1920s, for they were also collectors—in much the same way as the New Lost City Ramblers were to be twenty years later. But they did not recreate; rather, they assimilated and distilled. Their guitar and mandolin accompaniment neatly characterized their music as "folk" on their own terms (they retired in 1951 rather than switch styles). Occasionally a fiddle would join them, as on "Dust on the Bible," "Alabama," or "Kentucky" (Curly Parker).
Earl played bass runs and chords on guitar; Bill picked the melody. Their singing was carefully structured, with Earl on lead and Bill doing tenor, mostly derived from shape note sacred music. In fact, most of their work is such material (e.g., "S-A-V-E-D," the marvelous "Turn Your Radio On," "Take up Thy Cross," "Hymns My Mother Sang," etc.). Sweet and smooth harmonizing were developed for their popular songs ("Are You from Dixie?"), sentimental ballads, Child ballads ("Katie Dear"), American folk ("Down on the Banks of the Ohio"), etc. Overall,

with their overly sweet singing and their sad songs, plus their popularity and influence on others, they made a tremendous impact on the shape of country music in the 1940s—towards blander, "hurtin' " music. The 48 items here (with some slight duplications) were recorded 1936-1941.

F5.107   **Carter Family, v.1 and 3.** two discs. Country Music History CMH 112 and 116 (West German issue).

F5.108*   **Carter Family. A Collection of Favourites.** Ace of Hearts AH58 (British issue).

F5.109*   **Carter Family. The Legendary Collection, 1927-1934, 1941.** ten discs. RCA RA 5641-5650 (Japanese issue).

F5.110*   **Carter Family. 'Mid the Green Fields.** RCA ANL1-1071.

F5.111*   **Carter Family. More Favourites.** Ace of Hearts. AH 112 (British issue).
       The Carter Family exemplifies the transition of traditional music into commercial (but not modern) country music. Their total repertoire of some 275 plus songs is the greatest collection of all the ballads and lyric folk songs that were considered the roots in the rural areas of southeast America. Modern country music stems directly from Jimmie Rodgers, while traditional country and bluegrass have material provided by the Carters. *Everyone* in country music has at least one Carter song in his/her repertoire, and indeed, bluegrass groups have several. A major development in the history of country music, they influenced bluegrass music through the Louvin Brothers, Flatt and Scruggs, Bill Monroe, Bill Clifton, Doc Watson etc. They had a tremendous impact on folk music and the folk revival through Woody Guthrie, Pete Seeger, Bob Dylan, and Joan Baez. Their attempts at preservation (not entirely altruistic) deserve the heartfelt thanks of the entire American nation.
       There were three members of the Carters. Sara played banjo, second guitar, and autoharp. She sang lead—a great soloist who conveyed a sense of urgency tempe by a natural feel for the lyrics. Maybelle played lead guitar, banjo, and autoharp. She played the guitar in the "folk" style of slides and punctuated melody, which was quite advanced for the day (as was the style of Jimmie Rodgers). Her alto harmony in duets with Sara was important for both the blend and for the alternatin lines as in "Hello Stranger." Alonso Pleasant (A. P.) Carter sang bass in a tremulous style that resulted from his palsy. He was an excellent arranger and recomposer, and he imposed a stern discipline on the group. They rehearsed extensively for each recording session, and they were the first country group to do so. (Poole's North Carolina Ramblers were also disciplined, but they did not need to rehearse, as they were "professional" musicians performing all the time.) The Carters never performed much; they only recorded in isolation (indeed, despite Sara's divorce from A. P., they still united from time to time for recordings, and she had even remarried in California while the others stayed in the East). At the same time, they had *no* outside influences. They *never* went to the Grand Ole Opry, nor did they listen to the radio. They never experimented; they just improved in their

style that began in 1927. In other words, their 1941 recordings for Victor were the same as their 1927 first efforts, only better (and of course with different songs).

Because their style improved from one session to the next, their *best overall* recordings were in 1936-1938 for Decca (24 tracks are reissued on the two Ace of Hearts discs). By this time—a decade after beginning recording—their duets were perfect and the guitar stylings mastered. Changing record companies also gave them a chance to re-record their biggest hits. Here, then, are definitive polished versions of "Hello Stranger," "My Dixie Darling," "No Depression in Heaven," "My Home's across the Blue Ridge Mountains," and "Walking in the King's Highway." RCA ANL 1-1071 is a sort of "best hits" from their Victor recordings of *originals*, with their theme "Keep on the Sunny Side," "My Clinch Mountain Home," "Worried Man Blues," "Motherless Children," "Foggy Mountain Top," and "Wildwood Flowers." As mentioned above, the repertoire of the Carters was from the traditional area, as A. P. collated songs to provide sources for discs. A breakdown of their tunes shows great concern for the past, as in the hymns "Lonesome Valley" and "Little Moses" (see the Carters's annotation in the **Sacred** section); the songs of mother, death, home, lamented love; folk songs such as "John Hardy" or "Worried Man Blues"; and some Tin Pan Alley novelties, such as "Are You Lonesome Tonight?"

There was only one real influence on the Carters—Leslie Riddles, a black guitarist in Tennessee. The Carters recorded many of his tunes (with new words), and he had a profound influence on Maybelle's style. Her black-influenced guitar played the melody on the bass strings, while the rhythm was put out with chords on the treble strings. This reversal of the usual manner of guitar playing in the 1920s brought a *new* rhythmic beat to country music. Singers had previously made their instruments fit their voices and used open-tunings, which made the guitar a lot simpler to play in an accompanying role. A. P. adapted his songs, though, to Maybelle's guitar (again a reversal, aided by Maybelle's alto singing). Thus, many titles were reduced to a basic three chords (tonic, dominant, and subdominant) and were performed in a constant 4/4 time. The fragmented vocal-instrumental-vocal pattern of the then-current string bands, when coupled with a different tempo and rhythmic beat on the guitar, plus the low singing of Maybelle and the urgency of Sara, created a distinct sound that was immediately powerful and popular.

So popular were they, in fact, that the Carters were one of the few *groups* to record throughout the Depression (three people had to be paid, thus tripling recording costs over those for a soloist). Unfortunately, during this time, they were rushed into the ARC studios largely unprepared; and with poor sound, the resulting titles are among the lesser of their works. Yet they are still head and shoulders above many other groups. Any one interested in acquiring most of these titles will find them on Harmony HL 7280, 7300, 7396, and 7422, and on part of CMH 116 (v.3, noted above). The popularity of the Carters continued with their XERA radio shows (performed in Texas, but broadcast at 500,000 watts from Mexico, thus blanketing all North America). The Japanese RCA set of ten discs contains 148 songs, one take of all their Victor material. It is especially recommended because its scope embraces their entire career. In addition, it contains the two skits performed with Jimmie Rodgers ("The Carter Family and Jimmie Rodgers in Texas" and "Jimmie Rodgers Visits the Carter Family").

It is remarkable that the two pioneers in shaping country music, Rodgers and the Carters, first recorded for Victor on August 1, 1927, in Bristol, Tennessee, both being produced by Ralph Peer. Victor, then, had an immediate armlock on the public for country music, and this has continued to the present day with the likes of the Delmore Brothers, Bill Boyd, Monroe Brothers, Blue Sky Boys, Chet Atkins, Hank Snow, Jim Reeves, Eddy Arnold, etc. To make this a complete Carter set, there are also included the two Sara Carter-Jimmie Rodgers duets. The ten discs are in chronological and recording order, with excellent remastering and pressing. The booklet of some forty pages contains a biography, notes on each song (along with complete texts as transcribed, not as published), a song title index, and many, many photographs.

American RCA, as with the Jimmie Rodgers material, has reissued only a handful of Carter items (some more are on anthologies), chiefly on their budget Camden line. These are all in phony stereo, usually nine-ten tracks in each album— no notes, but plenty of other errors. For those interested, the Camden serial numbers are 586, 2473, 2554, ACLI-9947, and ACL 1-0501. Particularly unusual is the first one (586), for it was issued in Canada in 1961, a full six months before the U.S. set, and it was really the first old time music reissue from a major company. The American release was predicated on its success in Canada, where the Carter Family was immensely popular.

The Country Music History series presents items new to microgroove. Volumes 1 and 3 cover the Decca material that is so great; the other two volumes (2 and 4) now duplicate the Japanese RCA reissues (but not the U.S. reissues, as of 1976). As with the latter set, CMH issues come with notes, discography, and a chronological ordering. The Carter Family, to reiterate, was the single most important group in early country music, being responsible for such standards as "Wabash Cannonball," "I'm Thinking Tonight of My Blue Eyes," and "Jimmy Brown the Newsboy."

F5.112   **Tom Darby and Jimmy Tarlton.** Bear Family 15-504 (West German issue).

F5.113*   **Tom Darby and Jimmy Tarlton.** Old Timey OT 112.

The team of Darby and Tarlton had equally strong roots in black blues and traditional folk music. Tarlton, from South Carolina, was the stronger of the two guitarists; he merged the bottle neck slide of blues with the Hawaiian style of slide (which had been popular since the turn of the century). Darby, from Georgia, joined him in 1926, and they recorded for Columbia in 1927. Their first song— "Birmingham Jail," penned by Tarlton while an occupant there—was an enormous success and soon became a country standard. Typical followups included "Birmingham Jail No. 2," "New Birmingham Jail," "Birmingham Rag"—all to be found on these two discs. They recorded 75 items for Columbia (1927-1930), Victor (1931), and ARC (1933), and all of them fall neatly into the two styles exemplified by the reissued albums. The Bear Family set is mainly old time music, popular sentimental ballads (e.g., "After the Ball," "By the Old Oaken Bucket," "Louise," "Irish Police," "After the Sinking of the Titanic"). This disc emphasizes their unique vocal setting.

Darby sang lead, and Tarlton used a half-yodel, half-arhoolie falsetto for the harmony line. This exciting approach was, of course, supplemented by the superb steel guitar of Tarlton and the light airy touch of Darby. The Old Timey set features more of these guitars, with "Mexican Rag," "Heavy Hearted Blues," "Lonesome Railroad," plus uptempo titles like "Dixie Mail" or "Down in Florida on a Hog." Excellent guitar interplay and melodramatic vocals are emphasized here, and this disc is more in the black tradition than in the white. Indeed, "Ooze up to Me," with its ribald lyrics, is very close to "It's Tight Like That." These thirty reissued tracks are exceptionally important in the transformation and preservation of blues and country music. Good notes are on the Old Timey, and a booklet comes with the Bear Family.

F5.114*   **Kessinger Brothers. 1928-1930. County 536.**

Clark Kessinger, playing since the turn of the century, could draw on a wide repertoire of fiddle tunes. He showed much classical music influence, and he employed such techniques in his timing and tone, preferring a clear, sweet line that revealed controlled power and thematic variations that were cleverly planned in advance. He was then, the most proficient of all old time music fiddlers and also became influential in the early development of commercial country music, as a precursor to modern stylings with sweet and slick accompaniment. These are his first recordings, along with his *nephew* Luches on guitar (not his brother, but material was more marketable in those days if it was thought to come from sibling groups). During this time, the Kessingers would make seventy recordings—twelve on here, played with much exuberance and entertainment. No waltzes were chosen for this reissue (yet Kessinger favored the waltz time); instead, there are interesting thematic versions of "Cripple Creek" (entitled "Going up Bushy Fork" on the original issue), "Kanawha Rag," and the equally rag effort "Rat Cheese under the Hill" (which supposedly precedes bluegrass music by incorporating the rag aspects of jazz), the original "Everybody to the Puncheon," and the trick bowing of "Garfield March."

F5.115*   **Monroe Brothers. Feast Here Tonight. two discs. RCA AXM2-5510.**

The Monroe Brothers recorded many records for RCA; 32 of their 1936-1938 titles are on this collection. Overall, they did not write their own material, but they borrowed from Jimmie Rodgers, the Carter Family, the Skillet Lickers, etc.—the innovators in their fields. The Monroe Brothers took the material and shaped it to their own style. Charlie played a blues style guitar, with a modified Carter run that foreshadowed Lester Flatt's bass runs. Bill's mandolin—later to be so prominent in bluegrass music—was really advanced for the day, and he was highly noted for his improvisational work (again, with some blues feel through the flatted notes). Together, they provided a direct rhythm and drive at breakneck speed (such as on "Georgia Mail"). This meant, of course, that they could not sing ballads all the time, but when they did—to simple accompaniment—their harmony was masterful, with high and low tenor, as on "Weeping Willow Tree," where they sing in flat emotionless tones, but with clear and smooth voices and perfect enunciation. Other tracks display equal virtuosity: the blues of "Rollin' On" from the Prairie Ramblers, the harmonies of "He Will Set Your Fields on Fire," the sadness of "Goodbye Maggie," and so forth. In a word, their style was intense.

In 1938, the brothers broke up, Bill going into bluegrass style while Charlie continued with bluesy old music.

Standards

F5.116   **Allen Brothers**. Bear Family FV 15.501 (West German issue).

F5.117*   **Allen Brothers. The Chattanooga Boys**. Old Timey OT 115.
The Allen Brothers were a solidly respectable, old time music brother duo, playing guitar, banjo and kazoo along with the appropriate solo and duet vocals. They recorded in the 1927-1934 period, and their largely blues-style plus banjo predated bluegrass music. For that, they are important, if not vital or influential. Both albums present a total of thirty tracks with (unfortunately) nine duplications. Bear Family has an interesting booklet and discography; Old Timey has marginally better sound and liner notes. Strong collections of old time music will need both albums, not only for the unduplicated tracks but for the comprehensive notes, as little else has been written about the Allen Brothers. Overall, these records reflect their versatility, and themes include topical material ("Price of Cotton Blues," "Roll down the Line"), traditional ("Prisoner's Dream"), lowdown blues ("Rough Neck Blues" and "Chattanooga Mama"), plus some string band minstrelsy.

F5.118*   **Burnett and Rutherford. A Rambling Reckless Hobo**. Rounder 1004.
This popular duo performed old time fiddle and banjo music, mainly from southern Kentucky. They influenced many others through their archaic style, which preserved traditional tunes from the past. Dick Burnett was a blind banjoist who collected songs and did some compositions; his guitar style of playing the banjo predates 1900. Leonard Rutherford did the fiddling. The sixteen tracks are compiled from the 1926-1930 period, and feature such items as "Ladies on the Steamboat," "Cabin with the Roses on the Door," "Going around the World," "Two Faithful Lovers," and "Knoxville Rag." There is also a 12-page booklet with complete discographical information on their career, plus interviews, song texts, notes, and pictures.

F5.119   **The Callahan Brothers**. Old Homestead OHM 90031.
Homer and Walter Callahan came from the influential folk music state of North Carolina (after late 1941, they were also known as "Bill and Joe"; fourteen titles here, though, are derived from the 1934-1936 period, with one each from 1939 and 1941, before the name change). Singing was prevalent around their home, and they learned a vast number of folk songs, such as, "On the Banks of the Ohio." Their musical influences were Gid Tanner, Riley Puckett, Pop Stoneman, and, of course, Jimmie Rodgers. Walter played guitar exclusively, while Homer began on five string banjo, later moving to include mandolin, fiddle, ukelele, and guitar. They followed the route of other brother duos, performing on radio and making some 91 titles during 1934-1951; 150 titles were also created for radio transcriptions in the 1940s. Their style was characterized by fast uptempo selections that preceded bluegrass, with a heavy emphasis on both the blues and reinterpretations of songs from jazz and blues (such as "St. Louis Blues"). However, they added

diverse instrumentation during the war years, and by the end of their career, they sounded like a then-typical country band with steel guitar, rhythm guitars, pianos, fiddle, etc. The mixed titles here include "Gonna Quit My Rowdy Ways," "Corn Licker Rag," "Maple on the Hill," "The Dying Girl's Farewell," and "I Got Her Boozy."

F5.120   **Carter Family. 1936 Radio Transcriptions.** Old Homestead OH 90045.

F5.121*   **Carter Family. On Border Radio.** JEMF 101.
One of the questionable matters of compiling a recommended listing such as this one is the ever-present worry that "commercial" recordings might just not be representative of an artist's total capacity for creating music. Uncle Dave Macon never liked studio recordings and, consequently, rarely recorded his most favorite songs, preferring to perform them before a live audience. Charlie Poole was denied his preference for a quintet or larger group on Columbia records because the company liked the trio format (it sold well). During the Depression, companies could only afford to record soloists, and backing artists either worked for nothing or not at all. B. B. King and Muddy Waters had to forego their actual night club band and work with recording session men. Strikes by various musicians' and composers' unions shut down the industry at crucial times and *nobody* made any recordings.
The value of radio transcriptions, then, is immediate: they filled the gaps in repertoires, they were usually performed live, they were done in one take, and they usually had sympathetic musicians away from the whims of the producer. Nearly everyone in country music performed on the radio at some time or other, and it was a very influential medium—more so than the phonograph because it was cheaper, it played records anyway, and it brought live music plus news and weather to America's farms. The music's internal variations can also be noticed, as the programs went straight through for several selections without stopping. Before the long-playing record, listeners did not acquire the habit of listening to many records by just one group consecutively.
The Old Homestead issue allows us to listen to many songs that the Carter Family had not yet recorded, plus material associated with the Depression. The JEMF record is a scholarly presentation, as expected. At its founding, a decade ago, the Foundation expected to reissue early hillbilly material, since at that time, the field of folk, race, and old time music reissued material was barren. But since then, much has happened, and the JEMF was left behind to ponder the moral issues of reissued material. Here then is its first effort—taking into account "fair use" and "educational utility"—and it is a very important document.
XERA (Villa Acuna, Coahilla, Mexico), at 840 on the AM dial, started with 50,000 watts and had 500,000 watts (!) by 1935. It could be heard throughout the entire United States. It emphasized fraudulent advertising, old time and gospel music, fundamentalist religion, and politics. It started the chain of events that helped to break down regional barriers and let others hear southern and mountain music. The station produced 16-inch aluminum-based transcription discs as pre-packaged music; these were leased to stations and not available for sale to the public. (To ensure this, the casting cutting was lateral and the record played from inside

outwards to the rim.) The 23 selections on this disc were recorded 1938-1942. The importance of these transcriptions is vast.

Here is Carter Family material *not* found on commercial releases, such as "Old Ladies' Home." Three instrumentals were never recorded—Maybelle solos on "Honey Babe," Maybelle and Sara on guitars on "Del Rio," and a great "Chinese Breakdown" featuring Maybelle's flat-picking and Sara's autoharp. Some of the Carter children are heard here on solos and trios. There are also some *very* interesting A. P. Carter solos (he rarely recorded solos) that show his fondness for nineteenth century parlor songs. And, of course, there is some talking. All of this is wrapped up by a no-expenses-spared 60-page booklet describing the Carter Family, their songs (with historical notes and a traced discography of other artists who performed the same material, right through to 1972), the changes and differences between the various Carter versions, plus lyrics, scores, and American album reissue data.

F5.122   **Dixon Brothers.** two discs. RCA Bluebird AXM2-55- (in progress).

Howard and Dorsey Dixon were a brother guitar duo team, composers of the classic "Wreck on the Highway" (made more famous by Roy Acuff), which was sold for a flat sum, and other event songs such as "The Cleveland School House Fire." From 1936-1938, they recorded sixty titles for RCA, but other singers turned most of them into hits in the country field, while the brothers continued to perform in the old time tradition that made them one of the better duos. Dorsey always took the lead vocals, and he was a major rediscovery at Newport in the 1960s as part of the folk revival.

F5.123   **George Banham Grayson and Henry Whitter.** County 513.

This duo's repertoire was derived from the North Carolina area. Grayson was the fiddler; Whitter was the guitarist. The latter was the better known of the two, and he also pursued a solo career. He later claimed "Wreck of the Old 97" as being his own tune, and this started a long court battle. Typical material of this period included southern folk songs, British ballads, minstrel material, sentimental songs and topical songs—most of which were largely shaped by Grayson's archaic style, especially on the old ballads and sentimental numbers, such as "Ommie Wise," "Handsome Molly," "Where Are You Going Alice?" and "Dark Road Is a Hard Road to Travel."

F5.124   **Lester McFarland and Robert Gardner. Mac and Bob.** Birch 1944.

This duo recorded in the then-emerging urban style from 1926-1930; seven of these tracks are here, mainly slick ballads and sacred music such as "When the Roses Bloom Again." Their guitar and mandolin accompaniment was quite similar to that of other prolific duos at the time. During the 1930s, they were associated with the WLS Barn Dance. Two tracks here are from the 1940s, and in 1969, "Mac" recorded three solo efforts for Birch.

F5.125   **McGee Brothers. From Sunny Tennessee.** Bear Family 15517 (West German issue).

F5.126   **McGee Brothers. Milk 'Em in the Evening Blues.** Folkways. FTS 31007.

F5.127   **McGee Brothers. With Arthur Smith.** Folkways FA 2379.
    In the mid-twenties, the McGee Brothers recorded for Vocalion. In 1923,
they had met Uncle Dave Macon, and they became part of his Fruit Jar Drinkers off
and on for seventeen years. Sam's guitar was responsible for upgrading that instrument's role in early old time music, from rhythm accompaniment to lead instrument.
Kirk was proficient on clawhammer banjo. Their repertoire embraced country songs,
dance tunes, and guitar instrumentals. Both ragtime and blues—from black musicians—
helped to shape their style. The Bear Family album of sixteen tracks is from the
Vocalion period, and Uncle Dave Macon and Mazy Todd appear in accompanying
roles. Typical selections include "C-H-I-C-K-E-N Spells Chicken," "A Flower from
My Angel Mother's Grace," "Charming Bill," and "Chevrolet Car." In 1931, the
brothers teamed with Arthur Smith, a fiddler. This trio never recorded at that time,
though, and Smith split to play western swing music. In the late fifties, however,
Mike Seeger reunited them to record enough material for two long discs, mainly
instrumentals, and including "Easy Rider," "Memphis Blues," "Whistlin' Rufus,"
and "Charming Bill" again. After that, they hit the folk revival circuit of Newport,
Carnegie Hall, etc.

F5.128   **[Morris Brothers] Wiley, Zeke & Homer.** Rounder 0022.
    The Morris Brothers were once with J. E. Mainer. This disc finds them in 1972
playing all their old instruments in that North Carolina string band style, and with
Homer "Pappy" Sherrill assisting on fiddle. During the 1930s, they made several
good Appalachian type records for RCA Bluebird. The large amount of material
here (nearly 44 minutes) recreates their past successes, such as the fiddle pieces
"Rhoddish Schottische" and "Wednesday Night Waltz," or the traditional "Maple
on the Hill." The vocal trio is still strong, yet aging; the guitar-mandolin-fiddle combination (plus Ralph Lewis's string bass), still encouraging.

F5.129   **Tracy and Eloise Schwartz. Home among the Hills.** Big Bear 15.007
           (West German issue).
    Tracy Schwartz is the well-known member of the New Lost City Ramblers
and of the Strange Creek Singers. This is his first album together with his wife Eloise.
The fourteen tracks here are different from his usual recreations within the NLCR
framework; these tunes are reinterpretations in the style of old time music, and they
were not intended to be merely emulated. Thus the restrictions of the NLCR had
been lifted temporarily. And Schwartz is an excellent singer and multi-instrumentalist.
The program begins with "Home among the Hills," the ballad "Wild Bill Jones,"
the instrumental "Green Valley Waltz," sentimental songs ("Meet Me Tonight in the
Moonlight"), folklore ("John Henry"), and sacred ("How Beautiful Heaven Must
Be").

F5.130   **Strange Creek Singers.** Arhoolie 4004.
    Besides two-thirds of the New Lost City Ramblers (Mike Seeger and Tracy
Schwartz), the Singers also include Alice Gerrard and Hazel Dickens on vocals and
Lamar Grier on banjo. They are all multi-instrumentalists, collectively able to play
on anything ever used in old time or folk music. Many instruments are doubled,
and changing combinations of duos, trios and quartet lend great diversity to the
handling of the material. The scope of the NLCR has been widened considerably

with the inclusion of female singers, and new compositions and new forms of harmony predominate. Hazel Dickens, the only country-raised performer here, has a pure, anguished voice with superb intonation. She is at her best with the traditional "Will the Circle Be Unbroken?" and her original "Black Lung" (sung unaccompanied), the latter derived from her coal mining family's experiences. Schwartz's original "Poor Old Dirt Farmer" emphasizes a unique harmonica-violin duet, while the country version of "In the Pines" features a simulation of a train whistle by the performers. These are some of the roots of modern country music; the only type missing is the white blues.

F5.131*   **The Stripling Brothers. Old Time Fiddle Tunes, 1928-1936.** County 401.
    The Striplings, a duo based in Alabama, were quite similar to other brother combinations in the fiddle-guitar tradition (that is, similar in intent; the regional variations of the repertoire were, of course, different). Local traditions were very strong in this pre-radio, pre-record period when not everyone had access to the sounds of other regions and could begin to assimilate these "foreign" devices. The Deep South influence is here: there are blues ("Coal Mine Blues") and rags ("Kennedy Rag") and breakdowns for dances ("June Rose Waltz," "Ranger's Hornpipe," "Dance All Night," "Red River Waltz," etc.). Some local stylings manifest themselves in Charles Stripling's fiddle, such as the deep, dark tone that is characteristic of the Deep South, especially Mississippi ("Wolves Howling" is the best example of this).

BLUEGRASS MUSIC

BLUEGRASS MUSIC

> "We don't do anything different than we
> do on records. All the numbers are three
> minutes long."
> —Bill Monroe,
> explaining at the
> American Folk Festival (1963).

INTRODUCTION

"Bluegrass" is a narrowly defined term for a specific brand of old time music, the string band tradition. The name itself achieved commonality in the early 1950s and largely referred to the specific music of Bill Monroe. In a narrow sense, it is the music of Monroe and his Bluegrass Boys (Kentucky-based mountain music), but it can also embrace what some call "old grass" (traditional roots) and "new grass" (modern pop and country material). Basically, no matter how named, bluegrass is a highly structured vocal and instrumental treatment of a certain variety of traditional or folk-composed songs.

1. *Vocals* are extremely emotional phrasing in high-pitched singing. This projects a "high lonesome sound," especially in the tenor trio, where one person would sing lead, the other harmony, and a third sings high tenor lead to double the melody. This singing comes directly from church influences via the Carter Family. High lead singers are often adept at using unorthodox modal and minor intervals as well; their vibratoless phrasing can be very piercing. A variation on this tenor trio includes replacing the harmony tenor with a baritone below the lead, and adding a bass for sacred material. The bluegrass quartet, often a cappella, has this same make-up; though bluegrass trios usually harmonize in parallel thirds, the harmonizing described here is not limited to thirds.

2. *Instrumentation* features unamplified instruments, with the lead being handled by banjo, mandolin, and/or fiddle. Both the guitar and the bass are rhythm, and the former is plucked while the latter is slapped for downbeats. The guitar rarely takes the lead, although Flatt did introduce the catch-up run for a short bridge or guitar lick (the Lester Flatt G run, borrowed from the Carter Family). To compensate, the guitarist is almost always the lead singer, while the bassist is the comic relief and/or master of ceremonies. Thus all five performers have a fairly equally distributed work load, as the other three performers are soloists with harmonic singing duties. Another distinguishing characteristic is the use of the five string banjo for lead or background in all songs. "Scruggs-style" banjo is a three finger arpeggio picking style; Scruggs was not the first to use it (it is a Northern Carolina styling perfected by Snuffy Jenkins, who preached Scruggs), but he was the most successful at it (during his mid-1940s recordings for Monroe). His chromatic

stylings accent the melodic line to make this line featured in a veritable deluge of notes. His style is best adaptable to a fast tempo, and for effects, the strings can be alternately tightened and slackened. Done by a good performer, the ripple of notes from this three finger roll can be exceptionally smooth.

The violin wails through a series of devices such as odd double stops, slides, variations, blues tempos, and others that bear an uncanny relationship to Eck Robertson's techniques on "Sally Goodin" from 1923. Material favored by the fiddler includes breakdowns and jazz and blues items. It was Chubby Wise, Monroe's fiddler, who smoothed out the violin's approach by incorporating a more jazz-like feel of improvisation. The mandolin follows the banjo in creating drive in the music (although the banjo was a fast-paced instrument ten years before Scruggs played for Monroe). Like the banjo, it is mainly syncopated, and like the fiddle, it performs best on blues and breakdowns: it is an excellent middle instrument between the two. All of these instruments have a clearly defined role, and the nearest comparison is to New Orleans jazz, for bluegrass is also syncopated dance music with breaks, solo passages, and polyphonic ensemble work through the front line's contrapuntal complexity. This trio's overall effect on the rigid framework is to produce jazz's internal tension-musical interaction as expressed through much textural variation.

3. *Song patterns* cover the traditional form of verses and choruses (four lines), with three or four basic chords in 2/4 or 3/4 time. Instrumentals are almost always in 4/4 and performed at break-neck speed. A variety of tempi are used to fit the mood, and quite often, older songs can be given new life by varying the pace, changing the words, adding harmonies, or employing added instrumentation (such as the Dobro). Syncopated bluegrass, like ragtime and because of its formula structure, can be used as a style for almost any song from another musical genre. As a song can be "ragged," so too it can be "grassed."

4. Finally, *lyrics* reflect the reality of rural poverty. Topics deal with the loneliness in the mountains, aging parents, deep religious convictions, lost love, death, and catastrophes (which, when merged with religion, reveal that to die is to pass on to a better life; consequently, death is a reward), story ballads that have grim endings, and light-hearted songs that celebrate the past. Many contradictions abound, as pessimistic songs are performed at break-neck speed, normally associated with "happy" songs.

In its historical development, bluegrass music continued the social music of the late nineteenth century, along with the story ballads and sacred materials evolved through old time music. Most of the music was previously unaccompanied, but the advent of the guitar, mandolin, and string bass, plus the merger with dance music, created the need for a structured style. This fusion came about through Bill Monroe's Bluegrass Boys, and defined "classic bluegrass"—with Monroe's blues-style mandolin,

Scruggs's slurring banjo, Flatt's rhythm guitar and its runs, and Wise's jazz-style violin (1946-1947, for Columbia records). Spin-offs, cross fertilization, and imitations were inevitable with new bands such as Flatt and Scruggs's more polished style, Mac Wiseman's vocals, Jesse McReynold's adaptation of Scruggs's banjo style to his mandolin, Jimmy Martin's novelties, the Osborne Brothers' close harmonies, Don Reno's banjo, the Stanley Brothers' rural sound, and so forth.

By the late 1950s, bluegrass music seemed to be any music that exhibited at least *one* characteristic of the "classic" style, such as the singing of the Louvin Brothers or Charlie Monroe, or the use of less than the five basic instruments, in which case at least one person emulated the style of Monroe, Scruggs, Flatt, or Wise. In time, this meant a weakening of the original style, but it did set apart bluegrass music from Nashville country music or rock and roll. The traditional aspects of the lyrics plus the retention of such older instruments as the fiddle and banjo gave bluegrass its credibility in the ensuing folk revival. This preservation aspect excited urban singers, who really tried to like early American folk songs and British Child ballads but felt more at home with spicy bluegrass instrumentation. It is precisely this style of the music—this "grassifying" of songs—that resulted in the experimentation that led to the 1970s "new grass": Dobros, guitars, harmonicas, pianos, organs, accordion, instrumental duets, echo chambers, and even electrified instruments.

These changes had been evident since the 1950s, when Monroe sometimes used an accordion or required a two finger style banjo. In the 1950s, he used twin fiddling and recorded such modern country songs as "Four Walls" or such folk songs as "Danny Boy." With this stamp of approval by the master, other groups branched out, such as the Stanley Brothers recording rhythm 'n' blues material ("Finger Popping Time") or the shift of Flatt and Scruggs to pop in the 1960s ("The Ballad of Jed Clampett," "Memphis," "Detroit City") or the new troubador songs of John Denver ("Country Roads"), Steve Goodman ("City of New Orleans"), and John Prine ("Paradise").

The word newgrass first appeared in print on the second album put out by the Bluegrass Alliance. Essentially, newgrass changes the musical style and content of bluegrass to reflect both contemporary tastes and different versions of non-bluegrass songs (e.g., "Body and Soul"). The instrumentation is the same in the front line (banjo, violin, and mandolin), but others have been added (Dobro, harmonica, pedal steel guitar, drums, etc.) *and* most have been amplified for the same reason as for Chicago blues—to be heard over the noise in bars. In this sense, it is close to soft-rock music, since the same type of audience is being catered to. Musicians who have had great influence on the newgrass performing style include jazz violinist Stephane Grappelli (particularly with Django Reinhardt), mandolinist Jethro Burns (of Homer and Jethro, the country comics), and banjoist Bobby Thompson (whose pentatonic blues style can be heard with Jim and Jesse). Composers who have had their material sung include John Prine; Norman Blake; John Denver; Steve Goodman; John Hartford; Gordon Lightfoot; Simon and Garfunkel; Neil Young; Neil Diamond; John Sebastian; Buffy Ste. Marie; Crosby, Stills, Nash and Young; Leonard Cohen; James Taylor; Bob Dylan; and Johnny Cash—all falling within the troubador tradition.

Proponents of the updated electric sounds include the Allen Brothers and the New Grass Revival (particularly the dynamic Sam Bush). The younger groups appeal to the youth market, and, in the troubador tradition, they write their own songs, which tend to fall into the modern rock and roll field. Some of the older groups are content to impose the structure of bluegrass onto contemporary songs from country, folk, or mood genres (such as those active in the Washington, D.C.-to-Baltimore strip). Others, such as Johnnie and Jack, were essentially country groups attempting to broaden their horizons in search of a wider audience. Some were true eclectics, such as the Dillards, who promoted slick, polished interpretations of all types of songs beginning right in the midst of the folk revival period (1958-1963), and made solid contributions to the emerging folk-rock genre.

But one essential characteristic sets off bluegrass from newgrass. The latter is an arranged form best suited to the recording studio and exhibiting similar styles as rock music does in this context of "produced" music. The former is still a living form of music and finds its most common expression through amateur bands everywhere in the United States. Carleton Haney promoted the first all-bluegrass festival in 1965, and this revival linked bluegrass even more to the traditional revival meetings and medicine shows. There are now well over 150 such festivals a year throughout America, all with substantial attendance—and most of these fans play an instrument. Indeed, the literature on bluegrass shows a great concern for transcriptions, instrument care, manuals, song books, and personal contact with other, similar singers. Of all the musical genres dealt with in this book, bluegrass is the only one with highly active *participating* fans who know all about the music. This high level of awareness has helped to sustain the music and even extend it.

Literature

Bluegrass music is similar to ragtime, a clearly demarcated style, but it is only during the past few years that materials have been written, these mainly surveys. Sandberg and Weissman (77) give details of additional readings and recordings. Mitsui (60) wrote the first scholarly work on bluegrass in 1967. Artis (4) and Price (70) followed in 1975 with popular surveys. Rosenberg (74) has compiled an extensive discography of Bill Monroe's recordings, and he is also preparing a major scholarly work on bluegrass history for 1979. Rooney (73) has interviewed Bill Monroe, and Ralph Rinzler will publish Monroe's biography. Haglund (37) has compiled a virtually complete listing of bluegrass albums. Historical information is scattered through Malone (57), Malone and McCulloh (58), and Shelton (83), with biographic data up through 1967 from Stambler (86) and to 1972 from Shestack (84).

Bluegrass has two leading periodicals. *Bluegrass Unlimited* (2) is the oldest with excellent coverage of current performers and festival listings. *Muleskinner News* (15) used the in-depth interview technique and a good record review section (plus an annual directory). *Pickin'* (17) concentrates on the performing musician fan with articles on instruction, instruments, and interviews. Occasional articles can also be found in *Country Music People* (5), *Country Music Review* (6), *Journal of Country Music* (11), *Old Time Music* (16), and *Sing Out!* (20). Consult the *Annual Index to Popular Music Record Reviews* (3) and *Popular Music Periodicals Index* (69) for more details on records and articles.

ANTHOLOGIES

F6.1*   **American Banjo Tunes and Songs in Scruggs Style.** Folkways FA 2314.

F6.2*   **Banjo Classics.** Collectors' Classics CC 6.

F6.3   **Banjo Spectacular.** two discs. Starday 136.
    Scruggs-style banjo is the prime determinant of mainstream bluegrass music. The Folkways set of 31 tracks is a very important album, for it legitimatized bluegrass as "folk" music when the disc first came out in 1957. It added impetus to the bluegrass revival by employing the word "Scruggs" in its title. However, the record is mainly the North Carolina style of three finger picking, with younger, second-generation performers from the Virginia-Maryland area. Everything was collected by Mike Seeger (with notes by Ralph Rinzler), and there is some pre-Scruggs material as well. Performers include Larry Richardson, Don Bryant, Joe Stewart, Smiley Hobbs, and Snuffy Jenkins.
    The Starday reissue collects stunning commercial banjo songs (or tunes in which the banjo has some predominance) from Bill Clifton, the Stanley Brothers, Stringbean Akeman (who preceded Scruggs in the Monroe band), Connie and Joe, Jim Eames, Bill Harrell, and the Country Gentlemen. The Collectors Classic reissue of 1950s material is an instrumental album, with Flatt and Scruggs ("Dear Old Dixie's Farewell Blues"), the Stanley Brothers ("Hard Times," "Mastertone March"), Reno and Smiley ("Choking the Strings," "Banjo Riff," "Charlotte Breakdown"), and the McCormick Brothers ("Mad Banjo" and "Banjo Strut").

F6.4   **Bluegrass!** two discs. Pickwick PTP 2069.

F6.5   **Bluegrass Special.** World Pacific WPR 21898.
    These three discs are multi-purpose introductions to the "world of bluegrass." The Pickwick set is a budget issue put out to cash in on the bluegrass revival; it contains fine recordings from Mercury, mainly from the early 1950s and last reissued on Hilltop JS 6111, 6140 and 6156. Here are Flatt and Scruggs, the Country Gentlemen, Jimmie Skinner, the Stanley Brothers, Carl Story, etc. The World Pacific set collates offerings from Tut Taylor, the Kentucky Colonels, the Stoneman Family, Glen Campbell, and Clarence and Roland White—all from the early '60s.

F6.6   **Bluegrass Festival.** Nashville 2102.

F6.7   **Bluegrass Hall of Fame.** two discs. Pine Mountain 181 and 301.

F6.8   **Dueling Banjos.** Nashville 2114.

F6.9   **I'll Still Write Your Name in the Sand.** Nashville 2067.

F6.10   **More Bluegrass.** Starday SLP 272.

F6.11   **Stars and Hits of Bluegrass.** Nashville 2113.

These seven anthologies are budget reissues from 1950s and 1960s Starday material (Pine Mountain records are direct reissues). All are only ten tracks each, but most of these seventy cuts represent some pretty choice and classic bluegrass music from this period. Performers include Melvin and Ray Goins, the Cline Brothers and the Lonesome Pine Fiddlers, Hylo Brown, Flatt and Scruggs ("Foggy Mountain Breakdown" and "Roll in My Sweet Baby's Arms," both being re-recordings of their classics), Reno and Smiley, the Country Gentlemen, Bill Emerson, Grandpa Jones, Jimmie Skinner, Bill Clifton, latter-day J. E. Mainer, Stringbean Akeman, Red Allen, Jim and Jesse, the Stanley Brothers ("Ridin' That Midnight Train"), and Mac Wiseman ("'Tis Sweet to Be Remembered" and the title track of Nashville 2067).

F6.12   **Bluegrass for Collectors.** RCA APM 1-0568.

F6.13   **Bluegrass Music '52 and '53.** RCA RA 5508 (Japanese issue).

F6.14   **Bluegrass Music '54 and '56.** RCA RA 5505 (Japanese issue).

F6.15*   **Early Bluegrass.** RCA LPV 569.
    While RCA never really got into the bluegrass picture, they did record some fine examples from 1940 through the late fifties. These four discs cover that period, with no duplications. The last noted set begins in the 1940s, with pre-bluegrass stylings from the Morris Brothers, the Blue Sky Boys, Roy Hall, Bill Monroe, Jimmy Martin, and the Osborne Brothers. Of the four discs, this sixteen track anthology has the best notes. Much of the material's style is continued on the other domestic RCA offering, beginning with Bill Monroe's "In the Pines" and "Mule-skinner's Blues" (both poorly re-recorded). Charlie Monroe sings "Mother's Not Dead, She's Only Sleeping" and "This World Is Not My Home." Others are J. E. Mainer, Zeke Morris, Riley Puckett, and Gid Tanner.
    The two Japanese issues cover only four years, but their concentration is intense. Here are prime examples of a version of the Lonesome Pine Fiddlers (established in 1938 by the Cline Brothers) with Jimmy Martin and Bobby Osborne, the Osborne Brothers as a group, Martin himself (who also recorded as the Sunny Mountain Boys, a name he took with him to MCA), the Country Pardners, and others.

F6.16*   **Early Days of Bluegrass, v.1/5, 7/8.** seven discs. Rounder 1013-1017, 1019, 1020.
    This superb reissue series was conceived by Richard Spottswood, one of the primary experts on American folk music, who has worked on similar ventures with reissued recordings for Biograph and now for the Library of Congress. The series is also a good example of government-sponsored preservation of recorded materials, as it was partially financed by the National Endowment for the Humanities (youth grants), and should provoke other such projects from diverse small reissue firms. Each disc comes complete with a 12-page booklet of discographic information, biographies, photographs, and some texts. Each disc contains sixteen titles. (There is also a "volume 6," entitled *Have You Forgotten the Bailey Brothers?* in the same format and series, numbered as Rounder 1018.) These titles come from

Rich-R-Tone and Canary, 1947-1953; but as the album deals with only one group, it has been annotated separately, later on in this section. Even a casual listening to these seven discs will show that the independent labels of the U.S. South were instrumental in spreading the bluegrass genre. First, they recorded up-and-coming artists who would go on to greater things. Second, they furthered the creation of regional variances and stylings. And third, they distributed bluegrass recordings to listeners who could not get enough of what the larger companies had to offer.

The first three volumes are "devoted to the lesser known groups who helped create and popularize bluegrass music" through regional labels, radio and television (1013), honky-tonk clubs, dances, and so forth. Volume one is mostly from Kentucky of the early 1950s, and demonstrates the wide variety of instrumental styles and lyrics that were seminal in the development of modern bluegrass, such as the honky-tonk rendition of "Devil's Little Angel" by the Kelleys of Hazard, Kentucky (who, incidentially, had previously worked for Bill Monroe). This disc is noted for the famous sidemen, not too unusual in regional recordings where some money could be picked up by visiting performers. Thus, fiddler Tex Logan appears as well as Snuffy Jenkins, Pappy Sherrill, most of the Lonesome Pine Fiddlers, and Bea Lilly. The Lillys themselves are heard here on two sacred items: "They Sleep Together Now at Rest" and "What Are They Doing in Heaven Today?"

Volume two (1014) continues through the 1950s, with both Kentucky and North Carolina performers. There is Red Allen ("Preachin', Prayin', and Singin'," "Paul and Silas"—both sacred tunes), Frank Wakefield ("You're the One I See in My Dreams," "Leave Well Enough Alone," "New Camptown Races"), the Wright Brothers' epic "Island Creek Mine Fire," plus Dave Woolum, and the Brewster Brothers. Volume five (1017), subtitled "The Rich-R-Tone Story," is a collection of tracks from Jim Stanton's record company in Johnson City, Tennessee, a very important regional that starred many fine influential groups. The Stanley Brothers here have "Little Glass of Wine" and the Bailey Brothers, "Rattlesnake Daddy "; also here is sacred material from Wilma Lee and Stoney Cooper, Pee Wee Lambert's "Weary Hobo" and "Just a Memory" (modeled after Bill Monroe), Glen Neaves's "Black Mountain Rag," etc. Extensive notes are given on the company's history, and these clearly show the mountain market aimed for (Kentucky, East Tennessee, West Virginia, North Carolina).

F6.17*   Mountain Music Bluegrass Style. Folkways FA 2318.

The nineteen selections here are bluegrass versions of old time music, or that form of old time music that was also a transition to the bluegrass style. All were recorded in 1960, largely by Mike Seeger (who also furnished the notes detailing biographical sketches, the texts to the tunes, and discographic tracings to the original old time music 78 rpm discs). Here are some fiddle tunes by Tex Logan ("Natchez under the Hill"), Smiley Hobbs on several instruments ("Nine Pound Hammer," "Leather Britches"), Earl Taylor and the Stony Mountain Boys ("Short Life of Trouble," "White House Blues," "Fox Chase"), the Lilly Brothers with Don Stover ("Katy Cline" and "Bile 'Em Cabbage Down"), and so forth. This is both an exceptionally enjoyable record as well as an educational-instructional experience.

F6.18*   **Springtime in the Mountains.** County 749.
Subtitled "classics of early bluegrass," this album features a number of second-line but first-rate performers, largely from 1953 through 1965 (not quite the "early days"). There are three basic groups. Larry Richardson and Happy Smith recorded for Blue Ridge in 1953 and 1958. In addition to the superb clear, high singing of Richardson, the highlight here was the rarely used but effective combination of bluegrass and clawhammer banjo styles (both artists played banjo). Titles include the classics "Let Me Fall" and "Lonesome Road Blues" plus an instrumental. For the New River label, Ted Lundy cut a number of sides, and four appear here including the standards "Poor Ellen Smith" and "Dark Hollow." Red Allen only has three tracks, but "Lonesome Day" and "Keep on Going" are, again, standard classics of the bluegrass repertoire. His high tender lead is always exciting. Session men for Allen include Scotty Stoneman on dynamic fiddle and Frank Wakefield on mandolin. Scotty Stoneman reappears on the Richardson and Smith tracks, along with his brother Jimmy Stoneman, and two early founders of the Country Gentlemen: Charlie Waller and John Duffey. This anthology is one of the finest sets of bluegrass music ever released.

INNOVATORS

F6.19   **Red Allen.** County 710.

F6.20   **Red Allen. Bluegrass Country.** County 704.

F6.21*   **Red Allen. Solid Bluegrass Sound of the Kentuckians.** Melodeon MLP 7325.
Red Allen has the purest high tenor voice of any in bluegrass, and it is exceptionally unpolished rural singing; he was once with the Osborne Brothers before striking out on his own. The Melodeon set, one of his earlier recordings, is certainly his best, featuring an all star group comprising Wayne and Bill Yates, Bill Emerson, and fiddler Chubby Wise on one cut ("Hello City Limits"). All twelve tracks here are prime examples of solid, traditional bluegrass, especially the Georgia flavor of "Worry My Life Away," the patriotic "Down Where the River Bends," the old timey "Froggie Went A-Courtin'," and the very sacred "The Family Who Prays" and "Flowers By My Graveside." The two County records, with some of the same performers, include more diversified material by Bill Monroe, Jimmy Martin, Ernest Tubb, Jim and Jesse: "Milk Cow Blues," "Purple Heart," "Summertime Is Past and Gone," "Maiden's Prayer," and "Lonesome and Blue."

F6.22   **Country Gentlemen.** Vanguard VSD 79331.

F6.23*   **Country Gentlemen. Award Winning.** Rebel 1506.

F6.24*   **Country Gentlemen. Bluegrass at Carnegie Hall.** Starday SLP 174.

F6.25*   **Country Gentlemen. Country Songs—Old and New.** Folkways FA 2409.

F6.26   **Country Gentlemen. Yesterday and Today.** Rebel 1521.

    The Country Gentlemen were founded in 1957 by Charlie Waller, a guitarist strongly impressed by Hank Snow's music, and John Duffey, one of the best mandolinists in bluegrass music (now with the Seldom Scene). They sang in bars throughout the whole Baltimore-Washington area and strongly influenced the development of urban bluegrass and, in particular, "bluegrass bars." Formerly, much singing was done for radio, concerts and records. The popularity of singing in a saloon gave an added venue to many groups, but it also affected their material by creating a demand for "bluegrass" versions of folk and contemporary songs. But before all this began, the Country Gentlemen recorded some traditional albums for Folkways. Their first is their best, containing versions of "Roving Gambler," "Drifting Too Far," "Paul and Silas," and "The Story of Charlie Lawson."

    In 1960, Eddie Adcock's banjo arrived in the group, and their music took a stronger bluegrass bent. They began playing folk festivals and television in addition to their club routines. They also recorded for Starday, and this resulted in a recording of their dynamic Carnegie Hall performance, emphasizing their skillful selection of songs that formed a bridge between folk music and bluegrass music. Indeed, they became known as the most prominent interpreters of bluegrass-as-folk music through second-generation development (nobody disputed Monroe or Flatt and Scrugg, as the leaders in the "roots" of bluegrass and the originators). In the 1960s, they recorded widely for a variety of labels, and despite changing personnel (only Waller remained a constant), they became a very tight band always performing at the height of their powers. There were no off nights or recordings. Thus, they appealed to *both* the new and the traditional fans of bluegrass.

    By the late 1960s, they began to feel the feedback of contemporary music into bluegrass, and they recorded what some might call dubious material in a wide choice of traditional and popular titles. In so doing, they opened the way for "progressive bluegrass," which is mainly imposing bluegrass instrumentation and vocal styles on contemporary music (folk, rock, soul, etc.). Not too many people appreciated this, but the group kept it down to one or two items per album. At the same time, they began to parody both folk music and themselves with a fey version of "Big Bruce," a rollicking "Tom Dooley," a devastating "Duelin' Banjos," and the comic "Cripple Creek" played at half time. Their irreverent humor was very successful. The material for Rebel (some of it live) comes from 1963-1971 and includes "Walking down the Line," "Little Bessie," "Redwood Hill," "Country Roads" and "Slant of the Waterfall." Most of their work during this period was of more modern compositions. Their initial album for Vanguard assured them of worldwide distribution for the first time in fifteen years, and this fine disc includes sterling renditions of "Traveling Kind," "One Morning in May," and "The Leaves That Are Green." During the 1970s, the varying personnel of the group has included Waller, Adcock, Duffey, Ed Ferris on bass, Bobbi Woods, Doyle Lawson, and Mike Auldridge.

F6.27*   **Lester Flatt and Earl Scruggs.** Hilltop JS 6093.

F6.28   **Lester Flatt and Earl Scruggs. Carnegie Hall.** Columbia CS 8845.

F6.29   **Lester Flatt and Earl Scruggs. Foggy Mountain Banjo.**
Columbia LE 10043.

F6.30*   **Lester Flatt and Earl Scruggs. The Golden Years, v.1/2.** County/
           Columbia P 13810 and Rounder/Columbia P 13826.

F6.31   **Lester Flatt and Earl Scruggs. Songs of the Famous Carter Family.**
           Columbia LE 10026.

Lester Flatt and Earl Scruggs rose to prominence with the Bill Monroe
Bluegrass Boys. They were the first of the second generation group as they took
the ideas of Monroe and developed them a little further, after they split from Monroe
in 1947. Their "classic" recordings were the thirty titles done in 1948-1950 for
Mercury, followed by their initial Columbias, beginning in 1951. Earl Scruggs
was the banjoist who gave bluegrass its distinctive sound. His banjo is basically
in the North Carolina style (Scruggs was influenced by Snuffy Jenkins of North
Carolina) that developed from classical banjo performing and from minstrel shows;
it was very closely tied to fiddle music. Explained simply, the right hand picked the
strings with the thumb, index, and middle fingers ("three finger"). The other style
at the time was "two finger" (or brushing, drop-thumb, frailing, clawhammer, and
other such appelatives).

With "Scruggs Style"—as it became known—the melody could now be more
precise and syncopated. Monroe took advantage of this and showcased Scruggs's
banjo. Scruggs later developed a cam for the banjo that could create a *slide* effect.
Thus, not only could he pick out the notes with precision, but also he could deliberately slur them in a blues style. His lead guitar playing (heard generously on the
Carter songs album) was, in the main, a blues style influenced by Travis, Maybelle
Carter, and the Scruggs banjo itself. In no small way was Scruggs pushed into the
late fifties folk revival (and thereby, he extended the audience for bluegrass because
of its "pure" nature). Pete Seeger wrote a definitive banjo instrumental book and
coined the term "Scruggs Style." Mike Seeger produced Folkways FA 2314
American Banjo Scruggs Style, and both of these gave authenticity to Flatt and
Scruggs and to bluegrass music generally. At the same time, no electric instrumentation was used. The next crest in the career of Flatt and Scruggs was the television
show *The Beverly Hillbillies*, which used their bluegrass music and Scruggs's banjo
as background music. Many people even went so far as to only watch the opening
and closing titles to catch the music—until "The Ballad of Jed Clampett" was
recorded as a disc. The movie *Bonnie and Clyde* was their next peak, as that film
used the Mercury recording of "Foggy Mountain Breakdown" (1949 version,
found on the Hilltop album).

Lester Flatt was steeped in old time traditional music. Originally he was a
mandolinist and a tenor (as was Bill Monroe), but Monroe turned him into a guitarist and a lead vocalist. Flatt was most shaped by Monroe, perhaps more than any
other bluegrass musician who played with Monroe. Flatt's tenor lead vocal was
only possible because Monroe himself sang so high that Flatt could easily get under
him. Later, Flatt would create mellow and relaxed vocals. Monroe's fast mandolin,
though, meant that Flatt had trouble catching up; so, with Monroe's approval,
Flatt made up a fast guitar run to catch up. Often, only the end of the run was
audible after the last line of the verse. It was a dramatic effect, and coupled with
Scruggs's syncopated banjo, Monroe's fast mandolin, and Chubby Wise's jazz-blues
violin, bluegrass became a highly emotionally charged music. Flatt's guitar bass
runs were common in old time music (especially with Maybelle Carter and Charlie
Monroe), but Flatt brought them into bluegrass, and today it is often referred to

the "Lester Flatt G run." His guitar was not as driving or melodic as those of other guitarists in that period, but his timing was definitely better.

The first Flatt and Scruggs band for Mercury (heard on the Hilltop album) produced originals at breakneck speed, and often featured the high harmony of Everett Lilly and Curly Seckler. Typical titles included "My Little Girl in Tennessee," "Bouquet in Heaven," "Roll in My Sweet Baby's Arms" and "Pike County Breakdown." Their theme at the time was "Foggy Mountain Top." Other performers here included Mac Wiseman, and several were interchangeable with the Bluegrass Boys of Monroe. Many also came from Monroe's group to the Foggy Mountain Boys, but adjustments had to be made. There was little use made of the mandolin, for then the sound would be too close to Monroe's. They pushed the banjo to more prominence and later, for Columbia, developed the Dobro sound with Josh Graves. The comparison of the two leading bluegrass groups is unavoidable as Scruggs had created the bluegrass sound of the banjo. Other differences, though, included the fact that there was no longer any high, lonesome sound.

Throughout the 1950s and 1960s, success made the group lose their drive. Scruggs slowed down, and there was a distinct folk orientation to their early 1960s sound. When their popularity increased through their television theme, they became more widely known and recorded virtually anything their producer could come up with, even bluegrass music of slick pop material. While they were severely criticized for this, there was never any doubt that Flatt and Scruggs assisted in the spread of bluegrass through exposure on radio, television, and college concerts (they were the first bluegrass group to go on campus). In 1959, they appeared at the *first* Newport Folk Festival. Their *Carnegie Hall* recording ("Fiddle and Banjo," "Flint Hill Special," "Salty Dog Blues," "Yonder Stands Little Maggie") was authentic bluegrass, as was their Vanderbilt University recital. Their first Columbia records (on Harmony) included "Thinking about You," "On the Hills to the Poor House," "Dear Old Dixie," and "I'm Gonna Settle Down," and it extended their Mercury-type material. Curly Seckler was on mandolin and sang tenor, but when he left in 1962, the band declined in musical quality. Two good specialty albums of importance were *Foggy Mountain Banjo* (twelve instrumentals of such traditional items as "Sally Ann," "Reuben," "Cripple Creek," "Little Darlin' Pal of Mine," "John Henry," "Sally Goodwin," etc.) and the Carter album, which featured their songs and Mother Maybelle on autoharp. A decisive swinging style promoted such titles as "Keep on the Sunny Side," "On the Rock Where Moses Stood," "Worried Man Blues," "Jimmy Brown the Newsboy," and "The Storms Are on the Ocean."

F6.32   **Jim and Jesse. Bluegrass Special and Bluegrass Classics.** two discs. Columbia CSP 12641.

F6.33*   **Jim and Jesse. 20 Great Songs.** two discs. Capitol DTBB 264.
During the late 1940s and early 1950s, the McReynolds brothers turned to bluegrass music. This music, heard on the Capitol set, showed good duet singing of a pure, urban blend—not a rural sound, but one of smoothness, especially when Curly Seckler joined for the trios. Typical tunes included "A Memory of You," "Too Many Tears," "Just Wondering Why," "Are You Missing Me?," almost all in lamented love or "hurtin' " style. Of great value, though, was the mandolin picking of Jesse. He developed a cross-picking style that adapted Scruggs banjo

techniques to the mandolin by using a single straight pick to replace the thumb and finger pick. Thus, while more difficult to perform in that manner, the scope of the mandolin was considerably widened, and a good many younger mandolinists take after Jesse rather than Bill Monroe.

In the 1960s, they moved to Columbia and refined their style. Recognition came with performances at Newport in 1963 and 1966. The Virginia-born brothers added Vassar Clements on fiddle and Bobby Thompson on banjo. With them, Thompson developed the highly influential *chromatic* banjo, which played around the melody in a shower of notes. His finger patterns thereby produced a straight chromatic scale. Highlights from their only two real bluegrass albums for Columbia include more sentimental pieces, such as "The Little Paper Boy," "Just When I Needed You," "I Wish You Knew," along with the sacred ("Grave in the Valley") and the traditional ("Stoney Creek").

F6.34   Lilly Brothers. Bluegrass Breakdown. Prestige FL 14010.

F6.35*   Lilly Brothers. Early Recordings, with Don Stover. County 729.

F6.36*   Lilly Brothers. Folk Songs from the Southern Mountains. Folkways FA 2433.
(Mitchell) "Bea" and Everett Lilly, playing guitar and mandolin respectively, came from West Virginia, and together, they perpetuated the brother duo element in bluegrass music. Ev was with Scruggs in 1950-1952, but then decided to get his group together. Banjoist Don Stover, just back from Monroe's group, was asked to join in 1952, and he was later joined by Herb Hooven on violin. Originally, a good deal of their music was very much in the sacred tradition, and many such elements are continued on all of their albums. The Folkways set has side one devoted to old time duets by just the two brothers ("In My Dear Old Southern Home," "Forgotten Soldier Boy," "Where Is My Soldier Boy?," and "What Would You Give in Exchange?") and clearly shows the influences of the Carter Family, the Monroe Brothers and the Blue Sky Boys. Side two introduces Stover and Hooven for the traditional "Little Annie," "Barbara Allen," "Waves on the Sea," and "John Hardy." The County reissue collates eleven items done for the Event label in 1956-1957, and at such a time when Stover's banjo was exceptionally bluesy in style. Many melancholy songs abound, as well as the blues here: "Bring Back My Blue Eyed Boy," "Are You Tired of Me, My Darling?," "Little Annie," "Southern Skies," and "Tragic Romance." The moving harmonic structure of the duo was particularly adaptable to the tragic songs.

F6.37*   Jimmy Martin. Big 'n' Country. Instrumentals. MCA 115.

F6.38*   Jimmy Martin. Good 'n' Country. MCA 81.
Martin became lead singer for Bill Monroe's early Decca recordings (1949-1954). In this capacity, he was excellent, with a reedy voice capable of both sustaining notes and just getting under Monroe's high tenor harmony. Together, they sang some of the best of the Monroe classics, and these titles are repeated here (without Monroe): "Uncle Pen," "New Muleskinner Blues," and "River of Death." The main contributors are banjoist J. D. Crowe and mandolinist Paul Williams.

Despite criticism that Martin was too rigid and easily fell into a formula of non-creativity, he did present a suitable mixture of country and bluegrass music to the extent that his music could have been classed as "newgrass" except for the lack of electrical amplification. He was a hard taskmaster, and many musicians passed through his band, but not without getting some good, basic training. The instrumental album is one of the best efforts from the groups, which here consisted of J. D. Crowe, Bill Emerson, Vic Jordan, and Vernon Derrick. Included are "Big Country," "Uptown Blues," "You Are My Sunshine," "Going up Dry Branch," and "Union County." Of late, Martin has enjoyed a new audience from his contributions to the *Circle* set with the Nitty Gritty Dirt Band.

F6.39   **Bill Monroe. Father of Bluegrass. RCA CAL 719.**

F6.40*   **Bill Monroe. The Great. Harmony HL 7290.**

F6.41*   **Bill Monroe. 16 All Time Greatest Hits. Columbia CS 1065.**
     Monroe to bluegrass music is the "bossman," in much the same way as Muddy Waters to blues and Miles Davis to jazz. (The bossman sets the style and defines the field in his own terms; he develops his sidemen into a "school.") Notable alumni of Monroe's bands included Flatt and Scruggs, Mac Wiseman, Jimmy Martin, Clyde Moody, Sonny Osborne, Don Reno, Howdy Forrester, Chubby Wise, Vassar Clements, Kenny Baker, Red Smiley, Bill Harrell, and countless other, younger performers currently playing today (e.g., Roland White of Country Gazette, Bill Keith, Richard Greene, Pete Rowan, Byron Berline, etc.). The influences upon Monroe have been varied. His material is largely derived from rural string bands that played at square dances, the shape   note singing of church music, and more specifically, the blues violin and guitar of black performer Arnold Scholtz and the fiddle of his Uncle Pen Vanderver. All of this was distilled until Monroe produced a string band of driving speed, intricate instrumentation, and traditional lyrics. Despite the "modernism" of early bluegrass, Monroe has really been rooted in the past more than any other performer, and he has preserved many of his Uncle Pen's tunes that Pen learned before the turn of the century. Many of these are now non-mandolin tunes adapted from that violin.
     By category, Monroe's music concerns the old time or traditional pieces (e.g., "Katy Hill"), the sacred, the modern yodel songs of Jimmie Rodgers ("Muleskinner Blues"), contemporary original compositions, plus material submitted by his own band members, who often performed the relevant solos. His pattern—whether live or in recording sessions—is to mix all these and to keep the program varied. As outlined in the annotation for Flatt and Scruggs, Monroe actively encouraged his quartet to step out and solo. He fashioned many changes in the style of new band members (e.g., Scruggs-style banjo, Chubby Wise's jazz violin, Flatt's guitar run, etc.). His own style was for high tenor harmony over a lead tenor (thus projecting that "high lonesome sound"), plus lightning finger-picking on traditionally fiddle tunes, often employing the blues technique of alternating between minor and major thirds.
     In 1939, he joined the Grand Ole Opry and electrified the audience with his brilliantly fast rendition of "Muleskinner Blues," emphasizing fast, uptempo picking (which he had developed out of the former Monroe Brothers style) and the high

tenor harmony over tenor lead. His Victor recordings of 1940-1941, while not as important as his Columbia sessions of 1945-1949, were exceptionally polished for the time. The band only had four pieces (mandolin, violin, guitar, and bass) and, as such, it was a transitional group similar to J. E. Mainer's. During the Columbia period, Monroe added banjo and actively encouraged his other four instruments to solo, depending on the type of tune. This was his best period, and the best group here was the 1945-1946 ensemble of Chubby Wise's jazz-swing-blues fiddle, Lester Flatt's superb lead tenor (which blended exceptionally well with Monroe's high harmony), Earl Scruggs's three-finger syncopated blues banjo, and Monroe's syncopated blues mandolin, plus the rhythm of the stand-up bass violin. In singing patterns, they arranged themselves in duets, trios, and the marvelous sacred quartets. Original compositions were by Monroe and/or Flatt.

This group made 28 titles, and most—but not all—have been reissued on the above two Columbia sets. The Harmony has no duplications with the other Monroe reissues. Tunes include "Heavy Traffic Ahead," "Blue Yodel No. 4," "Goodbye Old Pal," "True Life Blues," plus the tune classics of "Footprints in the Snow," "Blue Moon of Kentucky" (later covered by Elvis Presley in the same uptempo speed), "Rocky Road Blues," "Will You Be Loving Another Man?," and the racing song "Molly and Tenbrooks," which was recorded *after* the Stanley Brothers pre-released it.

F6.42*   **Bill Monroe. Best.** two discs. MCA 2-4090.

F6.43*   **Bill Monroe. Bluegrass Instrumentals.** MCA 104.

F6.44*   **Bill Monroe. The High, Lonesome Sound.** MCA 110.

F6.45*   **Bill Monroe. Knee Deep in Bluegrass.** MCA Decca. DL 8731.

F6.46   **Bill Monroe and James Monroe. Father and Son.** MCA 310.

The Decca recordings of Bill Monroe are sufficiently different in intent from his on Columbia to warrant a separate annotation. First, Monroe moved to this company in 1950, and his 1976 recordings are quite similar to the early Deccas for conformity. It is just that he is better. He moved from Columbia because that company signed his closest rivals (the Stanley Brothers), who had taken some of his material to make recordings before he did. The decade of 1950-1960 was Monroe's most productive. He had physically matured, and he began to record many autobiographical songs that he himself called "true songs." Jimmy Martin was his guitarist and lead singer for the first five years of the Decca contract, and Martin gave the band new vitality with his pure vocals. Monroe, of course, developed many side men, and all contributed strongly to sacred music recording. During this period, "bluegrass" music was the appellative given to Monroe's style—named after his group the Blue Grass Boys. This was a distinct honor, and Monroe carried the name from early tent shows, radio, television, dances, college campus tours, and finally to the first bluegrass festival in 1965.

All of Monroe's Decca material is rated good to excellent. However, of the fifteen or so still in print, a few stand out for unique contributions to the field of bluegrass music. The *Best* twofer collates twenty of his well-known pieces and best selling singles. Some titles in this inexpensive introduction include: "Roane Country Prison," "Uncle Pen" (a salute to early influences), "Pretty Fair Maiden in the Garden," "Put My Little Shoes Away," and "The Girl and the Dreadful Snake." *High, Lonesome Sound* brings together eleven titles from 1950-1954 plus one from 1964, compiled and annotated by bluegrass historian Ralph Rinzler. Musicians included Jimmy Martin, Carter Stanley, Sonny Osborne, Vassar Clements, and Charlie Cline. Titles: "My Little Georgia Rose," "On the Old Kentucky Shore," "Memories of Mother and Dad."

Bluegrass Instrumentals, from the same time period, was a high water mark in bluegrass music. In addition to many of the above musicians, there were also Kenny Baker and Bill Keith. Great instrumentals—largely in a jazz-blues vein—included "Stoney Lonesome," "Tall Timber," "Big Man," "Scotland," and "Brown County Breakdown." In early 1958, Monroe recorded his first full album (all earlier efforts were singles and albums of singles): *Knee Deep in Bluegrass*. The eleven songs featured Monroe's vocals alone—no other lead or harmony. In a sense, it could be called a "concept" album. All the singing is of exceptionally high quality, and the instrumentation matches it. Of his modern recordings, the 1973 *Father and Son* disc stands out. Son James had previously played bass, but now he steps out on guitar and on vocals; nothing could probably have pleased his father more. The program is varied with fast and slow songs such as "Tall Pines" and "I Haven't Seen Mary in Years," respectively. Traditional duet items include "Banks of the Ohio," "Mother's Only Sleeping," and "What Would You Give in Exchange?" Of exceptional interest is "When the Golden Leaves Begin to Fall" for its auto-biographical material.

F6.47*   **Don Reno and Red Smiley.** two discs. King 552, 848.

F6.48*   **Don Reno and Red Smiley. Best.** Starday 961.

F6.49*   **Don Reno and Red Smiley. Together Again.** Rome 1011.

F6.50   **Don Reno and Red Smiley. A Variety of Country Songs.** King 646.
          Reno was Bill Monroe's first pick for a banjoist, but the army called during World War II, and Earl Scruggs became a last minute substitute—the rest is blue-grass history. Yet, Reno has been acknowledged as being the best all-round banjoist in bluegrass; he has been influenced by both Bill Monroe and Bill Bolick (Blue Sky Boys) in his singing style. Both he and Smiley were Carolina-born, a good source for bluegrass musicians. Reno is also considered to be the best writer of new, origi-nal bluegrass words and melodies, employing licks based on electric lead guitar and pedal-steel guitar techniques. He had the brilliant idea in the 1950s of turning honky-tonk music into bluegrass music, and in so doing, his group became the first progressive bluegrass band. Borrowing extensively from Ernest Tubb's urban life styles and Hank Williams's tearjerkers, both he and Smiley became a smoother and more urbane group than any other existing bluegrass ensemble. Their brilliant and polished recordings numbered in the hundreds, and featured exceptional duet singing, as on "I Know You're Married but I Love You Still."
          King 552 is an instrumental album featuring all original material: "Dixie Breakdown," "Charlotte Breakdown," "Double Banjo Blues," and the immensely

successfully executed "Little Rock Getaway." The ten selections on the *Best* album emphasized the tearjerkers "Talk of the Town," "One Teardrop and One Step Away," and "I Wouldn't Change You if I Could." Traditional motifs inspired "Springtime in Dear Old Dixie" and "Freight Train Boogie."

Reno and Smiley broke up but were later reunited; and in 1971, they recorded one of their last efforts together, this time with Bill Harrell and fiddler Buck Ryan. The material here is definitely superior to their latter-day King discs, and it features a traditional version of "Muleskinner Blues," Bill Monroe's "Shine Hallelujah Shine," and the instrumental "Riverdale Flash" and "Buck Ryan Rag."

F6.51*   **Ralph Stanley and the Clinch Mountain Boys. A Man and His Music.** Rebel SLP 1530.

F6.52*   **Ralph Stanley and the Clinch Mountain Boys. Plays Requests.** Rebel SLP 1514.

F6.53   **Ralph Stanley and the Clinch Mountain Boys. The Stanley Sound Round the World.** King Bluegrass KB 522.

After his brother Carter died in 1966, Ralph felt that he had no reason to go on. Carter had written the material, talked on the stage as m.c., and dominated Ralph in many other ways. Because they had begun as a young group, Ralph was only forty when he lost his brother. Eventually, though, with encouragement from fans and others, he rebuilt the band into a five piece unit including Roy Lee Centers on lead vocals (he, too, later died), Rick Skaggs on mandolin, and Curly Roy Cline on fiddle. Ralph, of course, played banjo and sang high tenor lead as poignant harmony. In many respects, this is the best traditional bluegrass group since 1950. Without Carter's domination, Ralph blossomed. His banjo style stuck to rural roots but it became exceptionally sure of itself, as befits the leader of a group. Stanley's style is the almost total absence of the choked or slurred notes put forth by Scruggs and others; these latter are mere effects. Stanley hits the specific tones *first*, occasionally sliding a note (called "pulling off" or "hammering on"). This left handed technique assists the more rigid, rural right hand style that Stanley uses, where the thumb stays on the fifth string while the entire melody is played by the index finger. This is a happy sound, for clarity of noting is emphasized with ringing tones in the melody lines.

All of the above discs are from the 1970s. *Plays Requests* are favorites from fans and includes fresh renditions of a number of older Stanley Brothers items such as "Man of Constant Sorrow," "Maple on the Hill," "Pretty Polly," "Little Maggie," and "Clinch Mountain Backstep." Cline plays hot fiddle, Centers accommodates nicely on guitar with some lead singing, and Jack Cooke handles both the bass fiddle and baritone vocals. This is a superb disc for modern reproduction of the rural sound. The other Rebel (1530) contains Ralph's personal favorites. Six tracks are from the Stanley Brothers repertoire; six others are traditional or contemporary, but played in Ralph's clawhammer banjo style. Here are "Shout Little Lucy," which honors his mother (who taught him the banjo), "Train 45," "John Henry," "Gold Watch and Chain," "Hard Times," and "Lonesome River." The King Bluegrass set returns more Stanley Brothers items from an out-of-print catalog. This, by now, very *professional* bluegrass band balances a number of traditional items ("Cumberland Gap," "Bill Cheatum") against Stanley material ("Loving You Too Well" and "Riding the Midnight Train") or Monroe epics ("On and On"). There are also two country items, both penned by Johnnie and Jack, perhaps the most underrated contributors to country music: "What about You?" and "Poison Love."

F6.54*   **Stanley Brothers.** CBS Sony 20AP14 (Japanese issue).

F6.55*   **Stanley Brothers,** v.1/2. two discs. Collector's Classics CC1/2.

F6.56   **Stanley Brothers. Long Journey Home.** County 739.

F6.57*   **Stanley Brothers. Their Original Recordings.** Melodeon MLP 7322.
    The Stanley Brothers perhaps remained closer to their country and traditional roots than other bluegrass groups. Their Appalachian, rural approach was broadcast on radio for twelve years from 1946 on, and it immensely affected the folk music revival as far as "honest and traditional" bluegrass music went. They formed the Clinch Mountain Boys and recorded in 1947-1948 for the Rich-R-Tone Company in Johnson City, Tennessee. All these tracks are on the Melodeon reissue. The Stanleys had been influenced by J. E. Mainer's Mountaineers (a pre-World War II transitional string band) and by the Monroe Brothers; but at this time, their own instrumentation was old-time, not bluegrass. Twenty-year-old Ralph's banjo was two finger clawhammer, not the later Scruggs style of three finger picking. Hence, they had the best old timey sound of any "bluegrass" group. In addition, Carter Stanley was beyond a doubt the best lead singer at that time in bluegrass music, and Ralph was technically proficient on banjo and as the very rural voice on the lonesome sound of high mountain harmony (especially on "I Can Tell You the Time"). In Pee Wee Lambert, they had an excellent mandolinist and high tenor singer. These classics are all excellent examples of the transition to modern bluegrass.
    The Stanleys sang the old songs ("Man of Constant Sorrow") and Monroe material, including the notorious "Molly and Tenbrooks," copied from a Monroe concert they had attended and released before Monroe even recorded it. The rivalry was so intense that Monroe quit Columbia when that company signed the Stanleys. With tunes such as "Little Maggie," "The Jealous Lover," a pre-Scruggs style "Little Birdie," and a transposed "Little Glass of Wine" by Carter (two versions heard here), the copying of the bluegrass sound was begun. With Columbia in 1949, the Stanleys now had a softer sound than Monroe, but it was more "lonesome" and rurally archaic despite some emulation of Monroe. They began to record sacred music, and some emotionalism spilled over to their other sessions.
    In 1953, they moved to Mercury, which signed them to fill the gap left by Flatt and Scruggs's moving to Columbia. They created many stirring items. The Collector's Classics are all Mercury items previously available as SR 60884 or MGW 12317, recorded in 1954-1956. Pee Wee Lambert was still with the group, but Howdy Forrester was added on fiddle. Ralph created some strumming instrumentals. His clawhammer style played with the back of his fingernails had given way to a modified Scruggs style (the clawhammer method, or frailing, was an old technique that emphasized the rhythm more than the melody). In line with the Stanleys' more traditional quality and their hymn-like sound, even in secular numbers,

Ralph now took an older approach similar to that of George Pegram and Bascom Lunsford. It was three finger style, but not as bluesy as the Scruggs style; there was double-thumbing and single-noting but little syncopation. Material from these sessions included "The Weary Heart You Stole Away," "Won't You Be Mine?," "Our Last Goodbye," "I'm Lonesome without You," "I Just Got Wise," "Calling from Heaven," "Lonesome and Blue," and "A Life of Sorrow."

The Stanleys toured in the 1950s and early 1960s, appearing at colleges, coffee houses, folk festivals, and even in Europe. The County reissue of Wango recordings done in 1961-1963, while reflecting their wider exposure, does show the intensity of their moral roots in the Virginia Clinch Mountain area, home of the Carter Family and the Stoneman Family. This is mainly a trio session, with the Stanleys and the guitar of George Shuffler. Yet, the range of tunes plus musical integration of a small ensemble clearly show the versatility of the Stanleys. Traditional items include "Will You Miss Me?," "Pretty Polly," "Wildwood Flowers," "East Virginia Blues," and "Cluck Old Hen."

F6.58*   **Stanley Brothers.** King 615.

F6.59*   **Stanley Brothers. America's Finest Five String Banjo Hootenanny.** King 872.

F6.60*   **Stanley Brothers. Best.** Starday 953.

F6.61*   **Stanley Brothers. Sing the Songs They Like Best.** Starday 772.

F6.62   **Stanley Brothers. Together for the Last Time.** Rebel SLP 1512.
Rockabilly music killed the career of the Stanleys, yet they stuck together as a group. Their Starday recordings were good music ("Rank Stranger," "How Far to Little Rock," "Shackles and Chains," and "Lover's Quarrel"), but they had little commercial success. They were asked to record many modern country items, they did so, and one result was a proliferation of low-keyed albums. Some of the best songs, though, were very good, such as "I'll Take the Blame," "Wild Side of Life," and "Mountain Dew"; and the Stanleys did more to bring country music and bluegrass together than any other group in either camp. Flatt and Scruggs at this time were mainly recording pop and r 'n' b material, and generally turning off the devoted "purist" fan. Yet the tolerant bluegrass collector will recognize older roots in commercial country music.

In the early 1960s, the Stanleys got caught up in the folk revival, which emphasized traditional sounds. As they were the most rural of groups, they were easily accepted by coffee houses and colleges. King 872, by its title, tried to cash in on this by presenting a program of all instrumentals, featuring Ralph's mountain style banjo. The best of all the recordings from the 1956-1966 period (from the end of the Mercury contract to Carter's death) was undoubtedly King 615, which included Ralph's very important instrumentals "Clinch Mountain Backstep," "Train 45," and "Mastertone March." Excellent vocals were done for "Midnight Ramble," "How Mountain Girls Can Love," "Keep a Memory," and "Think of What You've Done." Carter Stanley died in 1966. Their last live show together was at Bill Monroe's Brown County Jamboree in October of that year. The tapes, which show great involvement with the audience, include such instant classics as "Stone Walls and Steel Bars," some Carter Family (such as "Single Girl"), wonderful sacred items such as "Boat of Love" and "Take Me Home Savior," plus different remakes of "Little Birdie" and "Rovin' Gambler."

F6.63*   **Eric Weissberg. Dueling Banjos.** Warner Brothers BS 2683.
    This album is most of an earlier influential album entitled *New Dimensions in Banjo and Bluegrass* (Elektra 238; long deleted). It originally had eighteen tracks, but was cut down to sixteen to accommodate two tracks by Weissberg and Steve Mandel ("Dueling Banjos" and "End of a Dream") that had appeared in the film *Deliverance*. Otherwise, the sixteen reissued tracks comprise a set of some of the earliest and best examples of northern urban banjo music—mainly a show of technical skill. Marshall Brickman is the second banjoist, but he also plays solo on "Hard Ain't It Hard" and "Mountain Dew" (in both these cases, Weissberg is playing mandolin), or else he fingerpicks a guitar. Gorden Terry is the fiddler. In its original guise, this was a very important album for introducing bluegrass to folk music, and it ranks in impact with the Folkways anthology of Scruggs-style banjo.

STANDARDS

F6.64   **Bailey Brothers. Have You Forgotten?** Rounder 1018.
    This is volume six of the Early Days of Bluegrass series on Rounder Records. Charlie and Danny Bailey were a duo from Knoxville, Tennessee, and from 1947 through 1953, they recorded their brand of sweet harmonies for the Rich-R-Tone and Canary labels. Fourteen tracks from that period are here, such as "Rattlesnake Daddy Blues," "Happy Valley Special," "I Never Will Marry," and "Step out in the Sunshine." They were the first to bring the duo sound, as exemplified by the Blue Sky Boys and other brother duos, to the world of bluegrass. Their five piece ensemble included Carl Butler and Tater Tate. There are excellent notes in an attractive booklet.

F6.65   **Kenny Baker. A Baker's Dozen Country Fiddle Tunes.** County 730.

F6.66   **Kenny Baker. Portrait of a Bluegrass Fiddler.** County 719.
    Baker has been Monroe's fiddle player off and on since 1956. During his youth he absorbed many influences, including that of Django Reinhardt's hot string jazz band in France. For bluegrass, his prime influence has been the great Chubby Wise (with Monroe in the early 1940s, and later with Hank Snow). On both of these albums, Baker is backed by two completely different quartets—but then he is doing two different things involving different techniques for the country violin and the bluegrass violin. The former is on County 730, and it is a showcase for the country side of life, with emphasis on humor, dances, and skits (through Charlie Poole's "Ragtime Annie," "Sail away Ladies," "Greenleaf Breakdown," "Johnny the Blacksmith," and "Denver Belle"). County 719 has the bluegrass originals of Baker, often based on traditional tunes from a number of sources (his father, Bill Monroe, Red Herring, the Dillards, etc.). The group here is composed

of Del McCoury, Vic Jordan, Roland White and Doug Green. Both albums have twelve selections, and both provide a good contrast between the bluesy, hard edge of bluegrass and the sentimental sweetness of country music.

F6.67* **Kenny Baker and Joe Greene. High Country.** County 714.
Two of the leading bluegrass fiddlers combine here for a sterling, definitive set embracing the twin fiddle repertoire. Accompaniment on the other four traditional bluegrass instruments is provided by a Kentucky-based band. Of the two fiddlers, Greene is the one who has absorbed the most influences (bluegrass, Texas, Canadian, and western swing styles). Baker is more a pure performer in the old time music continuum, having played with Bill Monroe off and on for more than twenty years. Thus, the latter plays lead melody, while Greene weaves around with the harmony. Patterns are set up, and improvisation even appears possible. Dave Freeman provides good descriptive notes, both biographical and musical. The twelve selections include "Birdie," "Stoney Creek," "Boating up Sandy," "Friday Night Waltz," and the Greene composition "High Point."

F6.68 **Hylo Brown.** Collectors Classics CC 5.

F6.69 **Hylo Brown. Bluegrass Goes to College.** Starday SLP 204.
Hylo Brown was a very proficient singer and guitarist, with a mellow rustic voice that suited bluegrass music. In the 1960s, he went onto the college circuit and performed on many campuses. The Collectors Classics album is a reissue of his material from the 1950s. Thus, both albums survey a little more than a decade in his musical recording career. Included are "When It's Lamplighting Time in the Valley," "Gathering Flowers from the Hillside," "Put My Little Shoes Away," "The Old Home Town," and "Blue Eyed Darling."

F6.70 **Bill Clifton. Blue Ridge Mountain Blues.** County 740.

F6.71* **Bill Clifton. Carter Family Memorial Album.** Starday SLP 146.
Bill Clifton once led a recording group called the Dixie Mountain Boys in the United States, but now he resides in England. During his long career, he has shone both as a soloist and as a partner in a duo. He was one of the first organizers of bluegrass festivals, and he has traveled and recorded throughout the world. In all cases, he is a superb organizer and leader of bluegrass musical groups, and the County record is a prime example of this. These fourteen tracks were cut in 1957-1958 for Mercury and Starday; Clifton as leader retained the master tapes, and it is from these that this recording was re-pressed. Hence, the exceptionally clean sound. His accompanists were Ralph Stanley, Curley Lambert, John Duffey, etc.—all the leaders in second-generation bluegrass of the late 1950s. Not only did Clifton assemble the band, but his sure hand picked the material with an eye to solo material for each prominent performer. Included are "Cedar Grove," "Living the Right Life Now," "Another Broken Heart," "When You Kneel at Mother's Grave," and the title selection. In May of 1961, he was back in the Starday Studio to record several Carter Family tunes, for he was a Carter Family buff. This album in collating the different tracks, clearly shows the influence of the Carters on the bluegrass repertoire and on bluegrass guitars. For this occasion, Clifton used twin fiddles.

F6.72   **Connie and Babe. Basic Bluegrass.** Rounder 0042.
     Connie Gately and Babe Lofton have co-led this group since the late 1940s. Their style has not changed much, if at all, and there has only been one personnel change among the six players since they started more than thirty years ago. Along the way, they made a few recordings for the Republic and Starday labels. Their repertoire is tight and standard—really "basic." The twelve items are reflective of what bluegrass is all about. "Heavenly Light" is a traditional, camp-meeting uptempo hymn. "I'll Never Make You Cry" is recreated from their 1953 Republic session and has now entered the classic collection of early bluegrass. Instrumentals include the old time "Sail Away Lady" and a banjo-mandolin-fiddle version of "Auld Lang Syne." Apart from solid originals (mostly by Connie), there is also the contemporary "Are You All Alone?" (written by the great Ira Louvin). This disc is a solid example of the typical working bluegrass band whose members by now know each other's movements on an intimate basis.

F6.73*   **Stoney Cooper and Wilma Lee. Sunny Side of the Mountain.** Harmony HS 11178.
     This husband and wife team were probably the most traditional of all performers in the modern country music field. They believed in mountain ballads, Appalachian hymns, and uptempo instrumentals. Many later bluegrass musicians passed through their band. Stoney was a fiddler from West Virginia, and together with his wife, appeared on the WWVA Jamboree and other radio stations. They composed "Cheated Too," "I Tell My Heart," "Heartbreak Street" and "Loving You." Their version of "Midnight Special" was the best-known and best-loved of all traditional variants of this song. They have enormous respect from the bluegrass world.

F6.74   **Red Cravens and the Bray Brothers. 419 W. Main.** Rounder 0015.
     These recordings were made in Clinton, Illinois, at the address given in the title of the album, and they were originally meant for radio broadcasting in the mid-1960s. Nate Bray is a very good mandolin performer, guitarist Red Cravens sings lead vocals (as on the excellent "Pass Me By," a version of "Pass Me Not, O Gentle Savior"), John Hartford fiddles on five tunes, and Harley Bray and Francis Bray play banjo and string bass, respectively. This record is characterized by a dynamic verve and drive, especially in such breakdown songs as "East Virginia Blues," "Bluegrass Breakdown," and "Jingle Bell Breakdown." As was common with so many brother groups who have played for quite some time as a unit, the band is very tight.

F6.75   **J. D. Crowe. Bluegrass Holiday.** King Bluegrass KB 524.
     Crowe was the definitive banjo player behind Jimmy Martin for so many years. His group on this disc is the Kentucky Mountain Boys, and comprised Red Allen, Doyle Lawson, and Bobby Sloane. Together they are very effective on "Little Girl in Tennessee," "Philadelphia Lawyer," "Helen," and the Stanley Brothers' tune "Train 45." The music is built around Crowe's dynamic banjo, but he also contributes very much to the harmony singing, just under Red Allen's high tenor.

F6.76   **Dixie Gentlemen. Blues and Bluegrass.** Old Homestead 90024.
This group features Tut Taylor on Dobro and Vassar Clements on fiddle, plus the usual high harmonies of vocal lines. Tracks include "How Many Hearts Have You Broken?," "Little Green Pill," "Dixie Ride," "Soldier's Return," and "Flint River Ramble."

F6.77   **Lester Flatt. Best.** RCA APL1-0578.
All the material here comes from after the time that Flatt left Scruggs to pursue his own musical continuation in the mainstream of bluegrass. Thus, he had assembled some of the top session men in the music field, plus others who joined him on tours (such as Roland White, Howdy Forrester, and Josh Graves). Titles include one of his narrative religious stories ("Father's Table Grace") and "Backin' to Birmingham," "Cabin on the Hill," "The Country Boy," and a few standards earlier done with Earl Scruggs.

F6.78   **Alice Foster and Hazel Dickens. Won't You Come and Sing for Me?** Folkways FTS 31034.

F6.79   **Alice Gerrard and Hazel Dickens. Hazel and Alice.** Rounder 0027.
Both of these discs are a happy combination of old time and bluegrass music, which is not so unusual as the latter evolved from the former. But most new bluegrass records seem to have commercially derived, third generation materials. Alice Foster is city born, plays the guitar, and sings lead (somewhere along the line she changed her name to Gerrard). Hazel Dickens is country bred, plays the bass, and sings high tenor. Both are members of the Strange Creek Singers (Arhoolie 4004). The Folkways disc was recorded in 1967 and fills a decided gap in bluegrass music, which is usually a male preserve. It features top-flight bluegrass musicians such as Lamar Grier, David Grisman, and Billy Baker. They work on such items from the 1920s and 1930s as the delicately sacred title song, or, with bluesy harmony, perform "The One I Love Is Gone." The Rounder collection comes from 1973 and is a more polished performance. Besides a few unaccompanied duets of old time or blues materials, their backup players include Mike Seeger, Tracey Schwartz, and Lamont Grier. Original material is on the second side and is largely based on their own feminist experiences. Titles include "Mining Camp Blues," "Green Rolling Hills of West Virginia," "Two Soldiers," and "Tomorrow I'll Be Gone."

F6.80*   **Greenbriar Boys. Best.** Vanguard VSD 79317.
Formed in 1958 as a college-type bluegrass group with urban roots, the Greenbriar Boys featured Bob Yellin on loping banjo, Eric Weissberg, and the tenor lead of John Herald. Ralph Rinzler replaced Weissberg the next year, and Frank Wakefield replaced Rinzler in 1964. This album represents selections from their three discs for Vanguard, and the tracks did much to assist the revival of bluegrass during the folk boom of the early sixties. The group played at Newport, and they were recorded by a predominantly modern folk label. Tracks include "Blues My Naughty Sweetie Gave to Me" (a bluegrass version of the jazz classic), "Alligator Man," the folk story of "Stewball," "Levee Breakdown Blues," and the classic "Little Birdie."

F6.81   **Hodges Brothers. Watermelon on the Vine.** Arhoolie 5001.
The brothers—Felix (fiddle and vocal), Ralph (guitar, mandolin and vocal), and James (vocals)— compose a very pleasant and interesting old time style string band. The music is very listenable and provides a glimpse at the roots of bluegrass. Their repertoire is wide, encompassing fiddle tunes, instrumentals ("Bile Dem Cabbage Down" is memorable), ballads, blues, and gospel. Half the album was recorded in the early 1960s with John White's bass and vocals; the other half of the recordings were made in 1969 without White. The earlier songs work better both because of their harmony singing and, perhaps, more use of the mandolin than in the later songs. Good tunes include "Leaves Is Falling on the Ground," "It Won't Be Long," and "Little Church House on the Hill."

F6.82*   **Snuffy Jenkins. Carolina Bluegrass.** Arhoolie 5011.

F6.83   **Snuffy Jenkins and Pappy Sherrill. 33 Years of Pickin' and Pluckin'.** Rounder 0005.
These albums with Jenkins represent one of the earliest forms of bluegrass music. Indeed, Snuffy Jenkins influenced the young Earl Scruggs; however, the albums balance the rapid fire of Scruggs's style with selections that show an even earlier, less regular (and perhaps more interesting) technique. The fiddle playing of Homer Sherrill is also first rate (the first album does not give him a joint credit, but both performers have been playing together for over 33 years). He provides solid interplay with the other instruments, as well as taking some fine breaks. But perhaps the most interesting songs on the Arhoolie album are two guitar and washboard pieces, "Step It up and Go" and "Born in Hard Luck." The first is an old Blind Boy Fuller-Washboard Sam number; the second is a version of "Talking Hard Luck Blues," with Jenkins switching to guitar. This recording was made in 1962, with assistance from a string trio that pushes on harmony numbers. Titles include: "Watermelon Hangin' on the Vine," "Possum up a Gum Stump," "Big Eared Mule," and so forth—in the same vein as the Rounder album, recorded about eight years later, and featuring even more traditional songs that have since become classics in bluegrass: "Texas Quickstep," "Sally Johnson," "Cherry Blossom Waltz," "Alabama Jubilee," the western swing of "Beaumont Rag," the novelty of "When the Bumblebee Backed up to Me and Pushed," the blues of Kokomo Arnold and Cow Cow Davenport ("Milk Cow Blues"), Walter Davis ("C & W Railroad Blues"), and "Lonesome Road Blues" and "Model T Blues."

F6.84   **Bill Keith and Jim Rooney. Living on the Mountain.** Prestige FL 14002.
Forming this ad hoc bluegrass group was one of the first things that Bill Keith did after departing the Country Gentlemen. The other members were Joe Val and Herb Hooven, both later influences on the Boston bluegrass interpretative scene. Titles include "Devil's Dream," "One Morning in May," "Pretty Polly," and "Salty Dog." Emphasis was about equal for modern tunes and traditional bluegrass songs.

F6.85*   **Lonesome Pine Fiddlers. Collectors Classics CC 3.**
One of the best trios in the middle 1950s went under the name Lonesome Pine Fiddlers, and it was an odd assortment of anonymous performers. The

particular group here featured both Bobby and Sonny Osborne (who had played with Jimmy Martin and Bill Monroe, respectively, just prior to this recording). Red Allen completed the trio. By shifting the lead from tenor Allen to high tenor Bobby, smooth harmonies resulted. This simple exchange affected almost all of bluegrass in emulating the high lonesome sound of a vocal trio. Tracks here include "You Broke Your Promise," "Nobody Cares," "My Brown Eyed Darling," "Dirty Dishes," and "That's Why You Left Me So Blue."

F6.86   **Del McCoury. Sings Bluegrass.** Arhoolie F 5006
McCoury is a fine example of the continuing traditions of bluegrass; he took his early training with Bill Monroe before striking out on his own. This album features him on guitar and lead vocals with Billy Baker on fiddle, Bill Emerson on banjo, Wayne Yates on mandolin, and several session bass men. This is a conservative bluegrass release with many top-notch traditional songs: "You're a Flower in the Wildwood," "Fire on the Mountain," "Roll in My Sweet Baby's Arms," and "Prisoner's Song." The roots of the music predominate.

F6.87*   **Rose Maddox. Sings Bluegrass.** Capitol ECR 8178 (Japanese issue).
This is an unusual record on two counts. First, female leads in bluegrass music are rare. Second, Maddox is better known as a country singer; but here she assembled an excellent group, including the great Bill Monroe on mandolin, Red Smiley on guitar, and Don Reno on banjo. The time is 1962, and she sings lead on several Monroe numbers, including "Footprints in the Snow," "Molly and Tenbrooks," "My Rose of Old Kentucky," "Uncle Pen," and "Blue Moon of Kentucky." This is a first-rate disc that has been revered for years by cultists among bluegrass fans.

F6.88   **Charlie Monroe, v.1-2.** two discs. County 538/9.

F6.89   **Charlie Monroe. Sings Again.** Pine Mountain. PMR 272.
Charlie Monroe was the most aggressive of the Monroe Brothers. They recorded during 1936-1938 after a stint on radio, but Birch retired and Bill quit over musical differences. Charlie continued with a group called the Kentucky Pardners, and he recorded and performed his brand of country bluegrass through the 1940s, 1950s, and 1960s—with sidemen as important as Ira Louvin, Slim Martin, Curly Seckler, and Lester Flatt—for Decca, Starday, RCA, and a host of smaller labels. The two County issues are from 16-inch radio transcriptions done in North Carolina in 1944, and they are particularly instructive for a number of reasons. Monroe never actually recorded during this period, bluegrass music was in its formative stages, and many country stars were influential through the airwaves. Much of the music is lighthearted, in his bluegrass-country fusion. This important historical document illustrates the changes of mood and attitude throughout rural areas, a shift caused by the "Golden Age of Radio." Around forty titles are performed in all on this noonday show, and there are some revealing tracks performed by Lester Flatt before he joined the other Monroe brother. The brisk but fluid guitar style of Charlie Monroe is perhaps best heard on the Pine Mountain reissue of Rem and Starday material from the 1960s. Here, Monroe had returned to the studios to recreate his successes of the past, including "Down in the Willow Garden," "Phonograph Record," and "So Blue."

F6.90   **Clyde Moody. Moody's Bluesy Bluegrass.** Old Homestead OHS 90013.
Moody first recorded for ARC in 1935, which resulted in the brilliant
"Six White Horses," recreated here with a powerful driving rhythm. His career
included stints with Wade Mainer, five years as Bill Monroe's guitarist, and then
a spell with Roy Acuff at the Grand Ole Opry. He has the dubious distinction of
creating the modern country-sound ballad styling (with a firm, slightly nasal but
smooth baritone voice). At the same time, he did enough waltzes to become known
as the "Country and Western Waltz King." This present album contains superb
renditions of his 1947/48 hits "If I Had My Life to Live Over" and "Shenandoah
Waltz," which fall, respectively, into the above two categories. His bluesy style is
reminiscent of the "Nashville Stonewall Blues" type, but is more assertive and
wishful. Material here also includes traditional items like "Columbus Stockade
Blues," "Sitting on Top of the World," and "One Step More," among the thirteen
tracks.

F6.91   **Glen Neaves and the Virginia Mountain Boys. Country Bluegrass from
Southwest Virginia.** Folkways FA 3830.
Traditional music abounds here, from Child ballad derivations to basic
Appalachian-developed music. Neaves's expert fiddle provides that down home
bluegrass feeling so vitally needed for such items as the older "Barbara Allen,"
"Careless Love," and "Cripple Creek." Cullen Galyean (banjo), Ivor Melton
(mandolin), and Bobby Harrison (guitar) provide musical assistance for such other
tunes as "Don't Go out Tonight," "Drunkard's Dream," "Nigger Trader," and
"Drinking from the Fountain." As with all Folkways records, there are excellent
accompanying notes detailing the Virginia scene of bluegrass music.

F6.92   **Frank Necessary and the Stone Mountain Boys. Cimarron Bluegrass.**
Old Homestead OHS 90010.
This album is full of fine cross-fertilized music, especially bluegrass married
to western swing and the vocal stylings of the Sons of the Pioneers. There are
excellent arrangements of such numbers associated with the West as "Cool Water,"
"Cimarron," and "I'm So Lonesome I Could Cry," through which the strident
chords of bluegrass mandolin and banjo can be heard. Traditional items include
"Uncle Pen," "John Henry," and "Take This Hammer."

F6.93*   **Osborne Brothers.** MGM GAS 140.

F6.94*   **Osborne Brothers. Best.** two discs. MCA 2-4088.

F6.95   **Osborne Brothers. Bluegrass Instrumentals.** MGM SE 4090.
Bobby played mandolin and sang high lead tenor; Sonny played five string
banjo and sang baritone. The latter also performed with Bill Monroe at the tender
age of fourteen! Bobby was with Jimmy Martin. Together with Red Allen, they
formed a version of the Lonesome Pine Fiddlers, but later recorded under their
own names for MGM, beginning in 1956. The BAS 140 album collects a meager
ten items of "best" recordings, including George Jones's "White Lightning," Jimmie
Rodgers's "Muleskinner Blues," "Lost Highway," the country sounds of "Once
More" (with Red Allen), and the dynamic "Ruby Are You Mad," which featured

Bobby's pinched soaring high lead. As with many brother duos, there was an intricate relationship between their banjo and mandolin, and this is best revealed on the instrumental album, which contains "John Henry Blues," "Old Joe Clark," the fascinating "Banjo Boy Chimes," and the effervescent "Red Wing." In 1959, they began to establish themselves on the college circuit, and it was not long before they introduced electrified instrumentation, being the first bluegrass group to do so. They merged with aspects of the Nashville sound when they switched to MCA in 1969, recording the fast and sentimental "Rocky Top" (a perennial favorite at concerts), "Memories," "Roll Muddy River," and "Cuckoo Bird." Commercial drumming was also introduced as they became swept up in the folk-rock activities of the late 1960s. Later, in 1975, to the delight of older fans, they abandoned the electrified approach, but Sonny still retained his famous six string banjo (with an added low "G" string).

F6.96   **Olabelle Reed.** Rounder 0021.

F6.97   **Olabelle Reed.** Starday SLP 214.
       Banjoist Reed formed a duo with her brother Alex Campbell on guitar, and they performed a stream of North Carolina music, a variation on the mountain style of bluegrass music. The commercial album is the Starday, recorded in the 1960s with a Dobro supplied by Deacon Brumfield (heard on "Deacon's Dobro Boogie"). Yet she finally came into her own with the 1972 Rounder outing, recorded in Pennsylvania with members of the Reed Family. Only fiddler John Miller was not related to other members of the quartet. The traditional approach sums it all up: strength and sensitivity, depth of feelings, and true religion. Older songs include "The Soldier and the Lady" and "Rosewood Casket"; sacred numbers include "Wayfaring Pilgrim," "God Put a Rainbow in the Clouds," "My Epitaph," and "I Believe." Originals, almost all becoming standards in bluegrass music, include "High on a Mountain" and "The Springtime of Life."

F6.98   **Don Reno. Banjo Special.** King 787.

F6.99*   **Don Reno. Fastest Five Strings Alive.** King 1065.

F6.100   **Don Reno. Folk Ballads and Instrumentals.** King 579.
       Reno is perhaps the most brilliant and polished banjoist in all of bluegrass. He devised many innovative licks based on styles derived from electric lead guitar and pedal steel guitar techniques. These three discs highlight his long career with King records, during which time he perfected some of the most enduring bluegrass instrumentals, or " 'grass" versions of popular material, such as "Limehouse Blues," "Remington Ride" (borrowed from the pedal steel method), "Birth of the Blues," "Beer Barrel Polka," and "Carry Me Back to Old Virginia." Original material— he exhibited tremendous compositional skills—included "Banjo Signal," "Please Don't Feel Sorry," "Tennessee Cut up Breakdown," "Interstate 81," and "Washington and Lee Swing." On most of these recordings, he was accompanied by the urbane guitarist Red Smiley.

F6.101   **Don Reno and Bill Harrell.** Rural Rhythm RR 171.
When Red Smiley died, Bill Harrell assumed his place as partner to Don Reno. This disc presents nineteen (!) re-recordings of traditional materials by the new group, and it appears as if Harrell just stepped into the shoes of the deceased Smiley. Here are sterling renditions of "Nine Pound Hammer," "Great Speckled Bird," "Keep on the Sunny Side," "Man of Constant Sorrow," "Dill Pickle Rag," "Molly and Tenbrooks," etc.

F6.102   **Larry Richardson. Blue Ridge Bluegrass.** County 702.
For this set, Richardson concentrated on traditional materials delivered in a traditional style. His banjo was augmented by the swift guitar of Eddy Sharp in a program that included "Let Me Fall," "More Pretty Girls Than One," and the sacred "Paul and Silas."

F6.103   **Curly Seckler. Sings Again.** County 732.
Backed by the Shenandoah Cutups (Tater Tate, Billy Edwards, Hershel Sizemore, and John Palmer—all respected, working bluegrass players), Curly Seckler presents a varied program of music that he has been involved with in the past. For a dozen years he was tenor with Flatt and Scruggs, and indeed, he might just be the best tenor still actively performing in bluegrass. Items here include such F and S classics as "Don't This Road Look Rough and Rocky," "That Old Book of Mine," and "Old Salty Dog Blues." Many other tunes harken back to earlier recordings ("Moonlight in My Cabin," "You Took My Sunshine"). A good, tight little album, this will certainly bear many repeated playings.

F6.104   **Shenandoah Cut-Ups. Bluegrass Autumn.** Revonah 904.
Traditional bluegrass (including "Never Ending Love for You," "Banjolina," "Bluegrass Minor") here is sung and performed by a good group of second-line bluegrass artists—Billy Edwards, Tater Tate, Hershel Sizemore, and John Palmer.

F6.105   **Arthur Smith. Battling Banjos.** Monument Z 32259.
Smith is the person who originally co-authored "Duelin' Banjos" with Don Reno over twenty years ago, but today, he does not get the credit due. It is recreated here under its original title "Feudin' Banjos." Throughout this album, Smith is on tenor or four string, and his partner Bobby Thompson has a five string; the original melody was intended for two banjos, not banjo plus guitar. This is an instrumental album, with occasional rhythm accompanying the two banjos. It gets off to a weak start with polka material but picks up with "Just Joshin'," a rip-snorting, breakneck bluegrass item by Buck "Josh" Graves (once with Flatt and Scruggs). The second side is almost all bluegrass, with a superb "Foggy Mountain Breakdown" and a new "Ringing Banjos." A dazzling virtuosic record, this should not be ignored, but it has no liner notes.

F6.106   **Larry Sparks.** Starday 480.

F6.107   **Larry Sparks. The Lonesome Ramblers.** King Bluegrass KB 527.
Guitarist Sparks is ably assisted by diverse artists on these two discs from the beginning and middle of his career. The earlier Starday features "Six More Miles,"

"Faded Love," "Memories and Dreams," "Life of Sorrow," "I Am the Man," and "Just Because." With Wendy Miller on mandolin (plus banjoist Dave Evans, fiddler Ralph Meadows, and bassist Art Weidner), he recorded "Goodbye Little Darling," "Think of What You've Done," and "Dark Hollow" for King Bluegrass.

F6.108   Stoneman Family. White Lightning. Starday SLP 393.

Pop Stoneman had been a strong innovator and influence in old time music; by the 1960s, his style had transmuted into a mixture of old time music, bluegrass, modern Nashville, and Hank Williams's honky tonk styles. His family had grown up, and they were expressing their interests in an attempt to appeal to a wide-ranging audience. This combination of styles even led to a bizarre pop orientation in "Out of School." The late Scotty Stoneman held the group together with his flashy fiddle; after his father's and then his own death, the Family was never the same. This album from the 1960s included "Talking Fiddle Blues" (the best tune devised to show off the violin), "Little Susie," "Going Home," the story song "Sinking of the Titanic," and the perennial "Orange Blossom Special."

F6.109*   Don Stover. Things in Life. Rounder 0014.

F6.110   Don Stover. West Virginia Coal Miner's Blues. Old Homestead OHS 90011.

Stover has played banjo with a number of groups, including the illustrious Lilly Brothers. Basically, he's a non-aggressive "nice guy," a real gentleman in a musical genre known for its "country gentlemen." Unfortunately, though, this lack of push has led to few recordings under his own name. His clawhammer banjo is rare in bluegrass music; so much the better, for then it is a real pleasure to hear his infrequent stylings. The material on the Rounder issue is totally pure mountain and bluegrass, devoid of any trace of pop, urban folk, or country influences. David Grisman's mandolin solos are expert, and Dave Dillon provides a stunning tenor on the duets with Stover. Material is centered around Stover's West Virginia upbringing ("Old Coon Dog," "Birdie") and his early listening habits, plus serious additions to the coal mine repertoire ("Black Diamond," "Long Chain Charlie"—the latter with overdubbed blues guitar by Stover and a narrative story line). Most of the originals are instrumentals, and there are some sacred items as well.

Similar types of material appear on the Old Homestead. Most of it is traditional, such as "Salt River," "Greenback Dollar," and "Marching through Georgia," with some sacred ("Didn't They Crucify My Lord?"). Fiddler John Hall and vocalist-guitarist Dave Dillon (both also on the Rounder) project strong solo patterns. There are fewer originals than the first disc, but they appear to be more consistent with the old time themes of Old Homestead's record productions. His title cut is very well executed, adding to the string of mining lore songs. The highlight, though, is a stirring rendition of "Amelia Earhart's Last Flight," which is a very sympathetic reading.

F6.111   Joe Val and the New England Bluegrass Boys. One Morning in May. Rounder 0003.

This is one of the better issuances of second generation bluegrass. Joe Valliante and Herb Appelin, mandolin and guitar, team on some of the closest harmony duets yet heard. The soaring tenor of Val plus his stinging mandolin work is simply stunning. Along with Bob French and Bob Tidwell, the group returns to the Monroe and the Louvins' roots in the blue yodels on "Sparkling Brown Eyes," the close knit harmony on the Louvins' "I Don't Believe You've Met My Baby," and the haunting "Dark Hollow"—plus the title selection, the early British classic, "One Morning in May."

F.112*   **Mac Wiseman. 16 Great Performances.** Dot ABDP 4009.

Wiseman has had an exceptional recording career, beginning with Molly O'Day's first sixteen songs for Columbia in 1946-1947, a stint with Flatt and Scruggs in 1948, a tour with Bill Monroe in 1949, and his own solo work in 1950-1975 with Dot records (he recently changed labels). In his instrumental work, Wiseman has been influenced by Monroe; in his vocals and approach to music, he looks to Hank Snow. Half of the tracks on this album, which spans his career for Dot, are traditional. Some of the tunes are rare items from the past (Wiseman has only had one commercial hit: "Jimmy Brown the Newsboy" in 1959). Thus, "'Tis Sweet to Be Remembered" is handled in a traditional country style, while the uptempo "Bluebirds Are Singing for Me" is taken at the bluegrass clip. In most of his work, Wiseman used twin fiddling to complement his high voice and crystal phrasing. Other titles include "I'll Still Write Your Name in the Sand," "I Wonder How the Old Folks Are At Home," and "Where Is My Boy Tonight?"

NEWGRASS

F6.113*   **Red Allen and the Allen Brothers. Allengrass.** Lemco 612.

Allen had four sons whom he had literally trained in the 'grass tradition. They are all here, with occasional rhythm assistance from four other non-related performers: Red Allen himself has one of the highest, clear, pure tenors in the business, and the real key to the success of this album is the harmonizing of the two tenors (led by Red) and a baritone. Side one features Red and sons on five numbers, including the Louvin Brothers' "O Childish Love," the Callahan Brothers' "Story of Two," and the traditional "House of the Rising Sun." Rounding out the first side is the sixth cut, "Proud Mary," a weird breakneck version that is mercifully over in two minutes, but is representative of the "newgrass" approach. Side two is basically the four sons alone, singing original material except for Tim Hardin's "Reason to Believe." Neal Allen (who died quite recently) replaces his father on tenor; he also wrote most of the tunes here. Some drums, Dobro and electric bass appear on "Hobo Joe" and "Willy Boy."

F6.114   **Mike Auldridge. Bluegrass and Blues.** Takoma D 1041.

Auldridge is now the Dobroist with the Seldom Scene, but previously he had made two records for Takoma. This one features avid assistance from John Duffey, David Bromberg, Vassar Clements, and Linda Ronstadt (the latter providing harmony vocals). This is a very pleasant mixture of traditional and contemporary items in the "newgrass" form, such as "New Camptown Races," the soul hit "Killing Me Softly," "Eight More Miles to Louisville," and "Bottom Dollar."

F6.115   **Bluegrass Alliance. American Heritage. AH 401-21.**

F6.116   **Bluegrass Alliance. Newgrass.** American Heritage AH 401-30.
Dan Crary, an excellent flatpicker and superior vocalist, leads this progressive
bluegrass group through uptempo versions of "East Virginia Blues," "Beaumont
Rag" (the western swing number), "Red Haired Boy," and "Love Come Home."
The *Newgrass* album is more in the contemporary bag, with such items as "Where
Were You?," and "Gentle on My Mind."

F6.117*   **Country Gazette. A Traitor in Our Midst.** United Artists UAS 5596.
This quartet comprised Byron Berline (several times National Fiddle Champion), bassist Roger Bush, banjoist Alan Munde, and guitarist Kenny Wertz. Some
had played with the Flying Burrito Brothers; all were influenced by the fusion of
country-contemporary-bluegrass music. With the backing of a large company, they
easily became some of the leaders of the newer progressive bluegrass sounds. Titles
here include "Lost Indian," the Louvin Brothers' "I Wish You Knew," and "I
Might Take You Back Again."

F6.118   **Doug Dillard. Duelin' Banjo.** 20th Century T-409.
Dillard, master of the chromatic banjo and long a citified bluegrass hippy,
presents a varied program of bluegrass and 'grassified instrumentals. With Byron
Berline (once in the group Country Gazette, but not credited on this album) on
sweet violin, he romps through "My Grass Is Blue," which is based on Joplin's
ragtime epic, "The Entertainer." Assisting are brother Rodney (guitar and Dobro),
who also produced and arranged most of this disc, and several other performers,
depending on the instrumentation needed. This is sophisticated bluegrass, with
plenty of inside musical jokes scattered among the highlights. Interesting tracks
include "Bells of St. Mary's," which here gets its bluegrass outing twenty years
after the Drifters gave it an r 'n' b mode of attack. "Help Wanted" is a country
parody on such ditties, featuring Bill Martin reading classified ads. The title track
is notable for its honesty by remaining in the singular. There was only one banjo
in any version from 1973 or 1974; the original version was from the early fifties,
with Art Smith and Don Reno on, respectively, five string and tenor banjos—in
that case, two, not the present one.

F6.119   **Dillard and Clark. Through the Morning.** A & M SP 4203.
This lineup brings together Doug Dillard (the chromatic banjoist from the
Dillard Brothers), Gene Clark (from the folk-rock version of the Byrds), National
Fiddle Champion Byron Berline, Chris Hillman, and Sneeky Pete (on pedal steel
guitar). The latter three would form (or assist) the Flying Burrito Brothers, and
then transmute into Country Gazette. Their style here is a continuation of the folk
elements of the Dillards (Doug left because of musical differences, and the Dillards
without him pushed on to a harder, rock-oriented form of bluegrass); but it includes
profoundly slick, youth-oriented versions of such traditional songs as "Rocky Top"
and "Polly." Titles from this quintet include "No Longer a Sweetheart of Mine,"
"Corner Street Bar," "Kansas City Southern," and "Don't Let Me Know." This
is an engaging mixture of folk, bluegrass, and country elements, made the more
notable with the addition of the pedal steel guitar.

F6.120*   **Dillards. Country Tracks: Best of the Dillards.** Electra K 52035 (British issue).
The first version of the Dillards came together in 1958, with Doug's banjo and Rodney's guitar, plus Dean Webb on mandolin and Mitch Jayne on bass. Although most of the band's personnel was born in midwestern Missouri, they became California-based and were one of the first to engage in "progressive blue-grass" (later known as "newgrass"). Doug developed the chromatic banjo style that had a profound influence on upcoming performers who were disengaging themselves from the Scruggs style. In the chromatic version, notes are played with a ringing sound and also with an octave modifier. The 24 tracks here make this disc almost an hour long (good value here for the money), and many contrasts are presented as the evolution of the group becomes apparent. When Doug left, his replacement was Herb Pederson, and this presented a contrast in styles as well. Three instrumentals are of note here: the originals "Doug's Tune" and "Hickory Hollow," and the fast-paced version of "Duelin' Banjo" (note the singular title). Close harmony singing comes through on "Close the Door Lightly," "Dooley," and two Lennon-McCartney (Beatles') songs. The first is handled a cappella ("Yesterday"), while the second is given a fast bluegrass romp ("I've Just Seen a Face"). "I'll Fly Away" is also handled unaccompanied. Buddy Emmons contributes his pedal steel guitar on "Sundown."

F6.121*   **New Grass Revival.** Starday 482.
This 1972 recording was largely responsible for the emerging "newgrass" form of progressive music in the bluegrass genre. Just as Bill Monroe's group contributed the name "bluegrass," it looks as if mandolinist Sam Bush's group will contribute "newgrass." The basic characterization is fast picking and uptempo music with some electronic amplification for contemporary songs such as (heard here) "Body and Soul" (the jazz classic), "Great Balls of Fire" (the rock and roll classic), and the Leon Russell item, "Prince of Peace." Other material here comes from Vassar Clements in a western swing fusion that also included Norman Blake compositions, Dillard and Clark folk-rock songs, and some originals, especially Bush's own "I Wish I Said." Through overdubbing, Bush can be heard also on violin and guitar, as well as on his normal mandolin and vocals. The quartet includes Cortney Johnson (banjo), Curtis Burch (Dobro), and Ebo Walker (bass).

F6.122*   **Earl Scruggs. Family and Friends.** Columbia C 30584.

F6.123   **Earl Scruggs. I Saw the Light with Some Help from My Friends.** Columbia KC 31354.

F6.124*   **Earl Scruggs. Live at Kansas State.** Columbia KC 31758.
Scruggs-style banjo is mainly old timey in feel with a three finger approach; it is discussed at length under Flatt and Scruggs's material above (F6.27-31), but in the peculiar context of newgrass, Scruggs-style must be reiterated. It has a jazz-y, blues-y, and hence widely imitated, sound. The style fitted the banjo's sharp staccato sound, and highlighted ringing and slurring instead of "plunking" chord melodies. All virtuosity lies in the right hand. Through this style, Scruggs refashioned traditional, old time ballads and fiddle music into a banjo-emphasized

bluegrass music. During the 1960s, Flatt and Scruggs recorded highly commercial music, but musical differences split the group apart, and Scruggs began searching for "roots" and a musical genre.

The *Family and Friends* album comes from a 1971 National Educational Television sound track, and is perhaps the best transitional disc ever released. Earl was affected by his sons Randy and Gary plus all of the musical changes of the late sixties. In searching for musical peace, the Scruggs Family is assisted by contributions from Joan Baez, Doc Watson, the Byrds ("You Ain't Going Nowhere," by Bob Dylan), and the Morris Brothers ("Salty Dog") in a series of field recordings that even includes Dylan himself doing "Nashville Skyline Rag." There are also some conversational materials. KC 31354 carries this feeling along, with help from the country side of Vassar Clements, Norman Blake, Linda Ronstadt, and the Nitty Gritty Dirt Band. This is largely the electric bluegrass developed earlier by the Osborne Brothers (ranging from the traditional "Banks of the Ohio" to Johnny Cash's "Ring of Fire"). The *Kansas State* album puts it all together and fulfills his integration with early commercial country music, such as Jimmie Rodgers's "T Is for Texas," the traditional "Sally Goodwin," the jazz "Bugle Call Rag," and the modern folk of Dylan and of Joni Mitchell ("Both Sides Now"). Scruggs had by now assimilated many styles, and in doing so, he extended bluegrass to newgrass—the eclectic tastes of country-rock and folk-rock. Eventually, we suspect, all groups will be assimilated into one main sound.

F6.125   **II Generation. Head Cleaner.** Rebel 1533.

In the "newgrass" vein, this group promoted smooth, contemporary pop stylings with a bluegrass beat and feel. Titles include "Train," "Virginia," "If," and "Raining in Nashville."

F6.126*   **Seldom Scene. Acts One, Two and Three.** three discs. Rebel 1511, 1520, and 1528.

F6.127   **Seldom Scene. Old Trains.** Rebel 1536.

F6.128*   **Seldom Scene. Recorded Live at the Cellar Door.** two discs. Rebel 1547/8.

The Seldom Scene (with John Duffy and Mike Auldridge) began life as a group of professional people in the Maryland-Washington area, playing just for fun. They all had "day" jobs and rarely performed in person: they only recorded, for Rebel Records. All of their music is smooth, crisp, virtuosic, and in good taste. Their style is clearly eclectic and in the so-called "progressive" bluegrass, or new-grass, idiom. All of their first four albums contained minor gems of reinterpretation. The older songs were represented by "Darling Corey," "Another Lonesome Day," "Faded Love," and "Muddy Water." Sacred tunes included "House of Gold" and "Heaven." Bluegrass versions of contemporary hits included "Sweet Baby James," "City of New Orleans," "Mary Lou" (the Rick Nelson song), and "Early Morning Rain" (from Gordon Lightfoot).

Duffy took most of the vocals as well as playing his mandolin; John Starling played guitar, while both Mike Auldridge and Ben Eldridge contributed Dobros. Tom Gray was the rock steady bassist. Although many train songs are scattered throughout their works, a special concept album was recorded devoted to trains: "Appalachian Train," "Different Roads," "C & O Canal," "Traveling On and On," and "Pan American." Throughout, every note is in place and the harmonies are exceptional. In person, they are also very good, perhaps more entertaining than in the studio because they get a chance to relate to an audience. Some duplications exist on the 22-track double album from the studio versions, but there are outstanding renditions of "Baby Blue," "Grandfather's Clock," "Hit Parade of Love," and "Doin' My Time."

F6.129   **Cliff Waldron and Bill Emerson. The New Shades of Grass.** Rebel RLP 1485.

This is modern, but acoustic, bluegrass in the newgrass style. Assisting artists included John Duffey and Bill Baker, and this album is yet again another from the Washington-Maryland bluegrass scene. Material here includes Tom Rush's "If I Were a Carpenter," "A Message for Peace," "Our Darling's Gone," and "Fast Freight."

SOUTHWESTERN MUSIC

SOUTHWESTERN MUSIC

ORIGINS TO COUNTRY WESTERN

Southwestern music comprises a wide-ranging mixture of different types of materials. The earliest was probably the cowboy song of the trail drivers, ostensibly sung to keep the cattle at peace at night. This involved crooning and yodeling to some extent. Lyrics, often augmented by a solo guitar, concerned wide open spaces, lost love, and stories in songs picked up on the trail. During the Depression and with the advent of talking movies, the Hollywood cowboy became a marketable property and was exploited with occasional songs around the campfire. The professional singing cowboy developed, quite often as one who never left the movie lot. Instrumentation grew to accommodate contemporary popular musical practices of the time, as did group singing, such as by the Sons of the Pioneers, who also accompanied soloists (e.g., Roy Rogers). Gene Autry is usually thought of as being the typical tinsel cowboy. At the same time, lyrics shifted dramatically to take into account country music listeners' interest in the sentimental ballad, love, and novelties. By now, cowboy material was consistent with country music, and because cowboy music had a higher profile through nationally distributed films, several country music singers began to don garish cowboy outfits. The two musical streams thus merged as "country and western" or "c & w" music, and were virtually indistinguishable.

By the time of the first cowboy musical film, authentic cowboy music had ceased to be a recorded activity. Western swing was evolving from central and eastern Texas, the Panhandle and southern Oklahoma through the influence of radio dance music (especially from Fort Worth after 1933). It would later produce "honky tonk" music from Texas-born Ernest Tubb, which was transmitted to Hank Williams, and thence through to Texas-born Waylon Jennings and the "Nashville Outlaws" scene featuring story songs.

WESTERN SWING

Western swing developed in the American Southwest (Texas and Oklahoma) throughout the 1930s and 1940s. It was originally known as "Okie Jazz," "Tex-Mex Music," and "Southwestern Swing" before the rubric "western swing" became its accepted genre heading. Its immediate antecedents were the Texas fiddle-guitar duos of the 1920s, a musical development similar to that in the southeastern states with their Irish fiddle traditional old time string bands. An example of this is Bob Wills's Fiddle Band, a duo of the late 1920s. A piano and banjo were later added for house dances. At the same time, other groups, such as Prince Albert Hunt's Texas Ramblers, adapted popular songs of the day, borrowing both lyrics and melodies. Migrant workers moving from Louisiana because of the Depression's job shortage brought jazz to Texas. Consequently, these five piece groups (violin, guitar, banjo, bass, and piano) in the early 1930s began improvising "hot jazz" solos. Other influences at work besides fiddle bands included St. Louis style ragtime syncopations, the Texas blues of Blind Lemon Jefferson, the yodels of

Texan Jimmie Rodgers, jug band polyrhythms, vaudeville comedy, Hawaiian popular music and the steel guitar, German and Polish polkas and waltzes, Mexican mariachi bands, and of course, the swing riff being developed by the black territory bands centered in Kansas City (but traveling throughout the whole area).

Much was also learned from phonograph records. Putting all of these diverse influences together, along with added instrumentation of accordions, steel guitars, and drums, made western swing music one of the most widely-based dance forms in all of American music. It seemed to have a little bit of everything specifically designed for dancing: a vigorous rhythmic pulse that was insistent and infectious; relaxed vocals and lyrics that aided dancing; a wide repertoire of fiddle tunes, borrowed jazz standards, pop from the 1920s and 1930s, blues, and original compositions that were in the country mold (ballads, love songs and novelties); and improvised solos on a heavily bowed violin and a steel guitar.

Between 1932 and 1942, over fifty bands (of five to eight pieces) recorded some 2,000 sides, beginning with the Light Crust Doughboys' instrumentals for Victor through the traditional Bill Boyd's Cowboy Ramblers, the jazz of Milton Brown's Musical Brownies, and the blues inflections of Bob Wills. From 1942 through to 1955, this music became part of the big band idiom with reed and brass sections, and its popularity extended to the West Coast. At the same time, it became musically less interesting. In the 1950s, its expression was carried on by a more mature Bob Wills, by Leon McAuliff and his Cimarron Boys, and by Hank Thompson and his Brazos Valley Boys. But it was Bob Wills who became associated with the music (as Bill Monroe did with bluegrass music) and perfected the idiom, beginning with his radio work in Fort Worth in 1933. He introduced twin fiddles and gave prominence to the steel guitar.

LITERATURE

There are many cowboy song books, and much material can be found in books of general folk music. Sandberg and Weissman (77) point out a few, plus some recordings as well. Three very recent books cover both the streams of western swing and cowboy music. White (96) analyzes the songwriters of the American West and their songs. Townsend (90) writes about Bob Wills and the music of western swing. Griffis (35) meets them both halfway with his marvelous textual analysis, discography, and criticism of the commercial stylings of the Sons of the Pioneers. Biographical information can also be found in Gentry (30) and Stambler (86). Three good surveys of country music include references to cowboys and to swing: Malone (57), Malone and McCulloh (58), and Shelton (83).

Periodical articles are scarce in this subgenre. We know of nothing above the fanzine level, but scattered articles do appear in *Country Music People* (5), *Country Music Review* (6), the *Quarterly* of the John Edward Memorial Foundation (9), the *Journal of American Folklore* (10), the *Journal of Country Music* (11), and *Old Time Music* (16). Once again, the best places to look for retrieval are the *Annual Index to Popular Music Record Reviews* (3) and the *Popular Music Periodicals Index* (69).

COWBOYS

Innovators

F7.1*   **Authentic Cowboys and Their Western Folksongs.** RCA LPV 522.

F7.2   **Cowboy Songs, Ballads and Cattle Calls from Texas.** Library of Congress AAFS L 28.

F7.3   **Songs of the Mormons and Songs of the West.** Library of Congress AAFS L 30.

These three discs are about the only anthologies available of western and cowboy music. The RCA set is an annotated collection of sixteen titles, recorded in 1925-1934, and embraces mostly the nineteenth century repertoire. From 1925, Carl T. Sprague sings "When the Work's All Done This Fall," which was his first recording and biggest seller (both for him and for cowboy music), at over 900,000 copies. Mac McClintock performs "The Old Chisholm Trail" and the story of "Sam Bass." Jules Allen sings of "Zebra Dun" and "The Cowboy's Dream." Billie Maxwell relates "The Haunted Hunter," while J. D. Farley tells that "Bill Was a Texas Lad." Other performers here include Eck Robertson (fiddler) and Jack Webb. Sprague also contributes a compassionate "The Mormon Cowboy." There are excellent notes by Fred G. Hoeptner.

The two Library of Congress discs are, of course, non-commercial field trip recordings. The first record comprises thirteen tracks from 1941-1948, with most versions from 1942, and mostly recorded by John A. Lomax. Sloan Matthews of Alpine, Texas, has the most selections, including such traditional items as "The Texas Rangers," "The Cowboy's Life Is a Very Dreary Life," "The Dying Cowboy," and diverse cattle calls for starting, driving, and nightherding. The second set comes from 1938-1949, though mostly from 1946-1947. This period covers side one, and includes the Mormon songs collected by Austin E. Fife ("The Handcart Song," "The Utah Iron Horse"). The diverse material on the second side includes "Starving to Death on a Government Claim," "Custer's Last Charge," and "Freighting from Wilcox to Globe." Editorial work and notes were done by Duncan B. M. Emrich for both of the Library of Congress records.

F7.4*   **Gene Autry. Great Hits.** Harmony HL 7332.

F7.5   **Gene Autry. You Are My Sunshine.** Harmony HS 11199.

Texas-born Autry came from and presented an extremely eclectic musical background: sentimental ballads, novelty, topical, folk songs, country, and the blue yodels of Jimmie Rodgers. In 1931, he had his first real self-composed big hit—"That Silver Haired Daddy of Mine"—and sold over half a million copies. He had already been recording for two years, but now finally knew in what direction to pursue his singing career. In the 1930s, he became a western movie star, being featured in over 100 films. At the same time, he had a radio show, although he was erroneously billed as "Oklahoma's Singing Cowboy." By now he had developed the sincere, honest style that related to his screen and radio character—a far cry from the raunchy blues he recorded for ARC in 1929 in the first stage of his singing career. Next came the pre-war western and cowboy songs, followed by love songs during the war ("Tears on My Pillow"), and then the post-war children's songs ("Rudolph," "Peter Cottontail," "Frosty," "Here Comes Santa Claus")—all very popular.

He wrote over 300 songs, many early ones with a Jimmie Rodgers influence. Often dismissed as a trite singer, Autry had great importance in shaping tastes in country and western music. He appeared in four media (films, radio, records, television) and through these, he created the popular country and western song as a legitimate musical expression. His films gave both him and the music a positive respectability. Country music before Autry was essentially regional. He made it national in scope and was the key to adding "western" to "country and . . . ." He instilled a certain romanticism in western love and paved the way for such cowboy singers as Roy Rogers, Tex Ritter, Johnny Bond, the Sons of the Pioneers, Rex Allen, and Jimmy Wakely. In addition, he was solely responsible for the increased popularity of the guitar. Many hundreds of thousands were labeled "Gene Autry" and sold through Sears by mail orders. In the determination of influences, one should not forget all of these factors while listening to Autry's performances.

F7.6*   **Johnny Bond. Best.** Harmony HL 7308.

F7.7   **Johnny Bond. Best.** Starday SLP 444.
Bond was a guitarist from Oklahoma, and in the true tinsel cowboy tradition, he joined the Jimmy Wakely trio (1937-1940) before progressing to the movies with Gene Autry (1940-1954). During this latter period, he worked extensively for Columbia, having written and recorded such songs as "Divorce Me C.O.D.," "Smoke, Smoke, Smoke That Cigarette," and his greatest epic, "Cimarron." His style was part cowboy, part honky-tonk, and mostly western swing, with drinking songs such as "Ten Little Bottles" or "Set Em up Joe." He could be lyrical, as in "A Petal from a Faded Rose" or sentimental, as in "Oklahoma Waltz." The Harmony disc contains ten of his masterpieces from the 1940s. During his career, he wrote over 400 compositions, including "I'll Step Aside," "I Wonder Where You Are Tonight," "Tomorrow Never Comes," "Sad, Sad and Blue," the dynamic "Wildcat Boogie," and the smashing "Tennessee Saturday Night." These are on the Starday collection, beginning from 1954. Bond was a highly significant and influential fashioner of the honky-tonk genre.

F7.8   **Wilf Carter. First Five Sessions.** Country Music History. CMH 111 (West German issue).

F7.9   **Wilf Carter. The Next Sessions.** Country Music History. CMH 120 (West German issue).

F7.10*   **Wilf Carter. Montana Slim's Greatest Hits.** two discs. RCA ADL 2-0694.
Canadian singer Carter was known in the United States as Montana Slim. He has been an RCA artist in Canada for 45 years and has gained international respect in the country music world. Beginning as a rodeo cowboy from Nova Scotia, moving later to ranching in Alberta, Carter's brand of music concentrated

on campfire and roundup music through ballads, semi-folklore, and fast yodels. He has written over 600 songs, and while many were recorded for the budget Camden label in Canada, all are now deleted. He was on CBS radio in New York City, but an accident while driving severely restricted his career, and he returned to Canada.

Beginning with Victor in 1933, Carter is represented on the CMH set through 1934, judged to be his best recording years and the ones that Americans remember. Influences are many. "The Smoke Goes up the Chimney Just the Same" is a cowboy version of the Fiddlin' John Carson tune. "Hobo's Song of the Mounties" is a story of harassment of tramps by the RCMP in a Woody Guthrie vein (but before Guthrie's time, of course). "I Miss My Swiss" features trick yodeling, while "Lover's Lullaby Yodel" has triple yodeling. Sentimental songs include "My Little Grey Haired Mother in the West," "Cowboy Don't Forget Your Mother," "Old Shep," and "My Swiss Moonlight Lullaby." Cowboy tunes include "Twilight on the Prairie," "Yodeling Trailrider," "Pinto Pete," and "Calgary Roundup." Topical items include "The Capture of Albert Johnson" and "Life and Death of John Dillinger." The RCA set has his later pop material: "I'm Thinking Tonight of My Blue Eyes," the great "When It's Springtime in the Rockies," and the wonderfully inspiring "There's a Bluebird on Your Windowsill."

F7.11*   **Patsy Montana.** two discs. RCA Bluebird AXM2-55-- (in progress).

F7.12   **Patsy Montana. Sweetheart.** Starday 376.

Beginning with the National Barn Dance of WLS in Chicago the "Yodeling Cowgirl," as she was named, recorded in 1934 with the Prairie Ramblers quartet. In 1936, she established herself in the field by performing "I Want to Be a Cowboy's Sweetheart," the first hit sung by a woman in country music. It went on to become a million seller. Other popular tunes by this jaunty woman included "I'm an Old Cowhand" and "Singing in the Saddle." Montana was an early influence on Molly O'Day and also on virtually every other female singer in country and western music.

F7.13*   **Tex Ritter. An American Legend.** three discs. Capitol SKC 11241.

F7.14*   **Tex Ritter. The Singing Cowboy.** two discs. MCA 628.334 (West German issue).

Ritter, who died in January 1974, was a true collector of folk songs. His father knew most of the cowboy ballads, which could be traced back to 1830, and strongly impressed this love on Tex. By the time of his first recording for Decca in 1935, he was an expert on Texas (his home state) folklore, and in subsequent years, he would appear on radio and give lectures outlining the extent of Texas musical history. The thirty items on the MCA double set cover his career from 1935-1939, and include some film soundtrack masters of light, pleasant "cowboy" music, often with the Sons of the Pioneers. But the balance contain materials dealing with stories of western life, such as "Sam Hall," "Lady Killin' Cowboy," "Bill the Bar Fly," "The Oregon Trail," "The Hills of Old Wyoming," and "Arizona Days." Ritter became more of a movie star in the 1940s, with a recording career at Capitol beginning in 1941, when that company was founded.

His lyrics were both sentimental and impressive, full of stories about the old West, and his voice displayed the characteristic deep resonance of a tired ranch hand. He performed at many state fairs and rodeos, spreading his music around and bringing it to New York in a fusion of his western styling with the southeastern style of early country music developed by Jimmie Rodgers. His folklore background added tremendous authenticity to humorous songs, country dirges, love songs, and sacred music. He believed in what he sang—God, mother, home, and personal tributes. He also fashioned narrative epics such as "Pledge of Allegiance" and "Deck of Cards."

The three discs from Capitol span his entire career with that company. It is a representative sampling of 31 titles, beginning with early accompaniment furnished by guitarist Merle Travis: "There's a New Moon over My Shoulder," "One Little Tear Drop Too Late," "Someone," "Jealous Heart," "Blood on the Saddle," the 1948 "Rock and Rye Rag," the soundtrack version of "High Noon," the 1950 "Daddy's Last Letter," and the 1961 salute to country music's history in "I Dreamed of a Hillbilly Heaven." In this set, complete with descriptive notes, Ritter introduces each song by giving the story line and the circumstances of how he came to record it.

F7.15*   **Sons of the Pioneers.** JEMF 102.

F7.16*   **Sons of the Pioneers. Best.** Harmony HL 7317.

F7.17*   **Sons of the Pioneers. Best.** RCA LSP 3476.

F7.18*   **Sons of the Pioneers. Tumbleweed Trails.** Vocalion VL 3715.

The Sons of the Pioneers were first organized in 1933 as a trio, with Roy Rogers, Bob Nolan, and Tim Spencer. Through the years their personnel changed, beginning in 1937, when tenor Lloyd Perryman replaced Rogers, who pursued a solo movie career. Some were born in the American East and Canada (Bob Nolan), while others were born and raised in the West (Spencer, Perryman—the latter from the Ozarks—the Farr brothers who brought their Texas instrumental stylings, etc.). Overall, their music was a blend of southeastern and southwestern influences that merged into a western pop music. There were some old time music roots in the string band instrumentation as well. At the beginning, Rogers's strong voice and smooth solo work carried the melody with Nolan's baritone and Spencer's high lead voice.

Their success was due to three factors. First, their vocalizing in three-part harmony was entirely correct, with well-matched voices, perfect timing, and good coordination. Second, they had many superb compositions, largely written by Tim Spencer (over 400) and Bob Nolan (over 1,000), that were hauntingly beautiful and created from their actual experiences. For the most part, these were written for their movie roles as "lonesome cowhands." Third, the Farr brothers provided excellent musical accompaniment related to Texas string band traditions. All three factors put together made many of their songs very difficult for others to recreate, although to most people they "appeared" to be facile, and songs were brought off with ease. This harmonic singing was a direct influence on the entire West Coast mode of harmonic singing (Byrds; Buffalo Springfield; Crosby, Stills,

Nash and Young; et al.) that sprang up in the late 1960s, and it also spawned many such imitative groups in 1930s movies, such as the Riders of the Purple Sage.

The Harmony album covers ten tracks of their 1937 material for Columbia subsidiaries, all recorded in Los Angeles. Titles include such typical cowboy laments as "Let's Pretend," the sentimental ties of "When the Roses Bloom Again" and "Down along the Sleepy Rio Grande," and the western "epics" of "Open Range Ahead" and "Hold That Critter Down." In 1940, they made some radio transcriptions, and these are available from the John Edwards Memorial Foundation (along with a superb 16-page booklet authored by Ken Griffis). By this time, the singing trio had Hugh and Karl Farr on violin and guitar and personable Pat Brady on string bass. The selection of material here comprises all landscapes: prairie dogs, waterfalls, tumbleweed, trains, etc. The instrumental breaks are especially well-developed, with blues guitar licks and a jazz violin in the emerging western swing mode. The compositions are all largely by Spencer or Nolan, and the twenty tracks include "When Payday Rolls Around," "Song of the Bandit," "When the Prairie Sun Climbs out of the Hay," "The Texas Crapshooters," and "Love Song of the Waterfall." Although gloriously romantic and scenic, this material reflected more closely the type of music that the Sons were famous for singing at concerts and on the radio. Pop hit material that worked its way into other group repertoires is found on the commercial collections of "hits."

The Vocalion issue presents some twelve tracks, mostly from 1941 (with some from 1942, 1943, and 1954). These Decca recordings from their 1941-1943 period (the 1934-1937 Deccas are unavailable on microgroove) were perhaps the best titles ever in their simple period: "Tumbleweed Trail," "There's a New Moon over My Shoulder," "Cielito Lindo," "Lovely Rose of Mexico." With RCA since 1945, their music was complicated by more instrumentation, pop-derived material, and ever-changing personnel—offset, of sourse, by national exposure and more sales. The RCA disc covers originals up through 1963 (they are still recording today): "Cool Water," "No One to Cry To," "Tumbling Tumble Weeds," "San Antonio Rose," "Have I Told You Lately That I Love You?" Beginning in 1959, the existing Pioneers recreated many of their older classics in stereo, but not, of course, with the same voices. These can be found on RCA ANLI-1092 (*Cool Water*).

Standards

F7.19*   **Jules Allen. The Texas Cowboy.** Bear Family FV 12502 (West German issue).

This Texas-born successor to Carl Sprague provided colorful accompaniment to his cowboy singing, usually in the form of fiddle and/or harmonica. The jaunty spirit is evident on such items as "Gal I Left behind Me," which is much more in the western swing-type tradition of dance music. A slow tempo violin was used on the tragic songs, as in "The Dying Cowboy." Historical material includes "Days of '49," "Punchin' the Dough," and "Home on the Range"—all richly detailing life on the trail, especially for some of the non-cowboys, such as the cook. Much classic material was recorded at these 1928-1929 sessions, including "Cowtrail to Mexico," "Chisholm Trail" and " 'Long Side the Santa Fe Trail." The excellent liner notes were written by John I. White.

F7.20   Rex Allen. Mister Cowboy. MCA Decca 78776.

F7.21   Rex Allen. Sings and Tells Tales. Mercury SR 16324.
     Rex Allen is a modern performer deeply influenced by Gene Autry. He can display competence on both the guitar and the violin, and following in Autry's footsteps, he made 32 feature films. An anomaly, though, he was raised in the cattle country of Arizona but concentrated on singing country material rather than out-and-out cowboy epics. As a songwriter, he contributed over 300 compositions. The Decca album, recorded in 1958, includes remakes of some of his earlier successes, such as "Crying in the Chapel" (from 1953), "On Top of Old Smokey," "The Last Roundup," and "Softly and Tenderly." In a more modern vein by the 1960s, he recorded the Mercury album (1962), which played off his deep voice against contrasting instrumental backgrounds. During this period, he recorded the oft-mentioned "Money, Marbles and Chalk."

F7.22*   Bob Atcher. Best Early American Folk Songs. Harmony HL 7313.

F7.23   Bob Atcher. Dean of Cowboy Singers. Columbia CS 9032.
     Atcher was born in Kentucky, the son of a fiddle champion. He tried his hand at singing all forms of music (folk, country, western, and so forth), but he had most success with the cowboy song. During his long career, he operated out of Chicago at the WLS National Barn Dance. Typical efforts have included "Time Alone," "Don't Let Your Sweet Love Die," "Don't Rob Another Man's Castle," and traditional folk songs in a country vein.

F7.24*   Jenks "Tex" Carman. The Dixie Cowboy. Country Music History CMH
           2ll (West German issue).
     Carman was a very outgoing swing man who was an early proponent of the Hawaiian steel guitar. He was far ahead of his time, doing material in the 1940s that sounds just as fresh and alive today. He also was a strong influence on modern day Dobroists such as Tut Taylor and Mike Auldridge. Speed and special effects predominate on "The Artillery Song" and "The Caissons Go Rolling Along." Various dance stylings appear in "Kahila March," "Hillbilly Hula," "Locust Hill Rag," "Samoa Stomp," "Indian Polka," and "Sweet Luwana." Besides some stinging blues (:"Mississippi Valley Blues'" "Blue Memories"), he also contributed flash guitar to the railroad instrumental, as on "Fireball Mail" and "Dixie Cannonball."

F7.24a   Johnny Cash. Ballads of the True West. two discs. Columbia C2S 838.

F7.24b   Johnny Cash. Bitter Tears; Ballads of the American Indian. Columbia
           CS 9043.

F7.24c   Johnny Cash. Ride This Train. Columbia CS 8255.
     These discs by Cash were the first concept albums in country music, and each portrayed some part of the old West that appealed to him. As part Indian, he was naturally interested in the American Indian protest movement, and this 1964 set provides songs by another Indian—Peter LaFarge—and by Cash, as well

as with some narration. For the 1965 *Ballads* twofer, Cash sought the advice of Tex Ritter for a program of cowboy songs and folklore. However, neither album proved as popular as the 1960 *Train* disc. Here he relates stories and songs in a well-put-together package of narrative chatting and music. Most of the songs are either originals or obscure, such as "Loading Coal," "Dorraine of Point Chartrain," and "Boss Jack."

F7.25   **Slim Critchlow. Cowboy Songs: "The Crooked Trail to Holbrook."** Arhoolie 5007.

Critchlow is an authentic cowboy, but he was very old when he made this recording in the 1960s. Consequently, although he may have been influenced by outside events through the years, he can be thought of as transmitting the story songs of the trail and western landscapes. Typical stories include "Borax Bill, the Skinner," "Forty a Month and Found," "Windy Bill," "Snag Tooth Sal," "John Garner's Trail Herd," and "D-Bar-2 Horse Wrangler." These combine for an excellent program of life in the old West.

F7.26   **Al Dexter. Pistol Packin' Mama.** Harmony HL 7293.

Dexter began with the Texas Troopers in 1934, creating an uptempo style that later became known as western swing. In the 1930s, he recorded for Okeh and Vocalion, continuing that association in 1940 for Columbia when this company purchased the other recording corporations. His hard driving honky-tonk sounds may be heard here on such items as "Honky Tonk Blues," "Rosalita" (from 1942), "Too Late to Worry," "Guitar Polka," "Saturday Night Boogie," "Alimony Blues," and "Car Hoppin' Mama" (in addition to the title selection).

F7.27   **Harry Jackson. The Cowboy.** two discs. Folkways F 5723.

These two discs present a superb program of typical cowboy songs, ballads, and what is known as "brag" talk.

F7.28   **Leon Payne.** Starday 231.

Payne was a multi-instrumentalist (guitar, piano, organ, trombone, drums) who was also blind, like Riley Puckett and Doc Watson. He was the equal of these two in the field of western music, having developed an extensive repertoire by the late 1930s. In addition, he created thousands of songs (including "Lost Highway" for Hank Williams) and many were recorded by swing bands, including those of Bob Wills. Payne's own recording career began in 1939, and over the years, he has performed such minor classics as "I Love You Because," "Blue Side of Lonesome." "Things Have Gone to Pieces," and "Doorsteps to Heaven."

F6.29   **Goebel Reeves. The Texas Drifter.** Country Music History CMH 101 (West German issue).

Reeves was a colorful hobo and cowboy who recorded for Brunswick in the 1930s. He was one of the original "drifters" who preceded Woody Guthrie, although he normally restricted his songs to cowboys and hobos. Some of the songs that Reeves became famous for included "Miss Jackson, Tennessee" and "Little Joe, the Wrangler." He devised vocal showings such as the blue yodel so prominent in Jimmie Rodgers; he took poetic license with the rhythms and rhymes; he had a swoop falsetto. Some called him eccentric; others, eclectic—especially with material like "Mother-In-Law Blues" and the hoked-up broadcast of "H.O.B.O. Calling," plus the sexual fantasies of "I Learned about Women from Her."

F7.30*   Marty Robbins. Gunfighter Ballads and Trail Songs. Columbia CS 8158.
Arizona-born Robbins sings a wide variety of materials and stylings. Columbia has collated the western-cowboy aspect of his music into a single album, which includes such gems as "El Paso"—a tradition-breaking song as it was longer than 200 seconds but did not get less airplay on the radio—and "Big Iron." The former was a story about an outlaw involved with a Mexican girl named Felina; the latter concerns the fall and decline of an aging gunfighter. Other songs here include Spanish-influenced southwestern American stories, all composed by Robbins himself.

F7.31   Carl T. Sprague. The First Popular Singing Cowboy. Big Bear FV 15.001 (West German issue).
Born in 1895 in Texas, Sprague was largely responsible for preserving cowboy music through his recordings in the 1920s. For Victor, he made 28 titles in 1925-1929. Four of these are on RCA LPV 522 (noted in the anthology part of this section at F7.1). His first recording—"When the Work's All Done This Fall"—became the first million seller for both him and cowboy music. At this early stage (1925) he was mainly responsible for RCA's success in the cowboy music field. Yet his music is undeniably simplistic, with easy singing, easy chords, and a strong emphasis on story songs. Through the years, Sprague was impressed by Vernon Dalhart's "The Prisoner's Song" and John A. Lomax's publication *Cowboy Songs*. This German issue presents Sprague in his late seventies; half of the material is reworkings of older Victor items, and the balance is entirely new to his recorded repertoire. He is assisted by a second guitarist on only three tracks. His hands and his vocals are remarkably sure and deft, but since he had such a simple style to begin with, little could be lost through age. Everything here was recorded in March 1972, in Texas, and there are exhaustive notes by John I. White. Typical titles include "Home on the Range," "Following the Cow Trail," "Kissing," "Rounded up in Glory" (a perfectly marvelous sacred song), "Red River Valley," and "Roll on Little Doggies."

F7.32   Tex Williams. MCA MCFM 4295 (British issue).
Williams was one of the first California-based western singers. He starred in movies and television and, with his band, recorded for Capitol in 1946, later moving to MCA. His version of "Smoke, Smoke, Smoke" was the first million selling record for Capitol. His slick honky-tonk western swing music included such seminal commercial successes as "Rose of the Alamo," "California Polka," "Leaf of Love," and "Texas in My Soul."

WESTERN SWING

Anthologies

F7.33*   **Beer Parlor Jive.** String 801 (British issue).

F7.34*   **Rollin' Along.** Tishomingo 2220.
These two specialized anthologies concentrate on different aspects of western swing. *Beer Parlor Jive* collates fourteen items from the 1935-1941 period, thereby keeping to the strong band period and also to lesser-known names. The material here concentrates on blues and jazz elements. The bands were smaller, and hot dancing predominated, so most of the selections are uptempo all the way. Tunes include "Draggin' the Bow" and "When You're Smiling" (both by Cliff Bruner's Texas Wanderers), "Black and White Rag" and "Somebody's Been Using That Thing" (both by Milton Brown and his Brownies), "Chicken Reel Stomp," "Settle Down Blues," "Hi-Flyer Stomp," and "Sundown Blues." Tony Russell contributes excellent notes tracing historical milestones and a discography.
The Tishomingo set is more varied. Its sixteen tracks present an overview from the fiddle and small group of the Prairie Ramblers to the full band of Bob Wills. It is a well-planned program, emphasizing traditional European folk dance music via the German introduction of the accordion. Although this is primarily a dancer's album, thereby complementing the String album, it does present such different aspects as the blues vocal inflections on "Graveyard Blues" (by Bob Dunn's Vagabonds), the jazz of "Bring It on Down" (by Milton Brown and his Brownies), and pop material of "Juke Box Rag" and "Tickle Toe." The good notes are a pleasure to read.

F7.35   **Texas Country.** two discs. United Artists UALA 574-H2.
Although it could have been condensed by half to fit onto a single record, this anthology presents four well-known soloists or groups who performed in the southwestern style at one time in their careers. Side one presents early Willie Nelson ("Second Fiddle," "Hello Walls"); side two has the second generation sounds of Freddy Fender, who became influential as a chicano only after Rodriguez became famous and acknowledged Fender's influence ("Mean Woman," "Wasted Days and Wasted Nights"). Side three presents the other second generation sounds of Asleep at the Wheel, noted for their advanced western swing (Moon Mullican's "Cherokee Boogie," "Drivin' Nails in My Coffin"); side four gives some later-day renditions by Bob Wills and the Texas Playboys ("Milk Cow Blues," "San Antonio Rose," "Faded Love"). All of these total twenty tracks.

F7.36*   **Western Swing, v.1-3.** three discs. Old Timey OT 105, 116, 117.
"Western swing" often means Bob Wills and the more commercial Spade Cooley. Its main elements were Mexican influences from the border; the East European immigrant traditions of waltzes, marches, and polkas; and the lore of the American fiddle. Developing in the 1930s as popular dance music from a "hot" string band, its name came into being after World War II, when it spread from Texas and Oklahoma to the West Coast. This three-disc set covers the whole gamut of western swing. Volume one is essentially an important sampling of the genre

from 1935-1938. Thousands of records were made—mainly in Dallas, Houston, and San Antonio. Radio played an important role, and W. Lee O'Daniel (heard on this disc as a vocalist) later became governor of Texas, based on his popularity.

The most important group as noted above was Bob Wills and His Texas Playboys. His instrumentation included violins, guitars, piano, banjo, bass, drums, trombone, and saxophone for depth. He featured Leon McAuliffe, the master of the amplified steel guitar ("Steel Guitar Rag" and "Steel Guitar Stomp"). Music was sometimes borrowed from Blind Lemon Jefferson ("Swing Blues No. 1") and Jimmie Rodgers ("Never No More Blues" and "Never No More Hard Times"). Half of this initial disc is Wills; the balance comprises Bill Boyd, the Light Crust Doughboys, and Milton Brown—all leaders of the genre. More diverse material appears on the second and third volumes. The time period is later, and there are more groups, such as the Tune Wranglers ("Up Jumped the Devil"), Adolf Hofner ("Brown Eyed Sweet," "Alamo Rag," "Sage Brush Shuffle"), Hank Penny, the Nite Owls, Jimmie Revard, and Cliff Bruner. Both of these latter albums concentrate on ragtime items and blues in the hot dance mode, and there are excellent descriptive notes.

Standards

F7.37   **Norman Blake, et al.** Flying Fish HDS 701.

F7.38*   **Hillbilly Jazz.** two discs. Flying Fish 101.
Modern reinterpretations of western swing have come from the group Asleep at the Wheel, Merle Haggard, Commander Cody, and various Texans from the World Armadillo Headquarters in San Antonio. The group that recorded the above double set of 24 numbers is as yet untitled, but they are led by Vassar Clements, the well-known jazzy bluegrass fiddler, and Dave Bromberg, the rock-folk-country guitarist. The ten instruments here perform in a very eclectic style, expanding the parameters of western swing to include such hard core jazz items as "Cherokee," "Breakfast Feud," and "C Jam Blues." Other influences come from pop ("Sentimental Journey," "Back Home in Indiana," "Gravy Waltz"), blues ("Sitting on Top of the World"), plus western classics from Bob Wills ("San Antonio Rose," "Take Me Back to Tulsa"), Spade Cooley ("It's Dark Outside," "Crazy Cause I Love You"), and guitarists McAuliffe ("Panhandle Rag") and Remington ("Little Rock Getaway"). Everybody is having great fun in this superb set. A 20-page booklet by Rick Ulman accompanies the discs.

The single album, released in 1975 just after *Hillbilly Jazz*, is a further extension of the western swing amalgam. The album has no actual title, and the group again has no overall name. All performers are acknowledged leaders on their instruments, such as Blake on guitar, Sam Bush on mandolin, Vassar Clements on violin, Tut Taylor on Dobro, and David Holland (the superb jazzman) on bass. The eight selections—all instrumentals, like *Hillbilly Jazz*—include more jazz items, such as "Sweet Georgia Brown," "A Train," and even "Going Home" from Dvorak's *New World Symphony* (also found in the repertoire of Glenn Miller and others). There is only one distinctly old timey piece ("McKinley's Blues") that has been modified by Blake. Other tracks of equal importance are in the string jazz mold pioneered by Django Reinhardt and Stephane Grappelli. These originals are titled "Sauer Kraut 'n' Solar Energy" and "Vassar and Dave," the latter a fiddle-bass duo. Both albums have won acclaim in the jazz world as well as in the country sphere.

F7.39*   **Bill Boyd. Country Ramblers, 1934-1950.** Two discs. RCA Bluebird AXM 2-5503.

Boyd recorded about 300 titles for RCA over a 20-year period, in conjunction with a radio show he had for over thirty years (beginning in 1932). Of all the western swing groups, his was probably the most conservative, with its roots in the cowboy music of Texas. Any "hot jazz" they played used the occasional clarinet and ragtime-developed fiddle line. Normally, they simply modified the string band heritage found in the Southwest. At the beginning of his recording career, Boyd had a quartet (fiddle, tenor banjo, guitar and bass) in which he played guitar and brother Jim sang lead. As a document of transition, this 32-track compilation is important. A piano is added for percussive beats and the selection of songs in the group's book widens. Duet yodeling, obviously borrowed from the Sons of the Pioneers, is prominent, as on "Way out There." Twin fiddling develops, and Knocky Parker becomes the pianist, adding blues as on his solo of "Boyd's Tin Roof Blues" and "Mill Blues." Other performers join after leaving more important western swing outfits, such as Kenneth Pitts and Carol Hubbard (fiddles). Typical tunes here from the "cowboy" period include "I'm Gonna Hop off the Train," "The Rambler's Rag," and "The Windswept Desert." Swing includes "Saturday Night Rag," "Fan It," and "Beaumont Rag," as well as "Spanish Fandango" and "New Spanish Two-Step." Good notes and full discography are here, but the first 29 selections only go to 1938. The last three (from 1946, 1949, and 1950) seem out of place here.

F7.40   **Vassar Clements. Crossing the Catskills.** Rounder 0016.

The talented violin virtuoso Clements here leads a contemporary group that includes Dave Bromberg and Ev Lilly. He takes chances and usually pulls them off, mixing a variety of styles and types of compositions. He is very imaginative in treating the Beatles' "Norwegian Wood," done in Cajun style, or in "Corina, Corina," which is done in western swing style. Besides this mixture of traditional and contemporary, there are three improvisational jams (the title track, "Half and Half," and "Stumble") that show good stylings as each person solos. Clements' version of "Paddy on the Turnpike" has a good break featuring flatpicked fiddle. Everything here is enjoyable and danceable, in the true string band tradition.

F7.41*   **Spade Cooley.** two discs. Club of Spade 00102/3.

Spade Cooley was an exponent of commercial western swing music from Santa Monica. He was noted for several compositions, such as "Shame on You." All of his recorded material, unfortunately, has been long out of print; but in 1975, 26 items were released from private tapes. The first disc was recorded just before his sudden death in 1969; the second is composed of live recordings. During the 1940s, Cooley was extremely popular in California. His heritage is derived from Oklahoma old-time fiddling, and his band was very much into the "dance" aspect of music rather than the blues influence of Bob Wills and other western swing groups. All the tunes on these discs are fully orchestrated with multiple violins in unison. Only four tracks contain vocals: "San Antonio Rose," "Sugar Blues," "Que Sera Sera," and "Blue Skies." The balance are a judicious mixture of polkas, square dances, waltzes (mainly uptempo, as "Swinging the Blue Danube"), pop, jazz, and ragtime ("Pan Handle Rag" or "Dill Pickle Rag").

F7.42 **Johnny Gimble. Fiddlin' Around.** Capitol ST 11301.
Gimble is the greatest of the living western swing fiddlers (he plays, as of this writing, with the group Asleep at the Wheel). He is directly in the mold of Bob Wills. The ten tracks on this album include salutes to Wills such as "Beaumont Rag" and a Bob Wills medley.

F7.43 **Pee Wee King.** Starday 284.

F7.44* **Pee Wee King. Biggest Hits.** RCA Camden 2460.
King was an accordionist, a fiddler, a composer (of over 400 titles), and a superb bandleader who once employed Ernest Tubb and Eddy Arnold as vocalists. Beginning with Gene Autry in 1936 and moving to the Grand Ole Opry in 1940, he was effective in effecting many changes in country and western music. First, he made the accordion an acceptable western instrument at the Opry, transcribing western swing into honky-tonk country music. In 1940, he was also one of the first to employ the electric guitar at Nashville, bringing in ten gallon hats at the same time and thus advancing "costumes" at the Opry. In 1947, he added drums, creating great controversy. He was well-known for at least five monster tunes: "Bonaparte's Retreat," "Silver and Gold," "Bimbo," "Slowpoke" (from the mid-fifties), and "Tennessee Waltz," which, with Redd Stewart as vocalist, became one of the first country songs to cross over to the pop market (via Patti Page). The Starday album, recorded in 1963, repeats some of his earlier successes with new, updated material in a more "modern" vein.

F7.45 **Leon McAuliff. Mr. Western Swing.** Pine Mountain PMR 271.
McAuliff scored most of his successes as the very influential steel guitarist with the Bob Wills western swing band. He began his career with the Light Crust Doughboys, but it was with Wills that he composed his important "Steel Guitar Rag." With Wills he made over 200 recordings; on his own in the 1950s, he made forty titles under his own name. A dozen are here in this reissue of Starday 271, and this disc includes diverse instrumentals such as "Panhandle Rag," "I Don't Love Nobody," "Cozy Inn," "Shape up or Ship Out," and the perennial "Steel Guitar Chimes."

F7.46 **Hank Thompson.** Capitol SM 2661.

F7.47* **Hank Thompson. Golden Hits.** Capitol ST 2089.
In the best Bob Wills tradition of string band western swing, Thompson assembled the Brazos Valley Boys in the 1940s after leaving the Navy. Much of his early music was strictly dance, but by the 1950s, he had assembled a considerable corpus of vocal items with extended instrumental passages. His deep resonant baritone, which stretched upward from time to time, created many, many classics of the country *and* western repertoires: "Wild Side of Life," "A Lonely Heart Knows,"

"Today," "It Makes No Difference Now," and "Humpty Dumpty Heart." His voice was full of pain, but later he turned this to rawness for excursions into honky-tonk music, as on "A Six Pack to Go" or "Shot Gun Boogie."

F7.48*   **Bob Wills. Anthology.** two discs. Columbia KG 32416.

F7.49*   **Bob Wills/Asleep at the Wheel. Fathers and Sons.** two discs. Epic BS 33782.

   Wills was the popularizer of western swing music in much the same way as Monroe was for bluegrass music. By 1930, he had added the renowned vocalist Milton Brown to his Wills Fiddle Band. Later, Tommy Duncan replaced Brown, who left to form his own group. The Light Crust Doughboys, almost owned by W. Lee O'Daniel, were centered in Fort Worth, which could be likened to a cradle of western swing, for many groups were derived from the Doughboys. Wills joined, but then was fired by O'Daniel, and had to move to Tulsa, Oklahoma, to practice this style of music. O'Daniel had virtually all of Texas sewed up. From 1934-1958, Wills appeared on KVOO radio. His best years were 1934-1942, before the war depleted his band. Through this band passed some of the finest western performers: Johnnie Lee Willis (tenor banjo), Son Lansford (bass), Everett Stover (trumpet), Leon McAulliffe (steel guitar), Wills on fiddle, and Duncan as prime vocalist. During his long career, Wills recorded some 550 tunes, and on all of them he was fiddler or composer or band leader (or all three).

   In all of these titles, one can hear a clear integration of the black and white musical styles that were played on the radio and at dances throughout the Southwest. "Western swing" is mainly "southwestern dance music" related to breakdowns, waltzes, and western folk music played at ranch parties. Thus, Wills and his Texas Playboys were the ones who put "western" into "country and western" music. His basic style was derived from Texas fiddle ornamentation (he was born into a family of violinists). The Texas music scene seethed with diverse musical forms, and Wills pulled them all together. From the blues and the appeal of pure black music, he developed uninhibited freedom through slurring his fiddle. From jazz, he borrowed the characteristic style of New Orleans front and back line ensemble playing, with the strings (steel guitar, three-fiddle ensemble [his trademark], banjo, and guitar) at the forefront and the horns as a supplemental front line. The swing jazz of the Southwest provided him with a jazz beat in the rhythm section, led by Lansford's bass, and improvisation by the soloists was stressed. His "ah ha" sounds and vocal comments, which added spontaneity to the music, were actually cues to the band as to who was to solo next. Duncan's vocals were blues-tinged.

   By 1940, Wills added the horns, making fifteen to eighteen players the complement of the band. In that same year, with the new instrumentation, he recorded "New San Antonio Rose," which was originally an instrumental in 1938. This later version had a vocal line and catapulted him to lasting fame. The 24 items on the Columbia set were mainly recorded during 1935-1941 (two were from 1945), and five are issued here for the first time. Popular songs included "Mexicali Rose," "Sittin' on Top of the World" (from blues music), "Steel Guitar Rag," "Brain Cloudy Blues," and "Time Changes Everything." The double Epic release includes some previously available Wills material (from Harmony HS 11358, such as his ballads "Miss Molly" or "The Convict and the Rose") and the derivative revival group Asleep at the Wheel, a Texas-based 1970s swing outfit with the fiddle of Johnny Gimble plus electric amplification. Previously available as KE 33097, material here comes from the jazz world ("Jumpin' at the Woodside"), original Wills swing ("Miss Molly," also on the Wills disc in the same set), rhythm 'n' blues (Fats Domino's New Orleans-styled "I'm Gonna Be a Wheel Someday" or Louis Jordan's jump blues item, "Choo Choo Ch' Boogie"), plus original items in the tradition of western swing. Wills was a major influence on such performers as Hank Thompson and Merle Haggard, but especially on Bill Haley, who led the rockabilly vanguard in 1954. Wills thus provides an essential link between race music, rockabillies, and rhythm 'n' blues music. And this link can best be heard on the Tiffany transcriptions (Oakland, 1945-1948), the first of which was reissued on Tishomingo Records (BW01).

COUNTRY MUSIC

COUNTRY MUSIC

"Let's face it, most of us aren't singers, we're stylists."
—Bill Anderson,
country singer

ORIGINS

Country music resulted from the commercialization of the solo singer tradition in both folk and old time music. It is considered rural, southern, and Anglo-Saxon, but it has many roots and external sources, such as vaudeville, minstrel, and medicine shows; the Hawaiian steel guitar; the Celtic fiddle tradition; the Swiss yodel; the Spanish guitar; and the French concertina. In the past, it has gone under many names: hillbilly, rockabilly, mountain music, western swing, cowboy music, folk songs, sacred music, old time music, hill and range, bluegrass, "hurtin' music," honky-tonk, and so forth. Over 50,000 titles were recorded before World War II, and most of these fall into the genre of **Old Time Music** (see that section, p. 99). However, there is an obvious difference between the string band and the solo balladeer, which were the two main divisions. String bands evolved into bluegrass, while the soloist defined modern country music.

The end of World War II marked the beginning of modern country music. The major shift in white population patterns, in which rural people moved to urban centers, meant that they took their music with them, as did blacks in their migrations. The transplanted rural people fell prey to urban problems of disenchantment, alienation, and impersonality that led to rootlessness and loneliness, which were reflected in their singing and listening habits. The breakdown of regionalism meant the emergence of the Texas influence, and it all came together in the late 1940s through such performers as Ernest Tubb and Hank Williams. The roots of this music were in Texas black blues, the western swing of Bob Wills, the cowboy stylings of Carl T. Sprague and Gene Autry, the blues of Jimmie Rodgers, the pop of Vernon Dalhart, and the glamour of western clothes and films; and this followed through into the 1970s with the "Austin outlaws" branch of country music.

What follows, then, is a very brief history of country music. By the period of the Depression, recording companies began to run out of traditional songs. New compositions were needed, and there was extra money to be made by claims of copyright. The business of recording could not afford more than a singer-songwriter-musician (this was one person) who could functionally perform on the guitar, sing well, and employ some interesting lyrics. Jimmie Rodgers was the first and last who excelled in all three categories. Later, as expenses allowed, extra people were added to the discs. Brother duos began (they weren't to be paid as much as two unrelated people were) to perform the best of the old time music, but with guitars or mandolins rather than the string band's banjo-fiddle combination. This was smoother instrumentation in addition to the smooth and polished harmonic singing. Effective duos were the Delmores, the Mainers, the Bolicks (Blue Sky Boys), the Morrises, the Dixons, the Carlisles, the Monroes, and the Callahans.

By the time of the recording bans of the early 1940s, and with the desire of companies to seek national rather than regional markets, recordings had reached the stage of having larger, "acceptable" accompaniment that led to the same blandness that the pop market was suffering from. However, by this time, country music was largely being recorded by professional, experienced musicians whose sole job was music (i.e., it was no longer a hobby). Through the war years, several changes were ushered in. First, the spread of western swing by means of radio programs infused certain jazz and Mexican rhythms into the music. Second, many entertainers moved to urban areas such as Hollywood and New York. Third, the western element dominated much of the music, especially through road shows and sequinned costumes.

Thus, by the end of the war, a new breed of music had been fashioned— honky-tonk. This music was basically country plus western swing, with some roots in the 1930s boogie stylings in jazz and in the Delmore Brothers. Honky-tonk took western swing instrumentation (steel guitar, drums, horns), and added the thematic and vocal quality of a "cheating song" lyric. Thus, it was both raucous and sad at the same time, with a touch of introspective blues—Ernest Tubb was the leading exponent. King Records was one of the first independent labels, and it built a country roster around the honky-tonk motif. Later, this music would resurface in the late 1960s as "truck driving music." At this time, then, it was truly "country *and* western" music, and a golden period began that was to last for a decade. It included the performances of Tubb, Merle Travis, Hank Williams, and Webb Pierce. With much of the punch being taken out of pre-war ballad singing, it was not surprising that post-war honky-tonk developed in the direction of ballad singing. So crooners such as Eddy Arnold and George Morgan developed, and they were to have an impact on pop-derived styles.

In the 1950s, southeastern and southwestern music had merged together, and by this time, it no longer mattered in what part of the country a singer was brought up, just so long as he was exposed to music by record or radio. But by the mid-fifties, the emerging sounds of rock and roll took over and almost killed country music. There was little innovation after Hank Williams died in 1953, and the rockabilly sounds were the pop world's answer to honky-tonk music. Rockabilly was simply country music with a heavy dose of r 'n' b, a harder, more brittle form of honky-tonk that appealed to younger listeners. When it evolved into rock and roll, it also took several country singers with it, thereby creating a vacuum. The dilemma for country music was whether to continue with popular material and honky-tonk backing or to strike new ground.

At the same time, women singers began to perform in the genre, and most of them came from a church background or from singing families. Their material was basically the same as that for men: hurting, cheating, and drinking songs. (Rebellion and women's liberation were over a decade in the future.) But their impact was the contribution of naturally light voices and altos that never jibed with a honky-tonk backing (except for Wanda Jackson). Patsy Cline was the best during this period, and together with crooner Eddie Arnold, laid the foundations for the "Nashville sound"; this was an industry-wide position taken by the (then) recently-formed Country Music Association (put together to preserve country music) and developed by its leading architect, Chet Atkins. This sound emphasized the pop-ballad along with soft, discreet piano accompaniment, and later "sweetening" would be added (violins and horns).

Many years later, Atkins admitted that he was wrong to implement the ideas, but at the time it saved country music by eliminating the "*& western*" and moving it closer to the pop world of mood and mainstream material (which was also suffering from rock and roll). The appeal in the 1960s was to *both* the town and country audience, and it was palatable for all forms of radio as the singers (such as Jim Reeves) lost most of their rural and/or nasal twang. This movement accounted for the rise of country music radio stations, and its leading singers included Glen Campbell, Roger Miller, George Hamilton IV, early Waylon Jennings and Willie Nelson, and Eddie Arnold at the peak of his success. These slow, halting ballads had a profound effect on folk-rock of the time, especially on the Byrds, the Eagles, the Band, and Bob Dylan. Every singer of repute had to make the journey to Nashville in order to record at least one album there, and country music was riding high again, although it had reverted to the blandness that had affected it around 1940.

In the last decade, the "Nashville sound" received respectability through sales, cross-over artists using Nashville session men, national television shows, and the CMA. Films have brought forth the roots of modern country music, such as *Hud, Deliverance, Bonnie and Clyde,* and *The Last Picture Show.* But at the same time, these "roots" created an "uptown/ex-town" split between the sophisticated, urbanized country music singer and the disgruntled, counter-culture country singer. This latter movement has been shaping up since 1970, and its adherents go by such diverse names as "cosmic cowboys," "redneck rockers," "Nashville outlaws," and so forth. In 1975, it became centered in Austin, Texas, at the Armadillo World Headquarters, and now includes in its membership Jerry Jeff Walker and Kinky Friedman (both from the troubador genre), ex-rock star Doug Sahm, Asleep at the Wheel, Willie Nelson, and occasionally Waylon Jennings. In many respects, this new form of country music, with its rhythms and lyrics, is far in advance of contemporary country-rock, and it has proved more enduring through the decade of the 1970s.

It is very difficult to obtain earlier records of the 1930s and 1940s in the country music genre. Many are simply not available because the major recording companies will not issue them, and the smaller reissue companies think country music is too commercial and would rather reissue old time music or bluegrass. Thus, some of the early "stars" are virtually unobtainable today despite their original success: Patsy Montana, Molly O'Day, Moon Mullican, T. Texas Tyler, Tex Williams, Stuart Hamblen, Jimmie Dolan, Joe Maphis and Rosa Lee, and Rosalie Allen. CMH in West Germany has begun a massive reissue program covering Gene Autry, Hank Snow, Wilf Carter, etc., but many more singers need to be covered. Also, those that were reissued by the major companies are in danger of being let go into the "out of print" market.

NON-MUSICAL INFLUENCES

In such a heavily commercial field as country music, non-musical influences are also considerable. *First*, there was the advent of radio, since country life and the importance of radio in isolated areas made for a captive audience. Throughout the United States, radio programs sprang up everywhere, with enough power for each to blanket most of that part of the contiguous United States not covered by "border radio" (e.g., XERA). And all of this music was "live," creating a need for more and more performers and material. The first show was on WSB in Atlanta, which put old time music on the air in 1922, creating a local demand later supplied by Fiddlin' John Carson's recordings. This in turn established the field trip as the basis for recording old time music. The first regularly scheduled show of any sustaining power was the National Barn Dance on WLS (Chicago, 1924-1960), quickly followed by the Grand Ole Opry on WSM (Nashville, 1925-), and later the Country Jamboree on WWVA (Wheeling, West Virginia), the Midwestern Hayride on WLW (Cincinatti, 1938-1971, and also the first on television, beginning in 1948), the Big D Jamboree of KRLD (Dallas, 1947-1967), and the Louisiana Hayride of KWKH (Shreveport, 1948-1958 as a regular show). At opposite poles, there were many smaller, local "barn dances" on radio. And there was "border radio," a series of powerful transmitters in Mexico that completely blanketed all of North America with full-time country music and sacred music. The most famous of these was XERA. In 1948, one of the first radio surveys showed that the Grand Ole Opry was being listened to regularly in ten million homes, a phenomenon now only repeated through television. Economic conditions and television killed off many radio shows, but there emerged syndicated television shows by almost every top star in country music, as well as over 1,000 (!) radio stations playing country music full-time; New York City capitulated in 1974. *Second*, the demand for records did not slacken at all when these radio shows were in their heyday. It was obvious that listeners were attracted to particular singers, no matter what they sang, and the star cult was born. This tended to aggravate the situation by putting tremendous pressure on singers to rise to the top. *Third*, the breakdown of regional barriers (while regrettable) and regional markets created cross-fertilization potential between the different stylings of southeastern and southwestern music. Different musical backgrounds began to merge (Mexican, Creole, Anglo-Irish, black blues, European polkas, etc.) as well as to introduce different instrumentation. *Fourth*, jukeboxes began to add country music during the Depression and bars hired live music at the start of World War II, which encouraged new material. *Fifth*, the creation of the Country Music Association led to respectability. This industry group presented a united front of publishers, producers, musicians, writers, and singers in a successful attempt to upgrade the public perception of country music as it sought new markets and to create standards for the industry.

These five influences had an effect on the music by drawing listeners and performers who could or would fall into an acceptable pattern. In just about every case, the typical pre-1970 male country singer had generally the same background. He was poor, but had listened to country music radio shows and records. He borrowed, made, or bought a cheap guitar. He played by observing others, especially black performers. After memorizing the three basic chords, he performed at local dances and social events. He sang on fifteen minute radio shows and, maybe, on local television. He quite often got a job as a disc jockey; then, through this influence, he had enough clout to force a contract or to record a few songs for a (minor or major) company. Somewhere along the way, he would also have armed forces duty—in Europe, Korea, Viet Nam, or a routine foreign posting.

Here he would get lonesome and sing songs of home, with other soldiers listening and responding. Swapping songs and ideas was a common device, and many urban dwellers received their first introduction to country music in this manner. Also, many singers picked up regional variations that they would take back with them and composed many story songs.

MUSIC AND INSTRUMENTATION

In form, there are only three basic chords—the tonic, the dominant, and the sub-dominant (the 1st, 5th and 4th notes on the scale)—and all of these are relatively easy to perform. Key changes are effected through chromatic leaps rather than slow modulation (this also occurs in rock music). Influences come from rock and roll, folk music, and jazz, but the instrumentation itself is not complex. Originally, it was merely a guitar to accompany the singer, who often played that guitar himself. During the Depression, it was cheaper to record just one person who would also play, and he was not really required to play well. Imitators and second-generation singers followed this styling until the industry recovered and also perfected better recording equipment.

Instruments appear to have been added one at a time, first with another guitar or mandolin in the brother duos; then with string bass, fiddle, accordion, and slide guitar; and then the pedal steel guitar, followed by drums. In the late 1960s, horn and violin sections were added. But there are very few counter melodies and harmonies, and all of these extra instruments merely add punctuation or runs from one verse to another. Musicians borrowed much from the blacks, especially in the nineteenth century. Slaves who could fiddle created the difficult blue notes for the violin; the five string banjo was a black development from Africa; black railroad construction workers introduced the guitar to Appalachia and other workers brought it to the Cajun and southwest area. Many singers learned how to vocalize or play their instruments from local or migratory blacks (e.g., Bill Monroe, Jimmie Rodgers, Hank Williams, Charlie Rich). Others learned by listening to the records of Blind Lemon Jefferson, Georgia Tom Dorsey, the Mississippi Sheiks, and, in the 1950s, to Ivory Joe Hunter and Ray Charles. For all their influence, there have only been two blacks of note in country music—DeFord Bailey, who played harmonica on the Grand Ole Opry (1925-1941), and Charley Pride.

SONGS AND LYRICS

With roots in old time music and folk, early country music continued the instrumental tradition of blues, hoedowns, ragtime, and breakdowns. The vocal element comprised the ballad (weepers and heart songs), the cowboy song (ranchhouse life and the trail), topical songs, and event songs. In every respect, though, the basic element in the country song was the *lyric*. Performers could barely strum, and the tunes were repetitive and traditionally-based; however, the vocal lines were exceptionally strong. By the late 1940s, they reflected the country-to-city migrations and new stresses of the urban environment, creating a universality of meaning with conflicting ways of life (cheating on a spouse, excessive drinking, rowdiness, etc.). In most cases, the title of the song told the contents (e.g., "Cheatin' Heart," "We Had It All"). And it was through the country music industry that the songs of self-expression were turned into successful commercial vehicles.

Indeed, in the early 1950s, the songs published by the Acuff-Rose firm dominated the pop charts in addition to the country field. Through the years, the producer and a and r (artist-and-reportoire) man selected the material to control the singer. These men had dramatic impact on the choice of songs: for RCA, Steve Sholes, Chet Atkins, Ralph Peer; for CBS, Don Law, Art Satherley and Ralph Peer; for MCA, Dave Kapp, Paul Cohen, and Owen Bradley; for King, Sid Nathan; and for Starday and Mercury, Don Pierce.

Many songs were expressly written to order. In an analysis of 350 songs published by Southern Music-Peer International, plus 100 published by Hill and Range Songs Inc., 65 percent were found to be of the "hurtin' " music variety, 5 percent were optimistic, 4 percent were western, 5 percent were sacred, 1 percent were dance tunes, and 20 percent were miscellaneous. Horstmann (43) provides an invaluable guide to the topics of country music between 1940 and 1970. There are five chief concerns:

1. *Attitude towards life*, which is more pragmatic and realistic than in the pop music world (the sentimental song, the tragic song).

2. *Standards of conduct* show a dichotomy. On the one hand, rowdiness is openly discussed and commented on; on the other, there is a cultural transfer from medieval times through expressions of chivalry. Much of this leads to the familiar double standard.

3. *Ideals of behavior*, in which there is reverence for history and romanticism (hobos, trains, gun fighters) and a distrust of business (corruption by money, work-related migratory patterns).

4. *Social practices*, related to drinking and emotional displays.

5. *Family ties*, such as feelings about finances, open love ("barnyard imagery"), work (mining, taxi-driving, share cropping, farming, etc.), marriage (infidelity, triangles, divorce), and religion (immortality and reincarnation).

But in the last seven years, other forms have also developed. First, there has been a progressing adult movement toward *sexuality* that transcends the love category. Much has been fairly explicit, such as Conway Twitty's "You've Never Been This Far Before," Freddy Weller's "Sexy Lady," Tanya Tucker's "Will You Lay with Me (in a Field of Stone)?," and Charlie Rich's "Behind Closed Doors." Second, there has been a tremendous upsurge in the *loner* songs of hard times, alienation, truck-driving, gun-fighter ballads, prison songs, and so forth. Admittedly, many of these songs come from outside Nashville, such as those from the Austin, Texas scene (busker, or drifter, songs) or Bakersfield, California; and they also represent a revival of honky-tonk, social commentary (something new for country music), and story songs (as started by Tom T. Hall). And third, *women's songs* concentrating on liberation and stressing unequal relationships and partnerships. When viewed in light of real divorces among country stars, it appears as if the social fabric of America is degenerating into individualistic patterns rather than maintaining the collectivity so often stressed in pre-1970 country music. An indication of this is the disappearance of the song about children and about aging parents.

Whatever the topics or concerns of the country song, the format is nearly always the same. Folk, popular and religious sources are used for commercial music, with simple, direct, and easy lyrics that stress the sad and nostalgic side of life. There is a maximum of 200 seconds recording time to develop the story, so the narrative is far more important than the melody (which suffers from a lack of creativity). Indeed, an analysis of song timings shows that the greater the *hook* (catchy phrase, metaphor, or picturesque speech), the more condensed the song will be and the sooner it will be finished (after two minutes—120 seconds—just 60 percent of the limit imposed by AM radio). These phrases (Hoyt Axton's "bony fingers," Ray Price's "shoes keep walking back to you," Hank Snow's "married by the Bible, divorced by the law," Eddie Arnold's "thirty years married to the wrong woman," Dolly Parton's "go get her," and even satire on advertising such as "What Has Made Milwaukee Famous Has Made a Loser out of Me" or "I Was Raised on Country Sunshine") can either be opening lines or used to resolve some form of inner tension in the rhyming pattern. For rock music (in contrast), the hook is instrumental, and consists of the riff.

LITERATURE

Country music is based on folk, old time, bluegrass, and western music; hence, all previous materials apply for basic background in addition to what is listed here. The grandest scholarly work is Malone's (57) Ph.D. dissertation, published in 1968, which was a studious attempt to trace country music down through the years. This was later extended by other surveys, such as Gentry (30), Grissim (36), Malone and McCulloh (58), and Shelton (83). Biographical material includes a who's who (17), Gray's (32) pictorial work, Stambler's (86) entries for the pre-1968 period, and Shestack (84) through 1972. More specialized studies include Hemphill (39) on the Nashville sound, Horstman's (43) brief analysis of 300 songs, Kahn's (47) work on women, and Pleasants' (68) analysis of vocal singing style. Whitburn (95) gives basic hit chart data for the 1949-1971 period, all for single discs.

As with books, periodical literature in country music also includes folk, old time, western, and bluegrass histories. In addition to the magazines cited as being important to their respective fields, there are three main "country" publications. *Country Music* (4) contains popularly written articles about personalities, but with few historical approaches. *Country Music People* (5) and *Country Music Review* (6)—both from England—also include articles about old time music, bluegrass, etc. *The Journal of Country Music* (11) is devoted to the past, while *Popular Music and Society* (18) will detail sociological shifts in listener responses and marketing. The *Annual Index to Popular Music Record Reviews* (3) can be used to trace albums, while the *Popular Music Periodicals Index* (69) is useful for artists and discographies.

ANTHOLOGIES

F8.1   **Best of Music Country America.** MCA MCF 2599 (British issue).

F8.2   **Country Sides.** MCA 1929.
Anthologies are important sellers for the major recording companies, for through this means the public is "sampled" in the search for ever larger buying audiences. And it is a good way for collectors and libraries to build up a series of single hits that quite often either do not appear on albums or appear as the only good song on a collection of duds. These two collections from the MCA catalog are leading examples. Titles span twenty years, and include Patsy Cline's "Crazy," Red Foley's "Chattanooga Shoe Shine Boy," Bill Anderson's "Still," Kitty Wells's "It Wasn't God Who Made Honky Tonk Angels," Brenda Lee's "I'm Sorry," Loretta Lynn's "Trouble in Paradise," Jeanne Pruett's "Satin Sheets," and the duo of Conway Twitty and Loretta Lynn ("As Soon as I Hang up the Phone").

F8.3   **Canadian Country Music History, v.1.** Country Music History CMH 201 (West German issue).
This excellent introduction to the early Canadian music scene includes a hefty proportion of Wilf Carter ("Rescue from the Moose River Goldmine," "One Golden Curl"), along with one or two tracks from Hank Snow ("Prisoned Cowboy"), Orval Prophet, Stu Philips ("The Champlain & St. Lawrence Line"), Karl Lofstrom's patriotism ("Give Me Good Old Canada"), Luke Simmons, Donn Reynolds, and Stu Davis. Canadian country music has always been done in a looser style than that found in the United States Southeast.

F8.4   **Country Gals—Country Hits.** two discs. RCA ADL2-0177.

F8.5   **Country Music Hits.** Camden CAS 689.

F8.6   **The Country Stars! The Country Hits.** Camden CAS 793.

F8.7   **Grand Ole Country Hits.** Camden CAS 737.

F8.8*   **Stars of the Grand Ole Opry, 1926-1974.** two discs. RCA CPL2-0466.
The nature of the anthology in country music is diverse: they can be compilations of "the best of the year"; they are available in both budget and full-price lines; they can effectively deal with different themes and styles (sacred material, male singers, duets, women, etc.). RCA has one of the largest country catalogs, extending as it does over the past fifty years, and something from each time period appears on each one of these discs. ADL2-0177 gives a few hints of the power of women singers through renditions by Skeeter Davis, Davis Sisters, Norma Jean, Dolly Parton, Connie Smith, and Dottie West. The Camden budget discs—still in the catalog—comprise about 36 tracks of older songs from Eddy Arnold, Jim Reeves, Pee Wee King, Slim Whitman, Gid Tanner, Grandpa Jones, Elton Britt, Montana Slim, Bill Boyd, Chet Atkins, Jimmie Rodgers, Don Gibson, Roy Rogers,

Homer & Jethro, plus others. *Stars of the Grand Ole Opry* is a bit more cohesive, featuring Bill Monroe, Minnie Pearl, Eddy Arnold, Lester Flatt, Chet Atkins, and others in a wide-ranging program including such items as "Railroadin' and Gamblin'," "Jealous Hearted Me," "I'm My Own Grandpa," "I Don't Hurt Anymore," "Old Blue," "Down Yonder," "Send Me the Pillow You Dream On," and so forth.

F8.9*   **Country Hits of the 40s, 50s, and 60s.** three discs. Capitol ST 884/6.
     All the material in this thirty-year survey comes from the vault of Capitol records. Just by listening to the total of thirty tracks one can hear a mini-history of the changes in the sound of country music. Great tracks from the 1940s include Tex Williams's "Smoke! Smoke! Smoke! (That Cigarette)," the duo of Margaret Whiting and Jimmy Wakely singing "Slipping Around," Merle Travis's "Divorce Me C.O.D.," and Jimmy Davis's "You Are My Sunshine." Shifts in styles in the 1950s include Tennessee Ernie Ford's rendition of the Merle Travis tune "16 Tons," the honky-tonk swing of Hank Thompson's "Wild Side of Life," the early rock and roll of Sonny James's "Young Love," and the country duo of Jean Shepard and Ferlin Husky in "A Dear John Letter." With the 1960s came pop influences and the Nashville sound, such as Glen Campbell's "Gentle on My Mind," Faron Young's version of Willie Nelson's "Hello, Walls," the sentimentality of Tex Ritter's "I Dreamed of a Hillbilly Heaven," and the flash of Roy Clark's "The Tip of My Fingers."

F8.10*   **Diesel Smoke, Dangerous Curves and Other Truck Driver Favorites.** Starday SLP 250.

F8.11*   **18 King Size Country Hits.** Columbia CS 9468.

F8.12*   **Memphis Country.** Sun 6467.013 (British issue).
     These three discs present an excellent introduction to the best materials produced by the three leading independent country music record companies. The Starday catalog entry is wider than the "truck driving" songs would indicate (Willis Brothers, Dave Dudley); there are nine tracks here. The twice-as-big King catalog (distributed here by Columbia) includes performances dating back to the 1940s ("I'll Sail My Ship Alone" by Moon Mullican, "Blues Stay Away from Me" by the Delmore Brothers, "Signed, Sealed and Delivered" by Cowboy Copas, and items from Reno and Smiley, Grandpa Jones, Hawkshaw Hawkins, the Stanley Brothers, etc.).
     The immensely successful Sun catalog omits Elvis Presley (RCA bought his Sun masters), but does include Johnny Cash's "I Walk the Line," Jerry Lee Lewis's "You Win Again" (after Hank Williams), Charlie Rich's "Sittin' and Thinkin'," plus Carl Perkins, David Houston, and Roy Orbison.

F8.13*   **Grand Ole Opry Stars.** two discs. County 541/2.

F8.14*   **Grand Ole Opry Stars.** two discs. RCA Bluebird AXM2-55-- (in progress).
     These two albums span the early years of the Grand Ole Opry, but none of it was recorded "live"; all are studio versions. However, the performers on these sets were active until the war years. The 25 items on the County set include

DeFord Bailey (the first black country star—harmonica player and sometime-clown working at the Opry; Charley Pride would be the next black country star) with "Muscle Shoals Blues" and "Pan American Blues"; Dr. Humphrey Bate with "My Wife Died Saturday Night" and "Throw the Old Cow over the Fence" (a highly suspicious coupling); the Binkley Brothers' Dixie Clodhoppers with "Give Me Back My Fifteen Cents"; the Crook Brothers doing "Going across the Sea" and "Jobbin' Gettin' There"; Theron Hale and His Daughters singing "Jolly Black-smith" and "Hale's Rag"; plus others by Sid Harkreader, the McGee Brothers, Blind Joe Mangrum, and Fred Shriver. The 32 items on the Bluebird set include many of the above same performers doing different songs; in addition, there are Bradley Kincaid, Whit Graydon, Uncle Dave Macon, Arthur Smith, and Lasses and Honey. Both albums come with good notes, although the Bluebird compila-tion has lengthier texts. Both are excellent cross-sections of the type of music and material that went out over the airwaves from WSM in Nashville, although not everyone who appeared on the Grand Ole Opry was a big star.

F8.15   **Wanted! The Outlaws.** RCA APL 1-1321.
        This anthology neatly collates some prime, leading examples of the so-called "progressive country" or "Nashville outlaws" mode of singing. Waylon Jennings does "My Heroes Have Always Been Cowboys" and "Honky Tonk Heroes"; Jessi Colter (now Mrs. Jennings) performs "I'm Looking for Blue Eyes" and sings a duo with Waylon on "Suspicious Minds." Jennings also reappears with Willie Nelson on "Goodhearted Woman" and "Heaven or Hell." The collection concludes with Tompall Glaser selections loaned from MGM.

F8.16*   **Will the Circle be Unbroken?** three discs. United Artists UAS 9801.
        The Nitty Gritty Dirt Band (now simply the Dirt Band) assembled a key group of country musicians in Nashville in August 1971, and sat down to play with them. The resulting set highlights the careers of many performers, and the music thereon has to be rated as essential for any record collection dealing with country and bluegrass music. There is definitely no modern country "hurtin' " music here. The package itself, while physically awkward to manipulate, contains lots of photo-graphs, reprints of newspaper articles, and full personnel data. A brief rundown of the contents shows the variety here: Mother Maybelle Carter sings Carter Family favorites ("Keep on the Sunny Side," "I'm Thinking Tonight of My Blue Eyes," "Wildwood Flower") in her tired, worn voice, but with superb guitar. Jimmy Martin, the best performer on the set, sings three selections, including the lovely "You Don't Know My Mind." Earl Scruggs performs throughout and leads on "Nashville Blues" and "You Are My Flower." Roy Acuff, with a trembling voice that has to reach for even a medium high note, gives adequate force to "Precious Jewel," "Wreck on the Highway" and to Hank Williams's "I Saw the Light." (It was a shame that there was no one around to harmonize with him, for that's his main style.) Merle Travis repeats his classics "Dark as a Dungeon" and "Nine Pound Hammer," while Doc Watson wails away on "Tennessee Stud" and performs several instrumentals. All are backed by the rock solid, acoustic Nitty Gritty Dirt Band plus several key session men. The problem with voices is very evident; Carter, Acuff, and Travis no longer can reach the high, lonesome notes so characteristic of bluegrass and early country music. Sixteen of the 37

selections are instrumentals, and in this format, the best music is produced. Vassar Clements's fiddle on the oft-recorded "Orange Blossom Special" is a delight, and so is the interplay between various performers who have never before "jammed" on disc because of contracts with different recording companies.

Great emphasis is placed on the differences between country singers and the "long haired freaks," and on the fact that these differences dissolve when the music is laid down. The hype here is that this set is supposed to be a "back to the roots" trip, and the programming fits in with this. The opening selection is "Grand Old Opry Song" (which names most of the people of the Opry), and the closing selection is Earl's son Randy performing a solo guitar version of "Both Sides Now," as if to stress that both groups now appreciate and understand each other better. Both Acuff and Martin had a strong hand in persuading other older performers to participate in this session. Even so, Bill Monroe declined—and that might be the only foolish thing he has ever done, for the set ultimately sold more than a million units.

MALE SINGERS

Innovators

F8.17*   **Roy Acuff. Greatest Hits.** Columbia CS 1034.

Acuff has probably been responsible for most people's conception of country music as "hillbilly." He played a hot, wailing fiddle and sang in a nasal voice, both of which developed from his rural roots and the influence of the traveling medicine shows. His stage act with the Crazy Tennesseans went out over the airwaves for many years (a national show from 1934 and continuously on the Grand Ole Opry since 1940—almost 45 years!). He replaced Uncle Dave Macon as the most popular Opry regular. He perpetuated his image as a clown and entertainer by stressing *show business* above all else. The Opry was full of string bands until his arrival, but he quickly became its first *star* as he was a featured vocalist with a backup band. In his recording career, his most influential items were done for Vocalion, and these unfortunately are not yet available as reissues ("Steamboat Whistle Blues," "Wabash Cannonball" [on which he did the whistle while Dynamite Hatcher sang the vocal], "New Greenback Dollars," and "Steel Guitar Chimes").

Along with some 300 titles, Acuff re-recorded these originals, especially after World War II. On "Wabash," this latter time, he took the vocal, and perhaps this song (most associated with Acuff) illustrates what his music is all about: sincerity, where he shouts with emotion (later influencing Hank Williams); innovation, whereby he advanced country music beyond Jimmie Rodgers, especially with the introduction of the Dobro; compositional skills (he wrote and arranged over 100 songs, such as "Precious Jewel"); and musical synthesis, where he was being influenced both by Clarence Ashley and by carefully listening to the phonograph record while maturing. He thus becomes the transitional figure between the string bands of the Southeast (he had harmonica, mandolin, Dobro, banjo, etc., in his band) and the western swing of the Southwest style (through his humor, blues, and thematic material), ultimately blending both into "modern" country music. Some of his very important items include "Night Train to Memphis,"

"Muleshine Blues," "Smokey Mountain Rag," "Worried Mind," "Wreck on the Highway," and "Great Speckled Bird."

F8.18*   **Johnny Cash. At Folsom Prison and San Quentin.** two discs. Columbia CG 33639.

F8.19*   **Johnny Cash. Greatest Hits, v.1/2.** two discs. Columbia CS 9478 and KC 30887.
Cash came from a sharecropper family, and he was influenced by the Carter Family, Ernest Tubb, Hank Williams, Hank Snow, and Baptist hymns. With Luther Perkins (guitar) and Marshall Grant (bass)—known together as the Tennessee Two—he carved out several successful rockabilly hits for Sun records. With Columbia, after a mild flirtation with pop, he returned to uptempo country music with a rock beat, including such story ballads as "Don't Take Your Guns to Town" or "Frankie's Man Johnny." The earlier distinctively muffled plucking sound of his rhythm accompaniment gave way to a fuller musical background to augment his narrow baritone range, which deepened as the years passed. Surprisingly, his first Columbia album grossed 400,000 in sales—a record for country music at that time. His own songs largely emphasize droll humor (as on "Bad News") or male chauvinism (as on "Understand Your Man"), but he is occasionally sinful, as "Ring of Fire" testified.

Good written material from other composers included "Jackson," "Orange Blossom Special," some Dylan ("It Ain't Me Babe"), and "Green Green Grass of Home." His repertoire—perhaps the widest in all of country music—embraces sacred hymns, white blues, novelty songs, some topical items, traditional ballads, folk songs, story songs and sagas, and plain lyrical songs. He has often struck out in new directions, as by his appearing at folk festivals or appealing to urban dwellers. His 1968 Folsom Prison album (and the later San Quentin follow-up) was the first time the Cash road show was put on record, and they were also some of the first live albums in country music (Porter Wagoner in 1964 had the first one). Both were characterized at the time as being models of a performing style featuring precision and superb timing. They also started a barrage of prison concerts (and recordings) by other singers. Some prison songs are included on these discs as well as past hits, comedy items, and traditional ballads.

F8.20   **Delmore Brothers. 1934-1939.** two discs. RCA AXM 2-5541.

F8.21*   **Delmore Brothers. Brown's Ferry Blues, 1933-1941.** County 402.

F8.22   **Delmore Brothers. 16 All-Time Favorites.** King 589.
In style, the Delmore Brothers merged both blues and sacred music. Alton's tenor guitar (four strings) lead was modeled on the tenor banjo, but his brother Rabon's style was in the ragtime flavor of Blind Boy Fuller and other black rhythmic performers of the Piedmont area. Their Alabama heritage (as on "Back to Birmingham") was a great source of traditional material, but it was of the quick-step variety ("Don't Let the Deal Go Down" or "Step It up and Go") rather than sentimental songs. Harmonic expression was derived from the sacred tradition, with call-and-response patterns in the arrangements. Alton (lead vocal) had perfect

pitch, and coupled with Rabon's harmony, it formed a link of blues, ragtime, and sacred music through the transition period of the 1930s to the commercial sounds of the 1940s and to later bluegrass harmonizing.

Their guitars were rather prominent on such items as "Southern Moon" or "When It's Time for the Whipperwill to Sing," and they early established a boogie guitar style, heard on "The Nashville Blues." Later, for King, they recorded many spirited titles ("Freight Train Boogie," "Boogie Woogie Baby," "Used Car Blues," "Peach Tree Street Boogie") and some hit material ("Shame on Me" and the 1949 "Blues Stay Away from Me"). Alton composed over 1,000 songs, some recorded by Tennessee Ernie Ford, Glen Campbell, Bob Dylan, and Doug Sahm. He was also one of the few country performers who could read music. Brother Rabon wrote 200 songs himself. The Delmores were a very influential group, being one of the first brother singing acts (they recorded in 1931 for Columbia); they sang original songs, and they appealed to a largely diverse audience with their diverse material (sad numbers, blues, boogies, and harmony showcase pieces).

F8.23* **George Jones. Best.** United Artists UA 6291.

F8.24 **George Jones. Best of the Best.** RCA APL 1-1113.

F8.25 **George Jones. Greatest Hits.** KE 33352.

F8.26* **George Jones. Greatest Hits.** Mercury 60621.

F8.27 **George Jones. Greatest Hits.** Musicor 3116.

F8.28* **George Jones. Greatest Hits.** Starday SLP 150.

George Jones has recorded over ninety albums in his long career with many record companies, and we have selected a greatest hits album from each company. He has changed little over the years except to follow the whims of his diverse producers (such as echo, added instrumentation, sweetening of strings and voices, etc.). Essentially, he is a traditional singer from Texas who was heavily influenced by Roy Acuff and Bill Monroe. His sound is exceptionally rural, and he takes a fundamentalist sacred stance despite his reputation for fast living and hard drinking. Many of his songs relate to booze and despair, and in fact, his music is often known as "tavern music." His prolific recording output is no doubt related to the fact that he is a versatile singer, with a good span for both high and low vocals. His phrasing is exceptionally variable, so he can satisfy a wide-ranging audience.

His Starday years (1954-1957) were his most creative period. He had developed a harsh tone early in his career, being influenced by and extending the songs and nature of Hank Williams. The allusion, of course, was that Jones was Williams's successor, and in many ways, he was, with such classics as "Why, Baby, Why?," "Play It Cool, Man," "Rock It," "Maybe Little Baby," and "Ragged but Right"— all honky-tonk items—plus the sacred item "What Am I Worth?" Moving to Mercury (1958-1961), he used fiddler Link Davis and steel guitarist Herbie Remington to fashion "Treasure of Love," "Who Shot Sam," and his ultimate classic tavern song, "White Lightnin'." With Liberty (now United Artists) in 1961-1964, he continued his succession of hits with "Revenooer Man" and "Aching, Breaking Heart," but he also created more ballads, such as "A Girl I Used to Know," "She Thinks I Still Care," and "Tender Years." Sacred material included "Window up There." His Musicor career (1965-1967) returned him to more uptempo songs, such as "Love Bug," "Take Me," "Things Have Gone to Pieces," and the religious classic "You Can't Get There from Here."

Moving on to RCA (1968-1971), he concentrated on re-recording his earlier hits with different instrumentation and some sweetening. New material was scarce, but he included "Four-O-Thirty Three," "If My Heart Had Windows," "A Day in the Life of a Fool," plus more excellent sacred music. By now Jones had established a pattern for each album: some re-recordings in different stylings, some sacred items, and some new songs. In 1971, he went to his sixth record company, Epic. The pattern continued with a pleasant mixture of tender ballads and rousing uptempo songs. His biggest success from this period was "The Grand Tour," followed by the lyrically beautiful "These Days I Barely Get By" and "Nothing Ever Hurt Me Half as Bad as Losing You." With Epic, however, there is a distinct predominance of tearjerker ballads.

F8.29* **Louvin Brothers.** Hilltop JS 6036.

Charlie and Ira Louvin were a great singing team with two-tenor harmony. They began recording for Capitol in 1951, and they split their output between secular and sacred items. Their harmonies and fast tempo materials, such as "I Don't Believe You've Met My Baby" or "Hoping That You're Hoping," had a tremendous impact on bluegrass music, and now many such groups present or program Louvin Brothers' compositions. They served to reinforce the impact that duo singing has had on bluegrass, claiming that they, in turn, were influenced by the Delmore Brothers, the Wilburn Brothers, and the Blue Sky Boys. During their career, the Louvins received many awards for their performances. Also included on this 10-track set leased from Capitol records is the hurtin' music of "Here Today and Gone Tomorrow."

F8.30* **Webb Pierce. Story.** two discs. MCA Decca DXS 7181.

While Buck Owens may have had 27 consecutive "number one" hits, no other country singer has had a greater total number of them than Webb Pierce (at last count, 68!). His distinctive, wailing tenor voice can be heard on such early 1950s hits as "Slowly," the classic drink song "There Stands the Glass," the reworked Jimmie Rodgers classic "In the Jailhouse Now" (and other such prison songs as "Tupelo County Jail"), the ballads "Little Rosa" (with Red Sovine), "Missing You," "More and More," "You're Not Mine Anymore," and the uptempo honkytonk stylings of "I Don't Care," "Why Baby Why?," and "Any Old Time."

Pierce came from Louisiana and joined the Hayride. Early members of his personal band included Goldie Hill, Faron Young, and Floyd Cramer—all of whom went on to be stars in their own right. Recording for Decca in 1952 and joining the Opry in 1954, Pierce started his career with such epics as "Back Street Affair" and "Wondering." Unfortunately, Decca has never sought to put together his original materials. Most of the items on the above twofer (pre-1961 materials) are merely re-recordings with added strings and female chorus. This is a real shame, for Pierce, with his high voice and compositional skills (one of the first in country music) exemplifies the honest country singer of the late 1940s and 1950s. Unfortunate, too, was the fact that he never adjusted to the injurious impact of rock and roll music on country music.

F8.31* **Jimmie Rodgers. The Legendary Jimmie Rodgers' 110 Collection.**
eight discs. RCA RA 5459/66 (Japanese issue).
Rodgers took country music out of rural areas and into urban centers. He was a popularizer, aided by Ralph Peer (the first a and r man in country music), and as such, he was an *entertainer*, not just a country artist. He used a wide range of styles, with a distinct emphasis on non-traditional material. For this reason, he was obviously ignored by the folk revival in the late 1950s. Yet, his importance in country music is equal to that of the Carter Family in the creation of two distinct streams: modern country music began with Rodgers; traditional music was assimilated by the Carters to be heard and passed on by all. Country music is still caught in this dichotomy of modern vs old time, where the "Nashville sound" squares off against the "bluegrass sound."

Rodgers was involved in a number of highly significant innovations. His first releases (October 1927) were made with the electrical processes that made for good technical quality, especially important for first-time urban listeners to country, rural music. He was the *first* American singer to be internationally known despite the fact that he never toured much beyond the South, nor did he engage in much publicity or even radio work. In 1961, he was the first artist to be inducted into the Country Music Hall of Fame. His success was *entirely* based on his recordings. Other artists had to push to promote sales, but Rodgers simply sang great material. In fact, sales of his discs were best during the Depression years, because he consciously identified himself with the reassuring past. He created mournful songs of lost loved ones; sentimental songs of home, mom, and dad; the hobo and railroad song of wandering in a search for roots; and a very few western items. He sang few folk songs. In vocal technique, his sincerity appealed to the ordinary guy. He had a homesick quality to his voice, and his spoken comments made him seem to be even more informal.

His most popular best sellers were the thirteen songs in the Blue Yodel series; each was numbered and given a subtitle. He combined the blues and the yodel here, bringing both into the mainstream of country music. The resulting numbers were in 4/4 time and highly rhythmic, unlike the 3/4 tempo of the Alpine yodel original. From blacks in his native Mississippi, Rodgers borrowed blues lyrics, worksongs, and general laments. In common with blacks, he stretched or shortened syllables for syncopation. In this, he was widely imitated, especially by Cliff Carlisle, Gene Autry, Hank Snow, and Ernest Tubb. (Indeed, it has been estimated that 75 percent of all 1930s country singers were influenced by Rodgers and the yodel.) It was but one more step to tie in western and Texas music, emphasizing the cattle call as a modified yodel and promoting the self-styled individual who accompanied himself.

In the 1920s, much recording activity focused on groups, but with the Depression, it was economically sounder to record (and pay) only one person at a time. Yet Rodgers, before 1931, used a variety of settings. He put out a few jazz records with Louis Armstrong's cornet, clarinet, and string bass. He used the musical saw; he used black accompaniment; he used pianos, jug bands, banjos, and violins. He even used Hawaiian backing. (The Hawaiian guitar had already been introduced at the turn of the century, but Hawaiian music itself was slow to be featured on the mainland.) Rodgers promoted and spread this music by using Lani McIntyre's Hawaiians for accompaniment, with heavy emphasis on the steel guitar and ukelele.

Rodgers's career began in 1927, in Bristol, Tennessee, at the same time that the Carter Family started. It is as if fate had intended it so, for both were the "firsts" in the two diverse styles of country music today—yet they were recorded on the same day in the same place by the same person (Peer). (By the time of his death a mere six years later, Rodgers had sold over twenty million records.) "The Yodeling Cowboy" or "The Singing Brakeman" (he was know as both) was a most demanding pioneer. In 1929, he even made a film short, *The Singing Brakeman*— the first film to feature country music singing. Typical tunes of his included "T Is for Thelma," "Away out on the Mountain," "Standing on the Corner," "Peach Picking Time in Georgia," "The Soldier's Sweetheart," and "Ben Dewberry's Final Run"—and all of the rest of the 110 are equally great country music pieces. The earlier tracks feature self-accompaniment, and Rodgers's guitar finger picking was quite advanced for its time.

We have definite reasons for selecting only the Japanese RCA reissue. The work is complete, items are given in chronological order within a good boxed set, and there is a large booklet of texts to all the songs (as transcribed, not as published), two dozen photographs, and notes relating to a biography, a chronology, and a discography. The music is in monophonic sound, and the pressings are superb and clear. American reissues have few notes, are incomplete, have phoney stereo and distortion, and are haphazardly arranged, etc. Thus, the import is well worth seeking out. However, here are the RCA (American) serial numbers for the domestic albums: LSP 1232, 1640, 2112, 2213, 2531, 2634, 2865, and 3315.

F8.32*   **Hank Snow. Best, v.1/2.** two discs. RCA LSP 3478 and 4798.

F8.33*   **Hank Snow. This Is My Story.** two discs. RCA VSP 6014.

F8.34   **Hank Snow. The Yodeling/Singing Ranger, v.1/2.** two discs. Country Music History CMH 102 and 110 (West German issue).

F8.35   **Hank Snow and Jimmie Rodgers. All about Trains.** RCA ANL 1-1052.
Hank Snow was one of the first country singers to be strongly influenced by Jimmie Rodgers. *Trains* is an excellent collation of five songs apiece that illustrate the similarities of their styles, using the recurring railroad themes that figure prominently in both singers' careers. Rodgers's material includes "Ben Dewberry's Final Run," "Waiting for a Train," and "Hobo Bill's Last Ride." Snow items include "The Golden Rocket," "Fire Ball Mail," and "The City of New Orleans." Born in Nova Scotia, Snow ran away as a cabin boy and then began imitating Rodgers. He recorded for RCA in 1936, but only in Canada (his U.S. recordings would start in 1949, although he made his first U.S. appearance in 1944). From the beginning, he was a transmitter of the earlier tradition of the sentimental ballad.

The 48 tracks on the CMH set cover 1936 to 1947, and include such maudlin items as: "Someday You'll Care," "Broken Dreams," "Your Little Band of Gold," "Dry Those Tears Little Girl," "Darling I'll Always Love You," and "Broken Wedding Ring." The musical accompaniment was pretty much the same, with

steel guitar and rhythm guitars. Snow's voice over the years showed little development; it was a resonant baritone with faultless enunciation (listen to his later
"I've Been Everywhere," in which he rattles off the geographic names with lightning
speed) and a tendency to draw out his pronunciation in the slow songs with exagger-
ated stress. He was completely unmannered, even simple, and was one of the first
country singers who could be thought of as a "stylist," a personality with an instantly
recognizable voice. Indeed, every folksinger has a Hank Snow parody in his bag.
The CMH set presents Rodgers-derived material as well. There are no notes here,
but there is an excellent discography. During this time, Snow was known as "the
Singing, Yodeling Ranger."

In 1949, with his American recordings, his repertoire widened and today
he is exceptionally versatile. The old ballads are still there ("Married by the Bible,
Divorced by the Law"), but he has added tributes to people ("When Jimmie Rodgers
Said Goodbye"), religious items ("I Just Telephone Upstairs"), Hawaiian ("Bluebird
Island"), narration ("My Mother"), instrumentals (some with Chet Atkins) in his
distinctive picking style, and duets with Anita Carter ("Down the Trail of Broken
Hearts"). Snow's performing is versatile and professional; he always gives a good
show (even if he wears flashy cowboy outfits). His low whiny voice and his composi-
tional skills ("Marriage Vows," "I'm Moving On," "Rhumba Boogie," "Music
Makin' Mama from Memphis") were a direct influence on the young Johnny Cash.
In addition to the above cited songs, Snow was responsible for making many country
hits: "A Fool Such As I," "I Don't Hurt Anymore," "Tangled Mind," "These
Hands," "Conscience, I'm Guilty," "Cryin', Playin', Waitin', Hopin'."

F8.36*   **Merle Travis. Best.** Capitol SM 2662.

F8.37*   **Merle Travis. The Merle Travis Guitar.** Capitol SM650.
In a direct line of development from Kentucky mountain music, Merle Travis
was country music's first guitar virtuoso. He was an exceptionally heavy influence
on Chet Atkins, Doc Watson, and Jerry Reed, not to mention countless folksingers
throughout the land. Capitol SM650 collates twelve items in what is now known
as "Travis style," including the extremely important "Walkin' the Strings." All
tracks are unaccompanied electric guitar instrumentals, such as "Sheik of Araby,"
"Bugle Call Rag," "Black Diamond Blues," "Waltz You Saved for Me," "Steel
Guitar Rag," and "Blue Smoke." It is no accident that Travis excelled at jazz-
improvised tunes, for his style demands performances of lead, rhythm, and bass
lines all played simultaneously. His method was to use thumb and index finger
to pick several strings at once, both on the downstroke and on the upstroke.

As a singer, Travis found equal success with uptempo band versions of honky-
tonk songs dating from 1945, such as "Sweet Temptation," "So Round, So Firm,
So Fully Packed," "Divorce Me C.O.D.," "No Vacancy," and "Three Times Seven."
And yet a third successful career was opened to him with the late fifties folk revival.
His interest in mining songs led him to fashion many related songs, such as "Sixteen
Tons" (a monster hit song for Tennessee Ernie Ford), "Dark as a Dungeon,"
and "Nine Pound Hammer," which were performed and recorded for a decade
throughout the folk rush. Other diverse material includes the sacred item "I Am
a Pilgrim."

F8.38*   **Ernest Tubb. Story.** two discs. MCA 2-4040.

Tubb was strongly influenced by Jimmie Rodgers; indeed, he was the heir apparent, not only because of his singing style but also because Rodgers's guitar was given to Tubb by Rodgers's widow. Throughout the years, beginning with a 1940 Decca contract, he has recorded consistently. In 1941, he created a major hit with "Walking the Floor over You." With this song and subsequent titles, he transformed old time music into modern country music. He extended the Rodgers blues to uptempo melodies and fashioned "honky-tonk" music. His influence in Nashville is enormous (he was the second country singer to record here; Red Foley was the first). First, he visibly assisted many singers who performed in his style, and such well-known names as Hank Snow and Hank Williams became his protégés. Second, he directly influenced the national acceptance of western swing through his development of the honky-tonk style. Third, he was the first singer to use the steel guitar and electric guitar on his recordings. And fourth—and equally important—he opened a record store in Nashville in 1947 and made available a *national* mail order service for country and western music. His early catalogs of stocked records thus had an enormous impact on personal selection tastes for home listening. Also in 1947, he broke new ground by appearing at Carnegie Hall. Unfortunately, Tubb's original recordings have been unavailable for two decades; this twofer is a mid-sixties re-recording of his first 25 years of hits including "I'll Get along Somehow," "Slipping Around," "Don't Rob Another Man's Castle," "Tomorrow Never Comes," "Have You Ever Been Lonely?," "Filipino Baby," and "Blue Christmas."

F8.39*   **Hank Williams. Immortal.** ten discs. MGM MM 9097/9106 (Japanese issue).

F8.40*   **Hank Williams. In the Beginning.** Birchmount BM 705 (Canadian issue).

F8.41-3   Entries deleted.

Williams was basically a wandering, restless minstrel most comfortable on the road traveling from honky-tonk to honky-tonk. This was magnificently personified in the well-thought "Move It on Over," perhaps the best of his songs that dealt with his life. Throughout his six-year career (a length equal to the career span of Jimmie Rodgers) he recorded a total of 125 titles, plus radio shows; yet in the same time frame as Rodgers, he was equally important and influential as *the* shaper of modern country music. He was the very first country songwriter to influence pop singers and merge the streams of honky-tonk sentimentality (also known as "hurtin' music") and popular music (e.g., "Cold, Cold, Heart" went in 1951 to Tony Bennett, a prime example of agents talking to one another, as Williams's manager Fred Rose sold the song to Columbia's Mitch Miller).

Perhaps more than that of any other singer, Williams's music and popularity have outlived him. He continued the progression of country music, having been influenced by Roy Acuff, Ernest Tubb, and Jimmie Rodgers and, in turn, influencing Roy Price and George Jones, who both took Williams as a direct model. His own true personal popularity is somewhat questionable in light of the disgusting commercialism after his death. Williams reissues on American MGM came out in phoney stereo, with added strings and choir, with his son on one channel and Hank himself on the other (an eerie feeling), as on the "soundtrack" from *The Last Picture Show*. The Japanese set contains all of the MGM titles plus the four radio shows; the discography is in English, but the notes, unfortunately (for us), are in Japanese.

Williams, a master songwriter and performer, was unique at the time for singing almost exclusively his own material. His writing was dominated by four distinct themes: unrequited love ("Your Cheatin' Heart"), novelties ("Hey Good Lookin' " or "Kaw-Liga"), religious sacred music ("I Saw the Light"), or devotion to life, such as his Luke the Drifter maxims. All of these were written in plain and simple language, and all were shaped by Fred Rose, who supervised the recording sessions (selection of accompaniment, songs, arrangements, mixing, etc.). This was the first real occurrence of the iron will of the *producer*, the artist and repertoire (a and r) man, in country music, and Rose's diverse instrumentation (electric guitar or piano or string band), in addition to his concept of production, directly created the Nashville sound and the "tradition" of strong managers in the country field. (Colonel Tom Parker originally wanted to fashion another Hank Williams out of Elvis Presley, and taught Presley all of Williams's strange mannerisms.)

Williams's appeal was mainly an earthy one (through his lyrics), but there was also a raw sexual primitivism, and he could be thought of as the first sex symbol in country music. His style of crouching and use of the microphone were highly sexual for the time, and Williams acknowledged that he had borrowed them from black bluesmen he saw. He was hunched over the microphone, with his back bent, his eyes closed, and his knees dipping up and down in rhythm, and occasionally a pelvic twist was made during the uptempo numbers. From Williams to Presley to Beatles to rock theater—an impressive line that had black influences adding to the cumulative effect.

The closest one can come to these stage shows must be on the "live" portion of the Japanese MGM, an aural rendition of the total act. In addition to showing Williams as he was on tour *without* Fred Rose's strong command, these four radio shows (from WSM in Nashville in 1949) present the screams and utterances of the audiences at "sexual" moments. Besides his theme, "Happy Rovin' Cowboy," he presented a variety of material from diverse sources in a loose honky-tonk manner. There were the traditional "Joe Clark" and "Bill Cheatham," popular hits of the day ("There's a Bluebird on Your Windowsill," a duet with Audrey Williams), and always a sacred song or two. The good presence and sound of the assorted titles clearly show Williams to have had a *bona fide* touring act quite unlike the staged recordings that people remember best.

Indeed, the individual songs he recorded perhaps came off better because they were staged. For Hank Williams was basically a simple songwriter who needed assistance, and the emergence of the producer (in this case, Fred Rose) made it possible for *any* singer to be styled in a particular fashion. Williams's forte was that he could at least write simple endearing lines; and he was the first of his kind. His method of singing was to translate his down home speech into a trembling tear-stricken voice that relied on good phrasing, timing, and blues inflection

(Williams learned much from black music, as noted above). Good physical timing was also important. He recorded his first eight tracks in 1946-1947 for Sterling records (the Birchmount album, which also contains his first early MGMs) which were later reissued on MGM; presented were such titles as "Calling You," "Never Again (Will I Knock on Your Door)" and "Wealth Won't Save Your Soul."

His first major hit was "Move It on Over" for MGM. Fred Rose got him the contract and also persuaded MGM to put a lot of money into promotion as that company was new to country music. This meant exploring a lot of untapped markets, including popular mainstream areas. Thus, "Move" sold over a million copies, and MGM had a winner in many hitherto unrelated markets. Additional hits included "Honky Tonk Blues" (almost an anthem), "Jambalaya," "My Bucket's Got a Hole in It," "Half as Much," "Take These Chains from My Heart," "You Win Again," and "I Can't Help It if I'm Still in Love with You." These have all been recorded by other singers many times over. Other gems (but not "hits") include "Mansion on the Hill" and "Blue Love in My Heart" (the latter emphasizing his archaic guitar playing style). It is ironic that no comprehensive edition of his music has ever been available in his native land.

Standards

F8.44*   **Bill Anderson. Story.** two discs. MCA 2-4001.

Singer-songwriter Anderson possesses a degree in journalism, which helps to explain his vivid story songs and personal characterizations. In his stylings, he is reckoned as a traditional conservative, once making the point that there are no more country singers—just "country stylists" who have been pigeon-holed by their audiences. As a composer, he fashioned songs for Ray Price ("City Lights," 1958; "That's What It's Like to Be Lonesome," 1959), Jim Reeves ("I Missed Me," 1961), Roy Clark ("Tips of My Fingers," 1963), and Merle Haggard ("Strangers," 1965). On his own, he creatively performed "Still," "Mama Sang a Song" and the compassionate "Po' Folks." All these and others are on the 24-cut MCA collation.

F8.45   **Gene Autry.** two discs. RCA Bluebird AXM2-55-- (in progress).

F8.46*   **Gene Autry. Young Gene Autry.** Country Loon CSC 69.

Before becoming a noted western singer and film star, Autry was a very well-known stylist in the Jimmie Rodgers blue yodel mode. In fact, he was one of the very first cover artists in this genre. These two sets have over a dozen songs that were once recorded by Rodgers but here are handled in approximately the same manner by Autry. His recording career began in 1929, and the 44 tracks from that period (to 1933) here represent about half of his output. He was on the Gennett label (a predominantly black music company) with such items as "Money Ain't No Use Anyway," "Do Right Daddy Blues," "A Gangster's Warning," "Rheumatism Blues," and "She's a Low-Down Mama"—all raw and raunchy material for the 1931-1933 period. His guitar is heard throughout, and there is occasional assistance from Frankie Marvin (harmonica and steel guitar).

The Country Loon disc was pressed by RCA for a Texas-Oklahoma Autry fan club. The double RCA Bluebird leans more toward Rodgers covers and sentimental ballads, such as "My Old Pal of Yesterday," "That Ramshackle Shack,"

"Missouri Is Calling," "In the Shadow of the Pine," and so forth. Autry was a very significant, early imitator of Rodgers, but he shifted his career to western music with the big seller "That Silver Haired Daddy of Mine." For those who can't wait for completion of the Bluebird set, RCA LPM 2623, a "greatest hits" compilation, is available.

F8.47*   **Elton Britt. Best, v.1/2.** two discs. RCA LSP 2669 and 4822.
Britt was raised in Arkansas and Oklahoma near the Ozarks; his father was an old time fiddling champion. Recording since 1937 for RCA Victor, Britt amassed in 22 years a total of 672 songs and sixty albums. He became their top-selling artist during World War II, especially with "There's a Star Spangled Banner Waving Somewhere." This song alone got him an invitation to the White House in 1942, the first time a country performer had appeared there. Its success made the song the first national hit for country music (moving beyond regional stylings) since Vernon Dalhart's "The Prisoner's Song." Britt was a natural-born yodeler, modifying Rodgers's approach yet retaining its original Swiss flavor. In so doing, he became the highest yodeler in the world, bar none. Later Britt successes in the forties included "Chime Bells" (1948), "Candy Kisses" (1949), and "Quicksilver" (1950, with Rosalie Allen). Good tracks on these two discs also include "Detour," "I Hung My Head and Cried," "I Almost Lost My Mind," "Someday," and "Oklahoma Hills."

F8.48*   **Cliff Carlisle, v.1/2.** two discs. Old Timey X 103/4.
Carlisle broke into radio in 1931 as a direct imitator of Jimmie Rodgers. His range of material was quite similar: blues, hobo songs, Hawaiian guitar, cowboy music. Some typical tracks include "The Rambling Yodeler," "Mouse's Ear Blues," "Tom Cat Blues," "Goodbye Old Pal," and "Cowboy Johnny's Last Ride." With his brother Bill, he formed the Carlisle Brothers, a very typical duo in the 1930s; they resembled the Delmore Brothers in that they also sang extremely risqué items for the time, plus early honky-tonk and some sacred songs.

F8.49*   **Cowboy Copas. All Time Hits.** King 553.

F8.50   **Cowboy Copas. Story.** two discs. Starday S 347.
Copas was a top star in 1948 with such superb honky-tonk music as "Filipino Baby," "Juke Box Blues," "Honky Tonkin'," "Signed, Sealed and Delivered," and "Candy Kisses." In the 1950s, this Oklahoma-born guitarist (with an open string flat top guitar) saw his career completely collapse after his rendition of "Tennessee Waltz" with Pee Wee King. There was nothing for him to do in the pop field, which country music people tried to break into, and his decline was mirrored by the upsurge of rockabilly and rock and roll music. However, he did resurface in 1960 with the excellently rhythmic "Alabam," only to die in a car crash a few months later. The double Starday album repeats a few of the King efforts (as re-recordings) and it has as well some interesting material from the fifties and his last, but biggest, hit.

F8.51   **Jimmie Davis. Greatest Hits, v.1/2.** two discs. MCA DL 74978 and MCA 423.

Davis served as governor of Louisiana twice (1944-1948; 1960-1964). He was an exceptionally popular singer, and the composer of "You Are My Sunshine," "Worried Mind," and "It Makes No Difference Now." Many of his songs were recorded by Gene Autry. Since 1950, he has been singing sacred music almost exclusively, although these two records do contain a mixture of older materials plus some modern stylings (and reprocessed violins for sweetening, an attraction for newer tastes). Also of interest is "Nobody's Darlin' but Mine."

F8.52   **Jimmy Dean. Greatest Hits.** Columbia CS 9285.

With a national television show, Dean appealed to both country and pop music, although it must be said that his material fit into the later stages of the rock and roll merger with folk music. The former stream led to such titles as "Gonna Raise a Ruckus Tonight" and "Cajun Queen," while the latter led to "Big Bad John," "PT 109," and even "Dear Ivan."

F8.53*   **Little Jimmie Dickens. Greatest Hits.** Columbia LE 10106.

F8.54   **Little Jimmie Dickens. Greatest Hits.** MCA Decca DL 75133.

Dickens created real "hurtin' " music that was effective at grabbing one's heartstrings. This material included "My Heart's Bouquet," "Take Me As I Am," and "Just When I Needed You." His high vibrato came through best on his own composition "I'm Little but I'm Loud," which was exactly the case. Although born in West Virginia, he adopted the garish western garb of the cowboy. His other equally important song stylings concerned the rural humor and social commentary on rural childhood. Such novelty items included the 1949 "Take an Old Cold Tater," "Country Boy," the 1950 "A-Sleeping at the Foot of the Bed," and "Out behind the Barn."

F8.55   **Roy Drusky. Greatest Hits.** Mercury SR 61052.

A songwriter and jack-of-all-trades in the entertainment business (radio, television, disc jockey work), Drusky was an interpreter of the honky-tonk music and sentimental songs that were the main bulk of country music during the recovery period of the early 1960s. Included here are "White Lightnin' Express," "Such a Fool," "Anymore," and "Second Hand Rose."

F8.56*   **Tennessee Ernie Ford. Sixteen Tons.** Capitol T 1380.

Ford is the person most associated, by non-country music followers, with the rural brand of hillbilly music. His national radio shows and appearances, usually in a business suit, had created an image of a relaxed, soothing interpreter of music. Early on in his career, he actually studied voice, and his bass vocal lines are quite good and proper. Throughout the years he has been consistent with a semi-jaunty attitude to his singing, even in his biggest hit, the Merle Travis song "16 Tons." Titles include the original 1947 "Shotgun Boogie," the 1949 "Mule Train," the 1950 "The Cry of the Wild Goose," the 1956 "Rovin' Gambler," the 1958 "Sunday Barbecue," plus "Smokey Mountain Boogie" and "Anticipation Blues."

F8.57*   **Lefty Frizzell. Remembering the Greatest Hits.** Columbia. C33882.

F8.58   **Lefty Frizzell. Sings the Songs of Jimmie Rodgers.** Columbia C32249.

Frizzell's Texas roots prepared him for Jimmie Rodgers material. The originals, cut in the late twenties, had the country white blues punch typical of hard living and traveling. By the time Lefty got to them, the interpretation was more polished, in line with 1950s styles (when the bulk here was recorded; the others in 1953). The commercial country sound initiated by Rodgers and carried forth by Ernest Tubb, Gene Autry and Hank Snow (all had recorded Rodgers material in the thirties) had, by 1950, become identified with a "hurtin'" sound, and the most perfect voices for this were Webb Pierce and Lefty Frizzell. (Pierce recorded Rodgers material, but not with the same success as Frizzell.) In the history of country music, this very rural sounding music with a modern instrumental backup is an important document.

Having cut his teeth on Rodgers material, Frizzell went on to add more honky-tonk instrumentation. His characteristic "sound" was a nasal tenor, with bent notes and multi-syllable extensions from one note, such as "Always Late (with Your Kisses)." The archtypical honky-tonk number was his "If You've Got the Money, Honey, I've Got the Time" or "Give Me More, More, More of Your Kisses." But he could be tender as well, an observation based on his loving "Mom and Dad's Waltz" or "I Love You a Thousand Ways." Although quite often out of the country public's eye because of his nomadic existence, he did make a terrific impact on Merle Haggard, and he served as a transitional figure in the continuance of the rounder-bounder tradition that Haggard carried on through the 1970s.

F8.59   **Don Gibson. Best.** RCA LSP 3376.

Gibson began as a songwriter, with "Sweet Dreams" (sung by Faron Young) and "I Can't Stop Lovin' You" (sung first by Kitty Wells and then by Ray Charles). In 1957, though, he signed with RCA, and at Steve Scholes's suggestion, began writing faster, uptempo songs to compete with and counteract the rock and roll that was killing country music. Many of his songs then had cross-over potential, such as "Oh Lonesome Me," "Blue Blue Day," and "Just One Time"—all accented by his high, nasal, sad voice.

F8.60   **Stuart Hamblen. It's No Secret.** RCA LPM 1253.

Hamblen, like Elton Britt, once sang with the Beverly Hillbillies in the 1930s. His comeback began in the late 1940s with a series of his own compositions that provided a mixture of sentimental songs and sacred music, such as "This Ole House" (actually regarded as a religious song) and "Open up Your Heart and Let the Sun Shine In," plus "My Brown Eyed Texas Rose," "My Mary," "Just a Little Old Rag Doll."

F8.61*   **George Hamilton IV. Greatest Hits.** RCA APL 1-0455.

Hamilton has been very successful in finding appropriate songwriters for his performances; therein lies his strength—as an interpreter. "Urge for Going" was only the second recording of a Joni Mitchell song; Canadian composers also dominate with Ray Griff's "Canadian Pacific" and Gordon Lightfoot's "Early Morning Rain." Other material was contributed by John D. Loudermilk and Harlan Howard

("She's a Little Bit Country"). Hamilton is so successful in his consistent work that he has virtually complete control over his music—even to the extent that he now records solely for RCA of Canada (having signed a contract in Toronto) and utilizes Canadian studios, session men, and songs (while he still lives in Nashville). Hamilton began recording for RCA in 1961; consequently, the hit "Abilene" for 1963 is the original, but "A Rose and a Baby Ruth," originally made in 1956, is a country music remake on this disc.

F8.62   **Hawkshaw Hawkins. Legend.** King 850.
          Harold Hawkins's deep voice was influenced by Ernest Tubb. This West Virginia-born singer largely ignored folk roots, and concentrated on the then-popular honky-tonk music from the late 1940s to 1953 (for King records). He was one of King's top sellers during this period, with tragic songs ("Soldier's Last Letter," "I'll Get along Somehow," "Since You Went Away") and boogie tunes ("Mean Mama Blues"). His two biggest successes came near the end of his King contract, the 1952 "Slow Poke" and the Justin Tubb song "Lonesome 7-7203." After this, Hawkins moved to the major recording companies (RCA and Columbia) but didn't do so well. He was attempting a comeback when he died.

F8.63   **Johnny Horton. Greatest Hits.** Columbia CS 8396.
          Horton was a versatile honky-tonk performer who utilized a pop beat that fit in well with rock and roll. His early successes included "I'm Just a One Woman Man" (1957) and "All Grown Up" (1958). In 1959, he took the Jimmy Driftwood "Battle of New Orleans" and created a pseudo-folk song that lent credence to the resurging folk revival. Also in that year, he recorded "When It's Springtime in Alaska" and the first of his soundtrack epics, "Johnny Reb" (from the TV show). Other film songs, now assuming the proportions of folklore, included "Sink the Bismarck" and "North to Alaska."

F8.64*   **Ferlin Husky. Best.** Capitol SKAO 143.
          Husky was a showman with a high quavering voice. His popularity in the late fifties was partially a result of pop overtones in his work, which resulted in the sales of such cross-over recordings as the dramatic "Gone," "Fallen Star," and the gentle "On the Wings of a Dove." He was a steady performer, beginning with his first hit in 1953—"A Dear John Letter," sung with Jean Shepard and referring to a soldier's loss of love while fighting the Korean War. Husky's alter ego was Simon Crum, a humorist in the country music field who was full of corny aphorisms and hillbilly motifs. A surprising composition from the Crum recordings included the tribute "Country Music Is Here to Stay," an absolutely vital work that was greatly supportive during country music's darkest hours in the rock and roll period.

F8.65   **Stonewall Jackson. Greatest Hits.** Columbia CS 9177.
          Jackson had a grieving voice, plagued with pain. His first big performance was the prisoner song "Life to Go" in 1958, followed by "Waterloo" in 1959, and "A Wound Time Can't Erase" in 1962. In the low point of his career, though, he surfaced once more with "Mary Don't You Weep."

F8.66   **Jim and Jesse. Saluting the Louvin Brothers.** Epic BN 26465.

F8.67   **Jim and Jesse. We Like Trains.** Epic BN 26513.
The McReynolds Brothers were equally at home in both bluegrass and country music (although in the 1970s they have tried to program bluegrass music exclusively). Their pure urban style with few rural roots, coupled with an intensive mandolin and guitar accompaniment, gave them great distinction as interpreters (see the annotation of their bluegrass music at F6.32 and F6.33). The two discs here are among their finest country efforts. The first details their reinterpretations of the Louvin Brothers' singing (one of the most dynamic influences on modern country and sacred music). The ten titles include "I Don't Believe You've Met My Baby," "Cash on the Barrelhead," and "I'm Hoping That You're Hoping." The *Trains* set also includes some mid-tempo bluegrass renditions, such as Roy Acuff's "Wabash Cannonball"; but in general, it is mainly a collection of ten titles related to trains, such as Hank Snow's "The Golden Rocket" and Hank Williams's "I Heard That Lonesome Whistle" and his "Pan American."

F8.68   **Johnnie and Jack. Sing Poison Love and Other Country Favorites.** RCA Camden S 747.
Jack Anglin (who died in 1963) and Johnny Wright were a popular duo in the early 1950s. Wright married and now manages Kitty Wells, but at this time, he displayed his rural influences with Jack through "Crying Heart Blues" and "Poison Love" (1951). Other titles from among their 100 original compositions include "I Get So Lonely" and the frolicking "The Moon Is High and So Am I."

F8.69   **Grandpa Jones. An Evening With.** Decca DL 4364.
Jones worked with Bradley Kinkaid in 1935 at the National Barn Dance for WLS of Chicago. At the time though young, he had an "old" sounding voice, and since no one could see him on radio, he used it in an act. Thus, although he was only 23, he became an early rival to Uncle Dave Macon of the Grand Ole Opry, the other major radio program on country music. Like Macon, Jones played the banjo; unlike Macon, he also programmed more modern country material. His humor is not very brisk though, since he has not had Macon's experiences. Typical songs included "Good Ole Mountain Dew," "Going down in Town," "Old Rattler," "Eight More Miles to Louisville," and some yodeling songs.

F8.70   **Hank Locklin. Best.** RCA LSP 3559.
By the mid-fifties, Locklin was already forty years of age; he was a slow starter. But his career took off with some significant country songs, such as "Please Help Me I'm Falling," "Send Me the Pillow That You Dream On," and "It's a Little More Like Heaven"—all maudlin, sentimental songs.

F8.71   **Ronnie Milsap. A Legend in My Time.** RCA APL1-0846.
Milsap is one of the few emerging new country singers who performs in the older stylings of the immediate pre-Nashville sound days. He is a blind pianist who has a feel for older material (such as the wonderfully recreated "A Legend in My Time" and "Too Late to Worry, Too Blue to Cry"). The accompaniment is low-keyed and leaves plenty of room for Milsap to explore the possibilities of his voice.

F8.72*   **Moon Mullican. Unforgettable Great Hits.** Starday 398.

Mullican was once a church organist who later turned to country music. His piano style became part of the honky-tonk school in that it was performed with two fingers in a right-handed style (reminiscent of Horace Silver's later 1950s funk style in jazz). For King records (reissued on the Starday album), Mullican contributed significant and vast materials in a fusion of the southeastern and southwestern styles of country music during the 1940s, such as the 1947 hit "New Jole Blon" (from Cajun roots, but sung at a fast tempo with nonsense English words). Typical fast honky-tonk music included "Cherokee Boogie," a return to Louisiana with "Jambalaya," the significant love song "I Was Sort of Wondering," and the ballads "Sweeter Than the Flowers," "I'll Sail My Ship Alone," "Mona Lisa," and "Good Night, Irene."

F8.73   **Jimmy Newman.** MCA Decca DL 74781.

F8.74   **Jimmy Newman. Folk Songs of the Bayou.** MCA Decca DL 74398.

Newman was half French in ancestry, related to and coming from the Cajun stock in Louisiana. The material here comes from the mid-sixties, just before the entrance of Doug Kershaw, and it is more country-oriented than other Cajun music. He makes good, effective use of the "aieee!" screech call for added punctuation. Tracks include "Big Mama," "Alligator Man," "Bayou Talk," "Back Pocket Money," "Artificial Rose," and "Back in Circulation."

F8.75*   **Buck Owens. Best, v.1/3.** Capitol ST 2105, 2897, and SKAO 145.

Owens is a smart clown. He is seen on the nationally syndicated *Hee Haw* show; he projects a rural naiveté; many of his songs read like nursery rhymes (he's a prolific composer). For twenty years, he was with Capitol records, and they have issued over six collections of best hits through the years (as with most singers in country music, his earlier songs are his best). In chart action, Owens has had 27 number one hits in a row, a record for the Guinness book. His pop ballad style was one of the first to use drums, and he centered his music on Bakersfield, California, collecting others to present a viable alternative to Nashville (including such people as Merle Haggard, who later married Owens's ex-wife). He was projected to national prominence when the Beatles recorded his moderate western hit "Act Naturally" (actually, it was Ringo Starr, deeply influenced by country music, who sang the vocal, but it was issued under the Beatles' name). Representative tracks here from the thirty or so tunes assembled include his first hit "Under Your Spell Again," "Foolin' Around," "Excuse Me," "Above and Beyond," "Before You Go," "My Heart Skips a Beat," and "I Don't Care."

F8.76*   **Ray Price. All Time Greatest Hits.** two discs. Columbia KG 31364.

Part Cherokee Indian and from Texas, Ray Price was one of the greatest country music singers since World War II. His phrasing and magnificent voice mellowed honky-tonk and western swing into modern country music. He was strongly influenced by Hank Williams, Jimmie Rodgers, and Cliff Carlisle. His career began with the Big D Jamboree in Dallas. With a recording contract from Columbia, he went out and hired the best steel guitar players he could find (Jimmy Day and Buddy Emmons were two of them). This style led to an immense popularity and to his cross-over covers of pop music items, such as "Don't Let the Stars Get in Your Eyes." His colorful lyrics did lead to a closed style, but that was what the fans wanted. His metaphorical phrases have included "Crazy Arms" that won't let go, "My Shoes Keep Walking Back to You" independently of his heart, while "The Curtains in the Windows" wave goodbye after he leaves. It was almost as if he was embarrassed to come right out and state his love. Uptempo numbers, reminiscent of western swing, included "I'll Be There" and "Under Your Spell Again." Ballads included "Talk to Your Heart," "Release Me," "City Lights," and "One More Time."

F8.77   **Marvin Rainwater. MGM 4046.**
Country music attracts many native peoples, and Marvin Rainwater is a good example. His sweet voice attracted Arthur Godfrey's Talent Scouts and won him a contract with MGM, which promptly put out his biggest hit "Gonna Find Me a Bluebird." Follow-up songs reflected his early life and the great West, through "Albino Stallion," "Tea Bag Rodeo," and "Half Breed." His western style honky-tonk attempts to combat early rock and roll included "Whole Lotta Woman."

F8.78*   **Marty Robbins. All Time Greatest Hits.** two discs. Columbia KG 31361.
Originally known as "Mr. Teardrop" in 1952, because of his weeping ballad style ("Castles in the Sky," "Cryin' 'Cause I Love You 'Til the Day I Die," etc.), Robbins over the years has assumed the sobriquet "Mr. Eclectic," because he performs in vastly different styles depending on the type of song. He is an all-around country singer performing Hawaiian and Spanish love songs, basic rock and roll, ballads, country love-heartbreak songs, and cowboy materials. His early work is character-ized by a frenetic gospel style in the rockabilly and blues mode ("That's All Right," the Crudup song also recorded by Presley); "Knee Deep in the Blues" and "Singing the Blues"; "Story of My Life" and "White Sportscoat," both typical rock and roll songs; and "gunfighter ballads" based on his Arizona upbringing—these latter can be found annotated at F7.30. Other successes included "Tonight Carmen" and "Ribbon of Darkness," the latter written by Gordon Lightfoot.

F8.79   **Carl Smith. Greatest Hits.** Columbia CS 8737.
Tennesseean Smith grew up next to country music. He is a good mainstream performer, being noted for his full-throated vocal style, lusty intonations, and ballad singing. His instrumental accompaniment was distinctly honky-tonk in style; thus his material is mainly western swing songs plus ballads—and this from an Easterner! He was successful, then, in assisting the fusion of southeastern and southwestern singing styles. Representative tracks, beginning from 1951, include "Let's Live a Little," the uptempo "Hey Joe" and "Loose Talk," the ballad "Your Name Is Beautiful," and "If Teardrops Were Pennies."

F8.80   **Red Sovine. Music Time.** MCA Decca DL 74736.
Sovine rose through the Louisiana Hayride, being the replacement for Hank Williams after the latter left in 1949. During this period he met Webb Pierce, also at the Hayride, and together they began co-composing. Some of their better known efforts were "Little Rosa" and "Why, Baby, Why?" The uptempo honky-tonk music of Sovine made him popular, but success eluded him as much as it was

attracted to Pierce. Typical songs include "You Used to Be My Baby," "Don't Drop It," "My New Love Affair," "Long Night," and "Too Much."

F8.81   **Mel Tillis. Best. two discs. MCA2-4091.**

Tillis is best known as a composer. This Florida-born author penned over 450 songs, including forty for Webb Pierce, thirteen for Burl Ives, and some each for Ray Price, Carl Smith, etc. He is a singer and a versatile comedian. In real life, he stutters and does so also in his comedy sequences. He has turned his impediment into some measure of success. "Hurtin' " music is his forte, but done in the traditional style as influenced by Hank Williams, Ray Price, and even Bob Wills. The MCA reissue collates his Kapp recordings and includes "Heart over Mind," one of his greatest compositions. Others are "At the Sight of You," "Honky Tonkin'," "Detroit City," the painful "Half Laughing, Half Crying" and the equally so "All Right (I'll Sign the Papers)," and "Another Bridge to Burn."

F8.82   **T. Texas Tyler. Great Hits. Hilltop S 6042.**

As a proponent of the Texas-Oklahoma music scene in the 1940s, Tyler joined up with the Dixie Melody Boys (later, the Oklahoma Melody Boys) before passing on to movies and television. His stylings were recorded for Capitol records, and include 1948's "Deck of Cards," "Daddy Gave My Dog Away," "Bummin' Around," and the maudlin "Remember Me When the Candlelights Are Gleaming." This Hilltop reissue is from the Capitol days.

F8.83*   **Porter Wagoner. Best, v.1/2. two discs. RCA ANL 1-1213 and LSP 4321.**

Wagoner is renowned for sticking to his traditional music and traditional presentation (although he is ostentatious on stage with his sequined cowboy clothes). The bulk of his material comprises old style fiddle and steel guitar songs, very much related to Hank Williams in singing style and in writing ("Payday," "Uncle Pen"). The sentimental songs are of loneliness, such as "I Thought I Heard You Call My Name" or "Sorrow on the Rocks." Tragic songs, also a part of his repertoire, include "Misery Loves Company" and "Skid Row Joe" and "Cold Dark Waters Below." His blending of the various themes inherent in honky-tonk and mountain songs continues the assimilation of southeastern and southwestern strands in country and western music. Beginning with such songs as "Satisfied Mind" and "Eat, Drink, and Be Merry" for RCA in 1955, he continues to entertain via a syndicated television show plus tours of 230 or so days a year. Indeed, he was the first country artist to do a *live* record album (1964), which was so successful that others followed. In balance, adding up his roots, singing, repertoire, touring, and so forth, he can be personified as the best of all the country music stars in the modern idiom.

F8.84   **Jimmy Wakely. Slippin' Around. Dot 25711.**

Wakely was a movie star, appearing in over 100 westerns, and his musical career began in 1937 with Johnny Bond and Scott Harrel in a trio. During the 1940s, he had a significant band that blended western swing and pop. In the band were Cliffie Stone, Spade Cooley, and Merle Travis, who all struck out successfully on their own. Unfortunately, none of the records the group made have yet been issued on albums. In 1948, he began a solo career, with "I Love You So Much It Hurts," "Signed, Sealed and Delivered," and "Beautiful Brown Eyes." His highly significant 1949 duos with Margaret Whiting presaged the Lynn-Twitty duets of twenty years later, with classics such as "Slippin' Around" and " 'Til the End of the World." Again, unfortunately, these originals are unavailable except on anthologies. However, most of his hits were re-recorded for Dot, and these will have to do.

F8.85   **Wilburn Brothers. "A Portrait."** two discs. MCA 2-4011.
    Teddy and Doyle as a singing act are firmly within the realm of country pop. Before 1953, they were child singers with the touring Wilburn Family, a group that concentrated on sacred and old time music. Beginning in 1956, the duo sang for Decca with songs of lost love, such as "Somebody's Back in Town," "Which One Is to Blame," "Trouble's Back in Town." Their flat voices, ideal for old time music, created a detached feeling of resignation in these hurtin' songs. In this sense, their combination was perfect for this type of music, but not so good for other song genres.

F8.86   **Willis Brothers. Best.** Starday SLP 466.
    This trio, also known for their compositional skills, backed Hank Williams and Eddy Arnold on their early records in the 1940s. They came up in country music as studio session men for hundreds of recording dates in the decade before the "Nashville sound." They played guitar, violin, and accordion. With rhythm guitar from the featured lead singer, that instrumentation was all that was needed for a record. On occasion, they demonstrated a superb blending of voices, and all three could solo equally well as lead singers. The Starday material was recorded in the late fifties and represents a general summing up of the material that they performed, such as "Give Me Forty Acres," "Blues Stay Away from Me," and "Bummin' Around." The Willis Brothers were the best rhythm accompaniment in country music.

F8.87   **Faron Young. Best.** Capitol T 1450.
    Young's strong, virile voice made him a potentially good pop musician while still working within a country framework. After the impact of rock and roll, he was one of many singers to switch to a more uptempo format while still maintaining loyal country fans. This Capitol album documents his career since 1951, with such examples of romantic or maudlin songs as "Tattle Tale Tears," "Have I Waited Too Long?," "Hello, Walls," "Sweet Dreams" and "I Miss You Already." Two rocking numbers that he was known for are "If You Ain't Lovin' " and "Live Fast, Love Hard and Die Young."

CROONERS

Innovators

F8.88*   **Eddy Arnold. All Time Favorites.** RCA LPM 1223.

F8.89*   **Eddy Arnold. This Is. . . .** two discs. RCA VPS 6032.
    Arnold was the catalyst who deliberately created pop music out of country music, with a large assist from Chet Atkins (his arranger and producer during his 25-year stay with RCA). He developed after taking the "sweeter" aspects of the singing styles of Jimmie Rodgers, Gene Autry, and Red Foley. He extensively employed Roy Wiggins's electric steel guitar, but in the Hawaiian mode rather than in the western swing tradition. His smooth phrasing and exceptionally pleasant voice made him an early cross-over (1947) to mainstream popular music, and he thus made it easier for others to follow. Initial hits for the "Tennessee Plowboy" (his nickname) included "Anytime," "Cattle Call," "Richest Man," "This Is the Thanks I Get," and "I Really Don't Want to Know." His music and style directly inspired George Morgan, who took over where Arnold left off in the country music fold (but Morgan never did capitalize on the popular music scene, preferring to maintain his rural roots). In the 1960s, Arnold's work became sentimental in a syrupy sense, with such titles as "Make the World Go Away," "What's He Doing in My World?," and "The Last Word in Lonesome Is Me." Of all his "best hits" albums, the three discs cited above are perhaps the most faithful. The first captures his essence through 1958; the second set brings him up to the modern times. All other RCA collations are merely re-recordings in stereo, with sickly strings added for "sweetening."

F8.90*   **Chet Atkins. Best.** RCA LSP 2887

F8.91*   **Chet Atkins. Now and . . . Then.** two discs. RCA VPSX 6079.
    Atkins has recorded over 500 instrumental titles, all using his solid background of classical music upon which he modeled much of his technique. Early, as a guitarist, he played with Bill Carlisle and did some radio work. 1949 was a big year for him, as he signed with RCA and sold well with "Gallopin' Guitar," "Main St. Breakdown," and "Country Gentleman" (on LSP 2887). He shortly became a Nashville studio guitarist; then in 1952, under Steve Sholes's direction, he became an organizer of such sessions. In 1960, he became a producer and directly created the "Nashville sound." By 1968, he was a vice-president at RCA. Along the way, he also groomed such talent as Floyd Cramer, Roger Miller, Don Gibson, Connie Smith, Dottie West, and modern country's first black singer, Charley Pride.
    Atkins's greatest contribution was twofold, though. First, he developed the string-laden sweetening in Nashville to create a "sound" that had no tension. This relaxed music emphasized the piano (especially by Cramer) in an uptown, cocktail lounge style. No fiddle was used, and the guitars (led by Grady Martin) came from rock and roll. Constantly, the melody was emphasized for commercial appeal, which meant a loose beat on the drums and bass (normally, Buddy Harman and Bob Moore, respectively). This proved to be the salvation for country music, which had declined drastically with the advent of rock and roll. No more fiddle or

nasal singing: "country and western" was merged with the pop mainstream to become "modern country." In some respects, Atkins has since regretted his actions. Certainly the moralistic lyrical element was lost when the beat came into prominence. As he said, "the whole thing went too far."

His second contribution—and the one that directly concerns us—is his finger style in picking the guitar. An improvisor, he brought the guitar up from an accompanying to a solo role in modern country music. In fretting, he barely touches the strings, only enough so as to push down on them, and then lets his fingers up. This action was coupled with a pick on the thumb for playing rhythm on the bass strings. Through his method, and by using a vibrato on the Spanish guitar, he was able to use his classical training for speed, coordination, and precision. This is exemplified by his earlier work (on the RCA double set), with "Canned Heat" from 1947. This track clearly showed the influences of Merle Travis, Eddie Lang, and Django Reinhardt (especially on "Django's Castle"). Black styles were learned from Jim Mason of Kentucky. The 1952 "Chinatown, My Chinatown" introduces the listener to the Atkins electric guitar, and here the prime influence is Les Paul. Some 25 instrumentals are collated on the twofer up through "Knee Action" in 1972. Pop tunes include skillful recordings of "Mrs. Robinson," "Snowbird," and "El Condor Pasa" (the latter based on Simon and Garfunkel's version). Standard mood items on LSP 2887 include "Jitterbug Waltz," "Yankee Doodle Dixie," "Malaguena," and "Peanut Vendor."

F8.92*   **Jim Reeves. Best, v.1/3.** three discs. RCA LSP 2890, 3482, and 4187.

The attraction of Jim Reeves was his resonant, "touch of velvet" singing style on country pop and ballads. His voice was just a little bit lower than Eddy Arnold's and had none of the latter's accent. Indeed, he was closer to George Morgan in styling, but Reeves's producers early on decided upon the successful use of piano, discreet female voices, and a loose background to let the listener fully assimilate his vocal style. Because of both his style and his early death, he has become a cult figure. He has had more posthumous success than when he was alive, and much material has been recycled by RCA and his estate, such as "Distant Drums" (never released until after his death). In many ways, then, this has mitigated against a definitive set of four or so albums containing fifty or so of his best efforts. His loyal audience, though, keeps buying the reissued records. Of all country music stars, Reeves toured the most widely—Europe, South Africa, United Kingdom, Norway—and these places make the most demands for his material. From 1955 until his death in 1964, he had a constant stream of Top 10 songs: "Am I Losing You?," "Four Walls," "Blue Boy," "Billy Bayou," "Anna Marie," "He'll Have to Go" (his most successful), "Home," and "I Missed Me" among others. It is not insignificant that the greatest selling balladeer in country music came from Texas.

F8.93   **Slim Whitman. Golden Songbook.** United Artists UAD 29645 (British issue).

F8.94*   **Slim Whitman. Very Best.** two discs. United Artists UAS 29898 (British issue).

Florida-born Whitman is best known in England and in Australia, where he has a fanatical following. He has toured extensively throughout the years since

1949, mainly to Canada, Japan, Europe, South Africa, and Australia. His golden period was for Imperial in the 1950s (this material is now owned by United Artists), when he projected the image of a romantic cowboy singer. He did no honky-tonk or any novelty materials. He simply sang romantic sentimental songs perfectly suited to his high tenor voice and yodel, and to his good stage presence and handsome looks. Tracks here include, from several dozen good examples of the genre, "Rose Marie," "Secret Love," "Love Song of the Waterfall," "China Doll," "From a Faded Rose," "Northwind," and "Indian Love Call." This is a very strange mixture of romantic ballads from a Floridian in western garb, but if there is one idealist in the genre, then it must be Slim Whitman. He has very little material on domestic records currently available; the 34 tracks on these foreign releases contain all the above-mentioned titles.

Standards

F8.95   **Bobby Bare. Best.** RCA LSP 3479.
Pop-oriented Bare once wrote and performed the greatest rock and roll parody song ever made: "All American Boy" (1957). Since that time, he has written over 200 country songs that had mainstream appeal in the popular music arena. His first country hit, though, was the depressing title "Detroit City," penned by Mel Tillis in 1963. At that time, Bare was reacting to the rise of folk protest songs with a country beat, and indeed, he recorded "countrified" versions of "500 Miles," "Four Strong Winds," and others. He did continue with folk trends in "Streets of Baltimore" and "Come Kiss Me Love."

F8.96   **Jim Ed Brown. Best.** RCA APL 1-0324.
After breaking up the group, the Browns (F8.97), Jim Ed pursued a successful career with soft and intimate sounds in a pop vein. His main influences have been Red Foley, Eddy Arnold, and, of course, Jim Reeves. The twelve items on this disc include "Pop a Top," "Southern Loving," and "Regular on My Mind."

F8.97*   **The Browns. Best.** RCA ANL 1-1083e.
Jim Ed, Maxine, and Bonnie were siblings who merged soft, lyrical folk sounds with country music to produce winning versions of "Scarlet Ribbons," "The Old Lamplighter," and "Jimmy Brown" (a cross-over hit based on "Les Trois Cloches," from France). More uptempo and contemporary ballads included "I Heard the Bluebirds Sing," "Lookin' Back to See," and the Hank Locklin song, "Send Me the Pillow That You Dream On."

F8.98*   **Glen Campbell. Best.** Capitol ST 11577.
Campbell distinguished himself as a studio musician in the late 1950s, while also playing with a southwestern band. From 1960 on he was a sideman whenever a twelve string guitar was called for. Thus, he appeared on countless albums of country, rock, and pop music; in this capacity, he had a short tenure with the Beach Boys. He is exceptionally fluent on this difficult instrument, and at one time, recorded a solo instrumental album clearly showing his dept to Merle Travis. Beginning in 1967, he recorded vocals as well, possessing a characteristic high voice

that fit in well with the demands of younger listeners. The popularity of his television show increased his stature in the pop and country music world, and he sold equally well in both areas. The prime source for his material was mainly the folk-bluegrass influence of John Hartford ("Gentle on My Mind") or the soft-pop of Jim Webb ("By the Time I Get to Phoenix"). Also included here are "Wichita Lineman," "Galveston," "The Last Time I Saw Her," and "Rhinestone Cowboy."

F8.99 **Roy Clark. Greatest Hits.** ABC Dot DOSD 2030.
  The pop-oriented Clark has derived much success from his national exposure on the television show *Hee Haw* and his constant Las Vegas appearances. His banjo and twelve string guitar (he is exceptionally proficient on both instruments) reflect a downhome aura. His material is wisely chosen to enhance his rapport with the audience, and it includes some original comedy and novelty items. This 12-track collation begins with his first hit "The Tips of My Fingers" (1963), and continues with "I Never Picked Cotton," "Riders in the Sky," and "The Great Divide."

F8.100* **Red Foley. The Red Foley Story.** two discs. MCA2-4053.
  Foley, a baritone from Kentucky, was the first country singer to record in Nashville (1945), later bringing Ernest Tubb to that city and setting off a chain reaction that meshed perfectly with the Grand Ole Opry. Before joining the Opry, he had settled in Chicago and steeped himself in black blues and in the bottleneck guitar technique. Some of this influence shows on "Blues in My Heart," "Chattanooga Shoe Shine Boy," and even "Old Shep," a song that thus acquired a more mournful setting. In the 1950s, Foley became a crooner in the Eddy Arnold fashion. The 25 tunes on this set also include some sacred material in addition to such secular hits as "Salty Dog Rag," "Midnight," and "Tennessee Polka." His contribution to religious music was significant, as fully half his total recording output was of sacred materials (see the annotation for these at F9.38).

F8.101 Entry deleted.

F8.102 **Sonny James. Biggest Hits.** Capitol ST 11013.
  James made his debut as a four year old in a singing family performance. His broad Southern accent, though, sometimes impeded his success, and often his version deferred to more "pop" oriented versions from other singers; "Young Love" (1957), a bigger hit for Tab Hunter than for James, for example. Maudlin songs are James's forte, such as "First Date, First Kiss, First Love," "You're the Only World I Know," "Behind the Tear," and "Take Good Care of Her."

F8.103* **George Morgan. Remembering.** Columbia KC 33894.
  Morgan modeled himself on Eddy Arnold as a pop balladeer performing country-oriented material. He maintained his success (after World War II and through the fifties) for a decade. He had the soft, smooth vocal style of Arnold (as on "You're the Only Good Thing That Happened to Me") but retained the violin and the steel guitar. This may have contributed to his undoing, as the market for country ballads was exceptionally small until Jim Reeves came along in the late 1950s. Arnold succeeded in maintaining an audience primarily because of his

potential to cross over to the pop market, plus the fact that about half of Arnold's material was light, bouncy, and uptempo, while Morgan's material was slow and mainly concerned with romantic cheating and broken love affairs. Morgan's first big success, though, was the uptempo "Candy Kisses" from 1948 (also successfully covered by Cowboy Copas and Elton Britt). One of the significant aspects of this tune is the two fiddles softly playing in the background, one of the first examples of the later Nashville "sweetening" pioneered by Chet Atkins. Typical tracks here include "Slippin' Around" (a duet with Marion Worth), "Red Roses for a Blue Lady," "Bouquet of Roses," "Room Full of Roses," and "Almost"—the latter a prime example of Morgan's crooning style: quaint and old fashioned, in a sentimental way. In most respects, Morgan was a truer balladeer in the country music field than was Eddy Arnold.

F8.104*   **Charley Pride. Best, v.1/2.** two discs. RCA LSP 4223 and 4682.
      Although the publicists call him "black," Pride is part black, Indian, and white—and he has assimilated all of these stylings. While growing up, he heard many songs on the radio, but favored the country stream and thus was different from his family and friends in his musical appreciation. In early years, he was promoted by RCA as "Country Charley Pride" and his blackness was never speci- fied as he was at first soft-pedalled. Before that, he was turned down outright by many other companies (which are probably now kicking themselves). His is a smooth, pop style in the manner of Eddy Arnold and George Morgan, though his deep, resonant baritone voice is different from that of the normal balladeer. Excellent material has always been chosen for him (his first album comprised only previous hit songs from other singers, both to ensure a measure of success and to show that a black man could sing "white" music). Pride's controlled stage manner and flexible range (including yodels) was perfect for what he sings best and most: love songs. Smash successes from the past include "Does My Ring Hurt Your Finger?" and "Snakes Crawl at Night" (both 1966), "The Day the World Stood Still" and "Easy Part's Over" (both 1968), "All I Have to Offer You Is Me" (1969), plus "Just between You and Me" and the successful covers of "The Last Thing on My Mind," "Streets of Baltimore," and "Louisiana Man."

F8.105*   **Johnny Rodriguez. Greatest Hits.** Mercury SRM 1-1078.
      Rodriguez, with his first hit in 1973 ("Pass Me By"), was the first chicano to succeed in country music. He easily became the sex symbol of country music "Latin Lovers"—he has good looks, and he was only 21 years old when he first recorded. In some respects, he is pulling up other chicano singers (such as the older Freddie Fender), but they are not as handsome as Rodriguez, whose youthful, diverse audience demands pop-country-rock material. His producer uses the Texas stylings of pedal steel guitar and twin fiddling, and by so doing, Rodruguez has managed to synthesize the whole southwestern and Texas musical scenes, borrowing from old time blues, swing, and modern movements such as the Texas outlaws (Kinky Friedman, Jerry Jeff Walker, Willie Nelson, etc.). Although his material is eclectic by its very nature, his own compositions do very well on the themes of disappointed love and the rambling man image. Rodriguez's most prominent influences have been Merle Haggard, whose music is quite similar, and the dance halls of his youth. He records material in Spanish as well, thus assuring himself

of two markets. Representative tracks here include "Faded Love," "Ridin' My Thumb to Mexico," "That's the Way Love Goes," "Jealous Heart," and the Hank Williams classic "Born to Lose." In this day of the 9-track compilation, it is refreshing to see a company release a 14-cut (!) collation.

F8.106   **Floyd Tillman. Best.** Harmony HL 7316.
Tillman was one of the first cross-over composers. He initially wrote for the country market but sold mostly in the pop area, thereby garnering many airplay royalties. He was one of the prime people responsible for the shifts in country music to popular music. His lazy baritone drawl was perfect for tunes such as "I'll Keep on Loving You," the classic "It Makes No Difference Now," "Slippin' Around," "I Love You so Much It Hurts," and "I'll Never Slip around Again."

F8.107   **Conway Twitty. Greatest Hits.** MCA 52.
Through the years, Twitty sold sixteen million singles for MGM, mainly rock and roll items sung in a high vocal ballad style. In 1965, he moved to Decca, where he returned to his country roots, especially with the hit "The Image of Me." His music has been characterized as being contemporary in feel and lyrics (exceptionally strong in the latter), with a touch of introspection and closely guarded thoughts. Anyone who thinks country poetry is all maudlin lines certainly will not find them in Twitty's work. The eleven tracks here all concern stereotyped perceptions of the female: "I Wonder What She'll Think about Me Leaving," "Darling, You Know I Wouldn't Lie," "How Much More Can She Stand?," and so forth.

CONTEMPORARY "OUTSIDERS"

Innovators

F8.108*   **Commander Cody and His Lost Planet Airmen. Hot Licks, Cold Steel and Truckers' Favorites.** Paramount PAS 6031.

F8.109   **Commander Cody and His Lost Planet Airmen. Lost in the Ozone.** Paramount PAS 6017.
This group excels at parodies of country hurtin' music, especially the trucker and honky-tonk songs, such as the Merle Haggard-influenced "Mama Hated Diesels" or "Looking at the World through a Windshield." During the early 1970s, they were one of the finest and best of the country rock groups. Early in their career they adapted (or recreated) the rockabilly rhythms of Sun Records to the harder sound of rock music, through such seminal tunes as the old Presley number "Rip It Up" or the newer "Truck Stop Rock." With their rich steel guitar playing, they became the first of the long haired groups to cross the line into country and western music. Most of their materials quite often dealt with the common theme in hurtin' music: sleazy little places on the edges of town (as in "Back to Tennessee" or "Daddy's Gonna Treat You Right"). Often though, they would adapt older works to the country mode, such as their uptempo version of the swing tune "Beat Me Daddy Eight to the Bar," which Commander Cody turned into a country boogie opus.

F8.110*   **Merle Haggard. Best of the Best.** Capitol ST 11082.

F8.111*   **Merle Haggard. Strangers.** Capitol ST 2373.

F8.112*   **Merle Haggard. Swinging Doors.** Capitol ST 2585.
    Haggard has been called "the poet of the common man" or "the singing spokesman of the silent majority." By many, he is also referred to as the successor to Woody Guthrie although he never directly emulated Guthrie's lifestyle. In any case, he is extremely relevant for these times: there is no distinction between man and entertainer, for they are the same. Just about all of his varied repertoire is autobiographical—patriotic thoughts and songs, some in jest, such as "Okie from Muskogee"; prisoner songs: songs of working men and fugitives; lost love and unhappiness—all of which gives him an almost fanatical following in prisons, factories, and bars. Early on in his career, Haggard was strongly influenced by Texans Bob Wills and Lefty Frizell (he has both recorded with Wills and put out a tribute album to him).
    Haggard's first hit was in 1965, with "From Now on All My Friends Are Gonna Be Strangers"—a bitter song originally written by Bill Anderson. It eventually led to the name of his group (the Strangers) whose back-up style is the unique western swing/honky-tonk mode fashioned by Ernest Tubb, another Texan. Haggard himself centers his activity in Bakersfield, California, and both he and Buck Owens record there along with certain followers, creating an alternative structure to Nashville (as does Austin, Texas, with Willie Nelson, Waylon Jennings, Jerry Jeff Walker, et al.). Haggard has by now recorded over 35 albums and most of them are gems. He does not allow sweetening—just the sound of his band alone. His most personal material includes: "Branded Man," "I Take a Lot of Pride in What I Am," "I'm Gonna Break Every Heart I Can," "Swinging Doors," "Mama Tried," "I'm a Lonesome Fugitive," "Working Man Blues," "The Fighting Side of Me."

F8.113*   **Tom T. Hall. Greatest Hits, v.1/2.** two discs. Mercury SR 61369 and SRM 1-1044.
    Tom T. Hall is a contemporary storyteller who projects the general from the specific. Vocally, he is just an average singer with a limited range as has Rod McKuen. But as in the latter's work, Hall's voice and tunes are definitely subservient to the lyric—often, he is just talking to accompaniment, with his baritone like that of a radio announcer discussing the news of the day. His lyrical fashioning, though, is very alert, for many of the songs actually tell how they were written. In content, there is very little romanticism—just reality. All of his characters are *working* people, both real and familiar, as in the "Ballad of Forty Dollars," which is about a mourner (?) at the funeral of a man who owed him on a loan. *Cashbox* called his work "musical journalism," but with *no* editorials. He began writing his own material about life back home while he was in Germany with the Army. His homesickness led to his first hit composition (and only real successful song in terms of monetary gain): "Harper Valley P.T.A."
    Over the years, Hall has written many songs for others (over 200 have been recorded), and they are all basically the same ballads that emphasize wit, insight, and even inspiration. He writes no hurtin' music and few love songs, because he

believes that people should not moon over what is lost, but should appreciate and remember what they have. It is difficult to pick representative albums. As with The Band in the country rock genre, all releases are good. The two discs cited above are not "greatest" in the sense of money-makers or chart successes. They are his materials that people ask for constantly—the vignettes that are self-contained observations of human character, as when he states in one of his songs, "a man's not writing if he can't relate all the things he's seen in this world." If there is one weakness, it is that Hall will often use a cliché phrase to effect a rhyme, but that is forgivable.

"Pay No Attention to Alice" is the typical story of a wife who is also an alcoholic, but the main reason for her drinking is her husband's indifference. Other songs here include such descriptive titles as "Margie's at the Lincoln Park Inn," "The Year That Clayton Delaney Died," "Ravishing Ruby," "That Song Is Driving Me Crazy," "The Little Lady Preacher," and so forth. Diverse Nashville musicians provide discreet accompaniment and give some brightening to the mediocre tunes (fiddler Vassar Clements, harpist Charlie McCoy, and pedal steel guitarist Pete Drake).

F8.114*　**Waylon Jennings. Ladies Love Outlaws. RCA LSP 4751.**

F8.115*　**Waylon Jennings. Lonesome, Orn'ry, and Mean. RCA LSP 4854.**

F8.116*　**Waylon Jennings. Honky Tonk Heroes. RCA APL 1-0240.**
Jennings is largely responsible for the "Nashville Outlaws" movement. Born in Texas, he moved to Lubbock and played bass with Buddy Holly. Since 1965, he has recorded for RCA in a decade of changes in country music. His gritty lyrics and sandy vocal textures made him largely offensive to the "uptown" folk in country music; he was never bland and was definitely not country "pop." His ragged, highly individualistic attitude shows deep influences—such that he has independent production rights at RCA and can record what and how he wants. His deep voice fits in nicely with his style of rambling music, often suggestive of being drunk in a loose, but somehow precise, manner. His songs are mainly originals, but he does record both Willie Nelson and Billy Joe Shaver material. His impact and influence are tremendous because he still records in Nashville.

Some of his early work after his transition from country hurtin' music includes exciting versions of "Crazy Arms," Buck Owens's "Under Your Spell Again," and Mickey Newberry's "Frisco Depot." No matter what he sings, Jennings adds class and perfection to it. He has finely calculated the art of creating the "laid back" country sound, and finely complements the forceful, but subdued, instrumentation with vocals that never strain for dramatic effect. The boundaries of Jennings's music are always blurred. It is country, but a rock atmosphere prevails, as in "Are You Sure Hank Done It This Way?"—a song that questions the too-nice country pop—or as in the salute, "Bob Wills Is Still the King." A representative of the dissident groups in Nashville country music, Jennings is superb all the way.

F8.117   **Willie Nelson. Best.** United Artists UA LAO86-F.

F8.118*   **Willie Nelson. Phases and Stages.** Atlantic SD 7291.

F8.119*   **Willie Nelson. Shotgun Willie.** Atlantic SD 7262.
      Nelson is one of country music's truly eclectic performers. Texas-born, he has roots in blues, dance music, western swing, and rock 'n' roll—all forms of music—like so many other artists coming from that state. If any phrase can define his music, then, it must be "soul country." His early career, beginning in 1961 with Liberty records (reissued on United Artists), clearly showed that he was ahead of his time. A superb composer, he fashioned such instant classics as "Hello Walls" and "Three Days" (both hit titles for Faron Young) and "Crazy" (popularized by Patsy Cline). The thirteen titles on the United Artists disc, all with a spare backup of bass, drums, steel guitar, and piano (the latter featuring Leon Russell), were considered sad standards of the day, e.g., "Funny How Time Slips Away," "The Part Where I Cry," "Wake Me When It's Over," and "Darkness on the Face of the Earth." The material on this disc strongly influenced Kris Kristofferson, Mickey Newbery, and Billy Joe Shaver.
      Then, in a career miscalculation, Nelson spent ten lost years with RCA, slowly losing his touch although also slowly becoming transformed by all the social changes in the late 1960s. Thus, he left Nashville in 1972 for Texas, completely disillusioned with the attitudes, studios, and "sweetening" characteristics of Nashville music. His first real album recorded as such (the UA material was largely a compilation of his hit singles) was *Shotgun Willie*, prepared with the assistance of Doug Sahm, David Bromberg, and Waylon Jennings. One of the typical titles here was "Sad Songs and Waltzes Aren't Selling This Year"—a reflection on his RCA days. His attitude on this Atlantic disc was that of the honky-tonk cowboy concerned with sarcastic sentimentalism, alcohol, religion, and unrequited love. His instrumentation reverted to that of his Liberty days, with sparse, subdued accompaniment including only the addition of a fiddle. Such tunes as "Whiskey River," the western swing ballad "Stay All Night (Stay a Little Longer)" by Bob Wills and Tommy Duncan, and Leon Russell's "You Look Like the Devil" emphasize the solid creative musicianship and pleasant melodies. Even so, Nelson's next album was far better, and it is perhaps one of the few concept albums in country music. *Phases and Stages* used the Muscle Shoals rhythm section plus acoustic strings such as Johnny Gimble's fiddle and mandolin, Eric Weissberg's banjo (on "Down at the Corner Beer Joint"), and Nelson's own guitar. The disc was recorded in 1974 and predated the Gail Sheehy book *Passages*. As Willie says, "Phases and Stages circles and cycles scenes that we've all seen before" (liner notes). The album presents the woman's side of the story through "Washing the Dishes/Pretend I Never Happened/Sister's Coming Home," while the man's side is revealed when the disc is turned over through "No Love around/I Still Can't Believe You've Gone/Heaven and Hell." Nelson's keen incisiveness and concern are clearly evident in these two Atlantic offerings.

Standards

F8.120   Billy "Crash" Craddock. Greatest Hits. ABC 850.
Craddock combines the rock and roll feel in country music (actually, rocka-billy), with the softer sounds of modern ballads, as in "Don't Be Angry" or "Afraid I'll Want to Love Her One More Time." His style substitutes lead violins for the lead guitars and saxophones of the more raunchy days. His work is more uptempo than would appear, though, and often falls into the country-rock mold (except for the lyrics), as on " 'Til the Water Stops Runnin' " and "I'm Gonna Knock on Your Door."

F8.121*   Dave Dudley. Best. Mercury SR 61268.
With a deep voice and mumbles, Dave Dudley and the Roadrunners have carved out a style now known as "trucking songs." This sub-genre has, in some cases, merged with honky-tonk music and western swing to produce a rough, down-to-earth mixture that appeals to modern lifestyles. It has carried over to the rock world, where it is best expressed by such groups as Commander Cody and the Lost Planet Airmen, and to almost any singer-songwriter. Beginning in 1964, Dudley recorded songs embracing all aspects of the music through their lyrics: the Vietnam truck driver in "Operation X"; the disc jockey who provides company for the drivers in "D. J. Memphis Joe"; the hazards involved in "Jack Knife"; government legislation and regulation in "Speed Traps, Weigh Stations and Detour Songs"; celebration of the open life through "Six Days on the Road"; and personalities in "Truck Drivin' Son-of-a-Gun," his first big success from 1965. Tom T. Hall has written for Dudley, and these songs are the quieter, story songs that Hall is famous for. Dudley has been an innovator in his style, and one particular reason for this has been his effective use of the shotgun guitar, where the notes are literally fired off with a twang.

F8.122   Doug Kershaw. The Cajun Way. Warner Brothers WS 1820.
Cajun music is a proud music (see the section annotation at F1.6 and F1.7 for a review of the older forms of this music). The interpretations by Doug Kershaw, a native Cajun from Louisiana are in the pop-rock-country mold. This is a perfect blend of the two streams, along with amplification and Kershaw's stunning violin style. Most of the material is in English, and it contributes a substantial wealth of folklore and regional variations to the country music world. Kershaw and his brother write a significant amount of material and rework older variants, such as "Jole Blon" and the rhythmic "Louisiana Man." Most of the material here is of an autobiographical nature.

F8.123   John D. Loudermilk. Suburban Attitudes in Country Verse. RCA LSP 3807.
Loudermilk, known primarily as a composer of country music, came under diverse influences; among them were Eddy Arnold, Jimmy Reed (both from country music), and the r 'n' b stars of black music, Ivory Joe Hunter, Fats Domino, and Lloyd Price. Some of his greatest songs in the modern country vein have included "A Rose and a Baby Ruth" (recorded by George Hamilton IV), "Waterloo" (Stonewall Jackson), "Abilene" (Hamilton again) and "Bad News" (Johnny Cash).

He has recorded infrequently, but when he did, the resultant record was usually a minor gem. The above RCA disc has come in for some criticism as it is a sarcastically biting album.

F8.124   **Roger Miller. Golden Hits.** Smash 67073.
Humorist and eclecticist Miller seems to have found no place in country music. His gaffes and manners have made him appear to be an eccentric, and as a composer his music flashed across the country music sky during 1965 and 1966 (his two peak years)—"King of the Road," "Dang Me," "Chug a Lug," and "Engine, Engine No. 9"—all traveling songs.

F8.125   **Jerry Reed. Best.** RCA LSP 4729.
Reed is a clown and a honky-tonk singer, but equally at home with good picking at his guitar (in the tradition of Chet Atkins and Merle Travis). He has been responsible for much of the good uptempo country music of the 1960s, including "Guitar Man," "Tupelo, Mississippi Flash," "Georgia Sunshine," "Ko-Ko Joe," and "When You're Hot, You're Hot."

F8.126   **Del Reeves. Best.** two discs. United Artists UALA 235G.
Reeves began his career as a composer for Roy Drusky, Carl Smith, and Rose Maddox. It was more fashionable to sing, though, especially one's own compositions. Thus, he packaged a show for Los Angeles and Las Vegas, concentrating on what later became known as "trucking" songs (although they started out as uptempo honky-tonk). Titles here include "Girl on the Billboard," "One Bum Town," "A Dime at a Time," and "Looking at the World through a Windshield."

F8.127   **Billie Joe Shaver. Old Five and Dimers Like Me.** Monument KZ 32293.
Although Shaver has a not-too-unpleasant voice, he is better known as a composer, especially for Waylon Jennings. His material, whether here or for Jennings, quite often concerns interracial love and romance, plus the ubiquitous drug songs.

8.128*   **Tompall and the Glaser Brothers. Greatest Hits.** MGM SE 4946.
Chuck, Jim, and Tompall Glaser were a brother trio from Nebraska. At one time, they appeared as regulars on the Arthur Godfrey Show. Soon they were in the recording studios as session men/singers (they backed Marty Robbins on "El Paso"), later branching out to become producers and studio owners. They also honed their compositional skills and gave many songs to other performers. Eventually, they had their hands in most matters concerning country music, and demonstrated all-round versatility. The MGM disc comes mainly from the 1960s and includes such prominent titles as "Wicked California," "California Girl," "Rings," "Faded Love," and "The Moods of Mary."

FEMALE SINGERS

Innovators

F8.129* Patsy Cline. The Patsy Cline Story. two discs. MCA2-4038.
Cline was one of the first female country singers to invade the pop field, and thereby she started a whole line. Her untimely death in 1963 in a plane crash cut short a dramatic career that could have shifted the pop orientation of country music much earlier than it had actually occurred. She was strongly influenced by Patti Page and Kay Starr, but only by their country material (or popular versions of country music). Thus, the impact and feedback of country and pop on one another went full circle. Cline's tough vocal stylings were obviously derived from Starr. The 24 tracks here include many remakes of earlier country hits fashioned by others, mostly turned into a pop style, such as "South of the Border," "Sweet Dreams," "San Antonio Rose," and "The Wayward Wind." Her original hits included "A Poor Man's Roses," "I Fall to Pieces," and "Walkin' after Midnight."

F8.130* Loretta Lynn. Greatest Hits, v.1/2. two discs. MCA 1 and 420.
Lynn was a direct development from Jean Shepard and Kitty Wells, and she was the first challenge to Wells as "Queen of Country Music." She began recording in 1962 (the first female to talk of marriage and "rocky roads"), and her material is self-written and lyrical, both of these being a rarity among modern country performers. She is frank, and mentions brutal reality (e.g., "The Pill") but often she does it with grace and humor, as in "Don't Come Home A'Drinkin' (with Lovin' on Your Mind)" or "You Ain't Woman Enough (To Take My Man)." By looking after her image and using carefully written material, she appeals to all age levels. Horstmann has stated: "She expresses the outrage of the abused female faced with chauvinistic behavior, but she condemns only the abuse, not the system that permits it." Thus, while she is fighting for her rights in the face of change, her best material is still only halfway between "liberation" and "supplication." Overall, she provides a cop-out ending by suggesting that the usual result of misbehavior is that the "injured" partner leaves home or "walks out," which solves nothing. Her first hit was indicative of the future—"Success"— and later material was autobiographical, such as "Coal Miner's Daughter" or "Blue Kentucky Girl." The misleading "Happy Birthday" is a veiled threat to run around if her husband persists in his waywardness; "Your Squaw Is on the Warpath" is explicit. Lynn must be judged a transitional figure in the shaping of country music's recognition of equal rights for women, although it should be noted that she was breaking ground in even whispering discreetly about it.

F8.131* Molly O'Day. Unforgettable. Harmony HL 7299.
O'Day was probably the greatest woman singer in all of country music. She dealt mainly with western themes during her peak years of 1946-1952 (in later life, she was to become a full time sacred music singer; see her annotation under F9.63 and F9.64). Her traditional music, played on the five string banjo, has caused her to be known as a female Roy Acuff. She was a strong influence on Rose Maddox, Wilma Lee Cooper and, to some extent (although her style varied), Kitty Wells.

O'Day, with such titles as "Tramp on the Street" and "Don't Sell Daddy Any More Whiskey," was an emotional belter, well-known for her punch in delivery. She has been revered by bluegrass music fans for the quality of her banjo and for her performing style. In musical conception and delivery, she has been influenced by none other than Hank Williams, which shows on the murder ballad "Poor Ellen Smith," "Six More Miles to the Graveyard," and "I Don't Care If Tomorrow Never Comes."

F8.132*   **Kitty Wells. Story.** two discs. MCA2-4031.
Wells was one of the few consistent female singers in country and western music from the 1940s to 1965. She began radio work in the 1940s with the team of Johnny and Jack (and later married Johnny Wright of that duo). In 1952, she recorded for Decca, scoring instantly with an answer song to Hank Thompson's "Wild Side of Life," calling her song "It Wasn't God Who Made Honky Tonk Angels." She was 33 years old then and was considered elderly by many in the country field, especially for a woman singer. The only women of note who preceded her were Patsy Montana (from western music) and Molly O'Day (from country music). In effect, though, Wells was the first woman "star" in country music. The male guilt of "Honky Tonk Angels" (penned by a man, not by Wells) was emphasized by her high lilting quaver and forced singing, perhaps better revealed on "Repentin'," where an echo was also used.
"Honky Tonk Angels" could be considered one of the finest of the women's liberation songs, except that it occurred in 1952, much too early for the movement. Indeed, it was merely an oasis in a desert. Wells returned to the "straight and narrow" with songs of jilted love, unrequited love, and adultery—such titles as "Back Street Affair," "Mommy for a Day," "Lonely Side of Town," "Jealousy," "Making Believe," and "Repentin'." Her loyal fans stayed with her songs of the struggles of the cast-off woman attempting to rise in the world; but, of course, by 1965, not only was this old fashioned, it was derogatory. The 24 tracks here provide a strong look at a time that used to be, when a restrained voice and a nasal whine meant Kitty Wells. Because of her position (not necessarily the material), her pre-eminence was a goal for Loretta Lynn and Tammy Wynette to attempt to achieve.

F8.133*   **Tammy Wynette. Greatest Hits, v.1/3.** three discs. Epic BN 26486,
            E 30733, and KE33396.
Wynette was strongly influenced by her Mississippi upbringing in shape note religious songs. Hers is the cliché success story—advancing from being a hairdresser to being a queen of country music. With her emotional, powerful moans, she is the exponent of only *one* theme: the lonely, married housewife who always forgives any of hubby's foibles. Her "Stand by Your Man" (used in *Five Easy Pieces* and selling over two million copies) was the largest single seller performed by a woman in country music history. This theme translated Wynette into a stylist. Her management conducted a survey and found that not only are most of her listeners women between 22 and 45 years of age, but also that she is the one country star that most non-country fans can identify.

Under the influence of producer-composer Billy Sherill at Epic, Wynette was advanced as a package that harped on, but never changed, a winning idea. With titles such as "Elusive Dreams," "D-I-V-O-R-C-E" (spelled out in front of an infant), "Take Me to Your World," "(You Make Me Want to Be) a Mother," "Help Me Make It through the Night," "I'll See Him Through," "My Man (Understands)," and "He Loves Me All the Way"—all on her singular, best-selling theme—she provides an alternative to women's liberation. Indeed, she not only may have actually reinforced the male chauvinistic view but also lost ground already won by Kitty Wells, Loretta Lynn, and others. She has a tremendous voice, which is best heard *not* in her syrupy tunes, but on such items as "There Goes That Old Steel Guitar."

Standards

F8.134*   Rosalie Allen. Queen of the Yodelers. RCA LPM 1121.
Singer-guitarist Allen recorded with Elton Britt in the 1940s and early 1950s. She may be thought of as Britt's female counterpart during a time when female yodelers were relatively scarce. Her impressive solo work and range may be found on such classic items as "He Taught Me How to Yodel," "Rose of the Alamo," and "Yodel Boogie." Her best work with Britt includes the 1950 gem "Quicksilver," "The Game of Broken Hearts," "Tennessee Yodel Polka," and "Soft Lips."

F8.135   Lynn Anderson. Greatest Hits. Columbia KC 31641.
One of the more successful pop hitmakers in the country field, Lynn Anderson has been steeped in all aspects of the music. Her mother was a singer-songwriter; her father was a music publisher. Her own music is typed as "MOR [middle of the road] country" and includes "I Never Promised You a Rose Garden" (written by Joe South in 1970), "Listen to a Country Song," "Stay There 'till I Get There," and "You're My Man." She is one of the few country singers with a northern background, having been born and raised in North Dakota.

F8.136   Skeeter Davis. Best. RCA LSP 3374.
Skeeter was a member of the 1948 trio, the Davis Sisters, a group that produced a phenomenal disc in 1953 entitled "I Forgot More Than You'll Ever Know." As a solo singer, she has an appealing pinched voice, but her material dealing with country life, heartbreaks, honky-tonks, etc., was at variance with her personal convictions. For instance, she was a conservative in politics and would not perform anywhere that liquor was being served. Later in the 1970s, she became a stern religious fundamentalist, completely divorced from her songs. Included on this album are, then, sentimental numbers such as "The End of the World" (which crossed over to the pop charts), "Set Him Free," "I'm Falling Too," and "Homebreaker."

F8.137   Donna Fargo. Best. ABC DO 2075.
Fargo is one of a new breed of singers in country music, a breed that transcends the sex of the performer. She is among the few who can actually create their own

songs that are not based on traditional attitudes, tunes, wordings, or situations. She is a bit of a mystery and appeals to the intellectual side (such as it may be) of country music with songs that deal with suicide or are based on the writings of Camus. At any rate, her contributions, albeit depressing in tone, have been definite. The eleven tracks here contain her early hits (nine of them self-penned): "Happiest Girl in the Whole U.S.A.," "You Can't Be a Beacon (If Your Light Don't Shine)," "Funny Face," and "Superman."

F8.138   **Wanda Jackson. Best.** Capitol ST 2883.
    Jackson's raw voice suggests a hard rocker, and that is what she is best remembered for during the late 1950s. Indeed, many country and rock historians regard her as the one and only female rock and roll singer. Certainly she took the honky-tonk song and fashioned a career from it, beginning with Hank Thompson's brand of western swing in 1954. At the same time, she was an excellent composer, being responsible for "Kicking Our Hearts Around" and "In the Middle of a Heart-ache." Other tunes included "Right or Wrong," "The Box He Came In," and "Just Call Me Lonesome." (See her rock and roll annotation at R2.20 in the *Contemporary Popular Music* volume of this set.)

F8.139   **Rose Maddox. Best.** Harmony HL 7312.

F8.140*   **Rose Maddox. The One Rose.** Capitol ST 1312.
    In the western swing picture, Rose played with the Maddox Brothers (there were four of them) during the 1940s. Being influenced by the great Molly O'Day, she took on a honky-tonk style in much the same manner as Tubb did, combining western swing rhythms with black gospel music. In 1960, she teamed with Buck Owens in a series of memorable country duets ("Loose Talk" and "Mental Cruelty") and then made a bluegrass music album that was superb (see F6.87 for this latter annotation). Typical early material in the O'Day mold included "Philadelphia Lawyer" and "Honky Tonkin'."

F8.141   **Barbara Mandrell. Midnight Oil.** Columbia KC 32743.
    Mandrell emphasizes the beat in her music, much as rock singers do; in this manner, she is contributing greatly to the stylization of modern country music. In her lyrics, she is enlarging on the conscious concern about womanhood expressed by Loretta Lynn, taking it several steps further along the path to feminism. Some might say the numbers are even "provocative."

F8.142   **Anne Murray. Country.** Capitol ST 11324.
    Murray presented a problem to marketing experts. She has firm country roots in Nova Scotia, Canada, but also appealed to the middle of the road audience as well. Many of her successes were cross-over hits, but for many years, she was really in neither camp. Country music, though, has become respectable in the 1970s. To take advantage of this (and her "peaches and cream" attitudes), Capitol consolidated all of the distinctly country music versions of her material into one album and called it *Country*. In many ways, it can be considered a "best" album as all the material has been issued before. Criteria were obviously weighted toward those songs that had a country feel, sound, setting, or idea. Murray's deep alto

voice, unusual in country music today, does give her a distinctive style along with her feel for the music. Tracks include her first hit "Snowbird," the sacred "Put Your Hand in the Hand" (both tunes contributed by Gene MacLellan), the well-known country classic "He Thinks I Still Care," Loggins's "Danny's Song," and "Cotton Jenny." This is solid, middle of the road country music.

F8.143*   Dolly Parton. Best. RCA APL 1-1117.

F8.144   Dolly Parton. Hello I'm Dolly/As Long As I Love. two discs. Monument BZ 33876.
Dolly is everyone's favorite country singer—she is a gorgeous looking female exhibiting all the characteristics of a pinup girl, with long blond hair piled on top of her head. She personifies almost all female country music fans' dreams. Despite her knockout appearance, though, she comes from and still maintains a fundamentalist background. Almost all of her material is self-written in good, old time and simple fashionable style. Her early material for Monument was recorded when she was writing for others, and the twofer contains such tasty morsels as "Dumb Blonde," "Too Lovely Too Long," and "Daddy Won't Be Home Anymore." For RCA, she embarked on a series of duets with Porter Wagoner (see these under the annotation at F8.154) and contributed many solo efforts of her own, such as "Traveling Man," "Jolene," "Lonely Coming Down," and "Coat of Many Colors."

F8.145   Linda Ronstadt. Heart Like a Wheel. Capitol ST 11358.
Surprising to most people is the fact that Ronstadt is more of a country singer than Olivia Newton-John. This Arizona-born woman had been steeped in country and western swing since birth. After an abortive effort with the Stone Poneys (a soft-rock group) in 1965, she turned to Nashville in 1970, where she employed the finest session men and excellent materials. She hung out with the current country-rock singers and even assisted Earl Scruggs on one of his albums. She has been a slow builder in the country music field, but all of this paid off on her *Wheel* album, a brilliant merging of soft rock and country stylings, assisted by some familiar and some old material such as "I Can't Help It if I'm Still in Love with You" (from Hank Williams) and "When Will I Be Loved?" (from the Everly Brothers). Her honeyed voice is very feminine in the helpless sense. The title track here is performed with Maria Muldaur in a duet. For this album, she used some Hollywood session men, who have by now learned all of the skills employed in Nashville.

F8.146*   Jean Shepard. This Is. . . . Capitol T 1253.
Oklahoman Shepard has a tough voice (not a rough one: just tough) and used to play the string bass in her group. Her career began with Ferlin Husky in 1953, as the duo created the classic "A Dear John Letter," addressed to a soldier in Korea. Since then she has concentrated on songs of long suffering and the righteous woman, as in "Satisfied Mind" (1955) or "Beautiful Lies." She was one of the better female singers in the 1950s, second only to Kitty Wells. What is surprising, though, is that an examination of her songs from the 1950s shows that she was definitely ahead of her time in expressing concerns about the status of women. Many of them are quite valuable and in step with the 1970s.

F8.147   Connie Smith. Best. RCA LSP 3848.
Despite her activities as a committed Christian, Connie Smith has had a
very controversial personal life. This has been expressed time and again in her
songs, such as "Once a Day," "I Can't Remember," "Tiny Blue Transistor Radio,"
"Ain't Had No Lovin'," and "I'll Come Running."

F8.148   Dottie West. Best. RCA LSP 4811.
West is a songwriter whose roots are in poverty. Her church-soprano voice
reflects her warm style, characterized as "passionate and motherly." Her material
falls mainly into the romantic fantasy world, with some overtones of judgements
that all women are guilty of sin or error, such as "Love Is no Excuse," "Would
You Hold It against Me?," "Before the Ring on Your Finger Turns Green," the
tearjerker "Mommie Can I Still Call Him Daddy?," and "Gettin' Married Has Made
Us Strangers."

COUNTRY DUETS

F8.149   Carl and Pearl Butler. Great Carl Butler Sings. Harmony HS 11185.

F8.150   Carl and Pearl Butler. Honky-Tonkin'. Columbia CS 9769.
Butler, from Knoxville, Tennessee, was one of country music's premier
composers, creating songs for Roy Acuff, Carl Smith, Bill Monroe, Flatt and
Scruggs, and even Rosemary Clooney. On his own, he began a career with Columbia
in 1953 and was joined by his wife Pearl in 1962. His sentimental songs included
"Guilty Conscience," "Hold Back the Dawn," "Loving Arms," "If Tear Drops
Were Pennies," "River of Tears," and "Borrowed Love."

**F8.151*   George Jones and Tammy Wynette. Me and the First Lady/We Go
Together. two discs. Epic BG 33752.**
Originally available as two separately issued discs, these albums contain
vocals not only by some of the best country music singers in the business but
also perhaps the best all-around country duo. Their voices fit perfectly, as did
their marriage before 1975. All of the material here is modern country (from 1971
onwards).

F8.152   Lulu Belle and Scotty. Sweethearts of Country Music. Starday 206.
Beginning their association in 1934 with film work, Myrtle Eleanor and
Scotty Wiseman have progressed through the WLS National Barn Dance in Chicago
(for twenty years they were a fixture) to the modern era of bluegrass music, where
they are revered by fans. Country material predominates here, with the sentimental
"Remember Me," "Between You and Me," and "Mountain Dew," but a faster
pace and a banjo easily convert the music to bluegrass.

**F8.153*   Conway Twitty and Loretta Lynn. Lead Me On. MCA Decca DL
75326.**
This 1972 album is perhaps the finest representative of the modern, contemporary country duet. In the 1930s, a woman's voice was usually added for harmony

on the chorus. To some extent, she was replaced by the high lonesome tenor (over lead) in bluegrass music, or the yodel in country music. Then, with the resurgence of the female singer through Kitty Wells in the early 1950s, the woman in a country duet assumed some equality of expression, even if it was only to sing along with the man. Loretta Lynn developed a new tact, especially in her records with Ernest Tubb (which were largely unsatisfactory in terms of Tubb's vocals and the material presented). With this present album, though, the height of perfection has been reached. A male vocalist dealing with *persona* themes and the public and private perceptions of womanhood has been joined by the singer-songwriter of the country field who best presents the middle position of emerging womanhood. The two together can lead the way through to complete "emancipation" step by step without the crushing alienation of drastic changes. There are two basic themes on this disc. One is that of secret meetings, adultery, and/or playing around ("Playing House Away from Home," "Back Street Affair"). The other concerns eternal love and/or reconciliation (Bonnie and Delaney's "Never Ending Song of Love," "Get Some Loving Done," and the dramatic "You Blow My Mind," with its alternating lines approaching a crescendo). Excellent material, good voices and phrasing, and a real feel for the music lead us to ask: is this country soul?

F8.154 **Porter Wagoner and Dolly Parton. Best. RCA LSP 4556.**
Porter and Dolly were one of the most traditionally-oriented singing couples in country music, emphasizing sentimental and maudlin songs at the expense of the tragic or cheatin' songs. Titles include "Always, Always," "We'll Get Ahead Someday," "If Teardrops Were Pennies," and "Burning the Midnight Oil."

SACRED MUSIC

SACRED MUSIC

This section resembles the **Gospel** category in the *Black Music* volume of this set in that it annotates some of the better known forms of popular white religious music (including, to some extent, popular vocal renditions such as those by Perry Como). Stylistically, the differences between black and white religious music are in their modes of presentation. Gospel is relatively happy music, spreading the "good news"; sacred is more solemn and reverent, finer-paced without the call-and-response patterns established in gospel music. As pointed out in *Black Music*, gospel had only a few types of expression, whereas sacred music is more varied. The early practice of "shape note" singing, in which a soloist or group would sing the name of the note rather than a word or syllable, was particularly valuable in those times and places when people could not read, but could follow, the note patterns in music. Its importance, of course, was in celebrating God, despite the fact that the Bible was not read. However, all of the tunes in shape note singing came from standard hymns and white spirituals.

A second form was the "old timey call," also known as "linin' out." Again, this was a holdover from illiterate times. A reader would "line out" the words in a rhyme, and the chorus or congregation would sing them back to a standard, pre-established tune, and thus obviate the need for a hymnary. From this music developed the phrase "reading my lines." A third form was the choral song, which was sung by gatherings larger than most of the black groups had. A fourth form was the country and western hymn, a secular song of respect for some divine being, mother or home—not necessarily God, but dedicated to the righteous life in the spirit of Kant's categorical imperative. These were mainly slow tempo songs, and most country and western singers have an assortment of them in their repertoire. Most will sing one or two on each album recorded; a few will also sing entire sacred albums, or have collated their previous recordings in this genre. A fifth form of sacred music is the bluegrass hymn. It may be uptempo, but mostly it is slow and unaccompanied. Its main features are exceptional lyrics and four-part harmony by the bluegrass quartet. Most such songs are contemporary, especially the ones composed and sung by Carl Story.

This music has a very loyal but small audience, so there is no large marketing percentage in this genre for larger recording companies. In the 1970s, many country singers were able to assign their sacred music rights to Word Records of Waco, Texas. Thus, some (such as Ray Price) could continue to record secular material for CBS or MCA, and then do gospel records for Word (or its subsidiaries, Myrrh and Canaan). In this way, Word has managed to capture a good variety of singers, such as the Lewis Family and Anita Bryant. Other companies such as Rimrock and Pine Mountain do business with a mixture of reissues, country versions of bluegrass or old time music, and sacred music. Other forms of religious music are being produced by a new group of singers usually called "committed Christians," such as Pat Boone, Dale Evans, or Skeeter Davis. Some are for large companies; others are for independents.

ANTHOLOGIES

F9.1   **All Night Sing.** Camden CAL 767.

F9.2*   **The Family Gospel Album.** Rimrock 1002.

F9.3   **Greatest Gospel Hymns.** Pine Mountain 125.

F9.4   **Old Time Family Religion.** Camden CAL 816.
These discs contain some of the most beloved sacred music that has come down from traditional sources. The Carter Family predominates on the two Camden issues (from 1963 and 1964, respectively) with tunes such as "On the Sea of Galilee," "The Church in the Wildwood," "When the World's on Fire," "Let the Church Roll On," and "On My Way to Canaan's Land." The Pine Mountain issue presents latter-day Carter Family, as well as the Phipps Family, which sings in the Carter style. Carl Story, who has been performing sacred music for over 35 years, is joined here by Grandpa Jones. Primarily, groups are featured on the Rimrock reissue (Lewis Family, Masters Family, Blue Sky Boys), but there is also the great Molly O'Day, who made her comeback in the 1960s via sacred music.

F9.5*   **Country Gospel Song.** Folkways RBF 19.
This anthology presents both black and white performers, and it is the only anthology we could find that deliberately sets out to contrast the gospel and the sacred music approaches to traditional religious singing. Here are selections by Ernest Phipps, Blind Willie Johnson, the Smith Brothers, the Reverend J. M. Gates, Uncle Dave Macon, the Carter Family, and others. As with all RBF and Folkways discs, there are good notes for a comparison of the styles.

F9.6   **Country Stars Sing Sacred Songs.** RCA Camden CAS 2136.

F9.7   **Good Old Country Gospel.** RCA LSP 4778.

F9.8   **Gospel Song Styles of 12 Great Artists.** RCA LSP 3721.

F9.9   **Precious Memories.** two discs. RCA Camden CXS 9020.
RCA, with the largest country music catalog of all record companies, would naturally have the largest selection of sacred music. Several new companies such as the Word-Canaan complex may have more of this type of music, but as recent phenomena, they have yet to build up an historical collection. Just about the entire roster of RCA artists are here: Bobby Bare, Martha Carson, the Browns, George Hamilton IV, early Kitty Wells, Connie Smith, Don Gibson, Sons of the Pioneers, Porter Wagoner, Hank Snow, Skeeter Davis, Dolly Parton, Charley Pride, Jim Reeves, Dottie West, the Carter Family, Jimmy Dean, Stuart Hamblen, Hank Locklin, Norma Jean, and so forth. RCA LSP 3721 is particularly interesting, for the performers here either sing only sacred music in their performances or are strongly identified with sacred music. Here, then, are songs by the Billy Graham London Crusade Choir, George Beverly Shea, the Blackwood Brothers Quartet, the Speer Family, the Statesmen Quartet, and others.

F9.10*   **Fa-Sol-La Is Here to Stay.** Sacred Harp 105.

F9.11*   **Old Harp Singing.** Folkways 2356.

F9.12   **Sacred Harp Singing.** Library of Congress AAFS L 11.
     Sacred harp singing is also known as shape note singing. It was originally devised for people who could not read, but who could recognize the "shape" of the note and its position. Thus, only the notes themselves are sung, as in the title of the first album above. This demands intensive rigor and discipline for the multi-part harmonies. The Folkways album is traditional white religious music from Tennessee, including such selections as "Wondrous Love" and "Northfield" among many hymns, anthems, and fugues. The Library of Congress album contains much similar material for the 1930s, with many leaders and congregations in Alabama and Georgia among its nineteen tracks. The Sacred Harp album is from Bremen, Georgia; it is a more recent set with such items as "Coronation," "Faith and Hope," "The Child of Grace," "Christian Soldier," and "Infinite Day."

F9.13   **Gospel Music's Top Ten for 1970 and 1971.** two discs. Canaan CAS 9691 and 9710.
     Many companies put out annual compilations of sacred music, and the variety issues from Canaan records have always been the strongest in musical content and sincerity. These two years represent a high point in the Canaan story, for after this period, much commercialism began to intrude as the company found its marketing stride. Typical selections include "Sheltered in the Arms of God" and "The King Is Coming," both by the Speer Family, "He Touched Me" by the Statesmen Quartet, "The Night before Easter" by the Blackwood Brothers, and "Jesus Is Coming Soon" and "The Old Rugged Cross Made the Difference," both by the Oak Ridge Boys. Canaan Records produces a wide cross-section of sacred music groups, including many family singers.

F9.14*   **Preachin', Prayin', Singin'.** Starday 303.
     This is one of the few all-bluegrass sacred music anthologies. Here are most of the really popular groups of the late 1950s and early 1960s. Standouts are the melodies by the Stanley Brothers ("Let the Church Roll On"), the Country Gentlemen ("The Church Back Home"), Flatt and Scruggs (the title track), and Jim and Jesse ("You Can't Love Jesus More Than Me"). Others include Red Ellis, Hylo Brown, Carl Story, the Stoneman Family, the Blue Sky Boys, and the Lonesome Pine Fiddlers. There is also an excellent country sermon ("The Hell Bound Train") by Reverend Barney Pierce.

STANDARDS

F9.15*   **Roy Acuff. Waiting for My Call to Glory.** Harmony HS 11334.
     The high, penetrating voice of Acuff is ideally suited for sacred music. These recordings originally came from the 1940s, and they include "I Saw the Light," "Where Were You When They Crucified My Lord?," and the title selection.

F9.16   **Bill Anderson. Singing His Praise.** MCA Decca DL 75339.
Anderson, with his journalist's background, and his strong sense of styling, teams up with Jan Howard in this program of traditional singing.

F9.17   **Eddy Arnold. The Chapel on the Hill.** RCA LSP 1225.
The ever-popular Arnold—with his smooth as silk voice—projects here some of his earlier and best materials, with sparse accompaniment.

F9.18   **Bailes Brothers. Avenue of Prayer.** Audio Lab AL 1511.
The Bailes (Johnny, Walter, and Homer) are a traditional trio from West Virginia; they sing in an emotional style somewhat reminiscent of the Blue Sky Boys. Harmony predominates on such classics as "Dust on the Bible" and "Give Mother My Crown."

F9.19   **Bailey Brothers. Take Me Back to Happy Valley.** Rounder 0030.
This duet specializes in old time music and bluegrass. They are now semi-retired, but they once were with the Grand Ole Opry and WWVA Dances. Along with Tater Tate and others, they turn in sterling performances of "I'd Rather Have Jesus," "Sweet Allalee," "Heaven," "Whispering Hope" (with superb harmonies), and "He Whispers Sweet Peace."

F9.20   **E. C. Ball.** Rounder 0026.
Along with wife Orna and the Friendly Gospel Singers, E. C. Ball gives a program that is a judicious mixture of instrumentals and vocals in the old time music mode. The sixteen tracks include "When I Can Read My Titles Clear" (one of the oldest sacred music tunes), "Born to Serve the Lord," "Do You Call That Religion?," and the wonderful "I See God in Everything." This is North Carolina traditional music at its best.

F9.21   **Blackwood Brothers Quartet. Best.** RCA ANL1-1091.
This is an extremely popular quartet, somewhat commercial in that their records sell well and their concerts are always sold out. Over the years, they have recorded much good material. This disc from the 1950s includes twelve tracks, among which are "I've Got to Walk That Lonesome Road," "In Times Like These," "God Made a Way," "Precious Memories," and "The Lord's Prayer."

F9.22*   **The Blue Sky Boys. Precious Moments.** Pine Mountain PM 269.
The Bolicks (Bill and Earl) retired in 1951 rather than change their singing style (see their long annotation at F5.105, 106). In the early 1960s, though, they began to record once more, but this time, it was sacred music only. The Pine Mountain album is a straight reissue of Starday 269 from 1963, and it includes many earlier works re-recorded, such as "Radio Station," "S-A-V-E-D," "Come to the Savior," and "Last Mile of the Way."

F9.23   **Pat Boone. Hymns We Love.** Word WST 8664.

F9.24   **Pat Boone. Songs from the Inner Court.** Lamb & Lion LL 1016.
In the late 1960s, Pat Boone returned to his religious roots, and now he

concentrates solely on such material in his concerts and other performances. The first album here was previously released on Dot records and comes from the early 1960s, when he was beginning to recreate his lost popularity. The twelve selections are loosely religious, such as "Will the Circle Be Unbroken?," "Softly and Tenderly," "The Old Rugged Cross," and "Whispering Hope." This sacred music is most acceptable to the public at large because of the exceptional richness of the melodies and the harmony singing when groups perform it. The second album is more recent and more religious, with such offerings as "I Can Hear My Savior Calling," "I Am Thine, O Lord," "Does Jesus Care?," and "Fairest Lord Jesus."

F9.25   **Martha Lou Carson. Talk with My Lord.** Capitol T 1607.
A former country star in the honky-tonk mode, Carson has since turned to religion. Here are "I Can't Stand up Alone," "Satisfied," and "I'm Gonna Walk and Talk with My Lord."

F9.26*   **Carter Family. Great Sacred Songs.** Harmony HL 7396.
Although the Carter Family has been widely anthologized in sacred albums, this is the only strictly religious Carter Family album available. (It comes from 1935, when the Family recorded many older tunes from their repertoire for ARC records.) Thus, as mentioned in the **Old Time Music** section (F5.107-11), these are not their best efforts, but it is their only separately available sacred album. The ten tracks include "There'll Be No Distinction There," "River of Jordan," "The Storms Are on the Ocean," "God Gave Noah the Rainbow Sign," and "On the Rock Where Moses Stood."

F9.27*   **Johnny Cash. Sings Precious Memories.** Columbia C 33087.
The deep, husky voice of Cash is particularly attractive on these eleven tracks, but as with that of so many other popular singers, the material is not hard core sacred items. Rather, it includes such perennials as "Rock of Ages," "Old Rugged Cross," "Softly and Tenderly," "In the Sweet By and By," and "Amazing Grace."

F9.28*   **Perry Como. I Believe.** RCA ANL 1-1137.
The smooth sincerity of the Italian tenor of Como makes for some fine and easy listening of some popular sacred "hymns." He is well known for the title selection, and for closing each of his television shows with a "hymn." The twelve selections here—all from the 1950s—represent a wide variety of religions, such as "Onward Christian Soldiers," "Act of Contrition," "Ave Maria," "The Rosary," "Eli, Eli," and "Kol Nidrei."

F9.29*   **Country Gentlemen. Gospel Album.** Rebel 1497.
The Country Gentlemen are not too well-known for their sacred singing in the bluegrass area, but they do give fine, recent interpretations of such classics as "One Wide River to Cross," "Sunny Side of Life," "Little White Church," "Rank Stranger" (performed better by the Stanley Brothers), and "Are You Washed in the Blood?"

F9.30*   **Wilma Lee and Stoney Cooper. Sacred Songs.** Harmony HL 7233.
This fine traditional group blends country music with bluegrass, and their sacred singing fits into the same pattern. In these recordings from the 1940s, the emphasis is definitely on uptempo tunes. The traditional stylings here include the old time fiddle and the five string banjo. Selections include "I'm Taking My Audition," "Thirty Pieces of Silver," "What's the Matter with This World?," and the Hank Williams favorite—"Are You Walking and A-Talking for the Lord?"

F9.31*   **J. D. Crowe and the Kentucky Mountain Boys. The Model Church.** Lemco 611.
The bluegrass quartet nearly reaches its zenith with the close harmony singing on this album. Banjoist Crowe leads the way for "I'll Talk It over with Him," "Journey's End," "Let the Spirit Descend," "No Mother or Dad," and the title track.

F9.32   **Jimmie Davis. Christ Is My Sunshine.** Canaan CAS 9760.

F9.32a   **Jimmie Davis. How Great Thou Art.** MCA Decca 74322.
Former Louisiana governor Davis composes most of his own sacred music. The MCA collation is a retrospective covering his long career for Decca records. It includes "In My Father's Home," "Where Could I Go?," the dynamic "Supper Time," and "What a Happy Day." The Canaan collection is more recent, from the early 1970s, and while his voice is not as strong as it used to be, his material is as good as ever: "If You Love Him Let Him Know," "Because He Lives," "Welcome Home," "City of Gold," and "Will There Be Any Stars in My Crown?"

F9.33   **Skeeter Davis. Hand in Hand with Jesus.** RCA LSP 3763.
This perky singer had committed herself to Jesus by 1970. She now sings only sacred music in a deeply emotional style.

F9.34   **Little Jimmy Dickens. The Old Country Church.** Harmony HL 9025.
Dickens is a hillbilly-rural singer who specializes in novelty and humor. The other side of him is apparent here, in this reissued program of such sacred tunes as "No Tears in Heaven," "He Spoke Not a Word," "Take up Thy Cross," and "I Shall Not Be Moved."

F9.35   **Dale Evans. Heart of the Country.** Word WST 8658.
Surprisingly, Mrs. Roy Rogers has not recorded frequently, preferring the occasional number in movies or on television. For many years, she has been a committed Christian, but the material on this album is both loosely religious and partly patriotic, with such items as "This Land Is Your Land," "God Bless America," "Prayer for America," "I Am the United States." There are also two medleys, one of spirituals and one of Kris Kristofferson tunes ("One Day at a Time/Why Me, Lord?").

F9.36   **Lester Flatt and the Nashville Grass. Flatt Gospel.** Canaan CAS 9775.
This is Flatt's first solo sacred album, although he has sung sacred items on his secular albums. Curly Seckler is the tenor harmony here. "What a Friend We

Have in Jesus" is an instrumental, with Paul Warren on sweet fiddle. In addition to "Let the Church Roll On," "Awaiting the Boatman," and "He Didn't Stop at Calvary," there is the fine typical Flatt narrative (in his impressive deep and compelling voice) on "Call Me on Home Too."

F9.37*   **Flatt and Scruggs. Sacred Songs.** Harmony HL 7402
The Flatt and Scruggs bluegrass group was not too well-known for sacred singing and tunes, and it was mainly at the urging of Flatt that they did any religious numbers at all. Thus, this record of reissued earlier Columbia material from the 1950s is largely Flatt's effort. "You Can Feel It in Your Soul," "Gone Home," and "Give Me Flowers While I'm Living" are typical of the "mother/home" style of religious music closely related to those themes.

F9.38*   **Red Foley. Songs of Devotion.** MCA 86.
Nobody can deny that Red Foley was perhaps the most deeply committed Christian of 1950s country and western singers. This program is a superb collection of gospel music written by the Reverend Thomas A. Dorsey, and it includes "Take My Hand Precious Lord" (perhaps Dorsey's most widely known song) and "There'll Be Peace in the Valley for Me."

F9.39*   **Tennessee Ernie Ford. Hymns.** Capitol SM 756.
Ford has recorded many sacred tunes, and his deep, somber voice is particularly well-suited to this genre. His emphasis has been distinctly on the "hymn" approach and can be at times non-rural in flavor, with discreet backgrounds. The twelve selections here include "Who at My Door Is Standing," "My Task," "Ivory Palaces," and "In the Garden," as well as the more popular "Softly and Tenderly," "Rock of Ages," and "The Old Rugged Cross."

F9.40   **Goins Brothers. God Bless Her, She's My Mother.** Michigan Bluegrass MB 146.
Melvin and Ray Goins are accompanied by Joe Meadows (fiddle) and Harley Gabbard (Dobro) in this stunning program of "mother" and "sacred" material. Especially good are "Crying Holy," "Six Hours on the Cross," "I'll Fly Away," "Family Reunion," and "Death Came Creepin' in My Room."

F9.41   **Billy Graham. International Crusade Choirs.** RCA Camden ACL 1-0038.
Some of the best choral works have been assembled by Graham for his Crusade tours. The Choirs here perform at Charlotte, Frankfort, Sydney, Gothenburg, London, Louisville, New York, Melbourne, San Francisco Bay Cities, and the All-Scotland Crusades.

F9.42   **Stuart Hamblen. Hymns.** Harmony HL 7009.
Hamblen was another popular singer who later turned to sacred music after reaching middle age. Tunes here include "Near the Cross," "Just As I Am," "Abide with Me," "Softly and Tenderly," and "I Am Thine, O Lord"—all from the late 1940s.

F9.43 **Joe Isaacs and the Calvary Mountain Boys. Dreams of Home.** Old Homestead OHS 90015.

Isaacs once worked with Ralph Stanley and Larry Sparks; his knowledge of old time and bluegrass lead singing is impressive. The band members, from Kentucky and Ohio, are extremely tight-knit and perform the typical bluegrass four-part harmonies with skill. Included are "Dreams of Home," the Carter Family's "No Depression," "Land beyond the Sun," "Woe, Woe, Woe," and "No Mother or Dad."

F9.44 **Wanda Jackson. Now I Have Everything.** Myrrh MSA 6533.

Jackson used to be a tough-as-nails rocker in the late 1950s (indeed, she has been acknowledged as the *only* influential female in rock and roll music). She then made a religious commitment, and her music is now in that happy vein of new-found joy, with such uptempo items as "Heaven's Gonna Be a Blast" and "Jesus Put a Yodel in My Soul." To some, it may appear that this is gospel music in the black tradition. But she is equally convincing in solemn renditions of "Let This Be My Attitude" and "Pass Me Not, O Gentle Savior."

F9.45 **George Jones and Tammy Wynette. We Love to Sing about Jesus.** Epic KE 31719.

Except for the rowdy "Nashville outlaws," every country and western singer has some sacred numbers to sing, and George Jones and Tammy Wynette (the most successful duet in country music history) are no exceptions. This, their first and only religious album, was put out in response to many listener requests.

F9.46* **Lewis Family. Anniversary Celebration.** Starday SLP 161.

F9.47 **Lewis Family. First Family of Gospel Music.** Starday SLP 331.

The Lewis Family (father and seven children) hail from Georgia. They are showmanship personified, and their concerts are exceptionally well-attended and successful. Their earlier recordings for Starday are among their best efforts, for their 1970s material on Canaan appears to have been done in a highly commercial, slicked-up atmosphere. There is a bluegrass feel to the Starday recordings, including such songs as "In Heaven," "Wings of a Dove," "Child of the King," "Crying Holy unto the Lord," "His Blood Now Covers My Sin," and "Where Did You Get Your Religion?"

F9.48* **The Lilly Brothers. What Will I Leave Behind.** County 742.

This is a moving disc, reflecting the camp-meeting fervor and spirit of sacred music. The Lillys sing with vigor, and Everett does fine picking on the mandolin. As almost always, Don Stover on five string banjo is excellent. The joy and hope of this bluegrass sacred music is found through "What Would the Profit Be?," "The Great Reaping Day," "Will You Meet Me over Yonder?," and "I Have Found the Way."

F9.49*   **Louvin Brothers. The Family Who Prays.** Capitol SM 1061.

F9.50*   **Louvin Brothers. The Great Gospel Singing of the Louvin Brothers.** Capitol ST 11193.
     The high, tight harmony singing of the Louvin Brothers was very influential in the creation of latter-day bluegrass music. More than half of their recordings together were of sacred or religious music, and they promoted the concept of bluegrass talking-gospel and story-sacred songs, often concerned with sin and Satan. A number like "Love Thy Neighbor as Thyself" has already worked its way into the classic bluegrass repertoire. They wrote most of their own material, including the songs "Satan Is Real," "Make Him a Soldier," "Satan Lied to Me," "Just Rehearsing," "Satan and the Saint," and "God Bless Her ('Cause She's My Mother)."

F9.51   **Sam McGee and Bill Lowery. God Be with You until We Meet Again.** Davis Unlimited 33021.
     This album was recorded two weeks before Sam died (August 1975). McGee was a superb flat picker on guitar and a very religious man. (Perhaps he had a premonition.) This is excellent old time sacred music, and includes such items as "There Is a Fountain" and "How Great Thou Art."

F9.52   **Wade Mainer. Rock of My Soul.** Old Homestead OHS 90014.

F9.53   **Wade Mainer. Sacred Songs Mountain Style.** Old Homestead OHS 90016.

F9.54*   **Wade Mainer. Sacred Songs of Mother and Home.** Old Homestead OH 90001.
     Wade Mainer was the banjoist in the important transitional country group, J. E. Mainer's Mountaineers. Old Homestead has collated fourteen sacred songs he did from the 1935-1941 Bluebird period (eleven are from 1936-1937), from "Ship Sailing Now," his first recording at the first session, to "Precious Memories," the last. Such important titles as "If I Could Hear My Mother Pray Again," "Dear Daddy You're Gone," and "Dying Boy's Prayer" appear on this disc (OH 90001), and they clearly show the dominance that religious dedication has in and on country music. Most are duets, with Zeke Morris on guitar. Homer "Pappy" Sherrill, Steve Ledford, and J. E. Mainer also joined in from time to time. The other two discs contrast. Wade has retired and now only sings for church gatherings or records. *Rock of My Soul* (with "Diamonds in the Rough," "Great Caravan," "Keep Walking," "I'll Live Again," and "Scarlet Purple Robe") has bluegrass backing, while the third album, with "Shake My Mother's Hand for Me," "Beyond This Veil of Tears," "Oh Those Tombs," and "The Old Account Was Settled," has the more traditional old time music accompaniment. These are good records for the sacred music collection.

F9.55   **The Marshall Family.** Rebel 1541.
     The Marshall Family is firmly in the bluegrass tradition with such loosely religious songs as "Come Springtime" and "All I Can Do Is My Best" and the typical sacred items "I Just Want to Thank You Lord" and "I'll Be Coming Home."

F9.56   Jimmy Martin. This World Is Not My Home. MCA 96.
Martin, like many other popular bluegrass-country musicians and singers, is not really noted for sacred songs, but his voice is good and the accompaniment mostly uptempo. Typical tunes include "Prayer Bells of Heaven," "Give Me Roses Now," "Voice of My Savior," and "I'm Coming Home."

F9.57   The Masters Family. Sacred Songs. Harmony HL 7197.
This family stresses uptempo sacred music, getting away from the somber moods of other groups. Selections include "The Cry from the Cross," "Gloryland March," "Swing Wide Ye Golden Gates," "Noah and the Mighty Ark," and "While the Ages Roll On."

F9.58   Miller Brothers. Sacred Songs with a Down Home Flavor. Old Homestead OHS 90005.
With a feeling for reverence and that distinctive harmonic sound of the Louvin Brothers and the Blue Sky Boys, the Miller Brothers present dramatic old time music and bluegrass renditions of such songs as "Preaching by the Roadside," "Angel Band," "Some Glad Day," "Six More Miles," and "Tramp on the Street." As with the Louvins, the emphasis here is on the story song.

F9.59*   Bill Monroe. I'll Meet You in Church Sunday Morning. MCA 226.

F9.60*   Bill Monroe. I Saw the Light. MCA 527.

F9.61*   Bill Monroe. A Voice from on High. MCA 131.
The greatness, influence, and stylings of Bill Monroe have been discussed in the **Bluegrass** section of this book (F6.39-41). Of importance in his sacred music work are the quartet harmonies and that high, lonesome voice of his. The *Voice* album is his best work, with Jimmy Martin on lead, from 1950-1954. Titles are "I'm Working on a Building," "Walking in Jerusalem Just Like John," "River of Death," "Boat of Love," "Let the Light Shine down on Me," and "Get down on Your Knees and Pray," the latter with Carter Stanley. MCA 527 comes from the late 1950s and includes "I'll Meet You in the Morning," "I've Found a Hiding Place," "Lord Build Me a Cabin in Glory," and the definitive version of "I Am a Pilgrim." The first album listed above is 1960s material, with Kenny Baker and Del McCoury; it includes "Drifting Too Far from the Shore," "The Glory Land Way," "Master Builder," "We'll Understand It Better," and "Way down Deep in My Soul." Monroe wrote many of the best and most enduring sacred/mother/home songs in all of bluegrass.

F9.62   Charlie Monroe. Lord, Build Me a Cabin. Pine Mountain PMR 261.
In the 1960s, Charlie (brother of Bill) had a short career in a revival of bluegrass and sacred music. While his style is not as prominent as Bill's, he is held in a glowing light by devotees of bluegrass and old time music. Titles here include "Shake Hands with Mother," "Sing, Sing, Sing," and "New Beautiful Heaven"—all reissued from Starday Records.

F9.63*   **Molly O'Day. A Sacred Collection.** Old Homestead OHCS 101.

F9.64   **Molly O'Day. Heart and Soul.** Mastertone 80313.

O'Day was one of the leading country female singers of the 1940s, along with Patsy Montana. This Old Homestead collection is a reissue of 1940s material from Columbia, with Lynn Davis (now O'Day's husband) and the Cumberland Mountain Folks. It includes such non-religious items as her hit song "The Tramp on the Street," "I Heard My Mother Weeping," and "Mother Is Gone but Not Forgotten." The Mastertone album comes from the 1970s, after she had been retired for 25 years, and features discreet, simple accompaniment from Davis on guitar. After she quit country music by 1950, O'Day turned to religion full-time. Titles here include "I'll Shout and Shine," "When Judgment Reaches Home," and "Good Man of the House Is Coming Home."

F9.65   **Osborne Brothers. Favorite Hymns.** Decca DL 75079.

The Osbornes are not too well-known for their sacred materials. They feature a lot of uptempo bluegrass renditions of standard hymns, and the album was meant mostly for their fans. Included is a fast version of "I Bowed on My Knees and Cried 'Holy.'"

F9.66   **Reno and Smiley. Sacred Songs.** King 550.

F9.67   **Reno and Smiley. World's Greatest 15 Hymns.** King 853.

These two discs represent about half of the Reno and Smiley team's output of sacred music. Their style is characterized by restrained harmonizing, and while Reno is a master of the five string banjo, he used the guitar most of the time in sacred music. The first album is from the early 1950s, and these songs really started their career: "Get behind Me Satan," "The Lord's Last Supper," and especially "I'm Using My Bible for a Road Map." The second album is more in the "hymn" and solemn tradition: "Amazing Grace," "The Old Rugged Cross," "Jesus, Savior, Pilot Me," "Farther Along," and "River of Jordan."

F9.68   **Roy Rogers and Dale Evans.** Capitol SM 1745.

Their folksy style endears these two to a wide audience. These songs are some of the most popular ones that people grew up with: "The Bible Tells Me So" (which Dale wrote), "Whispering Hope," "Just a Closer Walk with Thee," "In the Sweet By and By," "Amazing Grace," "How Great Thou Art," etc.

F9.69   **George Beverly Shea. Best, v.1/2.** two discs. RCA LSP 2932 and 3904.

Shea is a strong singer and crusader, a performer of evangelical hymns. He has often performed with others, such as the Anita Kerr Singers and the Blackwood Brothers Quartet. He is equally at home with spirituals, such as "Everytime I Feel the Spirit." Typical titles here include "The King Is Coming," "Amazing Grace," "Whispering Hope," "How Great Thou Art," "I Believe," "There Is More to Life," and "I'd Rather Have Jesus."

F9.70   **Sons of the Pioneers. How Great Thou Art. RCA LPM 1431.**

F9.71   **Sons of the Pioneers. Hymns of the Cowboy. RCA LSP 2652.**
The Sons of the Pioneers are well-known for their intricate harmonizing and songwriting; both skills are evident in these two diverse collections of sacred music. The first album, a collation of twelve tunes recorded in 1947-1956, are in the traditional mold of "Little White Cross," "Power in the Blood," "Song of the Prodigal," "Read the Bible Everyday," and "The King's Highway." The second album, from 1963 and recorded as a unit of twelve songs, is more secular, and refers to the lonely cowboy out on the trail. Here are "God Speaks," "All the Wild Things," "Lord You Made the Cowboy Happy," and "The Woodsman's Prayer."

F9.72   **Larry Sparks and the Lonesome Ramblers. Where the Sweet Waters Flow. Old Homestead OHS 90035.**
Sparks is very strong in the bluegrass quartet of sacred music singing. He and his tight group produce some nice harmonies on "Get in Line Brother," "Don't Turn Him Away," "Where We'll Never Grow Old," and "There's Room at the Cross."

F9.73*   **Stanley Brothers, v.1. CBS Sony 20AP13 (Japanese issue).**

F9.74   **Stanley Brothers. Good Old Camp Meeting Songs. King 805.**

F9.75*   **Stanley Brothers. Sacred Songs from the Hills. Starday SLP 122.**

F9.76*   **Stanley Brothers. That Little Old Country Church House. County 738.**
These albums represent the vast repertoire of the Stanley Brothers through twenty years of singing and recording for many companies. Their emotional trios with Lambert, largely written by Carter Stanley, include "A Vision of Mother," "Drunkard's Hell," "White Dove," and "The Fields Have Turned Brown." The CBS Sony album is from this period (the late 1940s, for Columbia records) and includes "It's Never Too Late" and "Old Home." With King, they recorded "When He Reached down His Hand for Me" and "Heaven's Light Is Shining on Me," as well as "The Darkest Hour Is Just before the Dawn," "Few More Seasons," "Masters Bouquet," and the dramatic and best-loved Stanley sacred song, "Rank Stranger"—some reissued on Starday above. The County reissue comes from Wango recordings made in the early 1960s, and it includes Red Stanley on violin and Jack Cooke on bass. Material here is both traditional and old time music, along with many hymns contributed by Albert E. Brumley. Many items concern mother, e.g., "Shake My Mother's Hand for Me," "I Heard My Mother Call My Name in Prayer," and "Mother's Only Sleeping."

F9.77   **Ralph Stanley. Cry from the Cross. Rebel SLP 1499.**
After his brother Carter Stanley died in 1966, Ralph regrouped and continued to produce some exceptional sacred materials. With Roy Lee Centers on lead and Ralph's emotional and intense voicings, this Rebel album succeeds for twelve tracks in presenting a high standard of performance. Here are "Two Coats,"

"You're Drifting On," "Will He Wait a Little Longer?," "Stairway to Heaven," and "Take Your Shoes Off Moses."

F9.78   Statesmen. Best, v.1/2. two discs. RCA LSP 2933 and 3925.
Another popular singing group, the Statesmen were led by Hovie Lister and Tony Fontane. Titles include "No Greater Love," "Sing, Brother, Sing," "Standing on the Promises," "Taller Than the Trees," and "My God is Real."

F9.79   Statler Brothers. Holy Bible: New Testament and Old Testament. two discs. Mercury SRM 1-1051 and 1052.
This is an interesting concept put across by a prolific recording group. All of these titles describe stories from the appropriate parts of the Bible. The 24 tunes include "In the Beginning," "Eve," "Noah Found Grace in the Eyes of the Lord," "The Ten Commandments," "Song of Solomon," "The King Is Coming," "Beat the Devil," "The Brave Apostles Twelve," "The Lord's Prayer," and "How Great Thou Art."

F9.80*   Carl Story. Best. Starday SLP 956.

F9.81*   Carl Story. Gospel Quartet Favorites. Mercury MG 20323.

F9.82   Carl Story. Gospel Revival. Starday SLP 127.
Story has recorded over 700 songs and forty albums since he formed his first band in 1934, emphasizing the pre-bluegrass North Carolina style. His range is from countertenor falsetto to bass-baritone. His distinctive high pitch promotes a lovely lead and harmonizing singing, and he has produced some of the best and most-loved bluegrass sacred music. His early Mercury material had more polished vocal harmonies and exciting instrumentation, but the later Stardays are more rock steady and solemn, with assistance from Bud Brewster (banjo) and Tater Tate (violin). Typical tunes, at random, include "Light at the River," "The Old Country Preacher," "Family Reunion," "A Picture from Life's Other Side," "My Lord Keeps a Record," and "Lonesome Road." For over forty years, Carl Story has only sung sacred music.

F9.83   Porter Wagoner. The Grand Old Gospel. RCA LSP 3488.
Wagoner's rural roots reflect a deep commitment to sacred music. On this album, he is assisted by the Blackwood Brothers Quartet.

F9.84   Kitty Wells. Dust on the Bible. MCA Decca DL 78858.
With her husband, Johnny Wright, Wells continues to sing in her little girl voice with characteristic warbles. She has not been too prolific in the sacred music field, but is recognized as continuing such classics as the title selection and "God Put a Rainbow in the Clouds." If anything, she must be classified as "lightly religious."

F9.85*   Hank Williams. I Saw the Light. MGM SE 3331.
Williams's contribution to country music has been documented at F8.39-41. Despite his lifestyle (tough) he was deeply religious, and the emotional fervor of

his singing was nicely displayed with this type of music. All of it was distinctly uptempo and relatively happy, such as "Are You Walking and A-Talking for the Lord?," "How Could You Refuse Him Now?," "Jesus Died for Me," and "When God Comes to Gather His Jewels."

F9.86   **Mac Wiseman. Best Loved Gospel Humns.** Dot 25373.
    The strong, strident voice and guitar of bluegrass innovator Mac Wiseman are strongly displayed in this collection of twelve classics culled from his previous Dot albums.

F9.87   **Rual Yarbrough and the Dixiemen. The Greatest Day of My Life.** Old Homestead OHS 90026.
    Yarbrough approaches bluegrass gospel from the traditional Monroe-Stanley musical point of view. The group's harmonies are excellent, with some fine tenor work. Jake Landers, the guitarist, writes most of the material, which includes "Be a Rock unto Me," "After the Darkness," "I'll Follow Jesus," "Over in the Gloryland," and "Beyond the Gates." On this album, Vassar Clements joins in with his fiddle, and the counterpoint between him and regular fiddler James Bryan is delightful.

TROUBADOR MUSIC

TROUBADOR MUSIC

> "All a poet can do today is warn."
> —Wilfred Owen

INTRODUCTION

The singer-songwriter developed out of the folk and country tradition. Now called troubadors (or troubettes for some), they bring personal visions to listeners through their unique place and role in popular music. A popular song is a 50-50 relationship between words and music, as the words were not meant to be read as poetry. In the troubador's song, the lyrics *can* stand alone as poetry, or are poetry put to music. This is a crucial distinction, and it marks a dramatic shift in popular music history. Indeed, some of the strongest troubadors have been displaced poets: Richard Fariña, Bob Dylan, Leonard Cohen, Paul Simon, Tim Hardin.

To understand the troubador phenomenon, one must first understand the conditions of the late 1950s and 1960s folk revival. Folk purists either preferred "authentic" singers from the past (forgetting that these singers themselves were only interpreters) or memorizations of every phrase and nuance lifted off of Library of Congress or old commercial recordings. Audiences recognized both as "roots," with the memorizers standing in for the original performers. Thus, a clear fossilization of performing styles emerged. At the same time, Alan Lomax's philosophy of "to be folk, you live folk" found acceptance with other singers and audiences, so the dichotomy of "purism" vs. "life experiences" split the folk music world. The pattern for performers (which, incidentally, was established during the 1920s with old time music) was to listen to early records and to do imitations, with some singers *eventually* adapting the material creatively to develop their own musical styles. Such a process was common to blues, jazz, rock, etc., but it took Bob Dylan to put it all together. He made it possible for folksingers to emerge from their fossilized self-made traps to be singers with original words, music, styles, and variations. The existence of the troubador actually began with the folk revival during the Depression. In this earlier period, the stress was on *anonymity*. But in the 1960s, with increasing alienation from society on the part of singers, and with the emergence of protest songs, stress came to be on *individuality*. This shift came about through little-realized (at the time) extra-musical factors such as the civil rights movement, the impact of the Newport Folk Festival, mass media coverage in magazines and newspapers, the television blacklist of ABC's *Hootenanny* show, and the natural tendency towards a star system in the record industry. Musical factors included the emergence of rock music to supersede rock 'n' roll and purist folk music as popular music, and its parasitic spin-offs, blues rock (the traditional folk blues "House of the Rising Sun" by the Animals is an early example) and folk rock (the Byrds, Bob Dylan, etc.). Both are discussed in the **Rock** section of *Contemporary Popular Music*, but in essence, each was a fused music that took the material and traditions of the folk process and merged them with the electronic gadgetry associated with rock music.

Tom Paxton, Jimmy Driftwood, and Hoyt Axton were the first of the contemporary troubadors. They all used the folk form with new lyrics relating to contemporary life. Then Dylan's rough voice put it all together by presenting the song itself as having more meaning than the individual singer. He paid attention to the lyrics, with a great assist from the long-playing album, which allowed more time for a specific performance. Troubadors were mainly experienced performers, having put in years during the 1960s as folksingers in coffeehouses or as studio performers for session recording work.

Troubador song structure was mainly of the lyric poem type—a long, rambling, and non-repetitive (no choruses) free form association, often in the Dylan-type stream-of-consciousness mold. Unfortunately, this precluded any opportunity for the audience to sing along, and as the troubadors predominantly used the recording studio, there were also few mass meetings for audience participation. Troubadors shunned coffee houses in favor of auditoriums, for more revenue was generated for less work. The lyrical ballads of troubadors also look back to older British form for themes:

1. *Life and Nature*, which stresses that all natural phenomena are interdependent and sympathetic. This "pathetic fallacy" resulted in landscape and scenery songs, plus idyllic viewpoints. Three specific manifestations here include:
   a) the erotic songs (similes and images) concentrating on sexual euphemisms, such as germination or fruitfulness;
   b) ritualistic life cycle forms concentrating on dances, ceremonies, and "good times" generally;
   c) metaphoric extensions of the pleasures of love between partners to the whole natural environment (and vice versa), quite often as reinforcement;

2. *Pure Love*, dealing with stories of success, failure, and bitter frustrations, quite often presented in the first person;

3. *Psycho-analytic Autobiographies*, in which a selection of self-conscious expressions and subconscious ideas are presented in the manner of the bluesman, "to talk it out";

4. *Commentaries*, presenting some social criticism but offering few or no solutions. Most songs of this type are rhetorical in nature, indicating the condition and merely describing it. As most people have jobs and/or the basic necessities of life, then it is mainly imperfections of society that are pointed out in these songs rather than root evils. Alienation and outrage make this an individual discontent rather than the anonymous collective protest found in the 1930s. Three specific types here include:
   a) social commentary on the manner of urban life, in which the singer tries to define social reality;
   b) political commentary, where the essence of topical music is *to know the new facts early* in order, as Wilfred Owen said, to warn others;
   c) labor commentary about jobs, industries, capitalism, working conditions, etc.

Troubadors can promote many superficialties. In attempting to jump on the bandwagon, many have produced puzzling responses to situations, and one critic called them the "quack minstrels of a non-existent America." Something does appear to be out of sequence when the children of well-to-do parents start singing about "hard times" that they have never experienced. Other material falls into a too-common pattern: there is slight biographical material, meaning that the singers remain closed in their private lives; the Dylan "stream of consciousness" technique has been overdone by lesser mortals; much material concerns drugs, lost love, or country music influences; and the general pattern of many songs has been characterized as being "landscapes" or scenery songs. In fact, the standardization of the genre allows us to posit a set review of a troubador record: "This fine disc by (name) is yet another in a long list of troubador albums proclaiming, among other things, man's inhumanity to man, the 'downer' nature of life, unrequited love, rolling in the grass, dreaming, sunshine, drugs, and other similar and diverse topics. (Name)'s raw voice, sometimes in barren contrast to the strings and assorted session men, augments the gravity of the situations depicted. The self-composed materials are certainly expressive of (name)'s lifestyle, and for those who prefer to read, the lyrics are included." Such a review might commonly be applied to over several hundred singers in this musical area.

Literature

Troubador, or singer-songwriter, is such a new category that few materials exist outside recent folk or rock books. Laing (50) gives a superb account of the transmogrification of "folk into rock," in both Britain and the United States. Denisoff (18, 19, 21, 22) has done pioneering work (including a bibliography and discography) on songs of protest and war, from the American Revolution to the present. Biographical data—such as there are—can be located through Stambler's (86) encyclopedia through 1967, and his most recent one (84a) which goes from 1968 to 1973. Gray (33) analyzes the music of Dylan in the context of its time (impact and influence), while Sarlin (78) gives a critique of the lyrics of other troubadors in the early 1970s. Brand (9) comments on modern folk songs generally.

Periodicals are poorly represented here. *Sing Out!* (20) gives occasional coverage (plus lyrics and music) if the troubador has folk roots or has not gone commercial. *Rolling Stone* (19) and *Stereo Review* (21) give the best coverage through occasional articles. The only recourse to retrieving the odd article scattered in other magazines, such as country music magazines, is to examine the *Annual Index to Popular Music Record Reviews* (3) and the *Popular Music Periodicals Index* (69).

INNOVATORS

F10.1*   **Joan Baez. Any Day Now.** two discs. Vanguard VSD 79306/7.

F10.2*   **Joan Baez. Contemporary Ballad Book.** two discs. Vanguard VSD 49/50.
     Baez perhaps gave the greatest assist to Bob Dylan of anyone who aided him
early. She constantly exposed his music and, of course, was very influenced by it
herself. In the early sixties, she used to appear at his concerts, and, of course, it
would have been of great significance to their fans if the King and Queen of this
music ever got together on a permanent basis. *Any Day Now* is a double album of
sixteen well-chosen Dylan songs, with a mild country arrangement by Grady
Martin and several Nashville musicians. Included are "Love Minus Zero/No Limit,"
"I Pity the Poor Immigrant," "Love Is Just a Four-Letter Word," "Boots of Spanish
Leather," and the long "Sad-Eyed Lady of the Lowlands." The *Contemporary
Ballad Book* concentrates on singer-songwriter material (including four of Dylan's),
such as "Saigon Bride," "Birmingham Sunday," "The Lady Came from Baltimore,"
and two from Richard Fariña.

F10.3*   **Jackson Browne. Late for the Sky.** Asylum 7E-1017.

F10.4   **Jackson Browne. Saturate before Using.** Asylum SD 5051.
     Browne had been given the big hype by Tom Rush, yet he deserves it all,
and more. His quiet, shy nature is perhaps best suited for the landscapes that he
paints with his words; he has been quite often recorded by other artists, such as
Rush, the Byrds, the Eagles ("Take It Easy"), Johnny Rivers, Linda Ronstadt,
Bonnie Raitt, Gregg Allman, and the team of Brewer and Shipley, among others.
Browne began performing in 1967 as Nico's guitarist, and he became involved in
the Southern California scene of the time, promoting soft-rock and then later
country-rock. In style, he presents an interesting combination of folk and rock
and roll, blending the better elements of Dave Van Ronk and Bob Dylan. His vocal
style is very similar to Van Morrison's, and he projects a gospel voice on such as
"Rock Me on the Water" or "Under the Falling Sky."
     At other times, he has a flexible, crisp bluegrass sound to his vocals, particu-
larly the high bluesy style derived from Mississippi John Hurt. A certain amount
of mysticism came from the Incredible String Band, as in "Doctor My Eyes,"
recorded with a pronounced beat. In the main, his materials are ballads around
common themes of romantic moods that are perfectly adaptable by other singers.
(Indeed, the early part of Browne's career was as a straight songwriter.) Some of
the ballads are "Something Fine," "Jamaica Say You Will," and "Song for Adam."
The uptempo selections—where they exist—are characterized by smooth instrumentation. His lyrics have always been exceptional and articulate; not for him is the
cluttered line of Dylan, or the prettiness of James Taylor. His compactness leads
to order, and, as one critic noted, perhaps to universality.

F10.5*   **Leonard Cohen. Best.** Columbia PC 34077.

F10.6*   **Leonard Cohen. Songs.** Columbia CS 9533.
     Cohen is an established poet/novelist in his native country, Canada. He is

also a self-confessed "frustrated" singer-guitarist, often appearing at the Mariposa Folk Festival. Actually, many people and critics ignored him until he managed to get a contract from Columbia records and subsequently produced one of the finest of the troubador albums. None of the songs he sings (at least the ones that he sang earlier on, and the ones on which his reputation is based) were fashioned as songs. They were originally poems, and there are severe structural differences, which work in Cohen's favor. And Cohen was the master of gloom and the surreal subconsciousness. His major contribution was his appeal to the depressed and tormented. Most of his songs are full of self-pity and desperation, with touches of madness and paranoia. Cohen brought the psychological drama to its highest impact with such songs as "Suzanne" or "So Long, Marianne." The dreary nature of the songs' lyrics, coupled with both Cohen's monotonous voice and droning guitar, heightens this perception of life. Titles such as "Bird on the Wire" and "Hey That's No Way to Say Goodbye" actively advertise his sense of failure (Cohen should only be listened to by the mentally stable). His first album, *Songs*, is his best overall work from one period in time. The *Best* set of twelve comes largely from this album, but there are important later works and liner notes of interpretation by Cohen himself. A contribution by Cohen to the whole troubador scene was the awareness that one did not have to sing or promote tunes and lyrics in order to get a recording contract and become successful. But he had many imitators rather than actual followers.

F10.7   Donovan. Greatest Hits. Epic BXN 26439.

F10.8*   Donovan. History. Pye 502.
    A month after Dylan's first single hit the charts, Donovan appeared with "Catch the Wind." He was not only singing in the Dylan mold, but he also wore the same type of clothes and his folk-pop had that Dylan nasal twang. Immediately, the American press labeled him an imitator; yet, he was well-known in Scotland for many years before as just this type of person—a minstrel singing with Gypsy Davy, Shawn Phillips, and others as part of the British folk revival. He appealed to the same audience in the United States as Dylan did: he worked the protest song angle, Woody Guthrie numbers, plus dallying with folk rock. But then he switched over to whimsical fantasy with the song "Colours" (strongly rooted in the folk tradition), which appeared at the same time as Dylan's "Like a Rolling Stone." Here the twain parted. Yet Donovan stayed, with a more lyrical and better voice than Dylan. The pre-1965 period offered the above titles plus "Remember the Alamo" in the collection of subtle insights on Pye. Beginning in 1966, he recorded for Epic, and got enveloped in the drug/flower-power scene of incense, drugs, flowers, robes, and so forth. This shift was captured on such dope songs as "Mellow Yellow" and "Sunshine Superman." His whimsy and fantasy were still present, though, on such as "Sunny Goodge Street" and "Season of the Witch," along with other songs that bore references to early Scottish folk songs.

F10.9*   Jimmy Driftwood. Famous Country Music Makers. two discs. RCA DPS 2022 (British issue).
    Born in the Ozarks, Driftwood was a collector of folk songs who soon became fluent on guitar, banjo, and fiddle. But of all the folksingers and troubadors, he

appears to be the only one who actually created new story songs in the folk mold. This set contains two albums that Driftwood recorded in the late 1950s for RCA: *Newly Discovered Early American Folk Music* (LPM 1635) and *The Wilderness Road* (LSP 1994). Both feature his "new" folk songs, and from both, it is quite evident that Driftwood is perhaps the finest "folk poet" to have developed in America of the past 75 years. His biggest success was "Battle of New Orleans" (1815, in which Andrew Jackson defeated the British troops). The version here is the long one, with all verses intact. The song "Soldier's Joy" borrows some elements from this well-known instrumental, but then Driftwood adds lyrics based on the American Revolution (John Paul Jones, George Washington, General Cornwallis).

"I'm Too Young to Marry" and "Zelma Lee" are both excellent crosses between Carter Family traditional material and modern country music. The renowned "Tennessee Stud," also loosely based on a story from the Civil War, is here. "Bunker Hill" relates strictly to the American Revolution, but nothing in the song can be traced to any musical roots. Thus, it appears to be a brand-new contribution to the folk process. He has taken other melodies and made new songs, as with "Arkansas Traveler" and "Slack Your Rope" (the latter from Child 95). His accompaniment is mainly a string bass plus his own instrumentation. This is a very significant contribution to the folk process and to the troubador tradition.

F10.10   **Bob Dylan.** Columbia KCS 8579.

F10.11   **Bob Dylan. Another Side.** Columbia KCS 8993.

F10.12*   **Bob Dylan. Basement Tapes.** two discs. Columbia C2-33682.

F10.13*   **Bob Dylan. Blonde on Blonde.** two discs. Columbia C2S 841.

F10.14*   **Bob Dylan. Bringing It Back Home.** Columbia KCS 9128.

F10.15   **Bob Dylan. Free Wheelin'.** Columbia CS 8786.

F10.16*   **Bob Dylan. Greatest Hits, v.1/2.** three discs. Columbia KCS 9463 and KG 31120.

F10.17   **Bob Dylan. Highway 61 Revisited.** Columbia KCS 9189.

F10.18*   **Bob Dylan. John Wesley Harding.** Columbia KCS 9604.

F10.19*   **Bob Dylan. The Times They Are A-Changin'.** Columbia KCS 8905.
    Bob Dylan has had more impact and has been more influential than a simple appraisal of his recordings would seem to indicate. Indeed, very few of them were "best sellers" in the music world. However, his songs have been recorded many times over by others, and in this way, they became anthems: "Blowin' in the Wind" (against complacency, apathy, and non-involvement), "The Times They Are A-Changin'," "Ballad of a Thin Man" (with its references to a confused Mr. Jones), "Masters of War," "Don't Think Twice, It's All Right," and so forth. As a singer-

songwriter, Dylan made his pilgrimage to Woody Guthrie's sick bed and assumed Guthrie's mantle after a brief wrestle with Jack Elliott. In so doing, he became the Pied Piper of the 1960s, a multi-faceted talent who, although exceptionally weak on guitar and possessed of a weak voice, created superb images with his symbolism, which some critics have characterized also as a put-on, and others as a parody.

It is difficult to know what Dylan is saying at times and how he means it; almost any interpretation is now irrelevant as he has carved out five main styles and has used each one on virtually all of his records ever since they evolved. Thus, to some, he is a restless prober, striking out in all directions at once. This does become confusing to his devoted fans, and the impact was one of setting trends and opening up newly acceptable avenues, as when he appeared at Newport and Forest Hills in 1965 with an electric band (and was booed by the audience). The feeling here is simply, "What is Dylan up to? What is he going to do next?" In reality, Dylan is a shrewd performer who has finely honed his artistic phases. His career is a continuing one, and in more than fifteen years, he has "recreated" himself through re-evaluations. He has *not* become a stylist, sticking to just one fashion and cashing in on the accolades. Over a period of time, most such performers have tended to disappear after being absorbed into the mainstream, witness Phil Ochs.

The problem of Dylan's intentions again is complicated by his mysterious lifestyle (he actually made up stories about himself). This paranoia is most felt in the "stream of consciousness" style, upon which most of his reputation lies. Briefly, then, the styles and periods of his changes are:

1) The *folk narrative* songs on his first three albums, where he borrowed folk themes and delivered them in a blues style. His tough voice, although pinched, half-talked and half-sang the semi-protest and civil rights songs, which Dylan himself called "finger pointing songs." The first album by Dylan (1962, untitled) revealed the wide sources of his derivative materials, such as "She's No Good" (from Jesse Fuller's "You're No Good"), "Fixin' to Die Blues" (Bukka White), "See That My Grave Is Kept Clean" (Blind Lemon Jefferson), plus items by Little Walter, Sonny Terry, Mance Lipscomb, and Big Joe Williams—all from blues roots. Also there are "Freight Train Blues" (from Roy Acuff's folk tradition); items relating to Merle Travis, Hank Williams, and Jimmie Rodgers in the country field; material from the rockabilly giants (the country *and* blues fusion) the Everly Brothers, Carl Perkins, and Elvis Presley; and, of course, songs from ramblers Woody Guthrie and Jack Elliott. *Free Wheelin'* (1963), despite author credits for Dylan, is really a collage of new lyrics and old tunes. For example, "Girl from the North Country" from "Scarborough Fair," "A Hard Rain's A-Gonna Fall" from "Lord Randall," "Masters of War" from "Notamun Town," and "Don't Think Twice, It's All Right" from Johnny Cash's "Understand Your Man," plus directly related tunes such as "Corrina, Corrina" and "Oxford Town." This album, of course, is notable for the original "Blowin' in the Wind." *The Times They Are A-Changin'* (1964) appears to be entirely self-composed, reflecting more the story/ protest songs of "The Lonesome Death of Hattie Carroll" and the title track.

2) The *introspection* period, that begins with "My Back Pages" on *Another Side* (1964). The songs here, though, are based again on certain older variants ("I Shall Be Free, No. 10" from Leadbelly's version of "We Shall Be Free"; "To

Ramona" from the country classic "Anita"). *Bringing It All Back Home* (1965) is Dylan's first [half] rock album, with several uptempo, biting songs such as "Subterranean Homesick Blues" (his first commercial single), "Maggie's Farm," and the initially overlooked "Mr. Tambourine Man."

3) The *"stream of consciousness"* period, where the elusive narrative material was really understood only by the composer. Such items include dreams, nightmares, literary allusions, and paranoia. No clarification was ever given, but many people saw the music as "head" [LSD-inspired] music because of the electric accompaniment. What does come through is Dylan's harsh, whining voice on the verge of a breakdown, plus very negative attitudes toward women in general. *Highway 61 Revisited* (1965) introduces "superstars" Al Kooper on keyboard and Mike Bloomfield on guitar, with the epic "Like a Rolling Stone," "It Takes a Lot to Laugh, It Takes a Train to Cry," and "Queen Jane Approximately." Overall, its impressionistic blues are depressing, as with "Tombstone Blues," mainly a stream of consciousness. *Blonde on Blonde* (1966) is a double album—the first in the rock world—and was recorded in Nashville, with Kooper and some of The Band. Here are "Just Like a Woman," "Rainy Day Women, No. 12 & 35," and a whole side for "Sad-Eyed Lady of the Lowlands." Also, during this period, Dylan had his mysterious motorcycle accident and withdrew from live performances for four years.

4) His *consolidation and fusion* period (really a transition), in which he rested and retired to Woodstock in company with The Band. *Basement Tapes* (1967), long a best-selling bootleg,was finally officially released in 1975, seven years after its recording, and contained 24 tracks. Here, Dylan is accompanied by his touring group, which later evolved into The Band. Titles of new material include "The Mighty Quinn" (covered successfully by the British rock band Manfred Mann), "Tears of Rage," "This Wheel's on Fire," "I Shall Be Released" (all done by The Band on their *Big Pink* album, and co-written by The Band), and "You Ain't Goin' Nowhere." The marvelous laid-back feeling continues with the folk-inspired "Ain't No Cane (on the Brazos)" and Muddy Waters's "Long Distance Operator." This was a genuine period of relaxation and creativity. A major result was *John Wesley Harding* (1968), which relies once again on older tunes (e.g., "I Dreamed I Saw St. Augustine" from "I Dreamed I Saw Joe Hill," by Ed McCurdy) and country music roots in "The Ballad of Frankie Lee and Judas Priest" and the frankly sentimental "I'll Be Your Baby Tonight." This album has been acknowledged as his finest, most cohesive work—the "real" Dylan who has come to terms with his environment, as on "All along the Watchtower" or "As I Went out One Morning." His subdued and melancholic voice, now an octave deeper, had lost its hysterical whine. Overall, though, the mood is one of darkness.

5) And this leads—quite naturally—to the fact that, if Dylan is at peace with himself and his surroundings, then there really is no longer any need to involve the listener in his songs except to create a particular *mood*. These records, post-1969 material, were considered Dylan's "dropouts," and they started another trend, that of discovering roots and new meanings in what are essentially "mood" pieces, nothing less and nothing more. *Nashville Skyline* projects the contemporary country mood and back-to-the-earth movements (this was started earlier with his use of Nashville musicians on *Blonde on Blonde*). *Self-Portrait* and the atrocious *Dylan* were in a pop music/nostalgia mood, in which he sang other people's songs, such as "Blue Moon," "Let It Be Me," "A Fool Such As I," and "Can't Help

Falling in Love." And *New Morning* was definitely in the religious mood. At the same time, Dylan embroidered his fusion work by jumping around a lot. Several diverse periods can be found on his latest albums: *Planet Waves*, with The Band; *Blood on the Tracks*; and *Desire*.

Lyrically, Dylan is confusing. Many claims have been made that his songs are actually poems. But can pop music lyrics be poetry? Not according to the normal construction of popular songs, as practiced by tunesmiths. Yet *John Wesley Harding* combines the narrative story aspect of his early work with the imagery of the *Blonde on Blonde* set. This fusion is doubly important, for not only does it make *Harding* an exceptional album, it also makes Dylan easier to understand. The toughest criticism that can be leveled against Dylan is that during his early period before *Harding*—his most influential period—he projected too much imagery to be absorbed at once. It was a sensory overload, as it were, but with words. Once combined with electric rock music, as on *Blonde on Blonde*, it can be twice as deadly. Dylan's lack of discipline came from his inability to distinguish between the essential and the superfluous. No wonder much of this music was thought of as "head" music.

The *Greatest Hits* sets vary as to quality. The first one collates all the most popular tunes and hit singles from the folk and electric period. While not a good introduction to Dylan, it is more listenable for those in the mainstream of popular music. The second set (two discs) has selections from almost all of his albums through 1970. "Tomorrow Is a Long Time" gets its first official outing here (from a 1964 concert), as does "When I Paint My Masterpiece," plus some recordings of older material, with Happy Traum as second instrumentalist and on vocal harmonies.

As can be seen from this brief survey of Dylan's albums, his styles changed through the years and obviously had a pronounced impact on others in the troubador school and in the rock world. Topicality was introduced on *Free Wheelin'* (as well as self-composed songs); protest, with *The Times They Are A-Changin'*; rock (or at least electric amplification), with *Bringing It All Back Home* and "Mr. Tambourine Man"; and country, with *John Wesley Harding*. His non-musical impact was also enormous. He crystalized feelings in college students, and transformed alienation into social involvement (and occasional commitment). He brought seriousness to rock music. And he laid—single-handedly—the necessary ground work for the creation of rock culture as an intellectual and/or alternative lifestyle. In 1965, he legitimatized rock and pop for the folk world, and also brought folk into the pop world via the Byrds and "Mr. Tambourine Man." To many people, Dylan is the "main man."

F10.20*   **Woody Guthrie. Library of Congress Recordings.** three discs. Elektra EKL 271/2.

F10.21   **Woody Guthrie. Sings Folksongs with Leadbelly, Cisco Houston, Sonny Terry and Bess Hawes, v.1/2.** two discs. Folkways FA 2483/4.

F10.22   **Woody Guthrie. This Land Is Your Land.** Folkways FTS 31001.
Woody Guthrie personified the Homeric tradition in the American folk world, as he constantly created and refashioned many songs detailing the life of these

people in the first part of the twentieth century. He wrote new words and arrangements for traditional folk songs, thereby employing and fueling the folk process.
In this manner, he created about 1,000 songs that will live on in the memories
and singing of countless others in generations to come: "This Land Is Your Land,"
"Pretty Boy Floyd," "Reuben James," "Hard Traveling," etc. He was strongly
influenced by the Carter Family, especially Mother Maybelle's singing and guitar
playing. He took several of their tunes, such as "Wildwood Flower" (which became
"Reuben James"), "Little Darling Pal of Mine" (which became "This Land Is
Your Land"), and the "Wabash Cannonball" (which became "The Big Grand
Coulee Dam"). The Carters in turn had borrowed material for their own use,
thereby passing along traditional elements. As the greatest American folk balladeer,
Guthrie had many disciples. His hobo life since his Oklahoma birth, plus the
fact that he seemed to have done everything worth mentioning, influenced Pete
Seeger and Cisco Houston. A little later, it would be Jack Elliott, and at the turn
of the 1960s, it would be Bob Dylan, Mark Spoelstra, Phil Ochs, and Peter LaFarge.
   The Library of Congress recordings were done in 1940 for Alan Lomax,
Guthrie's good buddy. These were songs and conversations, with Guthrie reminis-
cing about the 1930s (he was still a young man, though) and singing 28 songs,
including "Railroad Blues," "Greenback Dollar," "So Long, It's Been Good to
Know You," "Hard Times," "Worried Man Blues," "Goin' down That Road Feeling
Bad"—and even "Foggy Mountain Top," later to be a bluegrass classic. An extensive
booklet accompanies the set. Among the essentials in folk music are input from and
interaction with other folksingers, so the songfest (or swap) helps to spread lyrics,
music, and styles around the world. The two Guthrie albums with Leadbelly (see
his annotations in the *Black Music* volume in this set) and others provide good
documentation, even to the point of comparison of "white" music and "blues"
music. Not everybody sings on every number, although the discs are assigned to
Woody Guthrie's name because he is on all of them, even if he merely accompanies
on his rarely-heard violin. Typical material here includes "Hard Traveling," "House
of the Rising Sun," "Brown Eyes," and "Oregon Trail"—all interspersed with
occasional instrumentals. Together, there are 29 selections here, along with notes
from Pete Seeger, tablatures, and texts.

F10.23   **Kris Kristofferson. Border Lord.** Monument KZ 31302.

F10.24*   **Kris Kristofferson. Me and Bobby McGee.** Monument Z 30817.

F10.25   **Kris Kristofferson. The Silver Tongued Devil and I.** Monument Z 30679.
   Kristofferson is a short-story teller in the Tom T. Hall mold, but he is more
romantic in his movements and seeks redeeming qualities in people. His scenarios
do not consider the foibles of life, but rather move on up to the astral level, as
on "Why Me Lord?" or "Just the Other Side of Nowhere." His witty lyrics, combined
with his sophisticated coverage in the singer-songwriter school, made him acceptable
to both the counterculture (which greatly affected him) and to the country music
world, which he strongly influenced through writing for Johnny Cash, Ray Price,
Roger Miller, and Bobby Bare.
   Kristofferson was born in Texas, like so many great popular music innovators.
Being influenced by Cash, he concentrated on simple, singable melodies like the

one for "Me and Bobby McGee" that even Janis Joplin could handle. His early work, which includes "Sunday Morning Coming Down" and "Help Me Make It through the Night," was characterized by some self-consciously poetic lyrics, but these were obviated by the direct themes of freedom and honesty in dealing with interpersonal relations. This endeared him to the "underground," and they promptly labeled him a "Nashville progressive." While his music was of the outlaw type that suited Jennings and Nelson, Kristofferson did record for a country label and that reinforced opinions that he promoted country music. "To Beat the Devil" proves this point, as it is a very good song dealing with both failure and subsequent loneliness. His country songs were thus accepted by country fans, and his folk-type songs were accepted by and large by both country and folk fans. The contrast lies in his romantically-inclined sentimental ballads being sung by his harsh, gravelly voice. In his country music, he tended to project a macho style and put women down; in his folk style, his lyrics are better than the music, but, unfortunately, they tend to be obscure and not reflect the scheme of the music. This is clear in the country "Jody and the Kid" and the song dedicated to all folksingers, "The Pilgrim—Chapter 33."

F10.26   **Gordon Lightfoot. Gord's Gold.** two discs. Reprise 2RX 2237.

F10.27*   **Gordon Lightfoot. The Very Best.** United Artists UALA 243-G.
    During his more than twelve-year recording career, Lightfoot sold more than ten million albums, and he has had more than 150 of his songs recorded by other artists. His track record is unbeatable, and his gospel was spread by Peter, Paul and Mary, Judy Collins, Johnny Cash, Harry Belafonte, George Hamilton IV, Waylon Jennings, Ronnie Hawkins, and Ritchie Havens. His music is really quite simple, and although there is an air of formula construction (and despite repetition), there is never the feeling of boredom. (As an experiment one day, we played every single Lightfoot record in order and not once did we yawn.) He employs simple, hummable melodies with plucked strings and a rolling rhythm guitar style (mainly twelve string). In his middle period he had supreme accompaniment from Terry Clements, Rick Haynes, and Red Shea. His vocals, although plain, were ornamented with an element of pleading and urgency. The tight rhythmic structures of Lightfoot and his accompanists made for seemingly effortless playing and a flawless perfor-mance. The lyrics mainly were story songs, raising the mundane to an astral level through the polished, mellow music and clever rhyme structures. Types usually included work songs, travel songs, and love songs.
    In his approach, Lightfoot was a skilled composer; but later in his career, he became self-indulgent and affected, even sentimental at times. This is clearly revealed on the Reprise twofer. Record one is a re-recording of his United Artists material with new arrangements (the five year contractual period was over) that fit into his current style: some slick strings and smooth phrasing, different tempi and emphases, and so forth. Record two is a collection of hits since 1970: "Cold on the Shoulder," "If You Could Read My Mind," "Circle of Steel," etc. Each disc has twelve cuts. The United Artists collection contains "Early Morning Rain," "For Lovin' Me," "Canadian Railroad Trilogy," "Did She Mention My Name?," "Black Day in July," "Last Time I Saw Her," etc.

F10.28   **Joni Mitchell.** Reprise RS 6293.

F10.29*   **Joni Mitchell. Blue.** Reprise MS 2038.

F10.30*   **Joni Mitchell. Clouds.** Reprise RS 6341.

F10.31   **Joni Mitchell. Court and Spark.** Asylum 7E-1001.

Rolling Stone captured the essence of Mitchell with the statement that "her primary purpose is to create something meaningful out of the random moments of pain and pleasure in her life." She quite literally burst upon the scene in 1968, when her compositions were performed by Judy Collins, Buffy Sainte-Marie, Tom Rush, Dave Van Ronk, and others. In 1969, she made her first record, which featured the pop oriented "Michael from Mountains," and introduced her wispy delicate voice to the folk world. Her swoops and falsetto singing have been characterized as pure, free, and sweet. The materials that she deals with all have good melodies in the highly romantic sense. They are hummable, which is a far cry from those of most troubadors, and she fell in with the trend by progressively adding more instrumentation and electrification until she reached the L.A. Express stage, with a horn section.

But the major importance of Mitchell lies in her lyrics (almost all of her albums have the texts reprinted on the liner sleeves). She deals mainly with sand-castles, tapestries, clouds, and other rich images that set her apart from the landscape artists. It is a dreamy world for Mitchell, with her earlier songs concerning stereo-typed lifestyles that were developing at the end of the 1960s (life in the city, the suburbs, communes, farms, etc.). Later, after the remarkable *Blue* album, she would attempt to recapture a certain amount of spontaneity in lyrics that dealt with plays, dances, and dreams. Titles on these albums include the successes "Both Sides Now," "Urge for Going," "Chelsea Morning," "Roses Blue," "Circle Game," and "Help Me." The *Blue* album was her stream of consciousness approach in the Dylan manner. This was the only mood album she did, the songs having definite unity, as half of them were about her lover, right from the first line of the first song, "All I Want." Latin touches augment and highlight the feeling of desperation, especially in "This Flight Tonight," "A Case of You," and the pain of "Blue." James Taylor accompanied on guitar, and Mitchell performed on piano for that extra wistful quality.

F10.32*   **Van Morrison. Astral Weeks.** Warner Brothers WS 1768.

F10.33*   **Van Morrison. Moondance.** Warner Brothers WS 1835.

F10.34   **Van Morrison. St. Dominic's Preview.** Warner Brothers BS 2633.

Van Morrison is one of the most expressive of the singer-songwriters. He has been influenced by the country and western music of Hank Williams and by the blues of John Lee Hooker, Leadbelly, Muddy Waters, and Sonny Boy Williamson, No. 2 (although his harmonica technique comes from Little Walter). Morrison is of Scottish ancestry, and he once formed the blues-based group Them. His high baritone is best on the slow moody songs, where he can display his dynamic phrasing and syntax: midphrase halts, word packing, and spreading in a continual expansion and contraction of syllables. Early efforts include "Brown Eyed Girl," "Coming Running," and "Domino." Each album dealt with a certain theme; for instance, *Moondance* is full of gospel-tinged ballads, while *Preview* is lyrically esoteric. He is expressively meditative in the 10-minute "Listen to the Lion" and the 11-minute "Alamo and Independence Day," yet in a mood of celebration for "Gypsy," with its double and triple time alternate rhythms.

F10.35*   **Fred Neil. The Dolphins.** Capitol ST 2665.

F10.36*   **Fred Neil. Everybody's Talkin'.** Capitol ST 294.

F10.37   **Fred Neil. Sessions.** Capitol ST 2862.
     Fred Neil has been called a legend and one of the most influential of the troubadors, having written hundreds of songs for dozens of recording artists (among them being Nilsson for "Everybody's Talkin'," used as the theme for the film *Midnight Cowboy*; Kenny Rankin; the Lovin' Spoonful; Peter, Paul and Mary; Frank Sinatra, José Feliciano; and even Mantovani and Roger Williams, the pianist). He even supplied material to Buddy Holly in the 1950s. In style, he is a blues-based, twelve string guitarist with a rich deep voice that developed in the Greenwich Village scene of the 1950s. He now lives in Florida as a quiet recluse, not bothering to record anymore. His topics are important in an understated way, with compassionate and vivid tunes highlighted by his intimate voice. In the main, they concern both life and love, but also include references to the high price that one must pay for enjoying both: "Faretheewell," "Sweet Cocaine," "The Dolphins," and "Green Rocky Road." He was immortalized for the rock world through the Jefferson Airplane's tribute, "Me and Pooneil."

F10.38*   **Randy Newman.** Reprise RS 6286.

F10.39*   **Randy Newman. Sail Away.** Reprise MS 2064.
     Newman personifies the singer-songwriter of the rough, ragged, hoarse voice. His laconic style was directly influenced by Dylan's recording his own music and starting the singer-songwriter cult, as in "I Think It's Going to Rain Today" (perhaps best performed by Judy Collins). His first album was released in 1968, one of the peak years for troubadors, and he was at once labeled a social critic in the H. L. Mencken style because of such items as "Love Story," "Living without You," "Cowboy," and "So Long Dad." Harry Nilsson did an entire album of Newman material, with Newman himself accompanying on piano. The Mencken pattern continued on *Sail Away*, Newman's most cohesive effort to date. These are twelve art songs, bitterly ironic and sentimental at the same time, as in "Last Night I Had a Dream" and "Lonely at the Top." Such songs as the title selection, detailing the arrival of blacks in Charleston Bay for purposes of slavery, are very American sounding in that he built a trap in reconciling the absurd with the tragic. This is continued with "Old Man" and "God's Song."

F10.40*   Phil Ochs. **All the News That's Fit to Sing.** Elektra EKS 7269.

F10.41*   Phil Ochs. **I Ain't Marching Anymore.** Elektra EKS 7287.

F10.42*   **Phil Ochs. In Concert.** Elektra EKS 7310.
    Phil Ochs was a bitter, disillusioned young man; he committed suicide early
in 1976, despondent over his lack of recent success. In the final analysis, though,
music history has been permanently shaped by this former journalist turned
composer. He was one of the first to promote the current event song of bitter
protest *and* be lyrical at the same time. He wrote material for Peter and Gordon,
Judy Collins, the Four Seasons, Anita Bryant, Ian and Sylvia, Pete Seeger, the
Brothers Four, Joan Baez, and others. In 1963, he appeared at Newport; in 1966,
at Carnegie Hall. He was the leading protest singer after Dylan, but always resented
the fact that he was not first. And in many ways he should have been, for his
material was well-crafted, lyrical, certainly topical (perhaps too topical: nothing
is as stale as yesterday's newspaper), but all with that morbid punch that makes
them unsingable by the uncommitted.
    Ochs was too specific in his striking out; Dylan was more general. Dylan knew
there was something wrong, but did not state what it was, which was left up to the
listener, and caught him up in some involvement with the song. Ochs was for
listening to and thinking, "Shame, shame, but what can I do? It's over and done
with." Together, the pair are superb, and a good meeting ground could be arranged
between the specific and the general. Later, for A & M, Ochs switched to general
social concerns when the protest song movement died. Roxon characterizes him thus:
"flat, deadpan, throwaway little boy voice." There was a certain charm in Dylan's
obscure voice that was lacking in Ochs's. The three discs here, most with some sort
of notes about the specific songs, include dramatic material in "One More Parade,"
"The Thresher," "Talking Cuban Crisis," "Draft Dodger Rag"; ballads in "Bound
for Glory" and his marvelous recreation of Alfred Noyes's poem "The Highwayman";
the humor of "Love Me, I'm a Liberal," and his three greatest songs about passing
through life: "There but for Fortune," "Changes," and "When I'm Gone."

F10.43   Tom Paxton. **Ain't That News.** Elektra EKS 7298.

F10.44*   Tom Paxton. **Ramblin' Boy.** Elektra EKS 7277.
    Paxton was one of the first folksingers to write his own material (his first
album came out in 1961). These modern compositions, the most effective being
"Rambling Boy" (also sung by the Weavers, Pete Seeger, and others), stressed the
beginning merger between current folk music and journalism. This harkened back
to the British broadsides days, a movement that never really affected America until
the turbulent 1960s. He eventually went on to write over 500 songs in a mixture
of love and compassionate ballads with the topical protest songs. Paxton was
influenced by Guthrie, Ed McCurdy, and Seeger, and, in turn, he was a powerful
influence on Dylan, Ochs, Baez, and Judy Collins. Some of his more restrictive
material (that seems old today) includes "High Sheriff of Hazard" (describing
labor conditions in a Kentucky coal mining town), "Talking Viet Nam Pot Luck
Blues," "Lyndon Johnson Told the Nation," and "What Did You Learn in School
Today?" Still valid are "A Rumblin' in the Land" (about social upheavals), the

anti-war "When Morning Breaks," and "Daily News" (an uptempo satire on conservative editorials). More romantic and in the folk tradition are "I Can't Help but Wonder Where I'm Bound," "The Last Thing on My Mind," and the classic salute to a hobo, "Ramblin' Boy," which foreshadowed "Me and Bobby McGee" by Kris Kristofferson.

F10.45*   Simon and Garfunkel. Bookends. Columbia KCS 9529.

F10.46*   Simon and Garfunkel. Greatest Hits. Columbia PC 31350.
   The duo of Paul Simon and Art Garfunkel had strong folk roots in the early 1960s. They began by singing both Dylan songs and Simon compositions with a distinct orientation toward the singer-songwriter emphasis. They just might have passed into oblivion like so many other duos (Peter and Gordon, Chad and Jeremy, etc.) if their 1964 "Sounds of Silence" had not been later given a rock backing. As part of the same CBS complex, Simon and Garfunkel, the Byrds, and Dylan were related. In 1965, with the powerful folk-rock rhythms of "Mr. Tambourine Man," Tom Wilson (a producer for Columbia) added electric amplification and drums to their 1964 song and re-released it. A clamor for more developed, and the second career of Simon was launched.
   "Sounds of Silence" perfectly summarized his music. The melody was superb; the lyrics and music were tightly composed and produced; the vocals were softly sweet (and on uptempo songs, they would be driving) with Art's high tenor; and the concerns of the lyrics were often expressed over and over again. Simon was a literate and sensitive writer, emphasizing meticulous construction that appealed to many college crowds. His themes dealt mainly with alienation, aging and the passage of time, love and its communication, death, and loneliness. After a period of time, though, it was felt that his material was too meticulous, that the metaphors and messages were too many to absorb (a similar criticism was made of Dylan), and that overall the music became very produced and bland, especially with "Bridge over Troubled Water," a monster of overproduction emphasizing Larry Knechtel's piano and Art's soaring tenor. The completely urban character of the music is revealed through "Fakin' It," a subtle song in which the slippery emphasis keeps changing—one cannot get a handle on it—or "At the Zoo," "Homeward Bound," "The 59th Street Bridge Song (Feelin' Groovy)," and even "Mrs. Robinson."

F10.47*   James Taylor. Sweet Baby James. Warner Brothers WS 1843.
   In 1970, the rise of Taylor started a massive chain reaction involving troubadors in the landscape-scenery school. The album here is basically a folk-type set with rock accompaniment, and can be likened as the successor to Bob Dylan's country-inspired folk art songs. The impressive "Fire and Rain" deals with drugs that Taylor used, and others such as "Rainy Day Man," "Night Owl," and "Knocking round the Zoo" showed alienation and rootlessness. Other songs detailed forests, streams, sunshine, lakes, and so forth in a vast array of happy styles, much in the John Denver mode of celebrating life. This was all augmented by Taylor's quiet, sensitive voice, reminiscent of Woody Guthrie and Jack Elliott.

STANDARDS

F10.48*   **David Ackles. American Gothic.** Elektra EKS 75032.

F10.49   **David Ackles. Road to Cairo.** Elektra EKS 74022.

F10.50   **David Ackles. Subway to the Country.** Elektra EKS 74060.
    Ackles has always been like a breath of fresh air among the pollution of records. His characteristic and compelling music, while outlining problems, also contains no solution; hence, the mood is at once dramatic and melancholy. Material on his first three records is somewhat reminiscent of Jacques Brel. The half-spoken, half-sung, piano-augmented tracks deal with down-home, Midwest life, with a touch of Woody Guthrie for good measure. Ackles's voice has always been well-recorded, and the accompaniment is very tasteful, with a wide variety of session men. "American Gothic" is a classic statement on non-communicative spouses: "they suffer least who suffer what they choose." "Ballad of the Ship of State" is a bitter analogy mocking the American way of war. He searches for his ancestors in the 10-minute tone poem "Montana Song"; he decides that he must leave love after a "One Night Stand"; he performs a Jolsonesque rollicking ditty on "Oh, California," completely awash with strings at the finale. In everything he does, Ackles is very positive, rarely negative, and is a strong force in the singer-songwriter tradition.

F10.51   **Eric Anderson. Best.** two discs. Vanguard VSD 7/8.
    Eric Anderson was one of the first folksingers to write his own material (and all the songs here are his except for one), beginning before the 1960s had even arrived. His character has been derived from Greenwich Village life, but he was subject to the usual Bob Dylan influences later in his career. His earlier works featured rhythm accompaniment, and these are on the first disc. The second disc contains his later electric rock sounds. Titles include "Violets of Dawn," perhaps his best-known song often recorded by others; "Thirsty Boots," recorded by Judy Collins; and the portraits created in "The Hustler," "A Woman Is a Prison," and "Dusty Box Car Wall." At this stage in his development, Anderson would be characterized as half-hobo (in the Guthrie tradition) and half-urban folkie (with certain roots in city living). This made some of his music appear both dichotomous (or "schizoid") in its approach, demonstrating the push-pull in life ("Cross Your Mind," "I Shall Go Unbounded," and "Hey Babe, Have You Been Cheating?").

F10.51a   **Hoyt Axton. Joy to the World.** Capitol SMAS 788.
    Axton has been a proficient worker in the field of folk-derived singing for about twenty years, yet his impact as a writer has been more pronounced than his own singing. (It was his *mother* who contributed "Heartbreak Hotel" to the Presley repertoire.) Many of his compositions were recorded by Three Dog Night, including the hits "Joy to the World," "Never Been to Spain," and "Have a Nice Day" (all sung on this disc by Axton, with a soft-rock background). In addition, in 1963, Axton wrote a most powerful anti-drug song—"The Pusher"—and these images were fashioned into a tortuous format by the hard rock group, Steppenwolf. In the main, Axton deals with wistful thoughts compounded by an uncanny sense

of reality and humor, such as the peacefulness of "Alice in Wonderland" or the compassion of "Ease Your Pain."

F10.52   **Tim Buckley. Goodbye and Hello.** Elektra EKL 7318.
Buckley was a singer-songwriter with a high-ranging voice, almost a counter-tenor with sweetish overtones. All of his music, blatantly sexual as women really loved him, was characterized by good production values and superb arrangements. Throughout, he strongly felt country music influences. Tracks include "Carnival Song" (about the effects of LSD), the hippie culture of "Pleasant Street," his experiences reflected in the title track, and bittersweet songs: "No Man Can Find the War," "Morning Glory," "Grief in My Soul," and "Knight-Errant."

F10.53   **Jimmy Buffett. Living and Dying in 3/4 Time.** ABC Dunhill DSD 50150.

F10.54*   **Jimmy Buffett. A White Sport Coat and a Pink Crustacean.** ABC Dunhill DSD 50132.
Buffett sings his story songs in a humorous vein, somewhat reminiscent of Will Rogers in his attempts at commenting on American life. Buffett, though, prefers to be "at peace in Florida," and one wonders if he comes into any sort of contact with Fred Neil, who is also in Florida. In many ways, the two men are remarkably alike. Buffett is the cowboy philosopher who has been influenced by Marty Robbins (such as in "Brand New Country Star," about sequined suits and the country music life, but also with the hook line, "he can either go country or pop"). The Tom T. Hall influence shows up in "The Great Filling Station Holdup," where the hero robs for the petty cash but then gets captured right away—so realistic that one can question whether it is a parody or not—and in "Peanut Butter Conspiracy," which details shoplifting in supermarkets. He is basically a celebrator of what to him is the good life, and rarely will he take things seriously, as in "Life Is Just a Tire Swing." In some ways, Buffett also falls under the Dylan influence in his shifting moods and advances, such as the long ribald song "God's Own Drunk," about drinking with a Kodiak bear who apparently then steals a still. Most of his songs, again in the Robbins style (note the title takeoff of Marty Robbins's first big hit, "A White Sports Coat and a Pink Carnation") are about "bad" people—but just barely bad, as in "Death of an Unpopular Poet," where he demolishes every singer-songwriter who ever existed.

F10.55   **Jim Croce. Photographs & Memories—His Greatest Hits.** ABC ABCD 835.
Croce achieved posthumous success through the "cult after death." He was influenced by the folk and blues materials of the 1960s, plus a good shot of Walt Whitman and Mark Twain. Others called him a scenarist and a short story teller. His songs range from the humor of the streets to fine ballads and pure love songs. As the cult grew, his material began to be covered by country and rock singers. His short, two-year career is reduced here to two sides of better-than-average material that may or may not last, depending on how well his vocals are accepted in the future. (Jim Reeves, for instance, has no real enduring influence, yet RCA has handled the material he laid down before he died in a very sincere fashion.) Some of the Croce songs that crossed over include "Bad, Bad Leroy Brown," "Operator

(That's Not the Way It Feels)," "I'll Have to Say I Love You in a Song," "You Don't Mess around with Jim," "I Got a Name," and "Time in a Bottle."

F10.56* **John Denver. Greatest Hits.** RCA CPL 1-0374.

The critics are always fickle. Less than a decade ago, John Denver was hailed as the redeeming singer who would stay Leonard Cohen's depressing influence. Denver celebrated what to him was the good life, in a nationalistic Thoreau-like sense. This was satisfactory for awhile, but for the critics, Denver seemed to make a lot of money and never considered the seedy side of life in his songs. No one, they said, can be perennially happy. Denver also brought a pop orientation to folk music, and a folk orientation to pop music in one of the most perfect examples of covering music in one genre with another. But Denver is very good at what he does, and a little of it goes a long way, as did his big success "Leaving, on a Jet Plane," "Take Me Home, Country Roads," and "Rocky Mountain High." All of the material on this album was re-recorded by Denver in 1974 because he felt his current style of interpretation was better than that of years earlier. Of course, this is true, as the material was sweetened with violins, and Denver's high pitched voice actually seemed higher with the lack of instrumental contrast. Other titles: "Poems, Prayers and Promises," "Sunshine on My Shoulder," and "The Eagle and the Hawk."

F10.57 **Mimi and Richard Fariña. Best.** two discs. Vanguard VSD 21/22.

The Fariñas were a husband and wife singing team until he died in 1965 in a tragic accident; she is Joan Baez's sister. Together, they had excellent potential, but perhaps they were better composers than performers at the time (although, now, with everybody singing, some dissonance in the music actually enhances its worth). There is a hymn-like quality to their music, superbly rendered on many original instrumentals in this repackaged set. Yet these melodies, like some of the more folk-type vocals, tend to be a little repetitious. Included are guitars, autoharp, and dulcimer for a chime effect. The balance of the collection has a sort of sweet rock background. Mimi's accompaniment is instrumental; her vocalizing is very discreet. There is a certain amount of old time music here, along with reworking of traditional music (e.g., "The Falcon," based on "The Cuckoo Bird"). The 26 tracks also include such originals as the droll "House Un-American Blues Activity Dream," "Hard Loving Loser," "The Swallow Song," "Sell out Agitation Waltz," and "Pack up Your Sorrows."

F10.58* **Steve Goodman. Essential.** two discs. Buddah BDS 5665-2.

This set is a reissue of Goodman's only two albums for Buddah (BDS 5096 and 5121), recorded in 1971-1972. He was one of the first of the singer-songwriters to employ a great many accompanists, some for only one track apiece. Many were from the Nashville area, such as Charlie McCoy, Kenny Buttrey, Grady Martin; others from contemporary bluegrass, such as Bill Keith, Vassar Clements, David Bromberg; vocalists such as Maria Muldaur; and even jazz musicians, such as Dave Newman, and a reed section. As a songwriter, Goodman contributed "City of New Orleans," a story song of the last train ride from Chicago to the Deep South (and recorded by well over a score of other singers). His high, humorous voice made for a great laid-back feeling; he casually avoids the scenery songs, eclectically preferring whatever moves him. Kris Kristofferson and John Prine have assisted with material and production work. Typical Goodman humor is exhibited on "Mind Your Own Business," "The Chicken Cordon Bleus" (about dieting), the Martin-Bogan-Armstrong song "The Vegetable Song or Barnyard Dance," and the very short but prophetic "I Ain't Heard You Play No Blues," a fragment detailing saving the lives of a bluesman and a non-bluesman.

F10.59   John Greenway. Talking Blues. Folkways 5232.
    The talking blues are a rhymed and rhythmic spoken form with a banjo or guitar accompaniment. In content, the material is comic or sarcastic, or else it deals with social protest material, as Guthrie's compositions did. Collector Greenway has assembled a number of these talking blues (some are his own) onto one album, and they deal with a wide variety of themes. Tracks include "Talking Guitar Blues," "Original Talking Blues," "Talking Butcher," Guthrie's "Talking Dust Bowl," "Talking Union," "Talking Miner," "Talking Social Worker," "Talking Inflation Blues," and "Dry Voters—Wet Drinkers."

F10.60*   Arlo Guthrie. Alice's Restaurant. Reprise RS 6267.
    Arlo Guthrie was in the tradition of both his father, Woody, and the urban folk protest. His early songs—among his best—are short story songs with a lyrical beat. Later in his career, he would turn to derivative country music, some of his father's material, and occasional self-penned items. Overall, he must be judged as a weak singer with minimal impact on the rock or folk world, except for two things. First, he was Woody's son, and that counted for a lot, as Woody Guthrie was hospitalized and inactive for the last twenty years of his life. Second, he gave a first rate account of the way in which he tried to beat the draft, which was of intense interest to younger audiences of the day. "Alice's Restaurant Massacree" (at 18:20) fills a whole side here, and it also became a movie with many of the original cast present. In format, it is an engaging story with a built-in rag riff for the musical accompaniment; indeed, it can be listened to many times without any monotony. The catch, of course, lay in the droll humor and the fact that the audience knew in advance what happened. And there was a certain "determinism," in that if Arlo got ahead of himself with the words over the music, we had "to wait until the melody came around again" before leaping in for the rest of the story. Déjà vu, and all that.

F10.61*   Woody Guthrie. Dust Bowl Ballads. Folkways FH 5212.

F10.62*   Woody Guthrie. Dust Bowl Ballads. RCA CPL1-2099.

F10.63   Woody Guthrie. Struggle. Folkways 2485.
    Guthrie, in common with Seeger and others in the late 1930s, became involved with unions and the American Left (he once wrote for the *Daily Worker*). He sang with Seeger, and they formed part of the Almanac Singers. Over the years in the 1940s, he fashioned many series of related songs, some on a commissioned basis, such as the hydro-electricity songs that led to "Elec-tric-i-ty" and "Bonneville Dam," the Sacco-Vanzetti saga songs, and his Dust Bowl ballads. The most popular, in terms of impact, were the ones dealing with the migratory workers and life in sixteen southwestern states hit by drought. In the midst of the Depression, these

areas became dry, parched, and could not sustain life. Yet there were few jobs, low pay, high prices, higher taxes, bum houses, and slummy houses. Disease was rampant. The eleven songs on the Folkways set reflect all this, such as the "Talking Dust Blues," the epic "Do Re Me," the important story song "Tom Joad," the rambling "I Ain't Got No Home in This World Anymore," and several others detailing dust storms and recoveries (if any). *Struggle* collates songs about the working man and the growth of trade unions. Whether he is singing about the tragedies of miners' lives in "Waiting at the Gate" and the "Dying Miner," or about the toll levied against unions in the early days in "The Ludlow Massacre" or the "1913 Massacre," one has to be moved and even outraged that some of these conditions still abound. Both Folkways albums are accompanied by booklets of notes and texts.

F10.64   **Tim Hardin. Best.** Verve 63078.
    Hardin developed in the Boston area as a white blues singer who was also into jazz and folk music materials. He was one of the very first of the troubadors to switch to electric guitar, far in advance of Dylan. In his lyrics, he presented a resigned view of life in his interpersonal relationships. His music is quite similar to Donovan's, but it is without the lyricism that Donovan adopted. Hardin played some role in influencing Dylan, particularly in Dylan's new-found calm after his motorcycle accident. Titles here include his best known song "If I Were a Carpenter," the 1966 "Don't Make Promises," "Lady from Baltimore," and "Speak Like a Child."

F10.65   **Richie Havens. Mixed Bag.** Verve FTS 3006.
    Havens was a black operating in urban folk music, and he was one of the few to do so. And he did not especially emphasize the urban blues either. 1968 was his best year, the time when troubadors peaked, when he began his gentle reinterpretations of Dylan's music ("Like a Woman," as found on the above eleven-item record). His self-taught guitar stylings were largely in a flail fashion, with an unorthodox open E tuning. In turn, he was one of the first troubadors to use the electric sitar, as it appeared on "Eleanor Rigby" and other rough personal songs that he was known for. Havens's blues and ballads had earlier been influenced by Paul Stookey (of Peter, Paul and Mary) and Len Chandler. Other titles here include "Morning, Morning," "San Francisco Bay Blues" (from Jesse Fuller), and the evocative "Three Day Eternity."

F10.66   **Cisco Houston. Sings American Folk Songs.** Folkways FTS 31012.

F10.67*   **Cisco Houston. Sings Songs of the Open Road.** Folkways FA 2480.

F10.68   **Cisco Houston. Songs of Woody Guthrie.** Vanguard VSD 9089.
    Houston once ran around with Woody Guthrie beginning in 1939, and they even served together in the Merchant Marine during World War II. His distinguished, husky, and resonant voice was more adaptable to sad or fast tunes, falling short of the mark on the slower or traditional materials. In his nomadic existence, Houston met many singers such as Niles and Leadbelly; he exchanged many songs; and he recorded for many labels (Decca, Stinson, Coral, etc.). His better efforts

have been for the largely non-commercial Folkways and Vanguard catalogs. FTS 31012 (a reissue of FA 2346) is second-generation American music that concentrates on tall tales, western ballads (or cowboy songs), southern ballads, work, prison, and railroad songs. FA 2480 is roughly similar, but substitutes "wandering" or "lonesome" songs such as "Hobo's Lullaby," "Travel On," "Soup Song," and "Mysteries of a Hobo Life." Between them, there are 27 selections of top-notch materials and interpretations, including his own marvelous composition "Rambling, Gambling Man." Of all the wanderers in folk music, only Utah Phillips and Jack Elliott remain.

F10.69   **Peter LaFarge. As Long as the Grass Shall Grow.** Folkways 2532.
    LaFarge was of American Indian ancestry. In 1963, he recorded this bitter album, but in 1965, at the age of 34, he was dead. LaFarge showed a great debt to Woody Guthrie for the rambling compositional styles, and he often showed up at coffee houses and at Newport, refusing to sing anything but his own material. This album, the best of his songs, concerns the American Indian through indicative titles: "Abraham Lincoln," "Vision of a Past Warrior," "Coyote," "Trail of Tears," "Custer," "Black Stallion," and the title selection. For Folkways, he also recorded other albums concerning the American West, women, cowboys, and protest.

F10.70*   **Harry K. McClintock. Haywire Mac.** Folkways FD 5272.
    This is an important documentary of the music of the International Workers of the World (IWW), performed by one of its original members. McClintock tells stories, sings songs, and generally spreads his message. The album, recorded off and on during the early 1950s (beginning in 1951) by Sam Eskin, is both informative and entertaining, being strong both in musical content and in sociological significance. McClintock was a hobo, with an interest in tramping through the country, the IWW (he was an exceptional writer of union songs), and the folk songs of the early southeastern United States. When he first recorded in 1927-1931 for Victor, he—like Uncle Dave Macon—was already past his prime of life. Thus he had many events to relate, such as "Subic" or a bluesy "Casey Jones," plus "Long Haired Preachers" and "Big Rock Candy Mountain." His folk material then was largely concerned with railroad cops, freight trains, and lonely hours. In his articulate recreations (usually prefaced by a narrative here), side one is IWW or labor-related. Side two—with "Utah Carl," "Poor Boy," and "Paddy Clancy"—contains his interpretations of songs gathered throughout his life.

F10.71   **Don McLean. American Pie.** United Artists UAS 5535.
    We hesitate to include this album, for all of it is bland if compared with the troubador traditions. Yet the highlight is obviously the title track selection, which goes on for over eight minutes and details the death of American rock and roll in a metaphorical fashion. A worthy purchase just for that long song.

F10.72   **Ralph McTell. 8 Frames a Second.** Transatlantic TRA 165 (British issue).

F10.73   **Ralph McTell. Not till Tomorrow.** Reprise MS 2121.
     McTell's troubador days concerned humanitarian songs. They were always thoughtful and intelligent, with a direct concern for the losers and underdogs in today's society. Not for him the pretty pastorale, but neither does he sing about the scum of life. His compassion centers on man's inhumanity to man, as in "Maginot Waltz" (about pre-World War I seaside trips) or "Michael in the Garden" (confusing madness with reality), or even "The Streets of London," a synoptic coverage of the passing human parade. Although British-born, he has been a "floater" and is popular in the United States as well as Britain.

F10.74   **Melanie. From the Beginning; 12 Great Performances.** ABC ABND 879.
     Melanie Safka had been characterized by her sweet voice and pretty face as the "girl next door." Yet, she was a notable songwriter who contributed many, many excellent songs to the troubador tradition of social protest: "Candles in the Rain," "Peace Will Come," and "Lay Down" (with the Edwin Hawkins Singers). Her slightly husky, nasal voice covers the gamut from love and hope to withdrawal and introspection. "Brand New Key" concerns a childish fantasy, while the others deal with a variety of issues and concerns developed by this eclectic performer. Many people, though, because of her success, had put her down as being a pop performer. The packaging of this album, or indeed any "best" album of a troubador, does nothing to dispel these images.

F10.75*   **Nilsson. Aerial Ballet.** RCA LSP 3956.

F10.76   **Nilsson. Harry.** RCA LSP 4197.

F10.77*   **Nilsson. Nilsson Sings Newman.** RCA LSP 4289.

F10.78   **Nilsson. Pandemonium Shadow Show.** RCA LSP 3874.
     Nilsson is the master of the romantically lush ballad, coupled with some wistful, naive children's songs. This apparent innocence, though, is purposeful, for it is needed in the careful calculation that underlies the creativity of his songs. His vocal lines are something to listen to: his soft rock songs use overdubbed Beatle harmonies, while his other uptempo items display his vocal acrobatics (three octaves). His first album, from 1967, (LSP 3874) featured the dramatic "Ten Little Indians" (written for the Youngbloods) and the tender "Sleep Late My Lady Friend." There are twenty voices here, all his through overdubbing. On the Beatles' "She's Leaving Home," he perfects four-part harmony. His perfect phrasing, as on "Without You" (written for Herb Alpert) is augmented by his scat singing and screams, as on his version of "River Deep, Mountain High." Another interesting song here is "Cuddly Toy," originally done for the Monkees. Others for whom he has written include the Ronettes, Blood, Sweat and Tears, Lana Cantrell, Jack Jones, Rick Nelson, and the Turtles.
     The thirteen tracks on *Aerial Ballet* include "Everybody's Talkin'," the Fred Neil song used in the film *Midnight Cowboy*; "Little Cowboy," written by

his mother; and some sarcastic items such as "I Guess the Lord Must Be in New York City." With *Harry*, Nilsson shows his lyrical inventiveness and diverse topical coverage, such as "Simon Smith and the Amazing Dancing Bear," "The Puppy Song," and "Nobody Cares about Railroads Anymore." To further display his vocal virtuosity, he undertook to record some Randy Newman songs. This is a ballad album, with jazz singing and Newman's piano, and contains excellent interpretations of nostalgic pieces that are at once poignant yet full of self-control. Throughout all of his music, Nilsson is the eternal optimist, once saying "hope is practical" in terms of his interpersonal relationships.

F10.79   **Laura Nyro. Eli and the 13th Confession.** Columbia KCS 9626.

F10.80*   **Laura Nyro. New York Tendaberry.** Columbia KCS 9737.
    The complex Nyro writes mainly about her environment (New York City)—the mood of the city's districts and its pulses. Her material has been recorded by such diverse groups as Blood, Sweat and Tears ("And When I Die"), the Fifth Dimension, Three Dog Night, and even Barbra Streisand. Nyro's black voice has been fully urbanized in her interpretations, using popular music derivations from the world of rock rhythms. She sings intricate harmonies and contrapuntal lyrics with herself, in addition to directing the musical accompaniment. Each recorded song is a minor gem, emphasizing a black soul sound, good melodies, and shifting moods. With "Sweet Blindness," "Poetry Train," and "Lovely Woman," the 13-item *Eli* album projects the theme of a young girl moving from childhood to womanhood, as Nyro herself was doing. The autobiographical caste also continues with *Tendaberry*, a more impressive album concerning social consciousness, especially in "Stoned Soul Picnic" (made into a hit by the Fifth Dimension), "Save the Country," and "Time and Love."

F10.81   **Utah Phillips. "Good Though."** Philco 1004.
    Bruce "Utah" Phillips has led a life rich in experience and adventures. He has gone the Guthrie route, and has hoboed his way around America, performed at free concerts, and played for unionists—all to the detriment of a comfortable personal life, for he believes strongly in what he does. His musical interests are union and railroad traveling songs, with the latter type here (plus the occasional train whistle and/or steam engine sound used between cuts). While the copious notes and lyrics describe the contents and atmosphere of each song, there is only one note to describe one train sound—the Nickel P. Plate Road, No. 759. Jane Voss, a Carter Family-influenced singer, is along for three harmony vocals, and there are occasional performers sitting in to fill gaps in the musical passages. "Cannonball Blues" is Phillips's opener, where he sings a verse and then goes into a jive talk-rap with the audience to gauge their reactions and thus set the tone for the balance of the performance. "Calling Trains," lifted from a Library of Congress disc, is a short piece from the 1930s in which a train caller rhymes off the names of station stops. Songs detail life on the hobo runs, giving tips on how to adjust and how to catch an old freight. Efficiency knows no sentiment, and while Amtrak may be trying its best to encourage passenger use of railroads, it also shut down the Wabash Cannonball (named after the song): Phillips's salute to its last run is here. Of course, hoboes are not affected by passenger runs. They

jump the freight, and there is as yet no danger of their demise as long as freights are still profitable for transport of goods. The railroad in folk song is an important genre, and Phillips nobly carries on the tradition. Soon, though, there may not be much more to sing about (one of his significant songs here is entitled "Daddy, What's a Train?").

F10.82*   **John Prine.** Atlantic SD 8296.
John Prine was touted as the "new Dylan" (as was early Bruce Springsteen). This might have been the automatic kiss of death, for both new performers quietly disappeared in 1976. Prine has had four discs, each one going downhill in the overall concept of what his albums should be like (according to him). Lyrics are good, very good: homey, with a lived-in look and feel that one can almost bite. Melodies are typically see-saw country, as found in any bar or saloon that featured honky-tonk music. Prine's voice has that 4 a.m., all night of smoking, drinking, and screaming feeling, which is always an asset for this type of music. The small group accompaniment is unusually super-slick (this would get worse in later albums, along with amplification, vocal choruses, and re-mixing). Stylistically, his bitter lyrics are on the negative side, yet he finds much inspiration in Carter Family songs and influences. "Your Flag Decal Won't Get You into Heaven Anymore" deals with death; "Six O'Clock News" is about a grim suicide; "Hello in There" concerns an old couple; "Donald and Lydia" deals with the fantasy of lovemaking; "Far from Me" indicates lost love; and "Illegal Smile" is a blues item.

F10.83   **Putnam String County Band.** Rounder 3003.
This is a personal project of John Cohen, one of the members of the New Lost City Ramblers. He joined here with Jay and Lyn Ungar and Abby Newton to create the spirit of old time music (as the NLCR had recreated) but applied it to rock music and topical folk. Typical "concerned" songs include "Last Go Round," "Nixon Daze," "The Candidate's a Dodger," "The Credit Card Song," and "Hi-Fi Stereo Color TV"—good sarcasm and satirical sketches.

F10.84   **Malvina Reynolds.** Cassandra CFS 2807.

F10.85   **Malvina Reynolds. Held Over.** Cassandra CFS 3688.
Reynolds had been singing social commentary folk-type songs for many years when her 1964 "Little Boxes" made an impact on an audience concerned with alienation and frustration in the urban environment. This pleasent little ditty tried to project, in what was essentially a children's song format, the horrors of suburbia and the tight constriction of office jobs in the big city. Reynolds acquired a Ph.D. in medieval folklore, and was also influenced by John Jacob Niles in the 1930s. She began to compose her own folk-type songs in 1943, submitting many to the Almanac Singers (in its latter stages of development), Woody Guthrie, and Pete Seeger. She began with soft ballads, but then moved to topical songs and then to protest songs, as American popular music entered the "Age of Protest" in the 1960s. Some of her most enduring titles as recorded late in her life for this California-based label include "What Have They Done to the Rain?," "The Albatross," "On the Rim of the World," "We Don't Need the Man," and "Look on the Sunny Side."

F10.86   **Tom Rush. Classic Rush.** Elektra EKS 74062.
Rush's began as pure folk music but then became electrified in 1965, like several others following Dylan's lead. Before appearing on the folk circuit of colleges, coffee houses and Newport, he had established a reputation in France as a major talent with folk materials. Some of these typical folk items are on the Prestige label, which collated his 1963-1965 career. With a shift to Elektra and seasoning in Cambridge, Massachusetts, Rush went electric and began both singing and promoting other (mainly unknown) troubador songs. The Elektra album noted above collects his "best" material: "Who Do You Love?," Joni Mitchell's "Urge for Going," "On the Road Again," "Something in the Way She Moves," "Sunshine Sunshine," "Circle Game," and "No Regrets."

F10.87   **Buffy Sainte-Marie. Best, v.1/2.** four discs. Vanguard VSD 3/4 and 33/34.
Buffy Sainte-Marie's strident but husky voice can be heard soaring over the percussive, repetitive beat of her music. While her melodies reflect her Cree Indian upbringing, her vibrato does not, and it rings through beautifully (even if it sometimes sounds like the voice of doom). Eight tracks here contain an electronic recreation of her voice, somewhat a gimmick, but also very effective. The variety of arrangements reflects her past decade's work: solo, medium rock background, orchestrated background, and finally, electronic manipulation. At times she could produce a heavy sound. Altogether, these 48 selections represent about half of her Vanguard output. Most songs are originals, but others are by Joni Mitchell, Patrick Sky, Richie Havens, and even Benjamin Britten. It was Sky who taught her how to use the Indian mouth-bow, and that instrument can also be heard here. Titles include "My Country 'Tis of Thy People You're Dying" (a bitter protest against atrocities committed on Indians), "Cod'ine" (based on her addiction when she was ill), "Now That the Buffalo's Gone," "Incest Song," "It's My Way," "Little Wheel Spin and Spin," her cloying "I'm Gonna Be a Country Girl Again," and the classic protest-topical song, "Universal Soldier."

F10.88   **Patrick Sky. Songs That Made America Famous.** Adelphi ADR 4101.
Multi-instrumentalist Sky, of Indian ancestry, developed the use of the Indian mouth-bow, introducing it to the world of folk and to Buffy Sainte-Marie. He made two reasonably good albums for Vanguard in 1965 as part of the folk revival in the troubador style. But his major importance will be for the above cited album, recorded sometime near the end of the 1960s at a low point in his career (but never released until 1973). All the material is "disgusting," but a reflection of then-current themes of American social disorders. He comments on all aspects of the recording industry, giving damning indictments of the various schlock styles and the audiences that respond to them. Throughout, he is bitter, commenting on the Viet Nam war, the Roman Catholic Church, education systems, racial strife, and so forth. Styles vary according to his subjects.
"Rock Star" takes the approach of heavy music and presents a disturbing picture of that industry; his emotionless country music approach to "Our Baby Died" deals with the lyrics of that industry ("it wasn't such a nice baby anyway"); "Child Molesting Blues" is a long piece of subtle recreation of the story of some rediscovered, aging bluesman who was pushing pencils outside a radio station.

It is an interview plus the "actual" 1927 record detailing what amounts to statutory rape. "Okie" deals with the conservatism of the West. (All thirteen tracks have specific points and can be considered dirty, so libraries may wish to audition the album.)

F10.89   Entry deleted.

F10.90*   **Cat Stevens. Greatest Hits. A & M SP 4519.**

F10.91   **Cat Stevens. Tea for the Tillerman. A & M SP 4280.**
      Stevens was a former folksinger with a Greek background. His songs are of the scenery type, touched with medieval minstrelsy. He derives romantic confessions from psychoanalysis and self-examination. Throughout his songs is a strong tendency toward sexualism and sexism, and his condescending sexual viewpoint has raised the ire of women's groups. His early music was in the rock mode, but this softened up with "Wild World," "Peace Train," and "Two Fine People." His distinctive voice and phrasing led to a number of AM hits, as collated on the anthology noted above. This is a pleasant mix of ballads and easy rockers. Other songs from the twelve cuts include "Moonshadow," "Morning Has Broken," and "Another Saturday Night."

F10.92*   **Jerry Jeff Walker. Mr. Bojangles. Atco SD 33-259.**
      Walker was an early folkie from the late 1950s who later turned to rock with Circus Maximus in 1966. He left that for the country rock music that was then starting. In essence, his work has always been that of the street singer. He recorded this album and made successes of the title track and "Gypsy Songman," "I Makes Money (Money Don't Make Me)," and "Round and Round." He has a warm, slightly nasal but husky, baritone that is really good when performing solo or with a small group. Accompaniment here includes David Bromberg on lead guitar. Walker has never ever equalled the success of this minor classic.

Citations,
Directories,
Index

BOOK CITATIONS

Most of the material in this book is based on a combination of readings from both book and periodical sources. In the listing that follows, the key books of concern to students of grass roots music and the folk process are numbered (after being alphabetized). Taken together, the books cited in the four volumes would constitute a library detailing popular music in America. We have excluded two categories of books. Generally, *biographies* have been omitted unless they deal substantially with an influence on other performers in the same genre. Thus, for example, we list in *Contemporary Popular Music* Gray's book on Bob Dylan rather than Scaduto's largely biographical offering. Second, we have omitted *songbooks* and instructional materials that look like songbooks, unless they deal substantially with the impact and influence of the music, such as Lomax's book.

It is very difficult to separate books about different musical genres, for there is much overlapping; thus, we discuss titles in the literature survey preceding each section by referring to a designated number, which then can be followed up here for source data and comment. At the same time, many books are called "reference works" (bibliographies, discographies) and "monographic surveys." To the student of music, these terms are interchangeable. In consideration of all of the above, a numerical reference listing seems the best way to handle the matter. At any rate, this is just a source list; please refer to the musical section for comments on the literature.

1 Abrahams, Roger D., and George Foss. Anglo-American Folksong Style. Englewood Cliffs, NJ: Prentice-Hall, 1968. 242p.

2 Ames, Russell. The Story of American Folk Song. New York: Grosset & Dunlap, 1960. 276p.

3 Annual Index to Popular Music Record Reviews, 1972– . Compiled by A. Armitage and D. Tudor. Metuchen, NJ: Scarecrow, 1973– .
This annual provides location to about 15,000 record reviews in about 55 magazines, noting for each review the reviewer's evaluation of the record. It provides a synoptic report on the year's music, pre-selecting the "best of the year" and indicating the length of each review.

4 Artis, Bob. Bluegrass. New York: Hawthorn Books, 1975. 182p.

5 Atkins, John, ed. The Carter Family. London: Old Time Music, 1973. 62p. illus. bibliog. discog. (Old Time Music Booklet No. 1).
An excellently-produced study of the importance and influence of the Carter Family, as revealed through their recordings (which are here critically analyzed).

6 Batcheller, John. Music in Recreation and Leisure. Dubuque, IA: W. C. Brown Co., 1972. 135p. paper.
A short treatise on the importance of music as a social function, with chapters on how to relax through music.

7 Blesh, Rudi, and Harriet Janis. They All Played Ragtime. 4th ed. New York: Oak, 1971. illus. bibliog. discog. music.
A pioneering work—the only one that provides a detailed history of its development as well as social commentary. The many special sections cover ragtime on record (both new and reissues), complete scores, rare photographs, and listings of performers and composers.

8 Bluestein, Gene. The Voice of the Folk; Folklore and American Literary Theory. Amherst: University of Massachusetts Press, 1972. 170p. bibliog.
Half of this book is devoted to folk music, and includes a study of blues as a literary tradition, the black influence, and rock as poetry.

9 Brand, Oscar. The Ballad Mongers; Rise of the Modern Folk Song. New York: Funk and Wagnalls, 1967. 240p.

10 Bronson, Bertrand Harris. The Ballad as Song. Berkeley: University of California Press, 1969. 324p.

11 Burt, Jesse, and Bob Ferguson. So You Want to Be in Music! Nashville, TN: Abingdon Press, 1970. 175p.
This career-oriented handbook does a good job of explaining the mechanics behind breaking into the business—songwriting, studio techniques, and so forth. Glossary of recording terms.

12 The Carter Family on Border Radio. Los Angeles, CA: John Edwards Memorial Foundation, 1972. 58p. illus. bibliog. discog. music.
A booklet designed to accompany the Foundation's recorded album of the same title (label number: JEMF 101).

13 Chasins, Abram. Music at the Crossroads. New York: Macmillan, 1972. 240p.
An appraisal of the current state of instrumental music, both classical and popular, with consideration of the effects of jazz-rock-folk on "serious" music.

14 Coffin, Tristram, ed. American Folklore. Washington: Voice of America, 1968. 325p. illus.
Based on the 1968 Forum Lectures; at least six have direct musical themes.

15 Coffin, Tristram. The British Traditional Ballad in North America. Rev. ed. Philadelphia: American Folklore Society, 1963. 186p.
A discussion on story variations in the Child ballads.

16 "Commercially Disseminated Folk Music Sources and Resources" (A Symposium). Reprinted from Western Folklore (July 1971). Los Angeles, CA: John Edwards Memorial Foundation, 1971. 75p. music. discog.
Covers various discographical projects, song folios, copyright, and radio and personal appearances.

17 Country Music Who's Who, 1976. New York: Record World Publications, 1975. 421p. illus.
A quadrennial, first published in 1960; this issue features a list of 2,000 hit songs of the last fifty years (with a comprehensive index), and capsule biographies of 300 prominent persons in the business.

18 Denisoff, R. Serge. Great Day Coming; Folk Music and the American Left. Urbana: University of Illinois Press, 1971. 220p.
Traces the use of folk music for socio-political ends from 1930 to the present.

19 Denisoff, R. Serge. Sing a Song of Social Significance. Bowling Green, OH: Bowling Green University Popular Press, 1972. 229p. illus. tables.
A series of papers about songs of persuasion and protest in American life.

20 Denisoff, R. Serge. Solid Gold; The Record Industry, Its Friends, and Enemies. New York: Transaction Book; distr. by Dutton, 1976. 350p.
Traces the steps through which a song goes to reach the public.

21 Denisoff, R. Serge. Songs of Protest: War and Peace; A Bibliography and Discography. Santa Barbara, CA: American Bibliographical Center-Clio Press, 1973. 88p. paper only.
Scope covers books, periodicals, songbooks, songs, and country and western music in the discography. This leads to a preliminary assessment of the role of music in American anti-war movements from the Revolutionary War to the present.

22 Denisoff, R. Serge, comp. The Sounds of Social Change; Studies in Popular Culture. Chicago: Rand McNally, 1972. 332p.

23 De Turk, David A., and A. Poulin, Jr., comps. The American Folk Scene; Dimensions of the Folksong Revival. New York: Dell, 1967. 334p. paper only.

24 Ewen, David. Great Men of American Popular Song. Englewood Cliffs, NJ: Prentice-Hall, 1970. 387p.
Mainly historical and biographical, this book does not attempt analysis. Its subtitle is: the history of American popular song told through the lives, careers, achievements, and personalities of its foremost composers and lyricists. There are 28 composers and thirteen lyricists covered.

25 Ewan, David. History of Popular Music. New York: Barnes and Noble, 1961. 229p. bibliog. paper only.
A brief introductory text to popular songs, the musical theater, and jazz in America from colonial times to 1960.

26 Fahey, John. Charley Patton. New York: Stein and Day, 1970. 112p. illus. bibliog. discog.
Includes a discussion of his lyrics, tuning, music, and influence in the Delta area.

27 Field, James J. American Popular Music, 1875-1950. Philadelphia, PA: Musical Americana, 1956.

28 Fuld, James J. The Book of World Famous Music: Classical, Popular and Folk. Rev. and enl. ed. New York: Crown, 1971. 688p. bibliog.
A discussion of 1,000 songs, primarily through tracing their roots.

29 Gammond, Peter. Scott Joplin and the Ragtime Era. New York: St. Martin's Press, 1975. 223p. illus. bibliog. discog.

30 Gentry, Linnell. A History and Encyclopedia of Country, Western and Gospel Music. 2d ed., completely rev. Nashville, TN: Clairmont Corp., 1969. 598p.
The first section contains 76 articles originally published between 1908 and 1968. The second section is largely biographical.

31 Goldstein, Richard. Goldstein's Greatest Hits. Englewood Cliffs, NJ: Prentice-Hall, 1970. 258p.
His collected writings from 1966-1968, originally published in the Village Voice, the New York Times, and New York Magazine.

32 Gray, Andy. Great Country Music Stars. London: Hamlyn, 1975. 175p. illus.

33 Gray, Michael. Song and Dance Man; The Art of Bob Dylan. London: Abacus, 1973. 332p. illus. discog. paper only.
An analysis of Dylan's songs, lyrics, music—placed in the context of his time (impact and influence).

34 Green, Archie. Only a Miner; Studies in Recorded Coal-mining Songs. Urbana: University of Illinois Press, 1972. 504p. illus. bibliog.

35 Griffis, Ken. Hear My Song; The Story of the Celebrated Sons of the Pioneers. Los Angeles, CA: John Edwards Memorial Foundation, 1974. 148p. illus. discog. paper only.

36 Grissim, John. Country Music; White Man's Blues. New York: Paperback Library, 1970. 299p. paper only.
This is very explicit and intelligent writing on the role that country music has played, with some emphasis on the ideas involved in cross-fertilization with blues and r 'n' b material.

37 Haglund, Urban, and Lillie Ohlsson. A Listing of Bluegrass LPs. Vasteras, Sweden: Kountry Korral Productions, 197? 72p.
A nearly complete list of albums issued in the United States and abroad.

38 Haywood, Charles. Bibliography of North American Folklore and Folksong. 2d ed. New York: Dover, 1961. 2 vols. discog.

39 Hemphill, Paul. The Nashville Sound; Bright Lights and Country Music. New York: Simon and Schuster, 1970. 289p.
Identifies country music in terms of the people involved in the music and the related industries.

40 Herdeg, Walter, ed. Graphics/Record Covers. New York: Hastings House, 1974. 192p. illus.
History and illustrations of record jacket designs.

41 Hoover, Cynthia. Music Machines—American Style; A Catalog of an Exhibition. Washington: Smithsonian Institution Press; distr. by Govt. Print. Off., 1971. 139p. illus. bibliog.
The exhibition portrayed the development of music machines from cylinders and player pianos to Moog synthesizers, and the effect of technology on performers and audiences.

42 Horn, David. The Literature of American Music in Books and Folk Music Collections: A Fully Annotated Bibliography. Metuchen, NJ: Scarecrow, 1977. 556p.
    A detailed listing of 1,696 books considered essential for a library on all aspects of American music: folk, country, blues, rock, musical stage, soul, jazz, etc. Strong annotations.

43 Horstman, Dorothy A., comp. Sing Your Heart Out, Country Boy. New York: Dutton, 1975. 394p. bibliog. discog. lyrics.
    An analysis of 300 country songs, arranged mainly by the original lyricist.

44 Howard, John Tasker, and George Kent Bellows. A Short History of Music in America. New York: Crowell, 1967. 496p. illus. bibliog. notes.
    A brief history that surveys folk, classical, spirituals, recorded music, and musical comedy.

45 Howes, Frank Stewart. Folk Music of Britain—and Beyond. London: Methuen, 1969. 307p.

46 Jasen, David A. Recorded Ragtime, 1897-1958. Hamden, CT: Archon, 1973. 155p. discog.
    This is an index to recorded ragtime, by composer and performer, with the normal discographical information (release label number, dates, and so forth). Coverage is limited to 78 rpm records only.

47 Kahn, Kathy. Hillbilly Women. Garden City, NY: Doubleday, 1973. 151p. paper only.

48 Karples, Maud. Cecil Sharp; His Life and Work. Chicago: University of Chicago Press, 1967. 228p. illus. bibliog.

49 Karples, Maud, ed. Cecil Sharp's Collection of English Folk Songs. New York: Oxford University Press, 1974. 2v. (1412 pages).

50 Laing, David, ed. The Electric Muse; The Story of Folk into Rock. London: Methuen, 1975. 182p. illus. discog. paper only.
    Coverage of the folk revivals in both England and the United States, plus the electric folk of Dylan, the Byrds, Fairport Convention, and Steeleye Span.

51 Lawless, Ray M. Folksingers and Folksongs in America; A Handbook, Biography, Bibliography, and Discography. New ed. New York: Meredith, 1965. 750p. illus. bibliog. discog.
    Evaluates some 300 songbooks and 700 albums (1948+)—with title listings, instruments, societies, and festivals.

52 Laws, G. Malcolm. Native American Balladry; A Descriptive Study and Bibliographical Syllabus. Rev. ed. Philadelphia, PA: American Folklore Society, 1964. 298p. bibliog.
    Classifications of event songs in America.

53 Lee, Edward. Music of the People; A Study of Popular Music in Great Britain. London: Barrie & Jenkins, 1970. 274p.

54　Lloyd, A. L. Folk Song in England. New York: International Publishers, 1967. 433p.

Examines the relationship of the evolution of English folk song and revolution in English society (ritual song to epic song to industrial song).

55　Lomax, Alan. Folk Song Style and Culture. Washington: American Association for the Advancement of Science, 1968. 363p. bibliog.

Stylistic aspects of folk songs are described in the context of sociological data, and they are related to social structure.

56　Lomax, Alan, ed. The Folk Songs of North America in the English Language. Garden City, NY: Doubleday, 1960. 623p. illus. bibliog. discog.

57　Malone, Bill C. Country Music, U.S.A.; A Fifty Year History. Austin: University of Texas Press, 1968. illus. bibliog. discog.

The definitive, scholarly study of country music, tracing its development from English ballads, commercial rural music, cowboys and bluegrass, and the start of the urban country music through the Nashville sound. The golden years were up through 1954.

58　Malone, Bill C., and Judith McCulloh, eds. Stars of Country Music; Uncle Dave Macon to Johnny Rodriguez. Urbana: University of Illinois Press, 1975. 425p. illus. bibliog. discog.

59　Mellers, Wilfrid. Music in a New Found Land. London: Barrie and Rockliff, 1964.

Here is wide coverage of the American musical tradition, relating classics to blues to jazz to pop.

60　Mitsui, Toru. Bluegrass Music. 2d ed. rev. Tokyo: Bronze-Sha, 1975. 222p. illus.

The first and only scholarly book on bluegrass music. Unfortunately, the text is entirely in Japanese. It was originally published in 1967, and the edition here covers newer bands.

61　The Music Yearbook: A Survey and Directory with Statistics and Reference Articles. 1972– . New York: St. Martin's Press, 1973– . 750p. average length.

This annual is the most up-to-date source of information on British music and musicians. Survey articles cover all aspects of classical and popular music, with lists of books and periodicals, addresses of relevant record companies, associations, halls, museums, etc. The American equivalent is The Musician's Guide, from Music Information Service.

62　The Musician's Guide. 1954– . New York: Music Information Service, 1954– . (available every four years. Last edition: 1976).

The basic directory of music information for the United States. Sections include data on record collections, various recording awards such as the "Grammies," addresses of groups, books to read, and so forth. The British equivalent is the Music Yearbook.

63　Nettl, Bruno. Folk and Traditional Music of the Western Continents. Englewood Cliffs, NJ: Prentice-Hall, 1965. 213p. illus. bibliog. discog.

64 Nettl, Bruno. Folk Music in the United States. 3rd ed. Detroit, MI: Wayne State University Press, 1976. 187p.

65 New York Library Association. Children's and Young Adult Services Section. Records and Cassettes for Young Adults; A Selected List. New York, 1972. 52p. paper only. discog.
Categories include rock, soul, blues, jazz, country and western, and various non-musical records and cassettes. Useful for the "now" sounds of 1972.

66 Passman, Arnold. The Dee Jays. New York: Macmillan, 1971. 320p.
He traces the evolution of the "disc jockey" from 1909 to the underground FM stations in San Francisco, with good detail on how songs are selected for airplay.

67 Paul, Elliot. That Crazy American Music. Port Washington, NY: Kennikat Press, 1970. 317p. bibliog.
Originally published by Bobbs-Merrill in 1957.

68 Pleasants, Henry. The Great American Popular Singers. New York: Simon and Schuster, 1974. 384p. illus.
The author examines the vocal tradition in popular music, the phenomenon of imitation breeding imitation, the meaning of "art" as applied to popular music, and various evaluations of 22 innovators in the fields of jazz, musical stage, blues, gospel, country, soul, and so forth.

69 Popular Music Periodicals Index, 1973– . Comp. by Dean Tudor and Andrew Armitage. Metuchen, NJ: Scarecrow, 1974– .
An annual author-subject index to sixty or so periodicals utilizing a special thesaurus involving musical genres.

70 Price, Steven D. Old as the Hills; The Story of Bluegrass Music. New York: Viking, 1975. 256p. discog.
A short historical work that is largely biographical, also provides the names and addresses of bluegrass clubs, magazines, and record companies.

71 Recording Industry Association of America. The White House Record Library. Washington: White House Historical Association, 1973. 105p.
A catalog of 2,000 records presented to the White House in March 1973. Categories include popular, classical, jazz, folk, country, gospel, and spoken word.

72 Rolling Stone Magazine. The Rolling Stone Record Review. New York: Pocket Books, 1961. 556p. paper only.

Rolling Stone Magazine. The Rolling Stone Record Review. v.2. New York: Pocket Books, 1974. 599p. paper only.

73 Rooney, James. Bossmen; Bill Monroe and Muddy Waters. New York: Dial, 1971. 159p. illus. discog.
Espouses the belief that "bluegrass" and "urban blues" came from these two men and from the various musicians they had employed over the past thirty years.

74 Rosenberg, Neil V. Bill Monroe and His Bluegrass Boys; An Illustrated Discography. Nashville, TN: Country Music Foundation Press, 1974. 120p.

75 Rublowsky, John. Popular Music. New York: Basic Books, 1967. 164p.
    Emphasis is on country and western, rock, and current popular materials.

75a Russell, Tony. Blacks, Whites and Blues. New York: Stein and Day, 1970.
    112p. illus. bibliog. discog.
    Examines the relationships of black blues musicians and white musicians,
emphasizing their traditions and differences. In Britain, CBS released an accompanying record.

76 Rust, Brian. The Victor Master Book. v.2 (1925-1936). Hatch End, Middlesex,
    1969. 776p.
    A complete listing, in numerical order, of every popular music record issued
by RCA Victor between 1925-1936.

77 Sandberg, Larry, and Dick Weissman. The Folk Music Sourcebook. New
    York: Knopf, 1976. 260p. illus. bibliog. discog.
    A guide to North American folk music (blues, old time music, bluegrass,
ragtime, jazz, Canadian, ethnic): books, instruments, recordings, films, instructional materials, societies, etc. Essentially updates Lawless's Folksingers and
Folksongs in America (New York: Meredith, 1965).

78 Sarlin, Bob. Turn It Up (I Can't Hear the Words); The Best of the New Singer/
    Songwriters. New York: Simon and Schuster, 1974. 222p. illus.
    A critique of the lyrics of troubador singing from the early 1970s.

79 Schafer, William J., and Johannes Riedel. The Art of Ragtime; Form and
    Meaning of an Original Black American Art. Baton Rouge: Louisiana State
    University Press, 1972. 249p. illus. bibliog. music.
    A more formal study that duplicates to some extent the Blesh and Janis
work.

80 Schicke, C. A. Revolution in Sound: A Biography of the Recording Industry.
    Boston: Little, Brown, 1974. 238p.
    A history of the recording industry, covering all forms of influences and
manipulation.

81 Scott, John Anthony. The Ballad of America; The History of the United
    States in Song and Story. New York: Grosset & Dunlap, 1967. 403p.

82 Seeger, Pete. The Incompleat Folksinger. New York: Simon and Schuster,
    1972. 596p. illus. bibliog. discog.
    A series of reprinted articles from diverse sources (mainly Sing Out!),
dealing with every conceivable aspect of folk, country, blues, and spiritual music,
including international music. Seeger's attitude toward folk music is well-known.

83 Shelton, Robert, and Burt Goldblatt. The Country Music Story; A Picture
    History of Country and Western Music. New Rochelle, NY: Arlington House,
    1971. 256p. illus.
    A general introduction that mainly provides a framework for the display of
about 370 photographs.

84 Shestack, Melvin. The Country Music Encyclopedia. New York: Thomas Y.
    Crowell, 1974. 410p. illus. discog.

84a Stambler, Irwin. Encyclopedia of Pop, Rock and Soul. New York: St. Martin's Press, 1975. 609p. illus.

85 Stambler, Irwin. Guitar Years; Pop Music from Country and Western to Hard Rock. Garden City, NY: Doubleday, 1970. 137p.
This short book is actually a compendium of bits and pieces dealing with guitar influences on music of the sixties.

86 Stambler, Irwin, and Grelun Landon. Encyclopedia of Folk, Country, and Western Music. New York: St. Martin's Press, 1969. 396p. discog.
About 500 entries for artists (most of them alive at the time of writing) plus extended lists of awards and records.

87 Strachwitz, Chris, ed. American Folk Music Occasional, No. 1 (from Arhoolie Records, 1964); No. 2 (from Oak Publications, 1970).
An irregular issue that lays stress on Strachwitz's interests: blues, Cajun music, chicano music, Austrian folk music.

88 Taubman, Howard, ed. The New York Times Guide to Listening Pleasure. New York: Macmillan, 1968. 328p. discog.
This is mainly a how-to guide for the novice record collector. A good two-thirds of the book deals with classical music; the balance concentrates on folk, jazz, Latin America, and the musical theater.

89 Tosches, Nick. Country; The Biggest Music in America. New York: McGraw-Hill, 1977. 224p. illus.
A readable account, tracing from the seventeenth century British ballad to the present day. Includes a chapter devoted to erotic records.

90 Townsend, Charles R. San Antonio Rose; The Life and Music of Bob Wills. Urbana: University of Illinois Press, 1976. 395p. illus. discog.

91 Tudor, Dean, and Andrew Armitage. "Best of the Year." LJ/SLJ Previews, April and May issues, 1974-1976.
A round-up of those years' best records, as reflected by the reviewing media.

92 U.S. Library of Congress. Checklist of Recorded Songs in the English Language in the Archive of American Folk Song to July, 1940. Washington: Govt. Print. Off., 1942. 3v.
This alphabetical list has a geographic index, and it is also available in one volume from Arno Press.

93 U.S. Library of Congress. Folk Music; A Catalog of Folk Songs, Ballads, Dances, Instrumental Pieces, and Folk Tales of the United States and Latin America on Phonorecords. Washington: Govt. Print. Off., 1964. 107p.

94 Wells, Evelyn Kendrick. The Ballad Tree; A Study of British and American Ballads, Their Folklore, Verse and Music. London: Methuen, 1950. 370p. illus. bibliog.
Discusses work by both Child and Sharp, with sixty musical examples.

95 Whitburn, Joel. Top Country and Western Records, 1949-1971. Menomonee Falls, WI: Record Research, 1972. 152p.
Arrangement is alphabetical by artist, and all tunes must have appeared on the Billboard charts. Annual supplements are available from the compiler.

96 White, John I. Git Along, Little Dogies; Songs and Songmakers of the American West. Urbana: University of Illinois Press, 1975. 224p. illus. discog.

97 Wilder, Alec. American Popular Song; The Great Innovators, 1900-1950. New York: Oxford University Press, 1972. 536p. illus.
   A study of important songs, grouped by their composers. Wilder believes that songwriting has deteriorated since 1950.

98 Wilgus, D. K. Anglo-American Folksong Scholarship since 1898. New Brunswick, NJ: Rutgers University Press, 1959. 466p. bibliog. discog.
   A very influential book on origins and critiques of folk music, this includes 138 albums in its listing.

99 Williams, Peter. Bluff Your Way in Folk and Jazz. London: Wolfe, 1969. 64p. paper only.
   A sometimes funny, but unwittingly serious, guide to "instant erudition." There is a checklist of techniques, heroes, names, glossaries, and recordings to mention at the next cocktail party. A very good overview.

100 Wolfe, Charles K. The Grand Ole Opry; The Early Years, 1925-1935. London: Old Time Music, 1975. illus. discog.

PERIODICAL CITATIONS

For many of the same reasons as in the Book Citations section, periodical titles here are listed alphabetically, sequentially numbered, and keyed to references in the section discussing musical genres. Periodicals come and go in the popular music world, depending on interests, finances, and subscriptions sold, and much valuable information is thereby lost. The following 21 periodicals show some stability and should at least be around when this book is two years old; consequently prices are not noted, nor are street addresses given for foreign publications that tend to move around. The annotations give a physical description of their contents, but please refer to the music genre for more complete details on specific articles or discussions. In addition to periodicals listed, about 40 more are printed in the English language (all are indexed in *Popular Music Periodicals Index*, 1973- ; Scarecrow Press), about 75 more in non-English languages, and countless scores of fanzine and very specialized publications.

1   Black Music. 1974–. Monthly. Sutton, Surrey, England.
    A glossy but expertly edited magazine concerned with blues, rhythm 'n' blues, soul, gospel, reggae, jazz, African music—all musical fields of interest to blacks. Good reviews of records and various current awareness services.

2   Bluegrass Unlimited. 1966– . Monthly. P.O. 111, Berke, VA 22015.
    Excellent articles on current performers plus record reviews. The oldest of the bluegrass magazines; this also has good concerts and festivals listings.

3   Contemporary Keyboard. 1975– . Bimonthly. P.O. Box 907, Saratoga, CA 95070.
    Emphasizes all aspects of keyboards (piano, organ, electronic music synthesizers, etc.) with reviews, articles on personalities in both popular and classical modes of music, plus performance tips and instructions.

4   Country Music. 1972– . Monthly. P.O. Box 2004, Rock Island, IL 61207.
    Popularly written articles about the many personalities in the country music world.

5   Country Music People. 1970– . Monthly. Sidcup, Kent, England.
    A British magazine that presents critical reviews and articles on all aspects of country music, including old time, western swing, instruments, etc.

6   Country Music Review. 1973– . Monthly. London, England.
    A British magazine that concentrates on the historical development of modern country music, with many articles on personalities from the 1930s, 40s, and 50s.

7   Guitar Player. 1967– . Monthly. 348 North Santa Cruz, Los Gatos, CA 95030.
    Emphasizes all aspects of guitars (bass, pedal, acoustic, electric, etc.) with reviews, articles on personalities in both popular and classical modes of music, plus performance instructional guidance.

8   High Fidelity. 1951– . Monthly. P.O. Box 14156, Cincinnati, OH 45214.
    A general magazine with slight coverage of popular music.

9   John Edwards Memorial Foundation. 1963– . Quarterly. Folklore and
    Mythology Center, University of California at Los Angeles, Los Angeles,
    CA 90024.
      A scholarly presentation of articles dealing with American folklore, old time
music, and early country music. Sections deal with discographies, commercial
graphics, histories of songs, etc.

10 Journal of American Folklore. 1888– . Quarterly. University of Texas
    Press, P.O. Box 7819, University Station, Austin, TX 78712.
      Scholarly articles and lengthy, comparative record and book reviews. Not
limited to music.

11 Journal of Country Music. 1970– . Quarterly. Country Music Foundation,
    700 - 16th Avenue South, Nashville, TN 37203.
      Devoted to interpretive articles treating subjects related to the country music
tradition (e.g., old time music, bluegrass, western swing, fiddle music, sacred
music, Anglo-American folk song, music research methodology, etc.).

12 Melody Maker. 1931– . Weekly. Sutton, Surrey, England.
      The best of the five British weeklies devoted to popular music. News, views,
and articles on rock, jazz, folk, blues, soul, reggae, country, etc. Unusually good
record veviews.

13 Micrography. 1968– . Quarterly. Alphen aan den Rijn, Netherlands.
      A new format in 1976 led to articles and discographic details concerning
the issuance of 78 rpms and air shots in the elpee format. A good service for tracking
down rare albums and duplications of tracks on reissued albums.

14 Mississippi Rag. 1974– . Monthly. P.O. Box 19068, Minneapolis, MN 55419.
      Subtitled "the voice of traditional jazz and ragtime." Good in-depth inter-
views and reviews, as well as historical articles and festival coverage.

15 Muleskinner News. 1970-1978. Monthly. Rt. 2, Box 304, Elon College, NC
    27244.
      Articles on bluegrass and old time music, favoring the in-depth interview
technique. Good record reviews. The March issue was an annual directory of people
in the whole bluegrass business. In October 1978, it became *Music City* and now
covers mainly country music.

16 Old Time Music. 1971– . Quarterly. London, England.
      Superb coverage of early American country music, with interviews, historical
articles, transcriptions, discographies, etc. Emphasis on string band music and duos,
plus some bluegrass.

17 Pickin'. 1974– . Monthly. 1 Saddle Road, Cedar Knolls, NJ 07927.
      Covers bluegrass and old time music, but concentrates on the performing
musician-fan, with articles on instruction, instruments, interviews.

18 Popular Music and Society. 1971– . Quarterly. 318 South Grove Street,
    Bowling Green, OH 43402.
      An interdisciplinary journal "concerned with music in the broadest sense
of the term." Scholarly articles.

19 Rolling Stone. 1968– . Biweekly. 625 Third Street, San Francisco, CA 94107.

America's strongest youth culture magazine, describing music as a way of life. Very opinionated, but only about one-third of it is now solely music.

20 Sing Out! 1950– . Bimonthly. 595 Broadway, New York, NY 10012.

News and articles on folk, blues and bluegrass, plus some ethnic articles. Very influential in the first fifteen years of its existence, with songs, some commentaries, transcriptions, etc.

21 Stereo Review. 1958– . Monthly. P.O. Box 2771, Boulder, CO 80302.

A general magazine favoring audio equipment, classical music, and popular music about equally.

DIRECTORY OF LABELS AND STARRED RECORDS

This directory presents, in alphabetical order, the names and addresses of all the American manufacturers of long-playing records cited in this set of books. Similarly, the starred records from all four volumes are listed here, not simply those for the present volume. British, Japanese, Swedish, French, Danish, etc., records can be obtained from specialist stores or importers. Other information here includes some indication of the types of popular music that each firm is engaged in and a listing in label numerical order of all the starred (special importance) records as indicated in the text, along with the entry number for quick reference. For this reason, starred foreign discs are also included in this directory/listing. This directory notes the latest **issuance** of a disc. Some albums may have been reissued from other labels, and they will be found under the label of the latest release. **In all cases, please refer to the main text.** Cross-references are made here where appropriate, especially for "family" names within a label's corporate ownership. To expedite filing and ease of retrieval, this listing of records follows the **numerical order of each label's issues**, ignoring the alphabetical initialisms.

A & M, 1416 North LaBrea Avenue, Hollywood, CA 90028
  specialty: general rock and pop

  SP 4245—Herb Alpert. Greatest Hits. P3.1
  SP 4251—Jimmy Cliff. Wonderful World, Beautiful People. B5.7a
  SP 4257—Fairport Convention. Liege and Lief. F2.49
  SP 4519—Cat Stevens. Greatest Hits. F10.90

ABC, 8255 Beverly Blvd., Los Angeles, CA 90048
  specialty: general

  S 371—Paul Anka. R2.15
  490X—Ray Charles. A Man and His Soul. two discs. B2.40
  654—Impressions. Best. B4.9
  724—B. B. King. Live at the Regal. B1.296
  780—Curtis Mayfield. His Early Years with the Impressions. two discs. B4.11
  781/2—Ray Charles. Modern Sounds in Country and Western Music.
    2 discs. B4.26
  ABCX 1955-1963—Rock 'n' Soul; The History of the Pre-Beatles Decade
    of Rock, 1953-1963. 9 discs. R2.12

Ace of Clubs (English issue)
  specialty: older popular music, jazz

  ACL 1153—Spike Hughes and His All-American Orchestra. J4.47
  ACL 1158—Django Reinhardt and Stephane Grappelli. J6.113

Ace of Hearts (English issue). recently deleted
  specialty: MCA reissues (all forms of popular music)

  AH 21—Andrews Sisters. P2.145
  AH 28—Jack Teagarden. Big T's Jazz. J3.91

Ace of Hearts (cont'd)
    AH 58–Carter Family. A Collection of Favourites. F5.108
    AH 112–Carter Family. More Favourites. F5.111
    AH 119–Jimmy Rushing. Blues I Love to Sing. B1.426
    AH 135–Uncle Dave Macon. F5.31
    AH 168–Jack Teagarden. "J.T." J3.92

Adelphi, P. O. Box 288, Silver Spring, MD 20907
    specialty: blues, folk

Advent, P. O. Box 635, Manhattan Beach, CA 90266
    specialty: blues music

    2803–Johnny Shines. B1.359

Ahura Mazda (c/o Southern Record Sales)
    specialty: blues

    AMS 2002–Robert Pete Williams. B1.130

All Platinum, 96 West Street, Englewood, NJ 07631
    specialty: blues and soul, mainly from the Chess catalog which it
    purchased; see also CHESS records

    2ACMB 201–Howlin' Wolf. A.K.A. Chester Burnett. two discs. B1.284
    2ACMB 202–Little Walter. Boss Blues Harmonica. two discs. B1.297
    2ACMB 203–Muddy Waters. A.K.A. McKinley Morganfield. two discs.
    B1.303

Alligator, P.O. Box 11741, Fort Dearborn Station, Chicago, IL 60611
    specialty: blues

    AL 4706–Koko Taylor. I Got What It Takes. B1.407

Angel, 1750 N. Vine Street, Hollywood, CA 90028
    specialty: classical and classical interpretations of popular music

    S 36060–New England Conservatory Ragtime Ensemble. Scott Joplin:
    The Red Back Book. J2.28

Antilles, 7720 Sunset Blvd., Los Angeles, CA 90046
    specialty: folk and pop

    AN 7017–Shirley Collins and the Albion Country Band. No Roses. F2.47

Apple, 1750 N. Vine Street, Hollywood, CA 90028
    specialty: rock

    SKBO 3403/4–The Beatles. 1962-1970. four discs. R4.3/4.

Argo (English issue)
    specialty: folk (British), classical, spoken word

    ZDA 66-75–Ewan MacColl and Peggy Seeger. The Long Harvest. ten discs.
    F2.23

Arhoolie, 10341 San Pablo Avenue, El Cerrito, CA 94530
  specialty: blues, old time music, ethnic music

  1001—Mance Lipscomb, Texas Sharecropper and Songster. B1.213
  1007—Mercy Dee Walton. B1.369
  1008—Alex Moore. B1.228
  1021—Fred McDowell. Delta Blues. B1.120
  1027—Fred McDowell. volume 2. B1.119
  1028—Big Mama Thornton. In Europe. B1.408
  1036—Juke Boy Bonner. I'm Going Back to the Country Where They Don't
    Burn the Buildings Down. B1.146
  1038—Clifton Chenier. Black Snake Blues. B1.324
  1066—Earl Hooker. His First and Last Recordings. B1.279
  2003—Lowell Fulson. B1.332
  2004—Joe Turner. Jumpin' the Blues. B1.431
  2007—Lightnin' Hopkins. Early Recordings, v.1. B1.182
  2010—Lightnin' Hopkins. Early Recordings, v.2. B1.182
  2011—Robert Pete Williams. Angola Prisoner's Blues. B1.131
  2012—Prison Worksongs. B1.55
  2015—Robert Pete Williams. Those Prison Blues. B1.134
  5011—Snuffy Jenkins. Carolina Bluegrass. F6.82

Arista, 6 West 57th St., New York, NY 10019
  specialty: rock, jazz, pop

  B 6081—The Monkees. Re-Focus R3.20

Asch *See* Folkways

Asylum, 962 N. LaCienega, Los Angeles, CA 90069

  SD 5068—Eagles. Desperado. R7.12
  7E-1017—Jackson Browne. Late for the Sky. F10.3

Atco, 75 Rockefeller Plaza, New York, NY 10019
  specialty: blues, rock, soul, rhythm 'n' blues

  SD 33-226—Buffalo Springfield. Again. R7.6
  SD33-259—Jerry Jeff Walker. Mr. Bojangles. F10.92
  SD33-266—King Curtis. Best. B4.44
  SD33-291—Cream. Best. R8.1
  SD33-292—Bee Gees. Best, v.1. R4.22
  SD33-371—The Coasters. Their Greatest Recordings: The Early Years. B2.27
  SD33-372—LaVern Baker. Her Greatest Recordings. B2.71
  SD33-373—Chuck Willis. His Greatest Recordings. B2.70
  SD33-374—The Clovers. Their Greatest Recordings. B2.26
  SD33-375—The Drifters. Their Greatest Recordings: The Early Years. B2.31
  SD33-376—Joe Turner. His Greatest Recordings. B1.430
  2SA-301—Otis Redding. Best. two discs. B4.28
  SD2-501—Wilson Pickett. Best. two discs. B4.27
  SD2-803—Eric Clapton. History. two discs. R5.16

Atlantic, 75 Rockefeller Plaza, New York, NY 10019
    specialty: jazz, blues, rock, soul, rhythm 'n' blues
        1224—Lennie Tristano. Line Up. J5.87
        1234—Joe Turner. The Boss of the Blues. B1.428
        1237—Charles Mingus. Pithecanthropus Erectus. J5.128
        1238—Jimmy Giuffre. Clarinet. J5.90
        1305—Charles Mingus. Blues and Roots. J5.125
        1317—Ornette Coleman. The Shape of Jazz to Come. J5.112
        1327—Ornette Coleman. Change of the Century. J5.108
        1353—Ornette Coleman. This Is Our Music. J5.113
        1357—Lennie Tristano. New. J5.88
        1364—Ornette Coleman. Free Jazz. J5.109
        1378—Ornette Coleman. Ornette. J5.110
        SD 1429—Modern Jazz Quartet and Laurindo Almeida. Collaboration. P3.15
        SD 1588—Ornette Coleman. Twins. J5.150
        S 1594—Roberta Flack. Quiet Fire. B4.64
        SD 1598—Gary Burton. Alone at Last. J5.143
        SD 1613—Turk Murphy. The Many Faces of Ragtime. J2.26
        SD 1614—Billie Holiday. Strange Fruit. J6.123
        SD 1639—Art Ensemble of Chicago. J5.136
        SD 1652—Modern Jazz Quartet. Blues on Bach. P3.14
        SD 7200—Crosby, Stills, Nash and Young. Déjà Vu. R7.10
        SD 7213—Aretha Franklin. Young, Gifted and Black. B4.67
        SD 7224—Blind Willie McTell. Atlanta Twelve String. B1.125
        SD 7225—Professor Longhair. New Orleans Piano. B2.67
        SD 7262—Willie Nelson. Shotgun Willie. F8.119
        SD 7271—Roberta Flack. Killing Me Softly. B4.63
        SD 7291—Willie Nelson. Phases and Stages. F8.118
        SD 8004—Ruth Brown. Rock & Roll. B2.73
        SD 8020—T-Bone Walker. T-Bone Blues. B1.315
        SD 8029—Ray Charles. What'd I Say. B2.41
        SD 8054—Ray Charles. Greatest. B2.39
        SD 8153—The Drifters. Golden Hits. B2.30
        SD 8161/4—History of Rhythm 'n' Blues, v.1-4. four discs. B2.13
        SD 8176—Aretha Franklin. Lady Soul. B4.66
        SD 8193/4—History of Rhythm 'n' Blues, v. 5-6. two discs. B4.3
        SD 8202—Booker T. and the MGs. Best. B4.8
        SD 8208/9—History of Rhythm 'n' Blues. v. 7-8. two discs. B4.3
        SD 8218—Sam and Dave. Best. B4.30
        SD 8236—Led Zeppelin. II. R8.8
        SD 8255—Champion Jack Dupree. Blues from the Gutter. B1.329
        SD 8289—Marion Williams. Standing Here Wondering Which Way to Go. B3.66
        SD 8296—John Prine. F10.82
        SD 18204—Aretha Franklin. 10 Years of Gold. B4.65
        SD2-305—Chick Corea. Inner Space. two discs. J6.128
        SD2-306/7—The Tenor Sax: The Commodore Years. four discs. J6.8
        SD2-316—Jazz Years; 25th Anniversary. two discs. J5.101

Atlantic (cont'd)
>SD2-700—Cream. Wheels of Fire. two discs. R8.3
>SD2-904—Carmen McRae. The Great American Songbook. two discs. P2.77
>SD2-906—Aretha Franklin. Amazing Grace. two discs. B3.39
>MM4-100—Mabel Mercer. A Tribute to Mabel Mercer on the Occasion of Her 75th Birthday. four discs. P2.78

Atteiram, P.O. Box 418, 2871 Janquil Drive, Smyrna, GA 30080
>specialty: bluegrass

Audiofidelity, 221 W. 57th Street, New York, NY 10019
>specialty: folk, jazz

Basf, 221 W. 57th Street, New York, NY 10019
>specialty: jazz

Bandstand (c/o Southern Record Sales)
>specialty: big bands
>
>7106—Screwballs of Swingtime. P4.3

Barclay (France)
>specialty: general
>
>920067—Stuff Smith and Stephane Grappelli. Stuff and Steff. J4.148

Barnaby, 816 N. LaCienega Blvd., Los Angeles, CA 90069
>specialty: rock and roll
>
>BR 4000/1—Cadence Classics, v. 1-2. two discs. R2.3
>BR 6006—Everly Brothers. Greatest Hits. two discs. R2.18

Barnaby/Candid (recently deleted from CBS)
>specialty: jazz, blues
>
>Z 30246—Otis Spann. Is the Blues. B1.310
>Z 30247—Lightnin' Hopkins. In New York. B1.183
>Z 30562—Cecil Taylor. Air. J5.132
>KZ 31034—Charles Mingus. The Candid Recordings. J5.126
>KZ 31290—Otis Spann. Walking the Blues. B1.311

Bear Family (West Germany)
>specialty: old time music
>
>FV 12.502—Jules Allen. The Texas Cowboy. F7.19
>FV 15.507—Dock Walsh. F5.79

Bearsville, 3300 Warner Blvd., Burbank, CA 91505
>specialty: rock

Bell, 6 West 57th Street, New York, NY 10019
specialty: general pop

1106—The Fifth Dimension. Greatest Hits on Earth. P2.137

Biograph, 16 River Street, Chatham, NY 12037
specialty: jazz, blues, popular

BLP C3—Boswell Sisters. 1932-1935. P2.135
BLP C4—Mississippi John Hurt. 1928: His First Recordings. B1.190
BLP C7/8—Ted Lewis. 1926-1933, v. 1-2. two discs. P5.13
BLP 1008Q—Scott Jopkin. Ragtime, v. 2. J2.10
BLP 12003—Blind Blake. v.1. B1.145
BLP 12005—Chicago Jazz, 1923-1929, v. 1. J3.63
BLP 12022—Ethel Waters. Jazzin' Babies Blues, v. 1. B1.411
BLP 12023—Blind Blake. v.2. B1.145
BLP 12026—Ethel Waters. v.2. B1.411
BLP 12029—Skip James, Early Recordings. B1.198
BLP 12031—Blind Blake. v.3. B1.145
BLP 12037—Blind Blake. v.4. B1.145
BLP 12043—Chicago Jazz, 1923-1929, v.2. J3.63
BLP 12050—Blind Blake. v.5. B1.145

Birchmount (Canada)
specialty: country and popular

BM 705—Hank Williams. In the Beginning. F8.41

Black Lion, 221 West 57th Street, New York, NY 10019
specialty: jazz and blues

BL 173—Barney Kessel and Stephane Grappelli. Limehouse Blues. J6.106

Black Lion (England)
specialty: jazz and blues

BLP 30147—Jimmy Witherspoon. Ain't Nobody's Business! B1.433

Blue Goose, 245 Waverly Place, New York, NY 10014
specialty: blues, jazz

Blue Horizon (England) recently deleted
specialty: blues

7-63222—Otis Rush. This One's a Good 'Un. B1.357
7-63223—Magic Sam. 1937-1969. B1.346

Blue Note, 6920 Sunset Blvd., Hollywood, CA 90028
specialty: jazz and blues

BST 81201/2—Sidney Bechet. Jazz Classics, v.1-2. two discs. J3.20
BST 81503/4—Bud Powell. Amazing, v.1-2. two discs. J5.31
BST 81505/6—J. J. Johnson. The Eminent, v.1-2. two discs. J5.64

Blue Note (cont'd)
    BST 81518—Horace Silver with the Jazz Messengers. J5.36
    BST 81521/2—Art Blakey. A Night at Birdland. two discs. J5.9
    BST 84003—Art Blakey. Moanin'. J5.8
    BST 84008—Horace Silver. Finger Poppin'. J5.35
    BST 84067—Jackie McLean. Bluesnik. J5.66
    BST 84077—Dexter Gordon. Doin' All Right. J5.56
    BST 84163—Eric Dolphy. Out to Lunch. J5.155
    BST 84194—Wayne Shorter. Speak No Evil. J5.161
    BST 84237—Cecil Taylor. Unit Structures. J5.135
    BST 84260—Cecil Taylor. Conquistador. J5.133
    BST 84346—Thad Jones—Mel Lewis Orchestra. Consummation. J4.171
    BNLA 158/160—Blue Note's Three Decades of Jazz, v.1-3. six discs. J1.6
    BNLA 401-H—Sonny Rollins. 2 discs. J5.76
    BNLA 456—H2—Lester Young. Aladdin Sessions. two discs. J4.124
    BNLA 507—H2—Fats Navarro. Prime Source. two discs. J5.26
    BNLA 533—H2—T-Bone Walker. Classics of Modern Blues. two discs. B1.313
    BNLA 579—H2—Thelonious Monk. Complete Genius. two discs. J5.24

Blues Classics, 10341 San Pablo Ave., El Cerrito, CA 94530
    specialty: blues, gospel

    BC 1—Memphis Minnie, v.1. B1.388
    BC 2—The Jug, Jook and Washboard Bands. B1.414
    BC 3—Sonny Boy Williamson, No. 1., v.1. B1.136
    BC 4—Peetie Wheatstraw. B1.253
    BC 5/7—Country Blues Classics, v.1-3. B1.14
    BC 9—Sonny Boy Williamson, No. 2. The Original. B1.318
    BC 11—Blind Boy Fuller. B1.168a
    BC 12—Detroit Blues: The Early 1950s. B1.58
    BC 13—Memphis Minnie, v.2. B1.388
    BC 14—Country Blues Classics, v.4. B1.14
    BC 16—Texas Blues: The Early 50s. B1.101
    BC 17/19—Negro Religious Music, v.1-3. three discs. B3.17
    BC 20—Sonny Boy Williamson, No. 1., v.2. B1.136
    BC 24—Sonny Boy Williamson, No. 1., v.3. B1.136

Blues on Blues (c/o Southern Records Sales) recently deleted
    specialty: blues

Bluesville (recently deleted)
    specialty: blues

    BV 1044—Lonnie Johnson and Victoria Spivey. Idle Hours. B1.208

Bluesway See ABC

Boogie Disease, Box 10925, St. Louis, MO 63135
    specialty: blues

Boogie Woogie (c/o Southern Records Sales)
  specialty: jazz and blues

  BW 1002–Meade Lux Lewis. J6.94

Brunswick (recently deleted); see also MCA
  specialty: jazz and soul

  BL 754185–Jackie Wilson. Greatest Hits. B4.32

Buddah, 810 Seventh Ave., New York, NY 10019
  specialty: pop, soul, gospel

  2009–Staple Singers. Best. B3.54
  BDS 5070–Edwin Hawkins Singers. Oh Happy Day. B3.40
  BDS 5665-2–Steve Goodman. Essential. two discs. F10.58

CBS, 51 West 52nd Street, New York, NY 10019
  specialty: general; formerly known as Columbia

  CL 997–Count Basie. One O'Clock Jump. J4.17
  CL 1098–The Sound of Jazz. J1.22
  CL 1228–Jo Stafford. Greatest Hits. P2.79
  CL 1230–Rosemary Clooney. Rosie's Greatest Hits. P2.96
  CL 1780–James P. Johnson. Father of the Stride Piano. J6.30
  CL 2604–Sophie Tucker. The Last of the Red Hot Mamas. P2.130.
  CL 2639–Chick Webb. Stompin' at the Savoy. J4.52
  CL 2830–Paul Whiteman. P5.19
  CS 1065–Bill Monroe. 16 All Time Greatest Hits. F6.41
  CS 1034–Roy Acuff. Greatest Hits. F8.17
  CS 8004–Mitch Miller. Sing Along with Mitch. P2.139
  CS 8158–Marty Robbins. Gunfighter Ballads and Trail Songs. F7.30
  PC 8163–Miles Davis. Kind of Blue. J5.151
  PC 8271–Miles Davis. Sketches of Spain. J5.85
  CS 8638–Mitch Miller. Mitch's Greatest Hits. P2.138
  CS 8639–Marty Robbins. Greatest Hits. R1.17
  CS 8807–Barbra Streisand. P2.126
  CS 8845–Lester Flatt and Earl Scruggs. Carnegie Hall. F6.28
  KCS 8905–Bob Dylan. The Times They Are A-Changin'. F10.19
  PC 9106–Miles Davis. My Funny Valentine. J5.153
  KCS 9128–Bob Dylan. Bringing It Back Home. F10.14
  PC 9428–Miles Davis. Milestones. J5.152
  KCS 9463–Bob Dylan. Greatest Hits, v.1. F10.16
  CS 9468–18 King Size Country Hits. F8.11
  CS 9478–Johnny Cash. Greatest Hits, v.1. F8.19
  G 31224–Count Basie. Super Chief. two discs. J4.18
  KG 31345–Johnny Mathis. All Time Greatest Hits. two discs. P2.13
  PC 31350–Simon and Garfunkel. Greatest Hits. F10.46
  KC 31352–Weather Report. I Sing the Body Electric. J6.138
  KG 31361–Marty Robbins. All Time Greatest Hits. two discs. F8.78
  KG 31364–Ray Price. All Time Greatest Hits. two discs. F8.76

CBS (cont'd)

    KG 31379—Mahalia Jackson. Great. two discs. B3.42

    KG 31547—Benny Goodman. All Time Hits. two discs. J4.58

    KG 31564—Eddie Condon's World of Jazz. two discs. J3.66

    KG 31571—Ethel Waters. Greatest Years. two discs. P2.86

    KG 31588—Percy Faith. All Time Greatest Hits. two discs. P5.79

    KG 31595—The Gospel Sound, v.2. two discs. B3.9

    G 31617—Teddy Wilson All Stars. two discs. J4.122

    KC 31758—Earl Scruggs. Live at Kansas State. F6.124

    KG 32064—Duke Ellington. Presents Ivie Anderson. two discs. P5.10

    KG 32151—Precious Lord; Gospel Songs of Thomas A. Dorsey. two discs.
       B3.19

    KC 32284—Clifford Brown. The Beginning and the End. J5.38

    KG 32338—Luis Russell. His Louisiana Swing Orchestra. two discs. J4.85

    KG 32355—A Jazz Piano Anthology. two discs. J6.12

    KG 32416—Bob Wills. Anthology. two discs. F7.48

    G 32593—Cab Calloway. Hi De Ho Man. two discs. P5.23

    KG 32663—Gene Krupa. His Orchestra and Anita O'Day. two discs. P5.36

    KC 32708—The Original Boogie Woogie Piano Giants. J6.91

    KG 32822—Benny Goodman and Helen Forrest. two discs. P5.11

    KG 32945—The World of Swing. two discs. J4.11

    CG 33639—Johnny Cash. At Folsom Prison and San Quentin. two discs.
       F8.18

    C2-33682—Bob Dylan. Basement Tapes. two discs. F10.12

    C 33882—Lefty Frizzell. Remembering the Greatest Hits. F8.57

    CS 9533—Leonard Cohen. Songs. F10.6

    CS 9576—The Byrds. Greatest Hits. R7.7

    KCS 9604—Bob Dylan. John Wesley Harding. F10.18

    PC 9633—Miles Davis. Miles Ahead. J5.83

    CS 9655—Art Tatum. Piano Starts Here. J6.38

    CS 9660—Ballads and Breakdowns of the Golden Era. F5.1

    CS 9670—The Byrds. Sweetheart of the Rodeo. R7.8

    KCS 9737—Laura Nyro. New York Tendaberry. F10.80

    LE 10043—Lester Flatt and Earl Scruggs. Foggy Mountain Banjo. F6.29

    LE 10106—Little Jimmie Dickens. Greatest Hits. F8.53

    G 30008—The Story of the Blues, v.1. two discs. B1.17

    G 30009—Big Bands Greatest Hits, v.1. two discs. P5.2

    C 30036—Bukka White. Parchman Farm. B1.257

    G 30126—Bessie Smith. Any Woman's Blues. two discs. B1.394

    KC 30130—Santana. Abraxas. R4.42

    KC 30322—Janis Joplin. Pearl. R5.20

    G 30450—Bessie Smith. Empty Bed Blues. two discs. B1.395

    C 30466—Maynard Ferguson. M. F. Horn. J4.168

    C 30496—Leroy Carr. Blues Before Sunrise. B1.107

    G 30503—Great Hits of R & B. two discs. B2.12

    C 30584—Earl Scruggs. Family and Friends. F6.122

    G 30592—The Fifties Greatest Hits. two discs. P1.5

    G 30628—Charles Mingus. Better Get It in Your Soul. two discs. J5.124

    G 30818—Bessie Smith. The Empress. two discs. B1.396

CBS (cont'd)

    KC 30887–Johnny Cash. Greatest Hits, v.2. F8.19

    KC 31067–John McLaughlin. The Inner Mounting Flame. J6.137

    G 31086–The Gospel Sound, v.1. two discs. B3.9

    G 31093–Bessie Smith. Nobody's Blues But Mine. two discs. B1.397

    KC 31170–Blood, Sweat, and Tears. Hits. R4.9

    KG 31213–Big Bands Greatest Hits, v.2. two discs. P5.2

    KC 33894–George Morgan. Remembering. F8.103

    PC 34077–Leonard Cohen. Best. F10.5

    KG ———Robert Johnson. Complete. three discs. B1.110 (to be released).

    C4L 18–Thesaurus of Classic Jazz. four discs. J3.86

    C4L 19–Fletcher Henderson. A Study in Frustration, 1923-1938. four discs. J4.41

    C3L 21–Billie Holiday. Golden Years, v.1. three discs. J6.121

    C3L 22–Mildred Bailey. Her Greatest Performances, 1929-1946. three discs. P2.87

    C2L 24–Joe Venuti and Eddie Lang. Stringing the Blues. two discs. J3.98

    C3L 25–Woody Herman. The Thundering Herds. three discs. J4.46

    C2L 29–Gene Krupa. Drummin' Man. two discs. J4.71

    C3L 32–Jazz Odyssey: The Sound of Chicago. three discs. J3.67

    C3L 33–Jazz Odyssey: The Sound of Harlem. three discs. J3.83

    C3L 35–Original Sounds of the 20s. three discs. P1.9

    C3L 40–Billie Holiday. Golden Years, v.2. three discs. J6.121

    GP 26–Miles Davis. Bitches Brew. two discs. J6.131

    GP 33–Bessie Smith. The World's Greatest Blues Singer. two discs. B1.393

    O2L 160–Benny Goodman. Carnegie Hall Concert. two discs. J4.38

    C2S 823–Tony Bennett. At Carnegie Hall. two discs. P2.2

    C2S 841–Bob Dylan. Blonde on Blonde. two discs. F10.13

    C2S 847–Eubie Blake. The Eighty-Six Years of Eubie Blake. two discs. J2.9

CBS Canada

    specialty: general; formerly known as Columbia

CBS (England)

    specialty: general

    52538–Charlie Christian, v.1. J5.10

    52648–Big Bill Broonzy. Big Bill's Blues. B1.152

    52796–Blacks, Whites and Blues. F3.32

    52797–Recording the Blues. B1.20

    52798–Ma Rainey and the Classic Blues Singers. B1.375

    63288–Screening the Blues. B1.36

    66232–The Story of the Blues, v.2. two discs. B1.17

CBS (France)

    specialty: general

    62581–Charlie Christian, v.2. J5.10

    62853–Benny Goodman. Trio and Quartet, v.1. J4.96

CBS (France) (cont'd)

    62876—Teddy Wilson. Piano Solos. J6.41

    63052—Django Reinhardt. Paris, 1945. J6.116

    63086—Benny Goodman. Trio and Quartet, v.2. J4.96

    63092—Clarence Williams Blue Five, with Louis Armstrong and Sidney
        Bechet. J3.50

    64218—Rare Recordings of the Twenties, v.1. B1.381

    65379/80—Rare Recordings of the Twenties, v.2-3. B1.381

    65421—Rare Recordings of the Twenties, v.4. B1.381

    66310—Miles Davis. Essential. three discs. J5.122

    67264—Duke Ellington. Complete, v.1. two discs. J4.27

    68275—Duke Ellington. Complete, v.2. two discs. J4.27

    80089—Roy Eldridge. Little Jazz. J4.25

    88000—Duke Ellington. Complete, v.3. J4.27

    88001/4—Louis Armstrong. Very Special Old Phonography. eight discs.
        J3.17

    88031—Buck Clayton. 1953-1955. two discs. J4.157

    88035—Duke Ellington. Complete, v.4. two discs. J4.27

    88082—Duke Ellington. Complete, v.5. two discs. J4.27

    88129—Erroll Garner. Play It Again, Erroll. two discs. P3.8

    88137—Duke Ellington. Complete, v.6. two discs. J4.27

    88140—Duke Ellington. Complete, v.7. two discs. J4.27

    J 27—New York Scene in the 1940s. J3.85

CBS (Japan)

    specialty: general

    20 AP 13/4—Stanley Brothers, v.1-2. F6.54 and F9.73

Cadence (recently deleted); most available on *Barnaby* label.

    specialty: pop

    3061—Andy Williams. Million Seller Songs. P2.67

Cadet (recently deleted); see All Platinum

    specialty: rhythm 'n' blues and soul

    S 757—Ramsey Lewis. The "In" Crowd. B4.53

Caedmon, 505 Eighth Avenue, New York, NY 10018

    specialty: spoken word, educational, folk music

    TC 1142/6—Folksongs of Britain, v.1-5. five discs. F2.9

    TC 1162/4—Folksongs of Britain, v.6-8. three discs. F2.9

    TC 1224/5—Folksongs of Britain, v.9-10. two discs. F2.9

Camden *See* RCA

Cameo (recently deleted)

    specialty: pop, rock and roll

    P 7001—Chubby Checker. Twist. R2.16

Canaan, 4800 W. Waco Drive, Waco, TX 76703
    specialty: sacred

Capitol, 1750 N. Vine Street, Hollywood, CA 90028
    specialty: general (country, rock, mood)
      SKAO 143—Ferlin Husky. Best. F8.64
      SKAO 145—Buck Owens. Best, v.3. F8.75
      ST 294—Fred Neil. Everybody's Talkin'. F10.36
      DTBB 264—Jim and Jesse. 20 Great Songs. two discs. F6.33
      DKAO 377—Peggy Lee. Greatest. three discs. P2.75
      SW 425—The Band. Stage Fright. R7.5
      SM 650—Merle Travis. The Merle Travis Guitar. F8.37
      SM 756—Tennessee Ernie Ford. Hymns. F9.39
      ST 884/6—Country Hits of the 40s, 50s, and 60s. three discs. F8.9
      SM 1061—Louvin Brothers. The Family Who Prays. F9.49
      ST 1253—Jean Shepard. This Is F8.146
      ST 1312—Rose Maddox. The One Rose. F8.140
      ST 1380—Tennessee Ernie Ford. Sixteen Tons. F8.56
      ST 1388—Les Baxter. Best. P5.78
      T 1477—Ray Anthony. Hits. P5.77
      SWBO 1569—Judy Garland. At Carnegie Hall. two discs. P2.69
      SWCL 1613—Nat "King" Cole. Story. three discs. P2.5
      ST 2089—Hank Thompson. Golden Hits. F7.47
      ST 2105—Buck Owens. Best, v.1. F8.75
      ST 2180—Kingston Trio. Folk Era. three discs. F4.11
      ST 2373—Merle Haggard. Strangers. F8.111
      ST 2422—Beatles. Rubber Soul. R4.7
      ST 2576—Beatles. Revolver. R4.6
      ST 2585—Merle Haggard. Swinging Doors. F8.112
      DT 2601—Dean Martin. Best. P2.54
      SM 2662—Merle Travis. Best. F8.36
      STFL 2814—Frank Sinatra. Deluxe Set. six discs. P2.16
      ST 2897—Buck Owens. Best, v.2. F8.75
      SKAO 2939—Cannonball Adderley. Best. J6.126
      SKAO 2946—Al Martino. Best. P2.58
      DTCL 2953—Edith Piaf. Deluxe Set. P2.113
      SKAO 2955—The Band. Music from Big Pink. R7.3
      STCL 2988—Judy Garland. Deluxe Set. three discs. P2.70
      T 10457—Django Reinhardt. Best. J6.110
      M 11026—Miles Davis. Birth of the Cool. J5.82
      M 11029—Gerry Mulligan. Tentette. Walking Shoes. J5.97
      M 11058—Duke Ellington. Piano Reflections. J6.17a.
      M 11059—Tadd Dameron. Strictly Bebop. J5.14
      M 11060—Lennie Tristano. Crosscurrents. J5.86
      ST 11082—Merle Haggard. Best of the Best. F8.110
      ST 11177—Supersax Plays Bird. J5.5
      ST 11193—Louvin Brothers. The Great Gospel Singing of the Louvin
        Brothers. F9.50
      SKC 11241—Tex Ritter. An American Legend. three discs. F7.13

Capitol (cont'd)

    ST 11287–Gene Vincent. The Bop That Just Won't Stop (1956). R1.18

    ST 11308–Les Paul and Mary Ford. The World Is Still Waiting for the Sunrise. P2.112

    SVBO 11384–Beach Boys. Spirit of America. two discs. R3.3

    ST 11440–The Band. Northern Lights. R7.4

    SKBO 11537–The Beatles. Rock 'n' Roll Music. two discs. R3.4

    ST 11577–Glen Campbell. Best. F8.98

Capitol (Japan)

    ECR 8178–Rose Maddox. Sings Bluegrass. F6.87

Capricorn, 3300 Warner Blvd., Burbank, CA 91505

    specialty: rock

    2CP 0108–Duane Allman. An Anthology, v.1. two discs. R4.20

    2CP 0139–Duane Allman. An Anthology, v.2. two discs. R4.20

    2CP 0164–Allman Brothers Band. The Road Goes On Forever. two discs. R5.12a

Charisma (England)

    specialty: folk, rock

    CS 5–Steeleye Span. Individually and Collectively. F2.58

Charly (England)

    CR 300-012–Yardbirds, Featuring Eric Clapton. R5.12

    CR 300-013–Yardbirds, Featuring Jeff Bech. R5.12

    CR 300-014–Yardbirds, Featuring Jimmy Page. R5.12

Checker (recently deleted); see All Platinum

    specialty: rhythm 'n' blues, soul

    3002–Little Milton. Sings Big Blues. B2.60

Chess (recently deleted, but many copies still available); see All Platinum and Phonogram

    specialty: blues

    1483–Muddy Waters. Folk Singer. B1.302

    1514–Chuck Berry. Golden Decade, v.1. two discs. B2.37

    1553–Muddy Waters. They Call Me Muddy Waters. B1.304

    2CH 50027–Sonny Boy Williamson, No. 2. This Is My Story. two discs. B1.319

    2CH 50030–The Golden Age of Rhythm 'n' Blues. two discs. B2.10

    60023–Chuck Berry. Golden Decade, v.2. two discs. B2.37

    60028–Chuck Berry. Golden Decade, v.3. two discs. B2.37

Chiaroscuro, 221 W. 57th Street, New York, NY 10019

    specialty: jazz

    CR 101–Earl Hines. Quintessential Recording Sessions. J6.26

Chiaroscuro (cont'd)
      CR 106—Don Ewell. A Jazz Portrait of the Artist. J6.53
      CR 108—Eddie Condon. Town Hall Concerts, 1944/5. J3.71
      CR 113—Eddie Condon. Town Hall Concerts, 1944/5. J3.71
      CR 120—Earl Hines. Quintessential Continued. J6.25

Chrysalis, 1750 N. Vine Street, Hollywood, CA 90028
    specialty: folk, rock

      CHR 1008—Steeleye Span. Below the Salt. F2.57
      CHR 1119—Steeleye Span. Please to See the King. F2.59

Classic Jazz, 43 W. 61st Street, New York, NY 10023
    specialty: jazz

Classic Jazz Masters (Denmark)
    specialty: jazz

      CJM 2/10—Jelly Roll Morton. Library of Congress Recordings. nine discs.
        J3.27

Collectors Classics (c/o Southern Record Sales)
    specialty: bluegrass

      CC 1/2—Stanley Brothers, v.1-2. two discs. F6.55
      CC 3—Lonesome Pine Fiddlers. F6.85
      CC 6—Banjo Classics. F6.2

Columbia *See* CBS

Columbia (England)
    specialty: pop, mood
      SCX 6529—Shirley Bassey. Very Best. P2.90

Concert Hall (France)
    specialty: jazz, pop
      SJS 1268—Tribute to Fletcher Henderson. J4.12

Concord Jazz, P.O. Box 845, Concord, CA 94522
    specialty: jazz

Contact (recently deleted)
    specialty: jazz
      LP 2—Earl Hines. Spontaneous Explorations. J6.27

Contemporary, 8481 Melrose Place, Los Angeles, CA 90069
    specialty: jazz

Contour (England)
    specialty: pop, rock

    2870.388—Dell-Vikings. Come and Go With Me. R2.31

Coral, 100 Universal City Plaza, Universal City, CA 91608
    specialty: reissues of MCA material; general

    CXB 6—McGuire Sisters. Best. P2.151

Coral (England)
    specialty: reissues of MCA material; general

    COPS 7453—Gospel Classics. B3.7
    CDMSP 801—Bing Crosby. Musical Autobiography. five discs. P2.11

Coral (West Germany)
    specialty: reissues of MCA material; general

    COPS 6855—Roy Eldridge. Swing Along with Little Jazz. two discs. J4.26
    COPS 7360—The Bands Within the Bands. two discs. J4.91

Cotillion, 75 Rockefeller Plaza, New York, NY 10019
    specialty: rock, contemporary folk

    SD2-400—Woodstock Two. two discs. R4.2
    SD3-500—Woodstock Three. three discs. R4.2

Country Music History (West Germany)
    specialty: old time music

    CMH 211—Jenks "Tex" Carman. The Dixie Cowboy. F7.24

County, Box 191, Floyd, VA 24091
    specialty: old time music, bluegrass

    402—Delmore Brothers. Brown's Ferry Blues, 1933-1941. F8.21
    404—Wade Mainer. F5.90
    405—The Hillbillies. F5.85
    505—Charlie Poole, v.1. F5.69
    506—Gid Tanner, v.1. F5.76
    509—Charlie Poole, v.2. F5.69
    511—Mountain Blues, 1927-1934. F5.15
    515—Mountain Banjo Songs and Tunes. F5.19
    516—Charlie Poole, v.3. F5.69
    518/20—Echoes of the Ozarks, v.1-3. three discs. F5.21
    521—Uncle Dave Macon. Early Recordings, 1925-1935. F5.35
    524—DaCosta Woltz's Southern Broadcasters. F5.61
    526—Gid Tanner, v.2. F5.76
    536—Kessinger Brothers. 1928-1930. F5.114
    540—Charlie Poole, v.4. F5.69
    541/2—Grand Ole Opry Stars. two discs. F8.13
    714—Kenny Baker and Joe Greene. High Country. F6.67
    729—Lilly Brothers. Early Recordings. F6.35

County (cont'd)
>   733—Clark Kessinger. Legend. F5.62
>   738—Stanley Brothers. That Little Old Country Church House. F9.76
>   742—Lilly Brothers. What Will I Leave Behind. F9.48
>   749—Springtime in the Mountains. F6.18

Creative World, 1012 S. Robertson Blvd., Los Angeles, CA 90035
>   specialty: progressive jazz, Stan Kenton

>   ST 1030—Stan Kenton. The Kenton Era. four discs. J4.173

Davis Unlimited, Route 11, 16 Bond Street, Clarksville, TN 37040
>   specialty: country, bluegrass, old time music

>   DU 33015—Fiddlin' Doc Roberts. Classic Fiddle Tunes Recorded during the
>   Golden Age. F5.99
>   DU 33030—Vernon Dalhart. Old Time Songs, 1925-1930, v.1. F5.29a

Dawn Club (c/o Southern Record Sales)
>   specialty: jazz reissues

>   DC 12009—Bud Freeman. Chicagoans in New York. J3.72

Debut (Denmark)
>   specialty: modern jazz

>   DEB 144—Albert Ayler. Ghosts. J5.140

Decca *See* MCA

Delmark, 4243 N. Lincoln, Chicago, IL 60618
>   specialty: jazz, blues

>   201—George Lewis. On Parade. J3.15
>   202—George Lewis. Doctor Jazz. J3.12
>   203—George Lewis. Memorial Album. J3.14
>   212—Earl Hines. At Home. J6.23
>   DS 420/1—Anthony Braxton. For Alto. two discs. J5.105
>   DS 605—Curtis Jones. Lonesome Bedroom Blues. B1.338
>   DS 612—Junior Wells. Hoodoo Man Blues. B1.370

Deram (England)
>   specialty: rock, folk, pop

>   SMK 1117—Shirley Collins. A Favourite Garland. F2.14

Dot, 8255 Beverly Blvd., Los Angeles, CA 90048
>   specialty: country, pop

>   ABDP 4009—Mac Wiseman. 16 Great Performances. F6.112
>   25071—Pat Boone. Pat's Greatest Hits. R2.26
>   25201—Billy Vaughan. Golden Hits. P5.91
>   25820—Original Hits—Golden Instrumentals. R2.10

Duke, 8255 Beverly Blvd., Los Angeles, CA 90048
   specialty: blues, soul

   DLP 71—Johnny Ace. Memorial Album. B2.48
   DLP 83—Junior Parker. Best. B1.352
   DLP 84—Bobby "Blue" Bland. Best, v.1. B2.49
   DLP 86—Bobby "Blue" Bland. Best, v.2. B2.49

Dunhill, 8255 Beverly Blvd., Los Angeles, CA 90048
   specialty: rock, folk

   DSD 50132—Jimmy Buffett. A White Sport Coat and a Pink Crustacean.
      F10.54
   DXS 50145—Mamas and Papas. 20 Golden Hits. two discs. R3.19

ECM, 810 Seventh Avenue, New Yorkl NY 10019
   specialty: modern jazz
   1014/6—Chick Corea. Piano Improvisations, v.1-3. three discs. J6.130
   1018/9—Circle. Paris Concert. two discs. J5.149
   1035/7—Keith Jarrett. Solo Concerts: Bremen and Lausanne. J6.64

EMI (Denmark)
   specialty: general

   EO 52-81004—Session at Riverside: New York. J4.164
   EO 52-81005—Bobby Hackett and Jack Teagarden. Jazz Ultimate. J4.142
   EO 52-81006—Session at Midnight: Los Angeles. J4.163

EMI (England)
   specialty: general

   Odeon CLP 1817—Django Reinhardt. Legendary. J6.111
   One Up OU 2046—Big 'Uns from the 50s and 60s. R2.2
   Starline SRS 5120—Wanda Jackson. R2.20
   Starline SRS 5129—Johnny Otis. Pioneer of Rock. B2.64

EMI (France)
   specialty: French music, general

   Pathe CO 54-16021/30—Swing Sessions, 1937-1950. ten discs. J1.5
   Pathe SPAM 67.092—Edith Piaf. Recital, 1962. P2.115
   CO 62-80813—Jay McShann's Piano. J6.67

ESP, 5 Riverside Drive, Krumville, NY 12447
   specialty: jazz

   1014—Sun Ra. Heliocentric Worlds, v.1. J5.130
   1017—Sun Ra. Heliocentric Worlds, v.2. J5.130

Eclipse (England)
   specialty: reissues of jazz and nostalgia

   ECM 2051—Django Reinhardt. Swing '35-'39. J6.112

Elektra, 962 N. LaCienega, Los Angeles, CA 90069
 specialty: folk, rock

 EKS 7217—Folk Banjo Styles. F3.30
 EKS 7239—Bob Gibson. Where I'm Bound. F4.9
 EKS 7277—Tom Paxton. Ramblin' Boy. F10.44
 EKS 7280—Judy Collins. Concert. F4.6
 EKS 7287—Phil Ochs. I Ain't Marching Anymore. F10.41
 EKS 7310—Phil Ochs. In Concert. F10.42
 EKS 74007—The Doors. R6.1
 EKS 74014—The Doors. Strange Days. R6.2
 EKS 75032—David Ackles. American Gothic. F10.48
 EKS 75035—Judy Collins. Colors of the Day: Best. R4.27
 EKL-BOX—The Folk Box. four discs. F3.7
 ELK 271/2—Woody Guthrie. Library of Congress Recordings. three discs.
  F10.20
 EKL 301/2—Leadbelly. Library of Congress Recordings. three discs. B1.209
 7E-2005—Paul Butterfield. Golden Butter. two discs. R5.8

Elektra (England)
 specialty: folk, rock

 K 52035—Dillards. Country Tracks: Best. F6.120

Enterprise, 2693 Union Avenue, Memphis, TN 38112
 specialty: soul, gospel

 1001—Isaac Hayes. Hot Buttered Soul. B4.51

Epic, 51 W. 52nd Street, New York, NY 10019
 specialty: general

 EE 22001—Johnny Hodges. Hodge Podge. J4.109
 EE 22003—Bobby Hackett. The Hackett Horn. J4.140
 EE 22005—The Duke's Men. J4.133
 EE 22007—Chuck Berry and His Stomping Stevedores. J4.131
 EE 22027—Gene Krupa. That Drummer's Band. J4.75
 BN 26246e—The Yardbirds. Greatest Hits. R5.12
 BN 26486—Tammy Wynette. Greatest Hits, v.1. F8.133
 KE 30325—Sly and the Family Stone. Greatest Hits. B4.31
 EG 30473—Johnny Otis Show Live at Monterey. two discs. B4.4
 E 30733—Tammy Wynette. Greatest Hits, v.2. F8.133
 KE 31607—Johnny Nash. I Can See Clearly Now. B4.56
 KE 33396—Tammy Wynette. Greatest Hits, v.3. F8.133
 PE 33409—Jeff Beck. Blow by Blow. R4.8
 BG 33752—George Jones and Tammy Wynette. Me and the First Lady/We
  Go Together. two discs. F8.151
 BG 33779—Jeff Beck. Truth/Beck-Ola. two discs. P5.14.
 BS 33782—Bob Wills/Asleep at the Wheel. Fathers and Sons. two discs.
  F7.49
 B2N 159—Those Wonderful Girls of Stage, Screen and Radio. two discs. P6.86

Epic (cont'd)
 B2N 164—Those Wonderful Guys of Stage, Screen and Radio. two discs. P6.87
 CE2E-201/2—Bing Crosby. Story. four discs. P2.8
 SN 6042—Swing Street. four discs. J4.10
 SN 6044—Jack Teagarden. King of the Blues Trombone. three discs. J3.93
 L2N 6072—Encores from the 30s, v.1 (1930-1935). two discs. P1.4 [v.2 never released]

Epic (France)
 specialty: general

 LN 24269—Johnny Dodds and Kid Ory. J3.24
 66212—Count Basie with Lester Young. two discs. J4.19

Eubie Blake Music, 284A Stuyvesant Ave., Brooklyn, NY 11221
 specialty: ragtime and reissues

Euphonic, P.O. Box 476, Ventura, CA 93001
 specialty: piano jazz, blues

Everest, 10920 Wilshire Blvd. West, Los Angeles, CA 90024
 specialty: reissues in folk, blues, and jazz

 FS 214—Charlie Parker. v.1. J5.71
 FS 216—Otis Spann. B1.305
 FS 217—Champion Jack Dupree. B1.327
 FS 219—Charlie Christian. At Minton's. J5.11
 FS 232—Charlie Parker. v.2. J5.71
 FS 253—Fred McDowell. B1.118
 FS 254—Charlie Parker. v.3. J5.71
 FS 293—Al Haig. Jazz Will O' the Wisp. J6.56

Excello, 1011 Woodland St., Nashville, TN 37206
 specialty: blues

 DBL 28025—Excello Story. two discs. B4.2

Extreme Rarities, c/o Ken Crawford, 215 Steuben Ave., Pittsburgh, PA 15205
 specialty: jazz and soundtrack reissues

Fantasy, 10th and Parker Sts., Berkeley, CA 94710
 specialty: blues, jazz

 9432—Woody Herman. Giant Step. J4.170
 9442—Staple Singers. The Twenty-Fifth Day of December. B3.57
 CCR-2—Creedence Clearwater Revival. Chronicle. two discs. R3.6
 F 24720—Jack Elliott. Hard Travellin': Songs by Woody Guthrie and Others. two discs. F4.30

Fat Cat's Jazz, Box 458, Manassas, VA 22110
 specialty: jazz

Flying Dutchman, 1133 Avenue of the Americas, New York, NY 10036
 specialty: jazz

 FD 10146—Coleman Hawkins. Classic Tenors. J4.99

Flying Fish, 3320 N. Halstead, Chicago, IL 60657
 specialty: bluegrass and Western swing, blues

 101—Hillbilly Jazz. two discs. F7.38

Flyright (England)
 specialty: blues, r'n'b

 LP 108/9—Memphis Minnie. 1934-1949. two discs. B1.389

Folk Legacy, Sharon Mt. Rd., Sharon, CT 06069
 specialty: folk

 FSB 20—Harry Cox. Traditional English Love Songs. F2.18
 FSA 26—Sarah Ogan Gunning. A Girl of Constant Sorrow. F3.66
 FSA 32—Hedy West. Old Times and Hard Times. F3.93
 FSI 35—Michael Cooney. The Cheese Stands Alone. F3.62

Folklyric, 10341 San Pablo Avenue, El Cerrito, CA 94530
 specialty: blues and folk reissues

 9001—Son House. Legendary, 1941/42 Recordings. B1.189

Folkways, 43 W. 61st Street, New Yorkl NY 10023
 specialty: folk, blues, jazz

 2301/2—Jean Ritchie. Child Ballads in America. two discs. F3.84
 2314—American Banjo Tunes and Songs in Scruggs Style. F6.1
 2315—Stoneman Family. Banjo Tunes and Songs. F5.74
 2316—Ritchie Family. F3.85
 2318—Mountain Music Bluegrass Style. F6.17
 2320/3—Pete Seeger. American Favorite Ballads. four discs. F4.65
 2351—Dock Boggs. v.1. F5.45
 2356—Old Harp Singing. F9.11
 2392—Dock Boggs. v.2. F5.45
 2395/9—New Lost City Ramblers. v.1-5. five discs. F5.66
 2409—Country Songs—Old and New. F6.25
 2426—Doc Watson and Jean Ritchie. F4.20
 2431/2—Newport Folk Festival, 1959/60. v.1-2. two discs. F3.15
 2433—Lilly Brothers. Folksongs from the Southern Mountains. F6.36
 2445—Pete Seeger. American Favorite Ballads. F4.65

Folkways (cont'd)
 2456—Pete Seeger. Broadsides. F3.89
 2480—Cisco Houston. Sings Songs of the Open Road. F10.67
 2492—New Lost City Ramblers. Play Instrumentals. F5.67
 2501/2—Pete Seeger. Gazette, v.1-2. two discs. F3.89
 2641/5—New Orleans, v.1-5. five discs. J3.2
 2801/11—Jazz, v.1-11. eleven discs. J1.9
 2941/2—Leadbelly. Last Sessions, v.1-2. four discs. B1.115
 2951/3—Anthology of American Folk Music. six discs. F3.4
 3527—Little Brother Montgomery. Blues. B1.223
 3562—Joseph Lamb. A Study in Classic Ragtime. J2.11
 3575—Irish Music in London Pubs. F2.35
 3810—Buell Kazee. His Songs and Music. F3.71
 3903—Dock Boggs. v.3. F5.45
 5212—Woody Guthrie. Dust Bowl Ballads. F10.61
 5264—New Lost City Ramblers. Songs of the Depression. F5.95
 5272—Harry K. McClintock. Haywire Mac. F10.70
 5285—Almanac Singers. Talking Union. F4.1
 5801/2—American History in Ballads and Songs. six discs. F3.21
 FTS 31001—Woody Guthrie. This Land Is Your Land. F10.22
 FTS 31021—Watson Family. F4.19

Fontana, 1 IBM Plaza, Chicago, IL 60611
 specialty: general
 27560—New Vaudeville Band. P2.153

Fontana (England)
 specialty: general
 STL 5269—Martin Carthy. F2.13

Fountain (England)
 specialty: jazz and blues reissues
 FB 301—Ida Cox, v.1. B1.401
 FB 304—Ida Cox, v.2. B1.401

Freedom (England)
 specialty: modern jazz
 FLP 40106—Cecil Taylor. D Trad That's What. J5.134

GHP (West Germany)
 specialty: old time music
 902—Riley Puckett. Old Time Greats. F5.39
 1001—Dock Walsh. F5.81

GNP Crescendo, 9165 Sunset Blvd., Hollywood, CA 90069
 specialty: jazz

GNP Crescendo (cont'd)
 S18—Max Roach-Clifford Brown. In Concert. J5.33
 9003—Coleman Hawkins. The Hawk in Holland. J4.101

Gannet (Denmark)
 specialty: jazz

 GEN 5136/7—Jimmy Yancey, v.1-2. two discs. J6.96

Good Time Jazz, 8481 Melrose Place, Los Angeles, CA 90069
 specialty: dixieland jazz, piano jazz

 10035—Luckey Roberts/Willie "The Lion" Smith. Harlem Piano. J6.34
 10043—Don Ewell. Man Here Plays Fine Piano. J6.50
 10046—Don Ewell. Free 'n' Easy. J6.49
 12001/3—Lu Watters. San Francisco Style, v.1-3. three discs. J3.59
 12004—Kid Ory. 1954. J3.42
 12022—Kid Ory. Tailgate! J3.46
 12048—Bunk Johnson. Superior Jazz Band. J3.10

Gordy, 6464 Sunset Blvd., Hollywood, CA 90028
 specialty: soul, blues

Greene Bottle (c/o Southern Record Sales)
 specialty: blues

Groove Merchant, Suite 3701, 515 Madison Avenue, New York, NY 10022
 specialty: jazz, blues

Gusto, 220 Boscobel Street, Nashville, TN 37213
 specialty: reissues of Starday and King records

Halcyon, Box 4255, Grand Central Station, New York, NY 10017
 specialty: jazz

Halcyon (England)
 specialty: reissues of jazz and nostalgia items

 HAL 5—Annette Hanshaw. Sweetheart of the Thirties. P2.104

Harmony (recently deleted); see also CBS
 specialty: budget line reissues of Columbia and Brunswick items

 HL 7191—Harry James. Songs That Sold a Million. P5.83
 HL 7233—Wilma Lee and Stoney Cooper. Sacred Songs. F9.30
 HL 7290—Bill Monroe. Great. F6.39
 HL 7299—Molly O'Day. Unforgettable. F8.131
 HL 7308—Johnny Bond. Best. F7.6
 HL 7313—Bob Atcher. Best Early American Folksongs. F7.22
 HL 7317—Sons of the Pioneers. Best. F7.16
 HL 7340—Lester Flatt and Earl Scruggs. Great Original Recordings. F6.30
 HL 7382—Gene Autry. Great Hits. F7.4

Harmony (cont'd)
    HL 7396—Carter Family. Great Sacred Songs. F9.26
    HL 7402—Lester Flatt and Earl Scruggs. Sacred Songs. F9.37
    HS 11178—Wilma Lee and Stoney Cooper. Sunny Side of the Mountain.
        F6.73
    HS 11334—Roy Acuff. Waiting for My Call to Glory. F9.15
    H 30609—Johnny Ray. Best. R2.22

Harmony (Canada)
    HEL 6004—Jazzmen in Uniform, 1945, Paris. J1.4

Herwin, 45 First Street, Glen Cove, NY 11542
    specialty: jazz and blues reissues

    101—Freddie Keppard. J3.6
    106—King Oliver. The Great 1923 Gennetts. J3.7
    202—Bessie Johnson. 1928-29. B3.43
    203—Sanctified, v.2: God Gave Me the Light, 1927-1931. B3.5
    204—Blind Joe Taggart. B3.61
    207—Sanctified, v.3: Whole World in His Hands, 1927-1936. B3.27
    208—Cannon's Jug Stompers. two discs. B1.419
    401—They All Played the Maple Leaf Rag. J2.8

Hi, 539 W. 25th Street, New York, NY 10001
    specialty: soul

    XSHL 32070—Al Green. Let's Stay Together. B4.48

Hilltop (recently deleted)
    specialty: Mercury budget reissues of country material through Pickwick
        records

    JS 6036—Louvin Brothers. F8.29
    JS 6093—Lester Flatt and Earl Scruggs. F6.27

Historical, P.O. Box 4204, Bergen Station, Jersey City, NJ 07304
    specialty: reissued jazz, blues, and country materials

    HLP 9—Benny Moten. Kansas City Orchestra, 1923-29. J4.83
    HLP 10—Chicago Southside, 1926-1932, v.1. J3.64
    HLP 24—The Territory Bands, 1926-1931, v.1. J3.103
    HLP 26—The Territory Bands, 1926-1931, v.2. J3.103
    HLP 30—Chicago Southside, 1926-1932, v.2. J3.64
    HLP 8001—Fields Ward. Buck Mountain Band. F5.101
    HLP 8004—Stoneman Family. 1927-1928. F5.73

Imperial (recently deleted); see United Artists
    specialty: blues and soul

    LP 9141—Smiley Lewis. I Hear You Knocking. B2.58

Impulse, 8255 Beverly Blvd., Los Angeles, CA 90048
    specialty: jazz (modern and mainstream)

    AS 6—John Coltrane. Africa Brass. J5.115
    AS 10—John Coltrane. Live at the Village Vanguard. J5.120
    AS 12—Benny Carter. Further Definitions. J4.24
    AS 77—John Coltrane. A Love Supreme. J5.121
    AS 95—John Coltrane. Ascension. J5.116
    AS 9108—Earl Hines. Once Upon a Time. J4.69
    AS 9148—John Coltrane. Cosmic Music. J5.117
    AS 9183—Charlie Haden. Liberation Suite. J5.156
    AS 9229-2—Pharoah Sanders. Nest. two discs. J5.158
    ASH 9253-3—The Saxophone. three discs. J6.5
    ASY 9272-3—The Drum. three discs. J6.2
    ASY 9284-3—The Bass. three discs. J6.1

Increase (recently deleted); see All Platinum
    specialty: rock and roll and rhythm 'n' blues in a disc jockey simulation

    2000/12—Cruisin', 1955-1967. thirteen discs. R2.4

Island, 7720 Sunset Blvd., Los Angeles, CA 90046
    specialty: folk and reggae music

    SW 9329—The Wailers. Catch a Fire. B5.9
    ILPS 9330—Toots and the Maytals. Funky Kingston. B5.8
    ILPS 9334—The Chieftains. 5. F2.39

Island (England)
    specialty: folk and reggae music

    FOLK 1001—The Electric Muse. four discs. F2.45
    HELP 25—Albion Country Band. F2.46a

Jamie (recently deleted)
    specialty: rock and roll

    S 3026—Duane Eddy. 16 Greatest Hits. R2.17

Jazum, 5808 Northumberland St., Pittsburgh, PA 15217
    specialty: jazz and nostalgia reissues

    21—Boswell Sisters. P2.136
    30/1—Boswell Sisters. two discs. P2.136
    43/4—Boswell Sisters. two discs. P2.136

Jazz Archives, P.O. Box 194, Plainview, NY 11805
    specialty: jazz

    JA 6—Charlie Christian. Together with Lester Young, 1940. J5.12
    JA 18—Lester Young. Jammin' with Lester. J4.127
    JA 23—Charlie Christian, with Benny Goodman's Sextet, 1939/41. J5.13

Jazz Composers' Orchestral Association, 6 West 96th Street, New York, NY 10024
specialty: modern jazz

JCOA 1001/2–Jazz Composers' Orchestra. two discs. J5.123

Jazzology, 3008 Wadsworth Mill Place, Decatur, GA 30032
specialty: jazz

Jazz Piano (Denmark)
specialty: piano jazz reissues

JP 5003–Library of Congress Sessions. J6.84

Jim Taylor Presents, 12311 Gratiot Ave., Detroit, MI 48205
specialty: mainstream jazz and blues

JTP 103–Olive Brown and Her Blues Chasers. B1.398

John Edwards Memorial Foundation, c/o Center for Study of Folklore &
Mythology, UCLA, Los Angeles, CA 90024
specialty: reissues of blues, and country and western material

Kama Sutra, 810 Seventh Ave., New York, NY 10019
specialty: rock and roll

KSBS 2010–Sha Na Na. Rock & Roll Is Here to Stay! R2.51
KSBS 2013–Lovin' Spoonful. Very Best. R3.18

Kapp (recently deleted); see also MCA
specialty: mood

3530–Roger Williams. Gold Hits. P3.24
3559–Jack Jones. Best. P2.48

Kent, 96 West Street, Englewood, NJ 07631
specialty: blues

KST 533–B. B. King. From the Beginning. two discs. B1.294
KST 534–Johnny Otis. Cold Shot. B1.351
KST 537–Jimmy Reed. Roots of the Blues. two discs. B1.232
KST 9001–Elmore James. Legend, v.1. B1.286
KST 9010–Elmore James. Legend, v.2. B1.286
KST 9011–B. B. King. 1949-1950. B1.291

Kicking Mule, P.O. Box 3233, Berkeley, CA 94703
specialty: blues, folk, and guitar albums

106–Rev. Gary Davis. Ragtime Guitar. J2.25

King, 220 Boscobel St., Nashville, TN 37213
specialty: blues, bluegrass and country music, soul

541–Hank Ballard. Greatest Jukebox Hits. B2.36
552–Don Reno and Red Smiley. F6.47

King (cont'd)

> 553—Cowboy Copas. All Time Hits. F8.49
> 615—Stanley Brothers. F6.58
> 826—James Brown. Live at the Apollo, v.1. B4.24
> 848—Don Reno and Red Smiley. F6.47
> 872—Stanley Brothers. America's Finest Five String Banjo Hootenanny. F6.59
> 919—James Brown. Unbeatable Sixteen Hits. B4.25
> 1022—James Brown. Live at the Apollo, v.2. B4.24
> 1059—Freddy King. Hideaway. B1.340
> 1065—Don Reno. Fastest Five Strings Alive. F6.99
> 1081—Little Willie John. Free At Last. B2.61
> 1086—Wynonie Harris. Good Rockin' Blues. B1.423
> 1110—James Brown Band. Sho Is Funky Down Here. B4.40
> 1130—Roy Brown. Hard Luck Blues. B2.38

King Bluegrass, 6609 Main Street, Cincinnati, OH 45244
specialty: bluegrass

Kudu, 6464 Sunset Blvd., Hollywood, CA 90028
specialty: soul

> 05—Esther Phillips. From a Whisper to a Scream. B4.74

Leader (England)
specialty: folk

> LEAB 404—Copper Family. A Song for Every Season. four discs. F2.16

Lemco, 6609 Main Street, Cincinnati, OH 45244
specialty: bluegrass

> 611—J. D. Crowe. The Model Church. F9.31
> 612—Red Allen and the Allen Brothers. Allengrass. F6.113

Library of Congress, Washington, D.C.
specialty: folk and ethnic music, blues; see also Flyright

> LBC 1/15—Folk Music in America, v.1-15. fifteen discs. F3.9 [in progress]
> AAFS L 26/7—American Sea Songs and Shanties, v.1-2. two discs. F3.25
> AAFS L 62—American Fiddle Tunes. F3.16

London, 539 W. 25th Street, New York, NY 10001
specialty: general

> NPS 4—Rolling Stones. Let It Bleed. R4.16
> PS 114—Edmundo Ros. Rhythms of the South. P5.112
> PS 483—Mantovani. Golden Hits. P5.100
> PS 492—John Mayall. Blues Breakers. R5.10
> PS 493—Rolling Stones. Got Live (If You Want It). R4.14
> PS 534—John Mayall. Alone. R5.9
> PS 539—Rolling Stones. Beggar's Banquet. R4.13

London (cont'd)
    NPS 606/7—Rolling Stones. Hot Rocks, v.1. two discs. R4.15
    XPS 610—Mantovani. 25th Anniversary Album. P5.101
    NPS 626/7—Rolling Stones. Hot Rocks, v.2. two discs. R4.15
    XPS 906—Mantovani. All Time Greatest. P5.99

MCA, 100 Universal City Plaza, Universal City, CA 91608
    specialty: general; formerly known as Decca, and consequently many older
    records were renumbered

    DL 8044—Kansas City Jazz. J3.101
    DL 8671—Gateway Singers. At the Hungry i. F4.8
    DL 8731—Bill Monroe. Knee Deep in Bluegrass. F6.45
    DL 8782—Sister Rosetta Tharpe. Gospel Train. B3.62
    DL 9034/8—Al Jolson. Story. five discs. P2.12
    DL 75326—Conway Twitty and Loretta Lynn. Lead Me On. F8.153
    DS 79175—The Who. Live at Leeds. R4.17
    DL 9221—Earl Hines. Southside Swing, 1934/5. J4.68
    DL 9222/3—Chick Webb, v.1-2. two discs. J4.51
    DL 9224—Duke Ellington, v.1: In the Beginning (1926/8). J4.28
    DL 9227/8—Fletcher Henderson, v.1-2. two discs. J4.40
    DL 9236—Jay McShann. New York—1208 Miles (1941-1943). J4.80
    DL 79237/40—Jimmie Lunceford, v.1-4. four discs. J4.77
    DL 9241—Duke Ellington, v.2: Hot in Harlem (1928/9). J4.28
    DL 9242—Big Bands Uptown, 1931-1943, v.1. J3.78
    DL 9243—Jan Savitt. The Top Hatters, 1939-1941. P5.44
    DL 9247—Duke Ellington, v.3: Rockin' in Rhythm (1929/31). J4.28
    1—Loretta Lynn. Greatest Hits, v.1. F8.130
    81—Jimmy Martin. Good 'n' Country. F6.38
    86—Red Foley. Songs of Devotion. F9.38
    104—Bill Monroe. Bluegrass Instrumentals. F6.43
    110—Bill Monroe. The High, Lonesome Sound. F6.44
    115—Jimmy Martin. Big 'n' Country Instrumentals. F6.37
    131—Bill Monroe. A Voice from On High. F9.61
    420—Loretta Lynn. Greatest Hits, v.2. F8.130
    527—Bill Monroe. I Saw the Light. F9.60
    2106—Neil Diamond. His 12 Greatest Hits. P2.33
    2128—Elton John. Greatest Hits. R4.10
    DEA 7-2—Those Wonderful Thirties. two discs. P1.14
    DXS 7181—Webb Pierce. Story. two discs. F8.30
    2-4001—Bill Anderson. Story. two discs. F8.44
    2-4005—Inkspots. Best. two discs. B2.22
    2-4006—Billie Holiday. Story. two discs. J6.122
    2-4008—Fred Waring. Best. two discs. P2.141
    2-4009—Buddy Holly. two discs. R1.8
    2-4010—Bill Haley and His Comets. Best. two discs. R1.7
    2-4018—A Jazz Holiday. two discs. J3.82
    2-4019—Art Tatum. Masterpieces. two discs. J6.36
    2-4031—Kitty Wells. Story. two discs. F8.132
    2-4033—Four Aces. Best. two discs. P2.149

MCA (cont'd)

    2-4038—Patsy Cline. Story. two discs. F8.129
    2-4039—Mills Brothers. Best. two discs. P2.140
    2-4040—Ernest Tubb. Story. two discs. F8.38
    2-4041—Guy Lombardo. Sweetest Music This Side of Heaven. two discs.
      P5.37
    2-4043—Bert Kaempfert. Best. two discs. P5.85
    2-4047—Ella Fitzgerald. Best. two discs. P2.68
    2-4050—Count Basie. Best. two discs. J4.13
    2-4052—The Weavers. Best. F4.21
    2-4053—Red Foley. Story. two discs. F8.101
    2-4056—Carmen Cavallaro. Best. two discs. P5.106
    2-4067—The Who. A Quick One (Happy Jack). two discs. R4.19
    2-4068—The Who. Magic Bus. two discs. R4.18
    2-4071—Eddie Condon. Best. two discs. J3.68
    2-4072—Xavier Cugat. Best. two discs. P5.107
    2-4073—Jimmy Dorsey. Best. two discs. P5.26
    2-4076—Glen Gray and the Casa Loma Orchestra. Best. two discs. P5.32
    2-4077—Woody Herman. Best. two discs. J4.43
    2-4079—Louis Jordan. Best. B2.45
    2-4083—Bob Crosby. Best. two discs. J3.54
    2-4090—Bill Monroe. Best. two discs. F6.42
    2-8001—American Graffiti. two discs. R2.1
    2-11002—That's Entertainment! two discs. P6.85

MCA (England)

specialty: general; formerly Decca American

MCFM 2720—Dick Haymes. Best. P2.45
MCFM 2739—Connie Boswell. Sand in My Shoes. P2.68a

MCA (France)

specialty: general; jazz reissues from American Decca

510.065—Lucky Millinder. Lucky Days, 1941-1945. B2.22a
510.071—The Swinging Small Bands, v.1. J4.93
510.085—James P. Johnson. J6.29
510.088—The Swinging Small Bands, v.2. J4.93
510.090—Kings and Queens of Ivory, v.1. J6.15 (set in progress)
510.111—The Swinging Small Bands, v.3. J4.93
510.123—The Swinging Small Bands, v.4. J4.03

MCA (West Germany)

specialty: general; reissued Decca material

628.334—Tex Ritter. The Singing Cowboy. two discs. F7.14

MGM, 810 Seventh Ave., New York, NY 10019
    specialty: general

GAS 140—Osborne Brothers. F6.93
SE 3331—Hank Williams. I Saw the Light. F9.85

MGM (cont'd)

SE 4946—Tompall and the Glaser Brothers. Greatest Hits. F8.128

MGM (England)

specialty: general; reissues of American MGM product

2353.053—Hank Williams. Greatest Hits, v.1. F8.40
2353.071—Billy Eckstine. Greatest Hits. P2.34
2353.073—Hank Williams. Greatest Hits, v.2. F8.40
2353.118—Hank Williams. Collector's, v.1. F8.39
2683.016—Hank Williams. Memorial Album. two discs. F8.42
2683.046—Hank Williams. On Stage! two discs. F8.43

MPS (West Germany)

specialty: jazz

20668—Oscar Peterson. Exclusively for My Friends, v.1. J6.69
20693—Oscar Peterson. Exclusively for My Friends, v.6. J6.69
206696—Oscar Peterson. Exclusively for My Friends, v.2. J6.69
206701—Oscar Peterson. Exclusively for My Friends, v.3. J6.69
206718—Oscar Peterson. Exclusively for My Friends, v.4. J6.69

Magpie (England)

specialty: blues

PY 18000—Robert Wilkins. Before the Reverence, 1928-1935. B1.129a

Mainstream, 1700 Broadway, New York, NY 10019

specialty: jazz and blues

MRL 311—Lightnin' Hopkins. The Blues. B1.181
MRL 316—Maynard Ferguson. Screamin' Blues. J4.169
MRL 399—Andy Kirk. March, 1936. J4.70

Mamlish, Box 417, Cathedral Station, New York, NY 10025

specialty: blues

S3804—Mississippi Sheiks. Stop and Listen Blues. B1.220

Master Jazz Recordings, 955 Lexington Avenue, New York, NY 10024

specialty: jazz

MJR 8116—Billy Strayhorn. Cue for Saxophone. J4.150

Matchbox (England)

specialty: blues

SDR 213—Little Brother Montgomery. 1930-1969. B1.222

Melodeon, 16 River Street, Chatham, NY 12037

specialty: blues, jazz, bluegrass reissues

MLP 7321—Skip James. Greatest of the Delta Blues Singers. B1.199
MLP 7322—Stanley Brothers. Their Original Recordings. F6.57

Melodeon (cont'd)
    MLP 7323—Blind Willie McTell. The Legendary Library of Congress Session, 1940. B1.127
    MLP 7324—Part Blues. B1.34
    MLP 7325—Red Allen. Solid Bluegrass Sound of the Kentuckians. F6.21

Mercury, 1 IBM Plaza, Chicago, IL 60611
    specialty: general

    MG 20323—Carl Story. Gosepl Quartet Favorites. F9.81
    60232—Dinah Washington. Unforgettable. B4.79
    60587—Frankie Laine. Golden Hits. P2.50
    60621—George Jones. Greatest Hits. F8.26
    60645—Sarah Vaughan. Golden Hits. P2.83
    SR 61268—Dave Dudley. Best. F8.121
    SR 61369—Tom T. Hall. Greatest Hits, v.1. F8.113
    SRM 1-1044—Tom T. Hall. Greatest Hits, v.2. F8.113
    SRM 1-1078—Johnny Rodriguez. Greatest Hits. F8.105
    SRM 1-1101—Bachman-Turner Overdrive. Best. R8.11
    SRM 20803—Jerry Lee Lewis. The Session. two discs. R2.49
    SRM 2-7507—Rod Stewart. Best. R4.44

Milestone, 10th and Parker Streets, Berkeley, CA 94710
    specialty: jazz and blues; reissues from the Riverside catalog

    M 2012—Earl Hines. A Monday Date, 1928. J6.21
    47002—Bill Evans. Village Vanguard Session. two discs. J6.55
    47003—Wes Montgomery. While We're Young. two discs. J6.108
    47004—Thelonious Monk. Pure Monk. two discs. J6.32
    47007—Sonny Rollins. Freedom Suite, Plus. two discs. J5.77
    47018—Jelly Roll Morton. 1923-1924. two discs. J6.33
    47019—Bix Beiderbecke and the Chicago Cornets. two discs. J3.53
    47020—New Orleans Rhythm Kings. two discs. J3.57
    47021—Ma Rainey. two discs. B1.392

Monmouth/Evergreen, 1697 Broadway, Suite 1201, New York, NY 10019
    specialty: jazz, reissued stage and show soundtracks, reissued nostalgia-pop music

    MES 6816—Ray Noble and Al Bowlly, v.1. P5.102
    MES 6917—Maxine Sullivan and Bob Wilber. The Music of Hoagy Carmichael. P2.82
    MES 7021—Ray Noble and Al Bowlly, v.2. P5.102
    MES 7024/5—Claude Thornhill. two discs. P5.89 and P5.90
    MES 7027—Ray Noble and Al Bowlly, v.3. P5.102
    MES 7033—Jack Hylton, v.1. P5.98
    MES 7039/40—Ray Noble and Al Bowlly, v.4-5. two discs. P5.102
    MES 7055—Jack Hylton, v.2. P5.98
    MES 5056—Ray Noble and Al Bowlly, v.6. P5.102

Monument, 51 W. 52nd Street, New York, NY 10019
  specialty: country music

  18045—Roy Orbison. Very Best. R2.21
  Z 30817—Kris Kristofferson. Me and Bobby McGee. F10.24
  Z 32259—Arthur Smith. Battling Banjos. F6.105

Motown, 6255 Sunset Blvd., Hollywood, CA 90028
  specialty: soul

  663—The Supremes. Greatest Hits. two discs. B4.12
  702-S2—Gladys Knight and the Pips. Anthology. two discs. B4.68
  MS5-726—Motown Story; The First Decade. five discs. B4.5
  782-A3—The Temptations. Anthology. three discs. B4.18
  793-R3—Smokey Robinson and the Miracles. Anthology. three discs. B4.29

Muse, Blanchris, Inc., 160 W. 71st Street, New York, NY 10023
  specialty: jazz and blues

  MR 5087—Elmore James/Eddie Taylor. Street Talkin'. B1.368

Muskadine, Box 635, Manhattan Beach, CA 90266
  specialty: blues reissues

Nonesuch, 962 N. LaCienega, Los Angeles, CA 90069
  specialty: mainly classical, but here includes ragtime music

  H 71305—Joshua Rifkin. Joplin Piano Rags, v.3. J2.23
  HB 73026—Joshua Rifkin. Joplin Piano Rags, v.1/2. J2.23.

Ode, 1416 North LaBrea, Hollywood, CA 90028
  specialty: popular

  SP 77009—Carole King. Tapestry. R3.15

Odeon *See* EMI Odeon (England)

Old Homestead, P.O. Box 100, Brighton, MI 48116
  specialty: bluegrass, old time music, sacred music, and reissues

  OH 90001—Wade Mainer. Sacred Songs of Mother and Home. F9.54
  OHCS 101—Molly O'Day. A Sacred Collection. F9.63

Old Masters, Max Abrams, Box 76082, Los Angeles, CA 90076
  specialty: jazz and pop reissues

  TOM 23—Ted Weems. 1928-1930. P5.46a

Old Timey, 10341 San Pablo Ave., El Cerrito, CA 94530.
  specialty: reissues of old time music and western swing

  OT 100/1—The String Bands, v.1-2. two discs. F5.24
  OT 102—Ballads and Songs. F5.3

Old Timey (cont'd)
>OT 103/4—Cliff Carlisle, v.1-2. two discs. F8.48
>OT 105—Western Swing, v.1. F7.36
>OT 106/7—J. E. Mainer's Mountaineers, v.1-2. two discs. F5.65
>OT 112—Tom Darby and Jimmy Tarlton. F5.113
>OT 115—Allen Brothers. The Chattanooga Boys. F5.117
>OT 116/7—Western Swing, v.2-3. two discs. F7.36

Oldie Blues (Holland)
>specialty: blues reissues

>OL 2801—Pete Johnson, v.1. J6.93
>OL 2806—Pete Johnson, v.2. J6.93

Onyx, Blanchris, Inc., 160 W. 71st Street, New York, NY 10023
>specialty: jazz reissues

>ORI 204—Red Rodney. The Red Arrow. J5.75
>ORI 205—Art Tatum. God Is in the House. J6.35
>ORI 207—Hot Lips Page. After Hours in Harlem. J5.67
>ORI 208—Don Byas. Midnight at Minton's. J5.42
>ORI 221—Charlie Parker. First Recordings! J5.28

Origin Jazz Library, Box 863, Berkeley, CA 94701
>specialty: blues and gospel reissues

>OJL 12/3—In the Spirit, No. 1-2. two discs. B3.13

Pablo, 1133 Avenue of the Americas, New York, NY 10036
>specialty: mainstream jazz

>2625.703—Art Tatum. Solo Masterpieces. thirteen discs. J6.39
>2625.706—Art Tatum. Group Masterpieces. eight discs. J4.155

Paltram (Austria)
>specialty: blues and gospel

>PL 102—Texas Blues. B1.97

Paramount, 8255 Beverly Blvd., Los Angeles, CA 90048
>specialty: popular, rock

>PAS 6031—Commander Cody and His Lost Planet Airmen. Hot Licks, Cold Steel, and Truckers' Favorites. F8.108

Parlophone (England)
>specialty: general, jazz reissues

>PMC 7019—Lonnie Johnson and Eddie Lang. Blue Guitars, v.1. B1.207
>PMC 7038—The Chocolate Dandies. 1928-1933. J4.55
>PMC 7082—The Territory Bands, 1926-1929. J3.104
>PMC 7106—Lonnie Johnson and Eddie Lang. Blue Guitars, v.2. B1.207

Parrot, 539 W. 25th Street, New York, NY 10001
    specialty: general

    XPAS 71028—Tom Jones. This Is P2.49

Peacock, 8255 Beverly Blvd., Los Angeles, CA 90048
    specialty: gospel

    136—Mighty Clouds of Joy. Best. B3.48
    138—Dixie Hummingbirds. Best. B3.33
    139—Five Blind Boys of Mississippi. Best. B3.36
    140—Golden Gems of Gospel. B3.6

Philadelphia International, 51 W. 52nd Street, New York, NY 10019
    specialty: soul

Philips, 1 IBM Plaza, Chicago, IL 60611
    specialty: general; see also Phonogram

    PHS 600.298—Nina Simone. Best. B4.70

Philo, The Barn, North Ferrisburg, VT 05473
    specialty: folk music

Phoenix, 7808 Bergen Line Ave., Bergenfield, NJ 07047
    specialty: jazz and blues reissues

    LP 7—Wynonie Harris. Mister Blues Meets the Master Saxes. B1.424

Phonogram (England)
    specialty: general, reissues of Philips and Chess materials

    6414.406—Alan Stivell. Renaissance of the Celtic Harp. F2.61
    6467.013—Memphis Country. F8.12
    6467.025/7—Sun Rockabillies, v.1-3. three discs. R1.5
    6467.306—Muddy Waters. At Newport. B1.300
    6641.047—Genesis, v.1. four discs. B1.275
    6641.125—Genesis, v.2. four discs. B1.276
    6641.174—Genesis, v.3. four discs. B1.277
    6641.180—The Sun Story, 1952-1968. two discs. R1.6

Pickwick, 135 Crossways Park Drive, Woodbury, Long Island, NY 11797
    specialty: reissues of Mercury and Capitol material, all fields

Piedmont (c/o Southern Record Sales)
    specialty: blues

    PLP 13157—Mississippi John Hurt. Folksongs and Blues, v.1. B1.191
    PLP 13161—Mississippi John Hurt. Folk Songs and Blues, v.2. B1.191

Pine Mountain, Box 584, Barbourville, KY 40906
    specialty: reissues of old time material

    PM 269—The Blue Sky Boys. Precious Moments. F9.22

Polydor, 810 Seventh Avenue, New York, NY 10019
  specialty: general pop and soul

  PD 4054—James Brown. Hot Pants. B4.39
  104.678—James Last. This Is P5.86

Polydor (England)
  specialty: pop and soul

  2310.293—Charlie Feathers/Mac Curtis. Rockabilly Kings. R1.14
  2384.007—Oscar Peterson. Exclusively for My Friends, v.5. J6.69
  2424.118—Jerry Butler. Best. B4.42

Prestige, 10th and Parker Streets, Berkeley, CA 94710
  specialty: jazz, blues and folk music

  7159—Thelonious Monk. Monk's Mood. J5.25
  7326—Sonny Rollins. Saxophone Colossus. J5.79
  7337—Stan Getz. Greatest Hits. J5.89c
  7593—Dickie Wells. In Paris, 1937. J4.156
  7643—Benny Carter. 1933. J4.20
  7827—Lee Konitz. Ezz-thetic. J5.92
  PR 24001—Miles Davis. two discs. J5.16
  PR 24020—Clifford Brown. In Paris. two discs. J5.40
  PR 24024—The Greatest Jazz Concert Ever. two discs. J5.6
  P 24030—Dizzy Gillespie. In the Beginning. two discs. J5.22
  PR 24034—Miles Davis. Workin' and Steamin'. two discs. J5.21
  P 24039—Eddie "Lockjaw" Davis. The Cookbook. two discs. P3.6
  P 24040—Buck Clayton and Buddy Tate. Kansas City Nights. two discs.
    J4.161
  P 24044—Sonny Stitt. Genesis. two discs. J5.80
  PR 24045—25 Years of Prestige. two discs. J5.104
  P 34001—Charles Mingus. The Great Concert. three discs. J5.127

Puritan, P.O. Box 946, Evanston, IL 60204
  specialty: bluegrass

Pye (England)
  specialty: general

  502—Donovan. History. F10.8

RBF, 43 W. 61st Street, New York, NY 10023
  specialty: jazz, blues and old time music reissues

  RF 3—A History of Jazz: The New York Scene, 1914-1945. J3.80
  RBF 8/9—The Country Blues, v.1-2. two discs. B1.11
  RBF 10—Blind Willie Johnson. B3.45
  RBF 11—Blues Rediscoveries. B1.10
  RBF 15—Blues Roots: The Atlanta Blues. B1.63
  RBF 19—Country Gospel Song. F9.5
  RBF 51—Uncle Dave Macon. F5.32

RBF (cont'd)

    RBF 202—The Rural Blues. two discs. B1.22

    RBF 203—New Orleans Jazz: The Twenties. two discs. J3.5

RCA, 1133 Avenue of the Americas, New York, NY 10036

    specialty: general; formerly known as Victor

    LSPX 1004—Guess Who. Best. R3.10

    LPM 1121—Rosalie Allen. Queen of the Yodellers. F8.134

    LPM 1183—Eartha Kitt. That Bad Eartha. P2.109

    LPE 1192—Glenn Miller. Plays Selections from "The Glenn Miller Story."
        P5.15

    LPM 1223—Eddy Arnold. All Time Favorites. F8.88

    LPM 1241—Artie Shaw's Gramercy Five. J4.146

    LPM 1246—Fats Waller. Ain't Misbehavin'. J4.117, P2.65

    LPM 1295—Muggsy Spanier. The Great Sixteen. J3.58

    LPM 1364—Duke Ellington. In a Mellotone. J4.32

    LPM 1649—Jelly Roll Morton. King of New Orleans Jazz. J3.26

    LPM 2078—Bunny Berigan. P5.5

    LPM 2323—Bix Beiderbecke. Legend. J3.88

    LPM 2398—Dizzy Gillespie. The Greatest. J5.53

    LSP 2587—Lena Horne. Lovely and Alive. P2.72

    LSP 2669—Elton Britt, v.1. F8.47

    LSP 2887—Chet Atkins. Best. F8.90

    LSP 2890—Jim Reeves. Best, v.1. F8.92

    LSC 3235—Spike Jones. Is Murdering the Classics. P4.8

    LSP 3377—Glenn Miller. Best. P5.14

    LSP 3476—Sons of the Pioneers. Best. F7.17

    LSP 3478—Hank Snow. Best, v.1. F8.32

    LSP 3482—Jim Reeves. Best, v.2. F8.92

    LSP 3766—Jefferson Airplane. Surrealistic Pillow. R6.7

    LSP 3956—Nilsson. Aerial Ballet. F10.75

    LSP 3957—Jose Feliciano. P2.40

    LSP 3988—Gary Burton. A Genuine Tong Funeral. J5.144

    LSP 4187—Jim Reeves. Best, v.3. F8.92

    LSP 4223—Charley Pride. Best, v.1. F8.104

    LSP 4289—Harry Nilsson. Nilsson Sings Newman. F10.77

    LSP 4321—Porter Wagoner. Best, v.2. F8.83

    LSP 4374—Nina Simone. Best. B4.69

    LSP 4459—Jefferson Airplane. Worst. R6.9

    LSP 4682—Charley Pride. Best, v.1. F8.104

    LSP 4751—Waylon Jennings. Ladies Love Outlaws. F8.11

    LSP 4798—Hank Snow. Best, v.2. F8.32

    LSP 4822—Elton Britt, v.2. F8.47

    LSP 4854—Waylon Jennings. Lonesome, On'ry, and Mean. F8.115

    ARL1-0035—Arthur Fiedler and the Boston Pops. Greatest Hits of the 20s.
        P5.81

    ARL1-0041/5—Arthur Fiedler and the Boston Pops. Greatest Hits of the
        30s, 40s, 50s, 60s, and 70s. five discs. P5.81

RCA (cont'd)
    KPM1-0153—Elvis Presley. The Sun Sessions. R1.11
    APL1-0240—Waylon Jennings. Honky Tonk Heroes. F8.116
    CPL1-0374—John Denver. Greatest Hits. F10.56
    APL1-0455—George Hamilton IV. Greatest Hits. F8.61
    APL1-0928—Neil Sedaka. His Greatest Hits. R2.42
    ANL1-1035—Spike Jones. Best. P4.7
    ANL1-1071—Carter Family. 'Mid the Green Fields. F5.110
    ANL1-1083e—The Browns. Best. F8.97
    APL1-1117—Dolly Parton. Best. F8.143
    ANL1-1137—Perry Como. I Believe. F9.28
    ANL1-1140—Vaughan Monroe, Best. P2.59
    ANL1-1213—Porter Wagoner. Best, v.1. F8.83
    CPL1-1756e—Russ Columbo. A Legendary Performer. P2.29
    CPL1-2099—Woody Guthrie. Dust Bowl Ballads. F10.62
    CPL1-5015—Cleo Laine. Live!! At Carnegie Hall. P2.74
    CPL2-0466—Stars of the Grand Ole Opry, 1926-1974. two discs. F8.8
    ADL2-0694—Wilf Carter. Montana Slim's Greatest Hits. two discs. F7.10
    VPS 6014—Hank Snow. This Is My Story. two discs. F8.33
    LSP 6016—Willie "The Lion" Smith. Memoirs. two discs. J6.74
    VPS 6027—Sam Cooke. This Is. . . . two discs. B2.42
    VPS 6032—Eddy Arnold. This Is. . . . two discs. F8.89
    VPM 6040—Benny Goodman. This Is. . . . , v.1. two discs. J4.62
    VPM 6042—Duke Ellington. This Is. . . . two discs. J4.33
    VPM 6043—This Is the Big Band Era. two discs. P5.4
    VPM 6056—Gene Austin. This Is. . . . two discs. P2.1
    VPM 6063—Benny Goodman. This Is. . . . , v.2. J4.62
    VPSX 6079—Chet Atkins. Now and . . . Then. two discs. F8.91
    VPM 6087—Tommy Dorsey. Clambake Seven. two discs. P5.9

RCA Bluebird (series devoted to reissues)
    AXM2-5501—Tampa Red. two discs. B1.242
    AXM2-5503—Bill Boyd. Country Ramblers, 1934-1950. two discs. F7.39
    AXM2-5506—Big Maceo. Chicago Breakdown. two discs. B1.283
    AXM2-5507—Fletcher Henderson. Complete, 1923-1936. two discs. J4.39
    AXM2-5508—Earl Hines. The Father Jumps. two discs. J4.65
    AXM2-5510—Monroe Brothers. Feats Here Tonight. F5.115
    AXM2-5512—Glenn Miller. Complete, v.1. two discs. P5.39 (in progress, about 20 discs)
    AXM2-5517—Artie Shaw. Complete, v.1. two discs. P5.45 (in progress, about 12 discs)
    AXM2-5518—Fats Waller. Piano Solos, 1929-1941. two discs. J6.40a
    AXM2-5521—Tommy Dorsey. Complete, v.1. two discs. P5.8 (in progress, about 12 discs)
    AXM2-5525—Blue Sky Boys. two discs. F5.105
    AXM2-5531—The Cats and the Fiddle. I Miss You So. two discs. B2.24
    AXM2-55??—Grand Ole Opry Stars. two discs. F8.14 (forthcoming)
    AXM2-55??—Patsy Montana. two discs. F7.11 (forthcoming)
    AXM6-5536—Lionel Hampton. Complete, 1937-1941. six discs. J4.97

RCA Camden (reissues)

2460—Pee Wee King. Biggest Hits. F7.44

RCA Vintage (jazz and blues and folk reissues; series recently deleted)

LPV 501—Coleman Hawkins. Body and Soul. J4.98
LPV 504—Isham Jones. P5.12
LPV 507—Smoky Mountain Ballads. F5.7
LPV 513—John Jacob Niles. Folk Balladeer. F3.79
LPV 519—The Bebop Era. J5.2
LPV 521—Benny Goodman. Small Groups. J4.95
LPV 522—Authentic Cowboys and Their Western Folksongs. F7.1
LPV 532—The Railroad in Folksong. F3.40
LPV 533—Johnny Hodges. Things Ain't What They Used to Be. J4.112
LPV 548—Native American Ballads. F5.5
LPV 551—Charlie Barnet, v.1. P5.21
LPV 552—Early Rural String Bands. F5.22
LPV 554—Fred Waring. P2.143
LPV 555—Paul Whiteman, v.1. P5.18
LPV 558—Johnny Dodds. J3.22
LPV 565—Leo Reisman, v.1. P5.17
LPV 566—Barney Bigard/Albert Nicholas. J4.132
LPV 567—Charlie Barnet, v.2. P5.21
LPV 569—Early Bluegrass. F6.15
LPV 570—Paul Whiteman, v.2. P5.18
LPV 581—Bunny Berigan. His Trumpet and Orchestra, v.1. P5.7
LPV 582—Artie Shaw. J4.86

RCA (England)

specialty: general

SD 1000—Frank Sinatra, with Tommy Dorsey. six discs. P2.14
INTS 1072—Gene Krupa. Swingin' with Krupa. J4.74
INTS 1343—Rudy Vallee Croons the Songs He Made Famous. P2.22
DPS 2022—Jimmy Driftwood. Famous Country Music Makers. two discs. F10.9
LSA 3180—Hoagy Carmichael. Stardust. P2.26
LPL1-5000—Cleo Laine. I Am a Song. P2.73
LFL4-7522—Perry Como. The First Thirty Years. four discs. P2.6

RCA (France)

specialty: jazz and blues reissues

730.549—Jelly Roll Morton, v.1. J3.25
730.561—Boogie Woogie Man. J6.82
730.581—Memphis Slim. B1.349
730.605—Jelly Roll Morton, v.2. J3.25
730.703/4—Original Dixieland Jazz Band. two discs. J3.51
730.708—Erskine Hawkins, v.1. J4.64
730.710—Barney Kessel. J6.101

RCA (France) (cont'd)
- 731.051/2–Louis Armstrong. Town Hall Concert, 1947. two discs. J3.38
- 731.059–Jelly Roll Morton, v.3. J3.25
- 741.007–Ethel Waters. 1938/1939. P2.85
- 741.040–Jelly Roll Morton, v.4. J3.25
- 741.044–Benny Goodman. The Fletcher Henderson Arrangements, v.1. J4.37
- 741.054–Jelly Roll Morton, v.5. J3.25
- 741.059–Benny Goodman. The Fletcher Henderson Arrangements, v.2. J4.37
- 741.061–Don Redman. 1938/1940. J4.50
- 741.070–Jelly Roll Morton, v.6. J3.25
- 741.073–Benny Carter. 1940/1941. J4.21
- 741.080–McKinney's Cotton Pickers. Complete, v.1. J4.48
- 741.081–Jelly Roll Morton, v.7. J3.25
- 741.087–Jelly Roll Morton, v.8. J3.25
- 741.088–McKinney's Cotton Pickers. Complete, v.2. J4.48
- 741.089–The Greatest of the Small Bands, v.1. J4.92
- 741.103–The Greatest of the Small Bands, v.2. J4.92
- 741.106–The Greatest of the Small Bands, v.3. J4.92
- 741.107–New Orleans, v.1. J3.3
- 741.109–McKinney's Cotton Pickers. Complete, v.3. J4.48
- 741.116–Erskine Hawkins, v.2. J4.64
- 741.117–The Greatest of the Small Bands, v.4. J4.92
- DUKE 1/4–Duke Ellington. Integrale. J4.31
- FPM1-7003–New Orleans, v.2. J3.3
- FPM1-7059–McKinney's Cotton Pickers. Complete, v.4. J4.48
- FPM1-7014–The Greatest of the Small Bands, v.5. J4.92
- FPM1-7024–Erskine Hawkins, v.3. J4.64
- FPM1-7059–McKinney's Cotton Pickers. Complete, v.5. J4.48
- FXM1-7060–Henry "Red" Allen, v.1. J3.33
- FXM1-7090–Henry "Red" Allen, v.2. J3.33
- FXM1-7124–The Greatest of the Small Bands, v.6. J4.92
- FXM1-7136–Jean Goldkette. 1928-1929. P5.28
- FXM1-7323–Big Joe Williams. B1.259
- FXM3-7143–History of Jazz Piano. three discs. J6.10
- FXM1-7192–Henry "Red" Allen, v.3. J3.33

RCA (Japan)
specialty: jazz, blues, and country

- RA 5459/66–Jimmie Rodgers. 110 Collection. eight discs. F8.31
- RA 5641/50–Carter Family. The Legendary Collection, 1927-1934, 1941. ten discs. F5.109

RSO, 75 Rockefeller Plaza, New York, NY 10019
specialty: rock music

- RSO 3016–Blind Faith. R8.12

Radiola Records

> 2MR 5051—The First Esquire All-American Jazz Concert, January 18, 1944. two discs. J1.19

Ranwood, 9034 Sunset Blvd., Los Angeles, CA 90069
> specialty: mood music

Rebel, Rt. 2, Asbury, WV 24916
> specialty: bluegrass

> 1497—Country Gentlemen. Gospel Album. F9.29
> 1506—Country Gentlemen. Award Winning. F6.23
> 1511—Seldom Scene. Act One. F6.126
> 1514—Ralph Stanley. Plays Requests. F6.52
> 1520—Seldom Scene. Act Two. F6.126
> 1528—Seldom Scene. Act Three. F6.126
> 1530—Ralph Stanley. A Man and His Music. F6.51
> 1547/8—Seldom Scene. Recorded Live at the Cellar Door. two discs. F6.128

Red Lightnin' (England)
> specialty: blues reissues

> RL 001—Buddy Guy. In the Beginning. B1.337
> RL 006—When Girls Do It. two discs. B1.274
> RL 007—Junior Wells. In My Younger Days. B1.371
> RL 009—Earl Hooker. There's a Fungus Amung Us. B1.281
> RL 0010—Clarence "Gatemouth" Brown. San Antonio Ballbuster. B1.322

Reprise, 3300 Warner Blvd., Burbank, CA 91505
> specialty: general, troubador music

> FS 1016—Frank Sinatra. A Man and His Music. two discs. P2.17
> 6199—Tom Lehrer. An Evening Wasted. P4.10
> 6216—Tom Lehrer. Songs. P4.11
> 6217—The Kinks. Greatest Hits. R4.11
> 6261—Jimi Hendrix. Are You Experienced? R8.4
> 6267—Arlo Guthrie. Alice's Restaurant. F10.60
> 6286—Randy Newman. F10.38
> 6341—Joni Mitchell. Clouds. F10.30
> 6383—Neil Young. After the Gold Rush. R7.19
> 6430—Pentangle. Cruel Sister. F2.53
> 2RS 6307—Jimi Hendrix. Electric Ladyland. two discs. R8.5
> MS 2025—Jimi Hendrix. Greatest Hits. R8.6
> MS 2038—Joni Mitchell. Blue. F10.29
> MS 2064—Randy Newman. Sail Away. F10.39
> MS 2148—Maria Muldaur. R4.35

Rimrock, Concord, AR 72523
> specialty: sacred, bluegrass

> 1002—The Family Gospel Album. F9.2

Rome, 1414 E. Broad St., Columbus, OH 43205
specialty: bluegrass

1011—Don Reno and Red Smiley. Together Again. F6.49

Roots (Austria)
specialty: blues and gospel reissues; old time music reissues

RL 301—Blind Lemon Jefferson, v.1. B1.112
RL 306—Blind Lemon Jefferson, v.2. B1.112
RL 317—Lucille Bogan and Walter Roland. Alabama Blues, 1930-1935.
B1.386
RL 322—Memphis Jug Band, v.1. B1.421
RL 330—Tommy Johnson/Ishman Bracey. Famous 1928 Sessions. B1.113
RL 331—Blind Lemon Jefferson, v.3. B1.112
RL 337—Memphis Jug Band, v.2. B1.421
RL 701—Riley Pickett. Story, 1924-1941. F5.40

Roulette, 17 W. 60th Street, New York, NY 10023
specialty: general and jazz

RE 124—Count Basie. Echoes of an Era: Kansas City Suite/Easin' It. two
discs. J4.166

Roulette (England)
specialty: general and jazz

SRCP 3000—Count Basie. The Atomic Mr. Basie. J4.165

Rounder, 186 Willow Avenue, Somerville, MA 02143
specialty: blues, old time music, bluegrass

001—George Pegram. F5.96
0011—Tut Taylor. Friar Tut. F5.44
0014—Don Stover. Things in Life. F6.109
0017—Almeda Riddle. Ballads and Hymns from the Ozarks. F3.83
1001—Blind Alfred Reed. How Can a Poor Man Stand Such Times and Live?
F5.41
1002—Aunt Molly Jackson. Library of Congress Recordings. F3.68
1003—Fiddlin' John Carson. The Old Hen Cackled and the Rooster's Gonna
Crow. F5.29
1004—Burnett and Rutherford. A Rambling Reckless Hobo. F5.118
1005—Gid Tanner. "Hear These New Southern Fiddle and Guitar Music."
F5.78
1006—Blue Sky Boys. The Sunny Side of Life. F5.106
1007—Frank Hutchison. The Train That Carried My Girl from Town. F5.30
1008—Stoneman Family. 1926-1928. F5.72
1013/20—Early Days of Bluegrass, v.1-8. eight discs. F6.16
2003—Martin, Bogan and Armstrong. Barnyard Dance. B1.218
3006—Boys of the Lough. Second Album. F2.10

Rural Rhythm, Box A, Arcadia, CA 91006
    specialty: bluegrass

Sackville (Canada)
    specialty: jazz

    2004—Willie "The Lion" Smith and Don Ewell. Grand Piano Duets. J6.76

Savoy, 6 West 57th Street, New York, NY 10019
    specialty: jazz; in the process of being reissued by Arista

    MG 12020—Dizzy Gillespie. Groovin' High. J5.54
    MG 12106—J. J. Johnson. Boneology. J5.63
    MG 14006—Clara Ward Singers. Lord Touch Me. B3.64
    MG 14014—Great Golden Gospel Hits, v.1. B3.11
    MG 14019—Sonny Terry and Brownie McGhee. Back Country Blues. B1.248
    MG 14069—Great Golden Gospel Hits, v.2. B3.11
    MG 14076—James Cleveland, v.1. B3.29
    MG 14131—James Cleveland, v.2. B3.29
    MG 14165—Great Golden Gospel Hits, v.3. B3.11
    MG 14252—James Cleveland, v.3. B3.29
    SJL 2201—Charlie Parker. Bird: The Savoy Recordings. two discs. J5.30
      [in progress]
    SJL 2202—Lester Young. Pres. two discs. J4.126
    SJL 2211—Dexter Gordon. Long Tall Dexter. two discs. J5.55
    SJL 2214—Billy Eckstine. Mr. B and the Band. two discs. P2.35
    SJL 2216—Fats Navarro. Savoy Sessions: Fat Girl. two discs. J5.27

Scepter, 254 W. 54th Street, New York, NY 10019
    specialty: pop

Shandar (France)
    specialty: modern jazz

    SR 10000—Albert Ayler, v.1. J5.139
    SR 10004—Albert Ayler, v.2. J5.139

Shelter, 100 Universal City Plaza, Universal City, CA 91608
    specialty: rock

    SW 8901—Leon Russell. R4.41

Sire, 8255 Beverly Blvd., Los Angeles, CA 90048
    specialty: rock

    SAS 3702—The History of British Rock, v.1. two discs. R4.1
    SAS 3705—The History of British Rock, v.2. two discs. R4.1
    SAS 3712—The History of British Rock, v.3. two discs. R4.1
    SASH 3715—Fleetwood Mac. In Chicago. two discs. R5.18

Solid State, 6920 Sunset Blvd., Hollywood, CA 90028
    specialty: jazz
    18048—Thad Jones-Mel Lewis Orchestra. Monday Night. J4.172

Sonet (Sweden)
   specialty: jazz and blues

   SLP 2547—Barney Kessel and Red Mitchell. Two Way Conversation. J6.107

Sonyatone Records (c/o Southern Record Sales)

   STR 201—Eck Robertson. Master Fiddler, 1929-1941. F5.41a

Smithsonian Classic Jazz, P.O. Box 14196, Washington, D.C. 20044
   specialty: jazz reissues

Speciality, 8300 Santa Monica Blvd., Hollywood, CA 90069
   specialty: rhythm 'n' blues, blues, soul, gospel music

   2113—Little Richard. Greatest 17 Original Hits. B2.46
   2115—Ain't That Good News. B3.1
   2116—Soul Stirrers and Sam Cooke, v.1. B3.53
   2126—Percy Mayfield. Best. B2.62
   2128—Soul Stirrers and Sam Cooke, v.2. B3.53
   2131—Don and Dewey. B2.53
   2177/8—This Is How It All Began, v.1-2. two discs. B2.4

Spivey, 65 Grand Ave., Brooklyn, NY 11205
   specialty: blues

   2001—Victoria Spivey. Recorded Legacy of the Blues. B1.405

Spotlite (England)
   specialty: reissues of bop jazz

   100—Billy Eckstine. Together. J5.49
   101/6—Charlie Parker. On Dial. six discs. J5.29
   119—Coleman Hawkins and Lester Young. J4.106
   131—Howard McGhee. Trumpet at Tempo. J5.23

Springboard, 947 U.S. Highway 1, Rahway, NJ 07601
   specialty: reissues of jazz and rock 'n' roll

Stanyan, 8440 Santa Monica Blvd., Hollywood, CA 90069
   specialty: mood

   SR 10032—Vera Lynn. When the Lights Go On Again. P2.76

Starday, 220 Boscobel St., Nashville, TN 37213
   specialty: country and western, bluegrass and sacred materials

   SLP 122—Stanley Brothers. Sacred Songs from the Hills. F9.75
   SLP 146—Bill Clifton. Carter Family Memorial Album. F6.71
   SLP 150—George Jones. Greatest Hits. F8.28
   SLP 161—Lewis Family. Anniversary Celebration. F9.46
   SLP 174—Country Gentlemen. Bluegrass at Carnegie Hall. F6.24
   SLP 250—Diesel Smoke, Dangerous Curves, and Other Truck Driver
      Favorites. F8.10

Starday (cont'd)
> SLP 303—Preachin', Prayin', Singin'. F9.14
> SLP 398—Moon Mullican. Unforgettable Great Hits. F8.72
> SLP 482—New Grass Revival. F6.121
> SLP 772—Stanley Brothers. Sing the Songs They Like Best. F6.61
> SLP 953—Stanley Brothers. Best. F6.60
> SLP 956—Carl Story. Best. F9.80
> SLP 961—Don Reno and Red Smiley. Best. F6.48

Starline *See* EMI Starline (England)

Stash, Record People, 66 Greene Street, New York, NY 10012
> specialty: jazz and blues reissues [thematic: drugs and alcohol]
>
> 100—Reefer Songs. P4.4

Stax, 2693 Union Ave., Memphis, TN 38112
> specialty: soul

Storyville (Denmark)
> specialty: jazz and blues
>
> 670.184—Boogie Woogie Trio. J6.83
> 671.162—Lonnie Johnson. B1.203

Strata East, 156 Fifth Avenue, Suite 612, New York, NY 10010
> specialty: modern jazz

String (England)
> specialty: old time music, western swing
>
> 801—Beer Parlor Jive. F7.33

Sun, 3106 Belmont Blvd., Nashville, TN 37212
> specialty: rock 'n' roll, rhythm 'n' blues, blues, country; see also Phonogram
>   and Charly for English reissues
>
> 100/1—Johnny Cash. Original Golden Hits, v.1-2. two discs. R1.13
> 102/3—Jerry Lee Lewis. Original Golden Hits, v.1-2. two discs. R1.9
> 106—Original Memphis Rock & Roll. R1.4
> 128—Jerry Lee Lewis. Original Golden Hits, v.3. R1.9

Sunbeam, 13821 Calvert St., Van Nuys, CA 91401
> specialty: big band reissues, Benny Goodman
>
> SB 101/3—Benny Goodman. Thesaurus, June 6, 1935. three discs. J4.61

Sussex, 6255 Sunset Blvd., Suite 1902, Hollywood, CA 90028
> specialty: soul

Swaggie (Australia)
> specialty: jazz and blues reissues

Swaggie (cont'd)

    S 1219/20—Sleepy John Estes, v.1-2. two discs. B1.164

    S 1225—Lonnie Johnson. B1.204

    S 1235—Cripple Clarence Lofton/Jimmy Yancey. B1.216, J6.98

    S 1242—Bix Beiderbecke. Bix and Tram, 1927/8, v.1. J3.87

    S 1245—Bob Crosby's Bob Cats. 1937-1942, v.1. J3.56

    S 1251/2—Django Reinhardt. two discs. J6.114/5

    S 1269—Bix Beiderbecke. Bix and Tram, 1927/8, v.2. J3.87

    S 1275—Count Basie. Swinging the Blues, 1937/39. J4.14

    S 1288—Bob Crosby's Bob Cats. 1937-1942, v.2. J3.56

Swing Era (c/o Southern Record Sales)

    specialty: reissues of big band material

    LP 1001—Themes of the Big Bands. P5.3

Takoma, P.O. Box 5369, Santa Monica, CA 90405

    specialty: folk guitar and blues

    B 1001—Bukka White. Mississippi Blues. B1.256

    C 1002—John Fahey, v.1: Blind Joe Death. F4.32

    C 1024—Leo Kottke. 6 and 12 String Guitar. F4.37

Tamla, 6464 Sunset Blvd., Hollywood, CA 90028

    specialty: soul

    S 252—Marvin Gaye. Greatest Hits, v.1. B4.46

    S 278—Marvin Gaye. Greatest Hits, v.2. B4.46

    S 282—Stevie Wonder. Greatest Hits, v.1. B4.62

    T 308—Stevie Wonder. Where I'm Coming From. B4.34

    T 313—Stevie Wonder. Greatest Hits, v.2. B4.62

    T 326—Stevie Wonder. Innervisions. B4.37

Tangerine, 8255 Beverly Blvd., Los Angeles, CA 90048

    specialty: soul

Tax (Sweden)

    specialty: jazz reissues

    m8000—Lester Young. The Alternative Lester. J4.125

    m8005—Cootie Williams. The Boys from Harlem. J4.87

    m8009—The Territory Bands. J3.107

    m8011—Cootie Williams. The Rugcutters, 1937-1940. J4.88

Testament, 577 Lavering Avenue, Los Angeles, CA 90024

    specialty: blues

    T 2207—Chicago Blues: The Beginning. B1.270

    T 2210—Muddy Waters. Down on Stovall's Plantation. B1.301

    T 2211—Otis Spann. Chicago Blues. B1.307

    T 2217—Johnny Shines and Big Walter Horton. B1.361

    T 2219—Fred McDowell. Amazing Grace. B3.46

    T 2221—Johnny Shines. Standing at the Crossroads. B1.235

The Old Masters *See* Old Masters

Tishomingo (c/o Southern Record Sales)
    specialty: western swing

    2220—Rollin' Along. F7.34

Topic (England)
    specialty: folk music

    12 T 118—Bert Lloyd. First Person. F2.21
    12 T 136—The Watersons. Frost and Fire. F2.31

Tradition, 10920 Wilshire Blvd., Los Angeles, CA 90024
    specialty: folk

    2050—The Clancy Brothers and Tommy Makem. Best. F2.40
    2053—Oscar Brand. Best. F4.5

Trip, 947 U.S. Highway 1, Rahway, NJ 07065
    specialty: reissues of Emarcy jazz catalog (Mercury)

    TLP 5501—Sarah Vaughan. 1955. P2.84

Truth (Austria)
    specialty: gospel music

    1002/3—Guitar Evangelists, v.1-2. two discs. B3.12

Twentieth Century, 8255 Sunset Blvd., Los Angeles, CA 90046
    specialty: general

Union Grove (c/o Southern Record Sales)
    specialty: material from the Union Grove Fiddlers' Convention

United Artists, 6920 Sunset Blvd., Hollywood, CA 90028
    specialty: general

    UAS 5596—Country Gazette. A Traitor in Our Midst. F6.117
    UAS 5632—Duke Ellington. Money Jungle. J6.18
    UA 6291—George Jones. Best. F8.23
    UAS 9801—Will the Circle Be Unbroken? three discs. F8.16
    UAS 9952—Miles Davis. two discs. J5.15
    UALA 089-F2—Vicki Carr. The Golden Songbook. two discs. P2.93
    UALA 127-J3—John Lee Hooker. Detroit. three discs. B1.175
    UALA 233G—Fats Domino. two discs. B2.44
    UALA 243-G—Gordon Lightfoot. The Very Best. F10.27

United Artists (England)
    specialty: general

    UAS 29215—Sound of the City: New Orleans. B2.19
    UAS 29898—Slim Whitman, Very Best. 2 discs. F8.94

United Artists (England) (cont'd)
> UAD 60025/6–The Many Sides of Rock 'n' Roll, v.1. two discs. R2.8
> UAD 60035/6–The Many Sides of Rock 'n' Roll, v.2. two discs. R2.8
> UAD 60091/2–Lena Horne. Collection. two discs. P2.71
> UAD 60093/4–The Many Sides of Rock 'n' Roll, v.3. two discs. R2.8

Vanguard, 71 W. 23rd Street, New York, NY 10010
> specialty: folk music and blues

> 2053/5–Newport Folk Festival. three discs. F3.15
> 2087/8–Newport Folk Festival. two discs. F3.15
> 6544–Bert Jansch and John Renbourn. Jack Orion. F2.50
> VSD 79144/9–Newport Folk Festival. six discs. F3.15
> VSD 79180/6–Newport Folk Festival. seven discs. F3.15
> VSD 79216/8–Chicago/The Blues/Today! three discs. B1.266
> VSD 79219/25–Newport Folk Festival. seven discs. F3.15
> VSD 79306/7–Joan Baez. Any Day Now. two discs. F10.1
> VSD 79317–Greenbriar Boys. Best. F6.80
> VSD 5/6–Ian and Sylvia. Greatest Hits, v.1. two discs. F4.35
> VSD 9/10–Doc Watson. On Stage. two discs. F4.18
> VSD 15/16–The Weavers. Greatest Hits. two discs. F4.22
> VSD 23/24–Ian and Sylvia. Greatest Hits, v.2. two discs. F4.35
> VSD 35/36–The Greatest Songs of Woody Guthrie. two discs. F3.37
> VSD 39/40–Max Morath. The Best of Scott Joplin and Other Rag Classics.
> two discs. J2.17
> VSD 41/42–Joan Baez. Ballad Book. two discs. F4.3
> VSD 43/44–Odetta. Essential. two discs. F4.45
> VSD 47/48–From Spirituals to Swing, 1938/39. two discs. J4.2
> VSD 49/50–Joan Baez. Contemporary Ballad Book. two discs. F10.2
> VSD 65/66–Jimmy Rushing. Best. two discs. B1.425
> VSD 79/80–Joan Baez. Lovesong Album. two discs. F4.4
> VSD 99/100–Vic Dickenson. Essential. two discs. J4.137
> VSDB 103/4–Buck Clayton. Essential. two discs. J4.158

Vanguard (England)
> specialty: jazz, blues and folk

> VRS 8502–Mel Powell. Thinamagig. J4.114
> VRS 8528–Mel Powell. Out on a Limb. J4.113

Verve, 810 Seventh Ave., New York, NY 10019
> specialty: jazz

> FTS 3008–Blues Project. Projections. R5.6
> VC 3509–Charlie Parker. J5.69
> V6-8412–Stan Getz. Focus. J5.89b
> V6-8420–Oscar Peterson. Trio Live from Chicago. F6.71
> V6-8526–Bill Evans. Conversations with Myself. J6.54
> V6-8538–Oscar Peterson. Night Train. J6.72
> V6-8808–Billie Holiday. Best. J6.120

Verve (England)
>   specialty: jazz, reissues of American Verve
>
>   2304.074—Stan Getz. Greatest Hits. P3.9
>   2304.169—Coleman Hawkins and Ben Webster. Blue Saxophones. J4.105, J4.119
>   2317.031—Woody Herman. At Carnegie Hall, March 25, 1946. J4.42
>   2610.020—Jazz at the Philharmonic, 1944-1946. two discs. J1.12
>   2682.005—Johnny Hodges. Back to Back/Side by Side. two discs. J4.107
>   2683.023—Ben Webster and Oscar Peterson. Soulville. two discs. J4.120
>   2683.025—Teddy Wilson and Lester Young. Prez and Teddy. two discs. J4.123, J4.128
>   2683.049—Ben Webster. Ballads. two discs. P3.21

Vetco, 5828 Vine Street, Cincinnati, OH 45216
>   specialty: old time music reissues
>
>   101—Uncle Dave Macon. The Dixie Dewdrop, v.1. F5.33
>   105—Uncle Dave Macon. The Dixie Dewdrop, v.2. F5.33

Vocalion, 100 Universal City Plaza, Universal City, CA 91608
>   specialty: reissues of MC material
>
>   VL 3715—Sons of the Pioneers. Tumbleweed Trails. F7.18
>   VL 73866—Jo Stafford. Sweet Singer of Songs. P2.80

. Virgin, 75 Rockefeller Plaza, New York, NY 10019
>   specialty: rock

Viva, 6922 Hollywood Blvd., Hollywood, CA 90028
>   specialty: reissues of nostalgia materials

Vogue (France)
>   specialty: reissues of jazz and blues
>
>   SB 1—Sidney Bechet. Concert à l'Exposition Universelle de Bruxelles, 1958. J3.19
>   LAE 12050—Gerry Mulligan. J5.95

Volt, 2693 Union Ave., Memphis, TN 38112
>   specialty: soul

Voyager, 424 35th Avenue, Seattle, WA 98122
>   specialty: old time music
>
>   VRLP 303—Gid Tanner. A Corn Licker Still in Georgia. F5.77

Wand (recently deleted)
>   specialty: rhythm 'n' blues
>
>   653—Isley Brothers. Twist and Shout. B2.34

Warner Brothers, 3300 Warner Blvd., Burbank, CA 91505
   specialty: general

   2WS 1555—Peter, Paul and Mary. In Concert. two discs. F4.13
   WS 1749—Grateful Dead. Anthem of the Sun. R6.5
   WS 1765—Petula Clark. Greatest Hits. P2.95
   WS 1835—Van Morrison. Moondance. F10.33
   WS 1843—James Taylor. Sweet Baby James. F10.47
   WS 1869—Grateful Dead. Workingman's Dead. R6.6
   BS 2607—Deep Purple. Machine Head. R8.17
   BS 2643—Bonnie Raitt. Give It Up. R4.39
   2LS 2644—Deep Purple. Purple Passages. two discs. R8.15
   BS 2683—Eric Weissberg. Dueling Banjos. F6.63
   3XX 2736—Fifty Years of Film Music. three discs. P6.79
   2SP 9104—Phil Spector's Greatest Hits. two discs. R2.11a

World Jazz, 221 West 57th Street, New York, NY 10019
   specialty: jazz

World Pacific Jazz (recently deleted)
   specialty: jazz

   1211—Cy Touff and Richie Kamuca. Having a Ball. J4.115

World Records (England)
   specialty: nostalgia, jazz, British dance bands; formerly World Record Club

   F 526—The Anatomy of Improvisation. J5.1
   SH 118/9—Golden Age of British Dance Bands. two discs. P5.93
   SH 146—Al Bowlly. P2.4
   SH 220—Original Dixieland Jazz Band. London Recordings, 1919-1920.
      J3.52
   SHB 21—Ambrose. two discs. P5.94

Xanadu, 3242 Irwin Ave., Knightsbridge, NY 10463
   specialty: reissues of jazz

Yazoo, 245 Waverly Place, New York, NY 10014
   specialty: blues

   L 1001—Mississippi Blues, 1927-1941. B1.84
   L 1002—Ten Years in Memphis, 1927-1937. B1.76
   L 1003—St. Louis Town, 1927-1932. B1.94
   L 1005—Blind Willie McTell. The Early Years, 1927-1933. B1.126
   L 1011—Big Bill Broonzy. Young. B1.155
   L 1013—East Coast Blues, 1926-1935. B1.65
   L 1016—Guitar Wizards, 1926-1935. B1.41
   L 1017—Bessie Jackson and Walter Roland. 1927-1935. B1.387
   L 1020—Charley Patton. Founder of the Delta Blues. two discs. B1.129
   L 1022—Ten Years of Black Country Religion, 1926-1936. B3.23
   L 1023—Rev. Gary Davis. 1935-1949. B3.31

Yazoo (cont'd)

    L 1024—Mister Charlie's Blues. F5.14
    L 1025—Cripple Clarence Lofton/Walter Davis. B1.215
    L 1033—Roosevelt Sykes. The Country Blues Piano Ace. B1.238
    L 1036—Leroy Carr. Naptown Blues, 1929-1934. B1.108
    L 1037—Blind Willie McTell. 1927-1935. B1.124
    L 1041—Georgia Tom Dorsey. Come on Mama, Do That Dance. B1.162
    L 1050—Furry Lewis. In His Prime, 1927-1929. B1.211

DIRECTORY OF SPECIALIST RECORD STORES

The record stores listed here handle orders for hard-to-find and rare items (primarily covering blues, country, ethnic, folk, and jazz). In fact, where many labels are concerned, record stores will be the only means of distribution. The following stores are highly recommended because of the superior service they give in obtaining issues from small, independent labels. Request a current catalog. (Note: These stores *may* offer library discounts, but since they are *not* library suppliers per se, this should be clarified at the outset of any transaction.)

UNITED STATES

County Sales
Box 191
Floyd, VA 24091

Rare Record Distributing Co.
417 East Broadway
P.O. Box 10518
Glendale, CA 91205

Roundup Record Sales
P.O. Box 474
Somerville, MA 02144

Southern Record Sales
5101 Tasman Drive
Huntington Beach, CA 92649

CANADA

Coda Jazz and Blues Record Centre
893 Yonge Street
Toronto M4W 2H2

GREAT BRITAIN (INCLUDING EUROPE)

Dave Carey—The Swing Shop
18 Mitcham Lane
Streatham, London SW16

Collet's Record Centre
180 Shaftesbury Ave.
London WC2H 8JS

Dobell's Record Shop
75 Charing Cross Road
London WC 2

Flyright Records
18 Endwell Rd.
Bexhill-on-Sea
East Sussex

Peter Russell Record Store
24 Market Avenue
Plymouth PL1 1PJ

ARTISTS' INDEX

Every performing artist in this book is listed alphabetically, and immediately following the name is a series of alphanumeric codes referring the reader to the appropriate annotation in the main text. Included are references to those annotations in which the artist is noted as having been influential or influenced, but does not necessarily appear on the relevant phonodisc. Also, in the case of annotations covering several offerings by one performer or group, the alphanumeric code here listed refers only to the *first* code of a series in which that first code is obviously the first entry of a combined review. The code numbers in boldface type refer to an artist's or group's major main entry phonodiscs (those items starred in text).

Mountaineers, F5.64, **F5.65**, F6.54
Muddy Waters, F3.8, F5.120, F6.39, F10.32
Muldaur, Geoff, F4.38
Muldaur, Maria, F4.38, F8.145, F10.58
Mullican, Moon, F7.35, F8.11, **F8.72**
Munde, Alan, F6.117
Murray, Anne, F8.142

Nagler, Eric, F3.48
Narmour, Willie, F5.11
Nashville Grass, **F9.36**
Neaves, Glen, F5.8, F6.16, **F6.91**
Necessary, Frank, **F6.92**
Neil, Fred, **F10.35-37**, F10.75
Nelson, Rick, F10.75
Nelson, Willie, F7.35, F8.9, F8.15, F8.105, F8.110, F8.114, **F8.117-19**
Nestor, J. P., F5.22
New Christy Minstrels, **F4.44**
New England Bluegrass Boys, **F6.111**
New Grass Revival, **F6.121**
New Humblebums, F2.44
New Lost City Ramblers, F3.21, F3.82, F5.55, **F5.66-68, F5.93-95**, F5.105, F5.129, F10.83
Newbury, Mickey, F8.114, F8.117
Newman, Dave, F10.58
Newman, Jimmy, F8.73, F8.74
Newman, Randy, F4.6, F4.26, **F10.38-39**, F10.77
Newton, Abby, F10.83
Newton-John, Olivia, F8.145
Nicol, Simon, F2.44, F2.46a, F2.47
Niles, John Jacob, F3.5, F3.15, F3.78, **F3.79**, F10.84
Nilsson, Harry, **F10.75-78**
Nite Owls, F7.36
Nitty Gritty Dirt Band, F4.38, F6.37, F6.122, **F8.16**
Nolan, Bob, F7.15
North Carolina Ramblers, F5.1, F5.11, **F5.69, F5.71**, F5.107
Northumbrian Barnstormers, F2.1
Nyro, Laura, F10.79, **F10.80**

Oak Ridge Boys, F9.13
O'Boyle, Andy, F2.36
O'Boyle, Sean, F2.9
Ochs, Phil, F3.7, F3.10, F4.6, F10.10, F10.20, **F10.40-42**, F10.43
O'Daniel, W. Lee, F7.36, F7.48
O'Day, Molly, F6.112, F7.11, **F8.131**, F8.132, F8.139, **F9.2, F9.63**, F9.64
Odetta, F3.37, F3.38, **F4.45**
O'Flynn, Liamm, F2.43
Oklahoma Melody Boys, F8.82
See also Dixie Melody Boys

Oklahoma Tornados, F1.6
Okun, Milt, **F3.80**
Orbison, Roy, F8.12
Osborne, Bobby, F6.12, F6.85, **F6.93-95**
Osborne, Sonny, F6.39, F6.42, F6.85, **F6.93-95**
Osborne Brothers, F6.12, F6.19, **F6.93-95**, F6.122, **F9.65**
Oswald, Brother
See Brother Oswald
Owens, Buck, F8.30, **F8.75**, F8.110, F8.114, F8.139
Ozark Strutters, F5.23

Page, Patti, F7.43, F8.129
Paley, Tom, F2.29, F3.30, **F3.82**, F5.66
Palmer, John, F6.103, F6.104
Parker, Chet, F3.8
Parker, Knocky, F7.39
Parton, Dolly, F8.4, **F8.143**, F8.144, F8.154, F9.6
Pate, Jim, F3.19
Patton, Charley, F4.32
Paul, Les, F8.90
Paxton, Tom, F3.15, F3.38, F3.80, F4.6, F10.43, **F10.44**
Payne, Leon, **F7.28**
Pearl, Minnie, F8.8
Pederson, Herb, F6.120
Pegram, George, **F5.96**, F6.54
Pendleton, Buddy, F5.91
Penny, Hank, F7.36
Pentangle, F2.44, **F2.52-54**
Perkins, Carl, F8.12, F10.10
Perkins, Luther, F8.18
Perryman, Lloyd, F7.15
Peter and Gordon, F10.45
Peter, Paul and Mary, F3.80, F4.2, F4.11, **F4.12**, F4.13, F10.26, F10.35
Philips, Stu, F8.3
Phillips, Bruce "Utah," F10.66, **F10.81**
Phipps, Ernest, F9.5
Phipps Family, F9.1
Pierce, Reverend Barney, F9.14
Pierce, Webb, **F8.30**, F8.57, F8.80, F8.81
Pitts, Kenneth, F7.39
Planxty, **F2.43**
Poole, Charlie, F3.4, F3.32, F5.1, F5.26, **F5.69, F5.70**, F5.120, F6.65
Pope's Arkansas Mountaineers, F5.21
Porter, Granny, F5.8, F5.104
Potts, Sean, **F2.39**
Prairie Ramblers, F7.34
Prater, Matthew, F5.11
Pratly, Gerald, F2.11
Preservation Hall Jazz Band, F3.8
Presley, Elvis, F6.39, F8.12, F8.39, F8.78, F8.108, F10.10